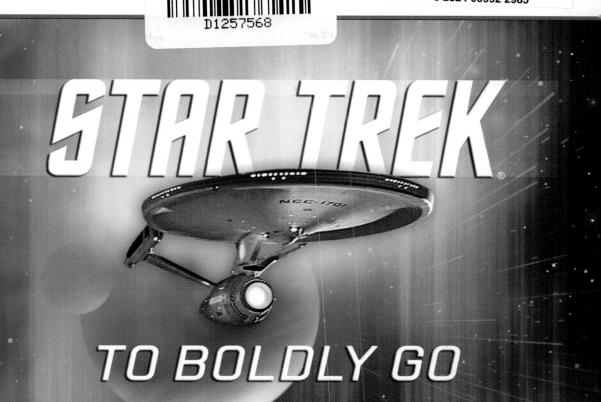

STAR TREK

TO BOLDLY GO

MIKE W BARR

TOM SUTTON

RICARDO VILLAGRAN

Titan Books

NANUET PUBLIC LIBRARY
149 CHURCH STREET
NANUET, NEW YORK 10954
845-623-4281

STAR TREK: TO BOLDLY GO

ISBN 1 84576 084 0

Published by Titan Books
A division of Titan Publishing Group Ltd.
144 Southwark St
London SE1 0UP

A CIP catalogue record for this title is available from the British Library.

This edition first published: July 2005
2 4 6 8 10 9 7 5 3 1

Printed in Italy.

Other titles of interest available from Titan Books:

Alien Legion: On the Edge (ISBN: 1 84023 765 1)

Alien Legion: Tenants of Hell (ISBN: 1 84023 811 9)

Battlestar Galactica: Saga of a Star World (ISBN: 1 84023 930 1)

Battlestar Galactica: The Memory Machine (ISBN: 1 84023 945 X)

What did you think of this book?

We love to hear from our readers.
Please email us at:
readerfeedback@titanemail.com, or write to us at the above address.

w w w . t i t a n b o o k s . c o m

REMEMBRANCE OF TIMES FUTURE

Walter Koenig – Star Trek's Pavel Chekov – discusses Star Trek II: The Wrath of Khan, the aftermath of which is the setting for the comics in this volume.

I bet the associate producer twenty dollars that the only stars that we would see after the release of our first movie were those that twinkle in the comatose brain of a beaten fighter. He never asked for payment. I guess he figured it was a sucker's bet. *Star Trek* has a way of climbing off the canvas, finding its feet and delivering a haymaker. *Star Trek II: The Wrath of Khan* was just such a film.

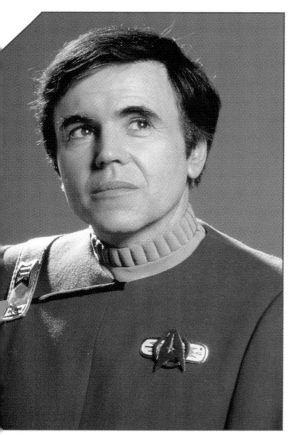

Introduction
by Walter Koenig

This picture had everything including, incidentally, a good role for Commander Chekov. Two elements in particular stand out for me: the character of the antagonist Khan as written and performed and a twenty-minute segment late in the story that emotionally battered the audience from ring-post to ring-post.

As to the first: writing and casting in film is frequently by shorthand – the hero is handsome, the heroine is beautiful and the bad guy has maggots squeezing between his molars. You don't have to write three-dimensional characters if the actors *look* the part. The fact is, the best writing and acting paints portraits with subtle hues and textures. The good guy is not without fault and the bad guy is not without honour. Kirk sent Khan into exile and the act led to the death of Khan's wife. Khan is merciless in his determination to destroy his adversary but it is grief over a lost love that fuels his hatred. Kudos to Jack B. Sowards, Harve Bennett, Nick Meyer and Ricardo Montalban for creating such a painfully compelling enemy.

As to the second: late in the story is the epic battle between Kirk's *Enterprise* and Khan's *Reliant*. It is beautifully staged, beautifully photographed and performed with monumental passion. Jeopardy has the audience holding its breath and victory has it sighing with relief. As a hand is raised in triumph, however, comes the sucker punch. Spock has left his post, Spock is sacrificing his life to save the ship, Kirk races to his side but must stand helplessly by as his friend perishes. Leonard Nimoy and Bill Shatner inhabit their characters with singular integrity and the audience is again staggering on wobbly pins. When you watch the film, see if it doesn't affect you that way.

I was proud to be a part of *Star Trek II*. I was particularly grateful for the opportunity to work with those two consummate professionals, Ricardo Montalban and Paul Winfield.

I started out thinking that *Star Trek III: The Search For Spock* was the B side of an old 1950s 45rpm record. Didn't we already do 'the bad guys want the bomb'

refrain in *Star Trek II*? I was wrong. It was considerably more than that. Although Kruge was pretty much standard villain fare, there was lot to be said for the evolving relationship between the captain and his newly discovered son. Good writing there and both well played and directed. It wasn't one of my favourite films for Chekov, though. After *The Wrath of Khan*, I thought that the only artistic direction for my character to go was up – after all, who else could have said, "Keptin, dey poot krechures in our ears," so brilliantly – somewhere contiguous with the furthest reaches of the galaxy. What I discovered instead was a ride in the back of the shuttlecraft. Oh, okay, there was that cunning pink outfit they gave me to wear. The Russian poet, Pushkin, was the inspiration, I understand. For some unfathomable reason, we got rid of it in a day. So you can see, not much to do, not many memories to savour. Of course, by contrast, that did make working on *Star Trek IV: The Voyage Home* that much sweeter. If I had the time and space (continuum) I could definitely rhapsodise about that experience.

A final word about these two films. Their success in no small part benefited from the work of many fine actors and principled human beings. Among them were DeForest Kelley, Paul Winfield, Bibi Besch and Merritt Butrick. Their loss is a source of enduring sadness but their contributions to the *Star Trek* universe remains a gift to be rejoiced in.

Walter Koenig, California, 2005

Walter Koenig is an actor and writer. His television work includes Dr. Novak, Jericho, The Star Lost, Babylon 5 *and, of course,* Star Trek, *where he played Pavel Chekov. His movies include the* Star Trek *series (up to* Star Trek Generations*),* Moontrap, Sworn to Justice *and* Drawing Down the Moon. *He is the author of* Warped Factors *and has also written episodes of* Star Trek, Land of the Lost, *and* The Powers of Matthew Star.

THE BEST OF TIMES

J ames Bond, Superman, Tarzan, Batman, Sherlock Holmes, Captain Kirk – these are the giants of our more recent mythology. They are legendary characters who captured our imaginations and became our heroes.

But there's an important difference between Kirk and the others.

"Actors come and go in these kinds of roles, but not so with Captain Kirk," says *Star Trek Generations* co-writer Ronald D. Moore. "Kirk is Shatner."

William Shatner interviewed by Pete Hull

He's right. Five actors have played James Bond, and there have been three Supermen. There have been numerous Tarzans, at least four Batmen, and several screen Sherlock Holmes. But there's only one Jim Kirk.

"But now, that character is dead," says Moore, "and in a way, it's like a real person has died."

So where does that leave the real person? Surely these are the worst of times for William Shatner. Without Kirk, what will Shatner do?

Perhaps we'll find him much like Bones found Kirk in an early scene from *Star Trek II: The Wrath of Khan*. Surrounded by a collection of his trophies from his *Star Trek* glory days, he's searching the channels for *Star Trek* re-runs, and hoping for the phone to ring with a call for a guest shot on *Star Trek: Voyager* or *Star Trek: Deep Space Nine*. One eye is on the television, the other on the phone.

It saddens one to think of it… but don't think about it too long, because nothing could be further from the truth. Forget Scotty's line, "Finding retirement a little lonely, are we?" Forget Spock's gift and the prospect of a leisurely evening with Charles Dickens' *A Tale of Two Cities*. Don't confuse fiction with fact, imagination with reality, because while you might not have noticed it, about six years ago William Shatner's career jumped to warp speed in a supernova of creativity that shows no sign of dropping to impulse any time soon. Still not with it? Take a look at these two snapshots:

1991: *Star Trek VI: The Undiscovered Country*, starring William Shatner, premières. His book, *TekWar*, is on the bestseller list. And he is hosting a show, *Rescue 911*, which is consistently ranked in the top 10 or 20 in the ratings battle. All this at the same time!

1994: During summer and autumn 1993, Shatner produced four television films from his *TekWar* series of books. In January 1994, they première on US television and capture top ratings slots. During the summer, he is involved in the filming of *Star Trek Generations*. He's still hosting *Rescue 911* and in September he directs

the first episode of a new series based on his *TekWar* universe. He has new fiction and non-fiction titles in the book stores, and two new *Star Trek* novels – his first ever – are on the way, the first, *Ashes of Eden*, released here last month. And he is leading Hollywood in its land rush to develop and market high-technology interactive entertainment. For William Shatner's career, these are the 'best of times'.

So how is life for William Shatner after *Star Trek Generations* – and is there anything about this actor that we don't know after all these years?

"I still love my character," Shatner says. "While there are many other things going on in my life that occupy my attention, when *Star Trek* does appear, I feel very fondly about it. I'm very happy with what I did in the film."

Even though Shatner has described his participation in formulating the *Star Trek Generations* story as "just the usual stuff between writers, producers and actors", his role was much more critical. "He recognised problems with the first draft of the script," says Moore. "Primarily, he didn't feel Kirk was integral to the plot and he had some problems with the way we presented his character. They were valid concerns and were interesting points of discussion. So it was clear that he was engaged in the story and was creatively interested."

Shatner's enthusiasm is legendary, and once problems with the script were resolved, he jumped into the film. Just take the orbital skydiving scene, cut from the final version of the film but used in several adaptations of the story and some early trailers.

"Bill couldn't stop talking," says James Doohan (Scotty). "You know, the excitement of what he had

just done, coming down from space, all this stuff."

"That shot was a tough one," agrees Shatner. "We were near Bakersfield, just outside Los Angeles in an area known as the Tejon Ranch. I'm up in the mountains in 110 degree heat, wearing a wet suit, a motorcycle helmet, mukluk winter boots, and dragging a parachute… while running uphill!" In fact, Shatner says that "the whole last part of the film was very challenging physically. Another day we were at 8,500 feet [at Whitney Portal, near Lone Pine, California] and I was chopping wood all through the scene."

The final fight scene with Malcolm McDowell and Patrick Stewart was filmed 65 miles outside of Las Vegas in a scenic, but tortuous, area appropriately called the Valley of Fire. Just getting there was difficult. The last 20 miles are on back roads, and the last half-mile is on foot. The temperature never dropped below 100 degrees Fahrenheit during the shoot, and there were some days when it was over 115 degrees.

"The intense heat and lack of humidity made doing a fight sequence that whole time a great challenge," says Shatner, with characteristic understatement. It was in those last days of filming that Shatner, Stewart and McDowell worked closely together.

"We spent lots of time together and we got to become friends – Patrick Stewart, Malcolm McDowell and I and everybody. It was just a wonderful professional experience. We all got very friendly. It will be a professional relationship that will last for the rest of our lives."

Prior to *Star Trek Generations*, Shatner had not worked with Stewart, nor had he watched *Star Trek: The Next Generation*. "I don't watch episodic television, so I'm not in the habit of turning on the television at the appropriate time. It doesn't have anything to do with whether I wanted to or felt I should have, I just haven't. It's just one of those things. Nevertheless, I think Patrick and I worked very well together."

Hollywood insiders wondered about one other relationship on the set: that of William Shatner and David Carson. While Carson had directed *ST:TNG* and *Star Trek: Deep Space Nine* episodes, Shatner had three decades of acting, producing and directing experience under his belt. Shatner had also directed *Star Trek* films; Carson had not. How would Shatner react to being directed by a relative newcomer?

"I didn't find it at all frustrating to work for someone else," says Shatner. "David is talented, very patient and very good."

In a rare bit of film trivia, Shatner revealed that someone very special to him made their film debut in *Star Trek Generations*. That beautiful, dark-eyed beauty… of a horse… that he's riding isn't some unnamed Hollywood stunt horse. That's Great Belles of Fire, and she's Shatner's pride and joy.

In 1985, Shatner purchased Belle Reve, a farm just outside Lexington, Kentucky, where he breeds and shows American Saddlebred horses.

"American Saddlebreds are very elegant, naturally high-stepping animals," says Pat Nichols, one of Shatner's neighbours and a spokesperson for the Saddle Horse Association. "American Saddlebreds are America's first native breed, and are only bred in America. Bill has been actively promoting them."

As with everything else he does, Shatner has been very successful with his horses. In fact, there are now three American Saddlebred classes named after him. The scene in which Kirk is riding Great Belles of Fire, seduced by the joy of the Nexus, and even the French name of his farm – which means 'Beautiful Dream' – might make you wonder: where is William Shatner's Nexus? What is his dream?

"I think if I were dissatisfied with my life I have the means to fix it," says Shatner. "I'm here in Los Angeles, working in show business in all its various forms. Then I grab a chunk of time with my horses and dogs, children and friends. So I must be in the ideal situation for me, otherwise I would have done something about it."

Throughout my research and during my conversations with Shatner and his friends, I discovered one constant – he creates his own destiny. Like Kirk, Shatner doesn't accept a no-win scenario.

"I'll certainly miss something that I haven't been doing for a long time," he says, when asked about the death of Kirk. "But the future has all sorts of interesting things in it – *TekWar* being one of them."

TekWar is now Shatner's universe. In 1988, the writers' strike brought the filming of *Star Trek V: The Final Frontier* to a grinding halt. Anyone else might have gone fishing, but he wrote an SF novel. And he created more than just a novel – he created an entertainment juggernaut.

"The concept came about by putting a policeman 200 years into the future – essentially, *TJ Hooker* into *Star Trek* [referring to his policeman television alter ego]," says Shatner. "I find that the stories appear in the newspaper headlines every day." His first book triggered a landslide. He has since written four more *Tek* novels, three of which have been turned into television films, and a series went into production late last year, scheduled for transmission in the United States in 1995. A comic book version of his first book appeared in 1992, with artwork by British artist Lee Sullivan (also known for his work on *RoboCop* and *Doctor Who*), and was scripted by Ron Goulart, who also played a cameo role in the first film.

"I realised when I spoke with Marvel Comics that if I put the stories fifty, rather than 200 years in the future, it would be easier if they were filmed," Shatner explains. "When the *TekWar* films were done, those fifty years became even more useful. Now that it is a series, it makes even more sense."

Shatner produced and directed the first film, *TekWar*, and also starred in it as Walter Bascom, the owner of the Cosmos Detective Agency. The film premièred in the US in January 1994, and was an instant hit. *TV Guide* gave

it an eight out of ten rating. It was placed in the ratings nationwide and earned newspaper praise from journals such as *The Hollywood Reporter*.

Three more films followed: *TekLords*, *TekLab* and *TekJustice*. "These four films were our pilot for the new series," explains Shatner, who now produces the show, and has directed the first and some later episodes.

Despite their similar sounding names, William Shatner's *Tek* universe and the *Star Trek* universe of Gene Roddenberry are nothing alike. "It never occurred to me that *Tek* might sound like 'Trek'. *Tek* was a technological drug; the concept was from television and the way television acts as a soporific for me. It's difficult for me to go to sleep without it on and by extension it could become the drug of the future. So it was from the word 'technology'. I was too involved in *Star Trek* for it to occur to me that the two seemed alike."

Shatner is also busy creating yet another universe for a whole new set of characters and stories. "I'm planning a new series of novels about a diplomat in the future," he says. "His problems will be dealing with entities that will have arisen fifty years from now."

Despite what might seem an impossible schedule of writing, producing, directing and starring in the *TekWar* world, Shatner is still very much alive in the *Star Trek* world.

"There are new boundaries that I am exploring," says Shatner. "One is *Star Trek* novels. Paramount Pictures are also interested in my book, *Star Trek Memories*, and it looks like we're going to do a television special based on that."

In addition to *Star Trek* and *Tek* books, Shatner has written yet another novel, *Believe*, which is about a *Scientific American*-sponsored contest to prove or disprove that life exists after death. The opposing champions? Harry Houdini and Sir Arthur Conan Doyle. How does he find the time to do all the things he does?

"It's a matter of focusing energies into what is needed," he says. "I'm all alone with a long legal pad and a dictation machine when I write."

In death, legends become greater than life. Shatner tells us so in his book, *Believe*. Doyle's and Houdini's legends "have grown in magnitude and poetry, like proverbial fish that get larger and larger through each retelling," he says.

And what about Jim Kirk's legend? Will William Shatner do something to bring him back to our screens someday in *ST:DS9* or *ST:VOY* or in a film script? Was an 'imprint' of him made in the Nexus, or will we see him in some future episode's holodeck fantasy?

"Probably not," he told me. "I don't think it would be appropriate. But stranger things have happened..."

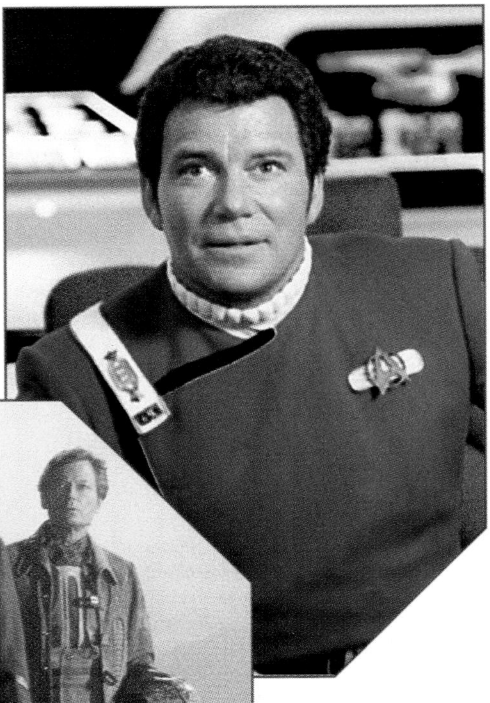

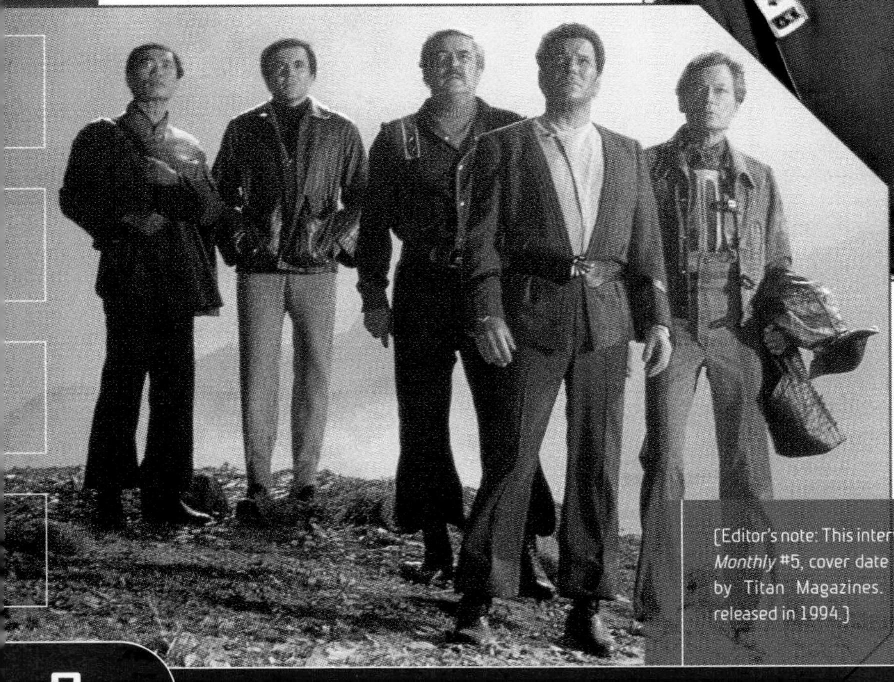

[Editor's note: This interview first appeared in *Star Trek Monthly* #5, cover date July 1995, published in the UK by Titan Magazines. *Star Trek Generations* was released in 1994.]

A SIMPLE COUNTRY DOCTOR

DeForest Kelley interviewed by Ian Spelling

Others have come after him and, in fact, another came before him. But in the hearts and minds of Trekkers everywhere, Dr Leonard "Bones" McCoy – and his actor alter ego, DeForest Kelley – is the be all and end all of *Star Trek* doctors. A terrific man of medicine, a rather crotchety guy, a loyal friend and a perfect human foil to that bastion of Vulcan logic, Mr. Spock (Leonard Nimoy), McCoy was, is and shall forever remain... McCoy. And the man behind McCoy is a soft-spoken Southern gentleman, a veteran character actor who virtually stumbled into his legendary role,

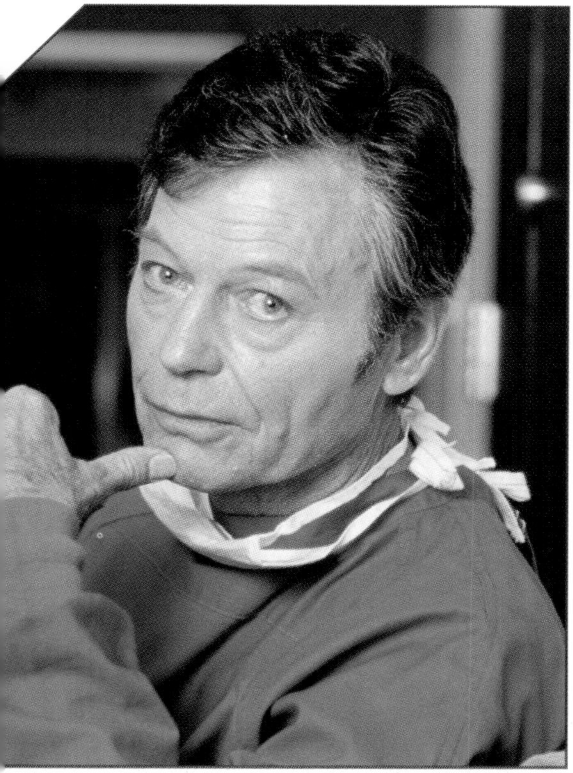

a man who could even have portrayed Spock had he desired that part.

The saga of Kelley's long association with *Star Trek* and its late creator Gene Roddenberry goes back even further than the 30 years of *Star Trek* now being celebrated. It's a familiar story; Kelley had been a film and television regular, often playing the villain, when he was introduced to a television producer named Roddenberry, who hired him for a pilot named *333 Montgomery Street* and another called *Police Story*. Neither pilot sold to US television, so Roddenberry moved on to his next project, something called *Star Trek*.

NBC nixed a first *Star Trek* pilot, *The Cage*, in which John Hoyt played the ship's doctor. After successfully pitching a second pilot, *Where No Man Has Gone Before*, Roddenberry was hunting for an actor to play the ship's doctor on a regular basis and thought of Kelley. He screened Kelley's performance as a good guy, a criminologist, in the *Police Story* pilot for NBC. The network gave Roddenberry the green light to cast Kelley – who had previously informed Roddenberry that he didn't want the Spock role – as Dr McCoy and the rest, to paraphrase McCoy, is history, dammit.

Following the demise of *Star Trek* as a weekly series, Kelley worked somewhat infrequently in other films and television shows. But he answered the call for every subsequent *Star Trek* incarnation, from the animated series to the first six films (he passed on *Star Trek Generations* because he didn't feel there was enough for him to do), and from a pass-the-torch appearance in the *Star Trek: The Next Generation* pilot *Encounter at Farpoint* to countless convention appearances around the world.

Over the past few years, Kelley has maintained a low profile, preferring instead to enjoy the quiet life with Carolyn, his wife of 50-plus years (they were married on 7 September 1945) and their pet turtle, Myrtle – "It's nice to have something around that's actually older than we are!" he jokes – at the California home they share. Still, Kelley is more than willing to look back at his days spent in the 23rd Century to his first encounter with Gene Roddenberry.

"I'd known Gene since 1959," recalls Kelley. "I knew him longer and probably better than anyone in the cast or anyone at Paramount Pictures. I'd done a couple of television pilots for Columbia, and they both sold. I was the heavy in them. The producers of those shows decided they were going to do a show about a criminal lawyer named Jake Erlich from San Francisco [*333 Montgomery Street*] and decided to test me for it.

"Before the test, Bob Sparks, one of the producers, said he wanted me to go out to Westwood and meet this writer, Gene Roddenberry. I went out there, went up this flight of stairs, and into this office. It was about seven feet by seven feet and there at this desk was this *huge* man. It was Gene, and he was sitting behind a typewriter. We had a long talk about the show and the possibility of my doing it. We shot the whole thing in San Francisco and we had the best time we ever had in our whole lives. Gene and I often reminisced about that."

When they first met, could he ever imagine how deep an impact Gene's relationship with him would have on his career and life? "Years and years later, I had dinner with him," Kelley recalls. "It was the night of his last public appearance at that huge *Star Trek* convention at the Shrine Auditorium, where 6,000-7,000 people gave Gene an ovation like you wouldn't believe. We were at Chasen's, Gene and [his wife] Majel [Barrett-Roddenberry], my wife and I, and another couple. We reminisced again about San Francisco, how it really had been one of the happiest times of our lives.

"Gene was not just a producer to me. He was a dear friend, a buddy, and his passing was a great loss to me and to a lot of people. He changed the course of my life, Leonard Nimoy's life, and that of everybody else in the show. None of us would be where we are today were it not for *Star Trek*, nor for Gene. God knows where we'd be today. Nobody knows. Also, he changed the lives of so many people who watched *Star Trek* and all of the other *Star Trek* shows that have come on since. He will be sorely missed."

Kelley was privileged to have seen *The Cage*, the first pilot, during the time it was being shown by Roddenberry to studio executives. He told one interviewer that he told *Star Trek*'s creator, "Well, I don't know what the hell it's all about, but it's gonna be either the biggest hit or the biggest miss God ever made." At that time he little suspected he would be an integral part of the big hit *Star Trek* was about to become.

When Kelley was first approached with *Star Trek* he was given the part of Spock to read, but he's more than happy he did not take the role. ("I don't think *anyone* could have played Spock better than Leonard Nimoy," he told US magazine *Starlog* in 1984). But there's a less familiar story about how Kelley had worked with Nimoy before *Star Trek* without even realising it. "That's true," says Kelley. "I did an episode of [the western TV series] *The Virginian* in which, oddly enough, I portrayed a doctor who was an alcoholic. In the story, I let one guy die in this so-called hospital we had. One day, we were on the set of the original show and Leonard said, 'Did you know that we worked

together before?' I said, 'Oh really? When?' He said, 'In *The Virginian*. You let a guy die and I was the guy who died.' I don't think Leonard had a line, hardly. I think he just groaned. I actually remembered it. I didn't know it was Leonard, but I did remember the scene. Leonard and I always thought that was just so ironic."

Over the years, Trekkers seemed to enjoy the brotherly bickering between Spock and McCoy. What would he say is his final word on the bond between these two individuals?

"It was always a love-hate relationship. Each of them maintained a great deal of respect for the other. I think there's that underlying thing, where you realise, 'Gee, Spock really does admire him,' or, 'Gee, McCoy really does admire Spock'. Really, Spock represents everything to McCoy that McCoy *hates*. In his eyes, Spock is something of a computer. I guess he's really, in McCoy's eyes, what Data is today. Leonard and I were very fortunate to be able to build the relationship between our characters over three decades. Not a lot of actors get an opportunity to do that."

Kelley elected not to appear in *Star Trek Generations* because he didn't think there was enough for McCoy to do. That left *Star Trek VI: The Undiscovered Country* as McCoy's final big-screen voyage. "I was *very* pleased that I went out with a movie that was a good, solid motion picture," Kelley says with a smile. "It's better than going out on a bummer! A bummer is bad any time, but especially if it's the last time out. I thought, for me, *Star Trek VI: The Undiscovered Country*, was as good as any a way to go. You never want to stay too long at the party."

Did he see *Star Trek Generations*? "Yes, I did go see that. I thought they did an excellent job. I saw it at Paramount on the première night. It was kind of fun to see Bill [Shatner] and Jimmy [Doohan] and Walter [Koenig] in it. As opposed to a lot of the criticism Bill got, I thought Bill gave it a lift."

And has he tuned into the other *Star Trek* series at all over the years?

"To tell you the truth, I haven't really watched much of *Star Trek: The Next Generation*, *Star Trek: Deep Space Nine* or *Star Trek: Voyager*," says Kelley. "I've seen one or two episodes of the shows and I remember watching the *ST:VOY* pilot. I thought that was very good. But you have to remember that I was never much of a science fiction aficionado, as such. I didn't connect with it at the beginning. I'd done all sort of things but science fiction, on film and television. Even when I started *Star Trek*, I was not into it at all until several months passed. Then I began to find what we were doing to be very fascinating. I began to enjoy what we did, but I was never one to follow up with it so much, to the point of watching other science fiction shows, even *Star Trek* shows. I'm just being brutally honest. It was a weird feeling when I first looked at *ST:TNG*. I remember thinking it was like walking back through time or something. It was like it was something we did before being done again. But they made it their own show over time, and so have the others."

Kelley is on record as recalling that he had "a feeling while making the first six episodes [of *Star Trek*] that we were doing something special… and it turned

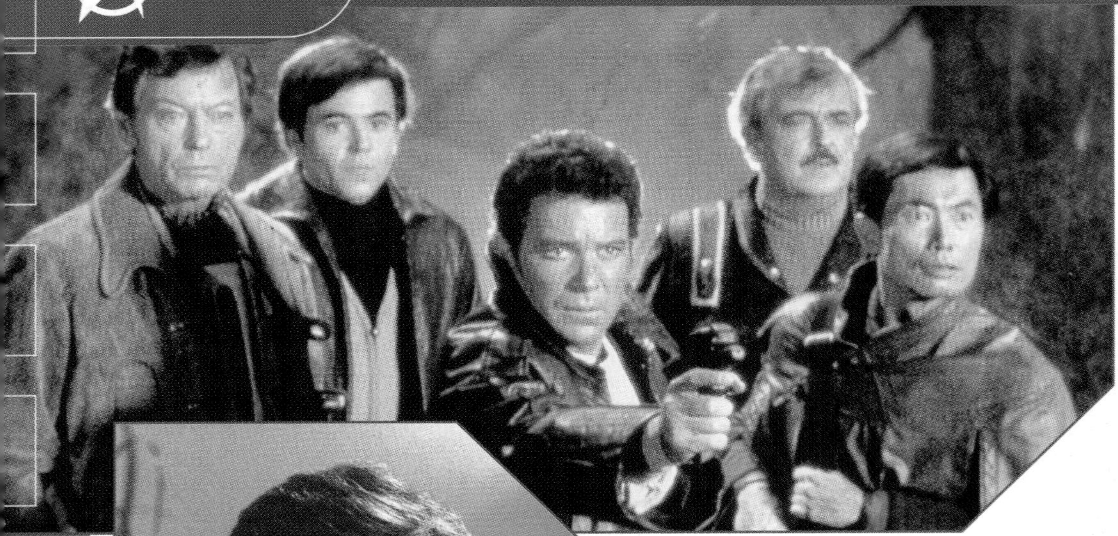

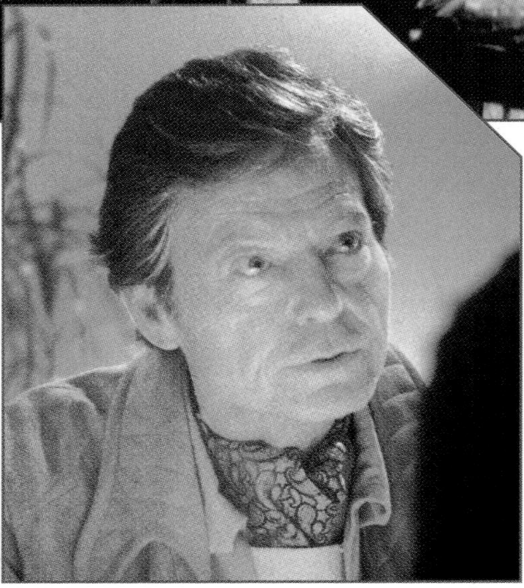

out to be more special than any of us ever dreamed." So it boggles the actor's mind that it's thirty years since *Star Trek* first beamed into his life and it's *still* as popular as ever before.

"It's very hard to believe," says Kelley. "Thirty years is a *very* long time. It's hard to explain, but that's a long time to be involved in something, even as scattered as we were over a certain number of years. The show folded in 1969 and we thought it was all over. Then the conventions started, and we started to see how these crowds were screaming for us." At one New York convention 10,000 fans showed up when only 600-700 were expected. "It made us think, or at least it made *me* think, *something* was going to happen with *Star Trek*. And it did. Then the *Star Trek* films happened throughout the years. It just seemed that, as I'd written in a poem I read at the conventions, *Star Trek* would always be there. I guess, in some ways, it always will be there."

Everyone knows that Kelley's favourite episode of the original series is *City on the Edge of Forever*. So, asking a different 'is there a favourite' question, is there one favourite memory he has from all of his *Star Trek* experiences?

"My absolute favourite memory? I don't know." The actor pauses for thought, then: "One that stands out, though, was something that happened during our third year of the series. We knew we'd be dropped at the end of the season, but we were still shooting the show. There was a television set around and we watched one of the NASA missions, maybe the one where they landed on the Moon. Here we were, standing there in our far-out costumes, filming a show about the future, watching the astronauts walking around, for real. That always amazes me, that memory."

Kelley has said in the past that with each passing day, it's more and more unlikely that he'll act again. If his career as an actor is truly over, how does he look back on his 50-plus years spent before the camera?

"I've always had a very positive attitude about my career and I believe I've had a good run, that I did well as an actor," says Kelley. "Not acting any more doesn't frighten me. Old actors don't really retire. They just die.

"I don't know that I've wanted to do anything else after *Star Trek VI: The Undiscovered Country*, which may be why I haven't done anything. I've been offered a few things, but nothing that really interested me enough to do it. I've just stayed at home with my wife, messed around with my roses, and let it go. God knows that we, I, had all the adulation an actor could want because of *Star Trek*. We couldn't have any more adulation, recognition than we've gotten from that. We've had some experiences some other actors have *never* experienced and never will. I also had a very good role to play over many years, and I got to work with people I consider dear friends many, many times. So, I'm not badly off!"

[**Editor's note:** This interview first appeared in *Star Trek Monthly* #18, cover date August 1996, published in the UK by Titan Magazines. *Star Trek Generations* was released in 1994.]

CREATOR BIOGRAPHIES

...LET'S BE CRAZY.

MIKE W. BARR is perhaps best known for writing DC's first ever graphic novel publication, *Camelot 3000*, but in a career spanning twenty years – and counting – Barr has written a wide range of comics, including adventures for Batman (in *Batman* and *Detective Comics*, where his "Year Two" story formed the basis for the animated movie, *Mask of the Phantasm*) and Superman (in *Action Comics*, and with Batman in *World's Finest Comics*). He has also written issues of *The Brave and the Bold*, *Green Lantern*, *House of Mystery*, *Mystery in Space*, *Secret Origins*, *The Shroud*, *Star Wars* and *Weird War Tales*.

TOM SUTTON's range of work is astonishing. Known primarily as one of the comics industry's foremost horror artists, with work including such classic comics as *Creepy*, *Eerie*, *Ghostly Tales*, *House of Mystery*, *Midnight Tales*, *Supernatural Thrillers*, *Vampirella* and *Werewolf By Night,* he has also worked extensively in the superhero and Western genres. In the former, he has pencilled issues of *Avengers*, *Batman*, *Captain Marvel*, *Doctor Strange*, *Ghost Rider* and *Silver Surfer*, as well as anthologies such as *Marvel Comics Presents*; his Western work includes *Butch Cassidy*, *Kid Colt – Outlaw*, *Rawhide Kid* and *Western Gunfighters*. Sutton has also branched into contemporary, adult-oriented material with *Grimjack*; satirised other comics in *Not Brand Ecch*; and even made a foray into the world of giant monsters with *Godzilla*. Sadly, Tom passed away – still at his drawing board – in May 2002.

RICARDO VILLAGRAN has worked on countless comics both as a penciller and/or inker, including *Airboy*, *Atari Force*, *Batman*, *Captain America*, *Conan the Barbarian*, *Darkhawk*, *Deadbeats*, *Elvira: Mistress of the Dark*, *Hawkman*, *Mighty Crusaders*, *Phantom of Fear City*, *Savage Sword of Conan*, *Skywolf*, *Solar: Man of the Atom* and *Tarzan*.

STAR TREK®

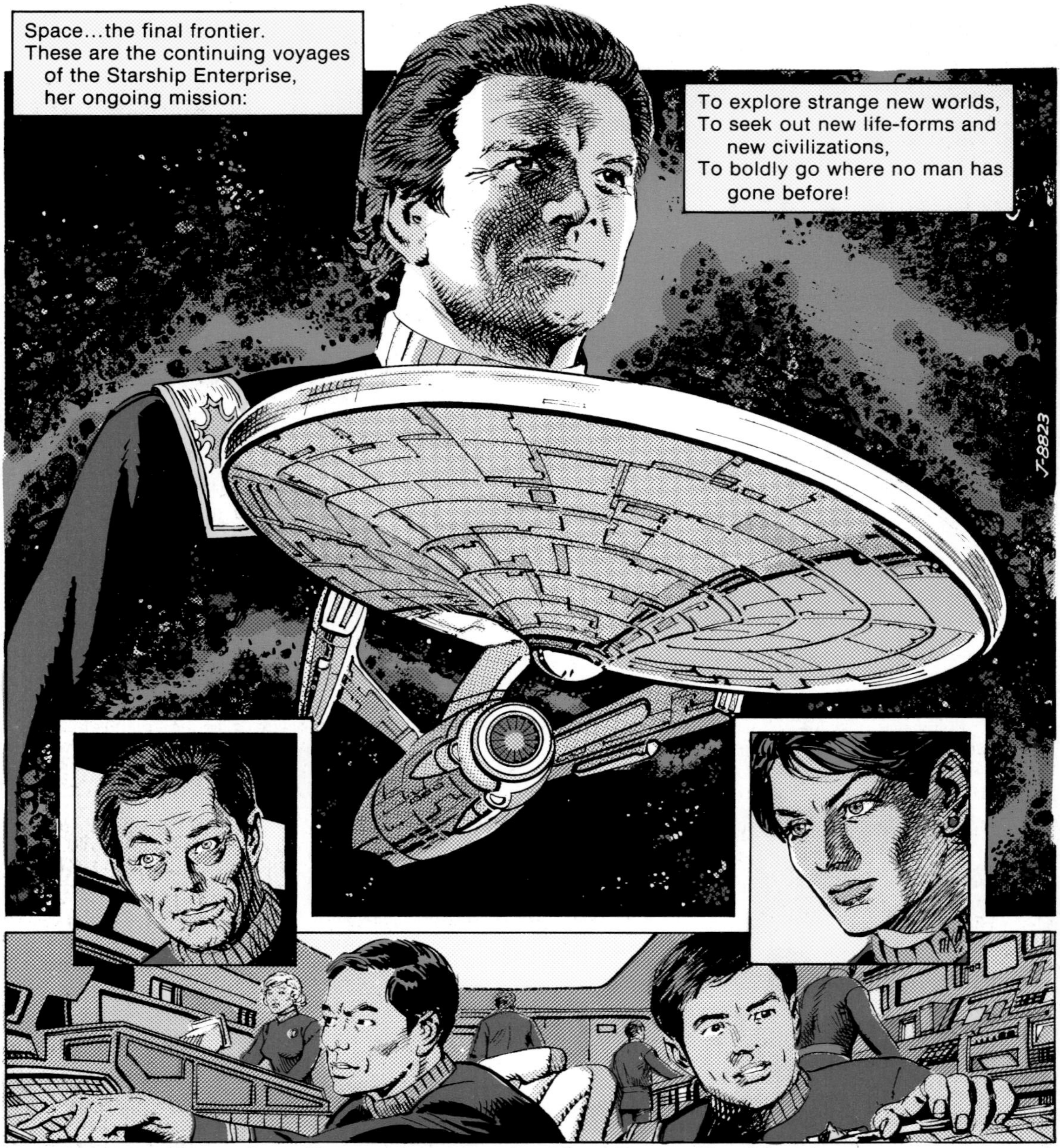
Space...the final frontier.
These are the continuing voyages of the Starship Enterprise, her ongoing mission:
To explore strange new worlds, To seek out new life-forms and new civilizations, To boldly go where no man has gone before!

Based on the series created by **Gene Roddenberry**

MIKE W. BARR * **TOM SUTTON** & **RICARDO VILLAGRAN**
Writer — Artists

JOHN COSTANZA * **MICHELE WOLFMAN** * **MARV WOLFMAN**
Letterer — Colorist — Editor

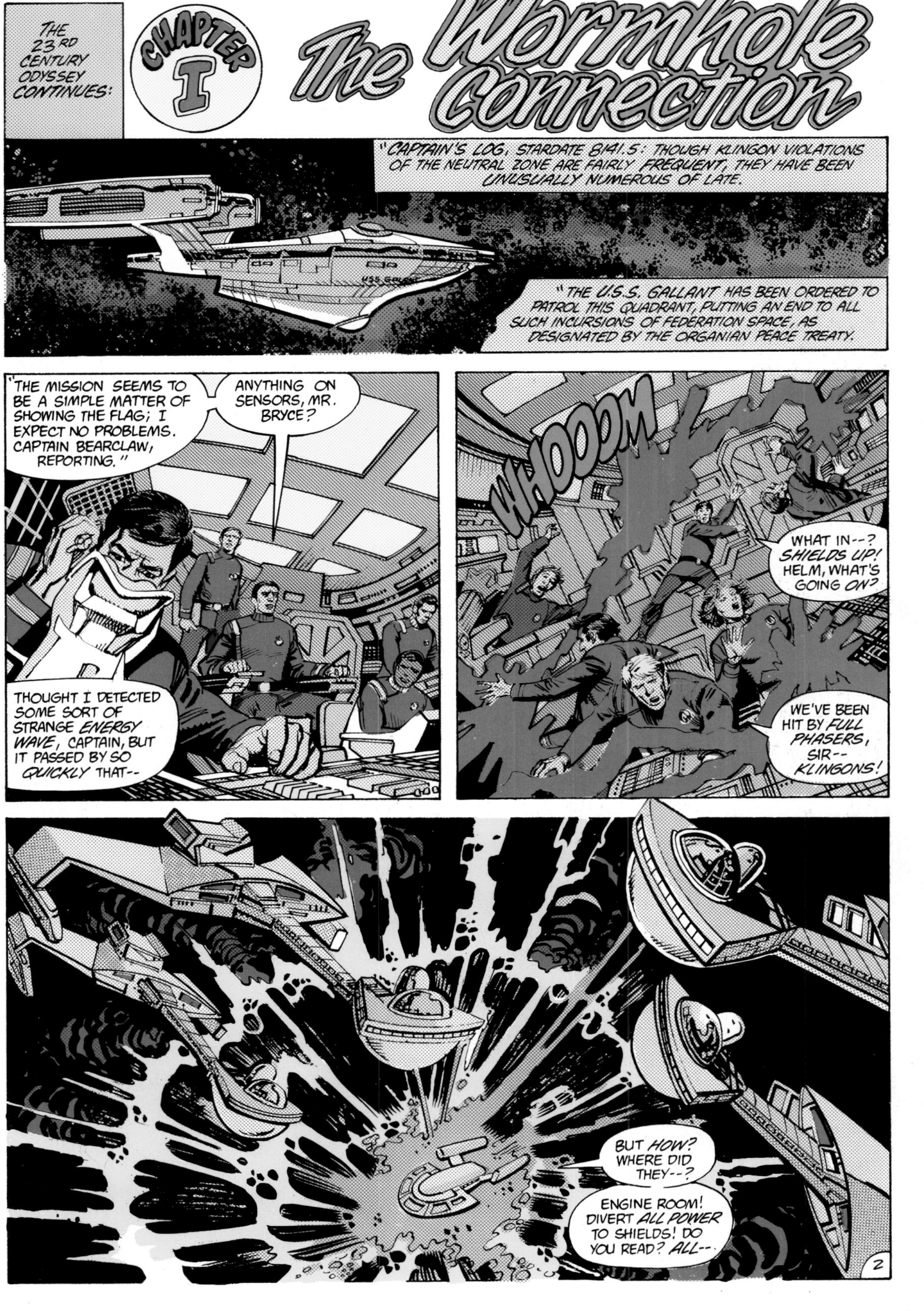
THE 23RD CENTURY ODYSSEY CONTINUES:
CHAPTER I
The Wormhole Connection
"CAPTAIN'S LOG, STARDATE 8141.5: THOUGH KLINGON VIOLATIONS OF THE NEUTRAL ZONE ARE FAIRLY FREQUENT, THEY HAVE BEEN UNUSUALLY NUMEROUS OF LATE.
U.S.S. GALLANT
"THE U.S.S. GALLANT HAS BEEN ORDERED TO PATROL THIS QUADRANT, PUTTING AN END TO ALL SUCH INCURSIONS OF FEDERATION SPACE, AS DESIGNATED BY THE ORGANIAN PEACE TREATY.
"THE MISSION SEEMS TO BE A SIMPLE MATTER OF SHOWING THE FLAG; I EXPECT NO PROBLEMS. CAPTAIN BEARCLAW, REPORTING."
ANYTHING ON SENSORS, MR. BRYCE?
THOUGHT I DETECTED SOME SORT OF STRANGE ENERGY WAVE, CAPTAIN, BUT IT PASSED BY SO QUICKLY THAT--
WHOOOM
WHAT IN--? SHIELDS UP! HELM, WHAT'S GOING ON?
WE'VE BEEN HIT BY FULL PHASERS, SIR-- KLINGONS!
BUT HOW? WHERE DID THEY--?
ENGINE ROOM! DIVERT ALL POWER TO SHIELDS! DO YOU READ? ALL--

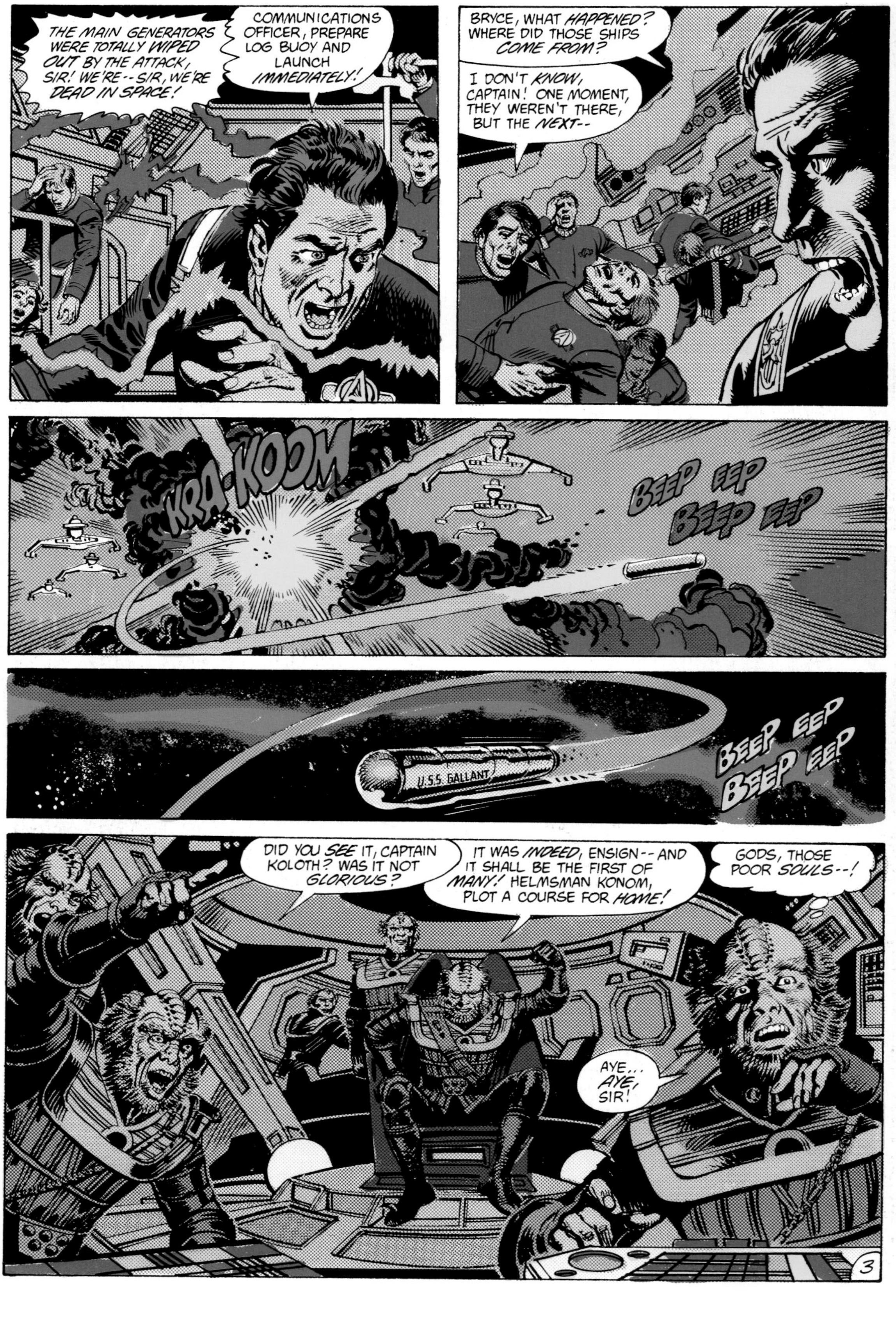
THE MAIN GENERATORS WERE TOTALLY WIPED OUT BY THE ATTACK, SIR! WE'RE--SIR, WE'RE DEAD IN SPACE!
COMMUNICATIONS OFFICER, PREPARE LOG BUOY AND LAUNCH IMMEDIATELY!
BRYCE, WHAT HAPPENED? WHERE DID THOSE SHIPS COME FROM?
I DON'T KNOW, CAPTAIN! ONE MOMENT, THEY WEREN'T THERE, BUT THE NEXT--
KRA-KOOM
BEEP EEP
BEEP EEP
U.S.S. GALLANT
BEEP EEP
BEEP EEP
DID YOU SEE IT, CAPTAIN KOLOTH? WAS IT NOT GLORIOUS?
IT WAS INDEED, ENSIGN--AND IT SHALL BE THE FIRST OF MANY! HELMSMAN KONOM, PLOT A COURSE FOR HOME!
GODS, THOSE POOR SOULS--!
AYE... AYE, SIR!

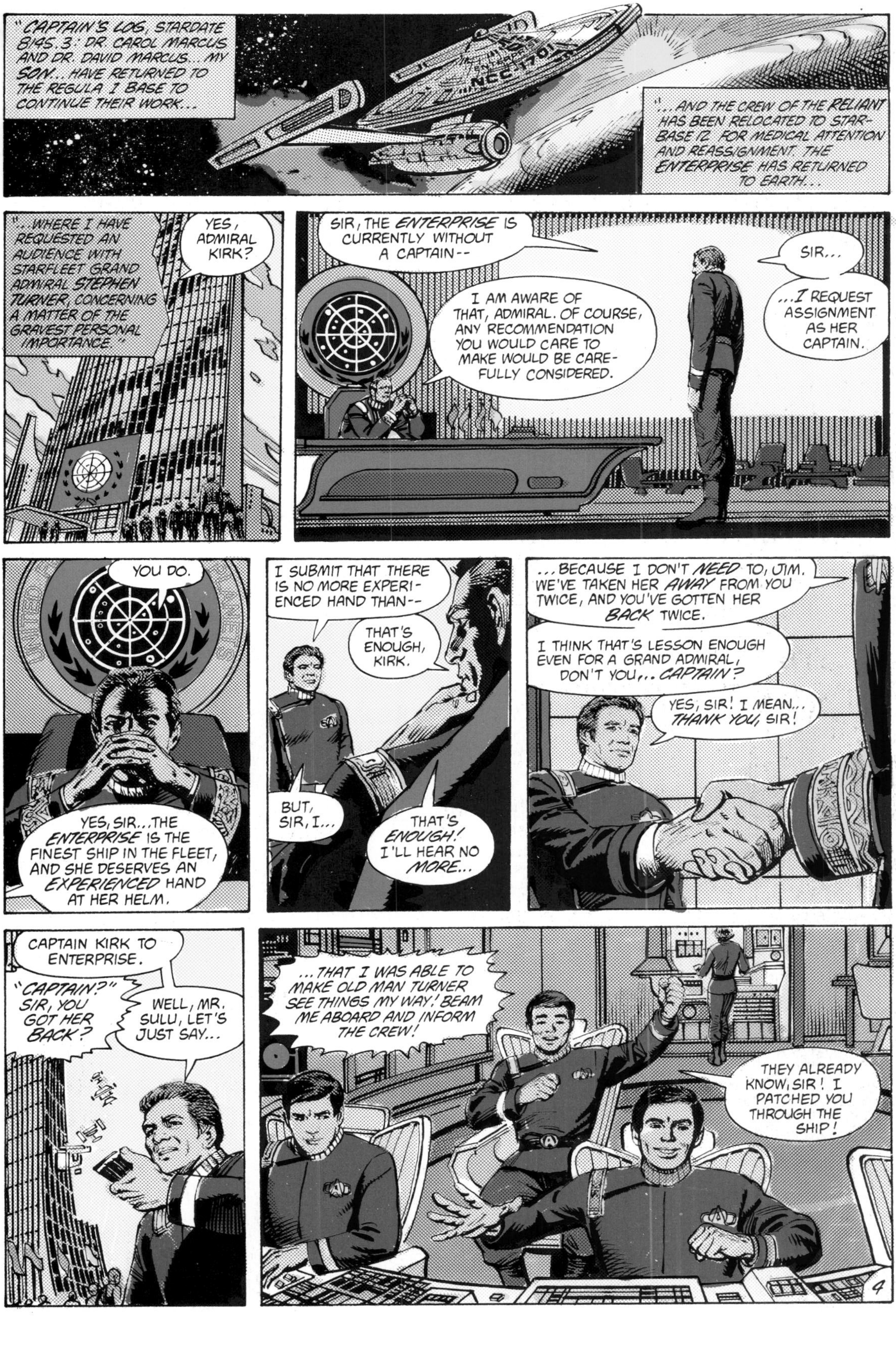
"CAPTAIN'S LOG, STARDATE 8145.3: DR. CAROL MARCUS AND DR. DAVID MARCUS... MY SON... HAVE RETURNED TO THE REGULA I BASE TO CONTINUE THEIR WORK...
"...AND THE CREW OF THE RELIANT HAS BEEN RELOCATED TO STAR-BASE 12 FOR MEDICAL ATTENTION AND REASSIGNMENT. THE ENTERPRISE HAS RETURNED TO EARTH...
"...WHERE I HAVE REQUESTED AN AUDIENCE WITH STARFLEET GRAND ADMIRAL STEPHEN TURNER, CONCERNING A MATTER OF THE GRAVEST PERSONAL IMPORTANCE."
YES, ADMIRAL KIRK?
SIR, THE ENTERPRISE IS CURRENTLY WITHOUT A CAPTAIN--
I AM AWARE OF THAT, ADMIRAL. OF COURSE, ANY RECOMMENDATION YOU WOULD CARE TO MAKE WOULD BE CAREFULLY CONSIDERED.
SIR...
...I REQUEST ASSIGNMENT AS HER CAPTAIN.
YOU DO.
YES, SIR... THE ENTERPRISE IS THE FINEST SHIP IN THE FLEET, AND SHE DESERVES AN EXPERIENCED HAND AT HER HELM.
I SUBMIT THAT THERE IS NO MORE EXPERIENCED HAND THAN--
THAT'S ENOUGH, KIRK.
BUT, SIR, I...
THAT'S ENOUGH! I'LL HEAR NO MORE...
...BECAUSE I DON'T NEED TO, JIM. WE'VE TAKEN HER AWAY FROM YOU TWICE, AND YOU'VE GOTTEN HER BACK TWICE.
I THINK THAT'S LESSON ENOUGH EVEN FOR A GRAND ADMIRAL, DON'T YOU... CAPTAIN?
YES, SIR! I MEAN... THANK YOU, SIR!
CAPTAIN KIRK TO ENTERPRISE.
"CAPTAIN?" SIR, YOU GOT HER BACK?
WELL, MR. SULU, LET'S JUST SAY...
...THAT I WAS ABLE TO MAKE OLD MAN TURNER SEE THINGS MY WAY! BEAM ME ABOARD AND INFORM THE CREW!
THEY ALREADY KNOW, SIR! I PATCHED YOU THROUGH THE SHIP!
4

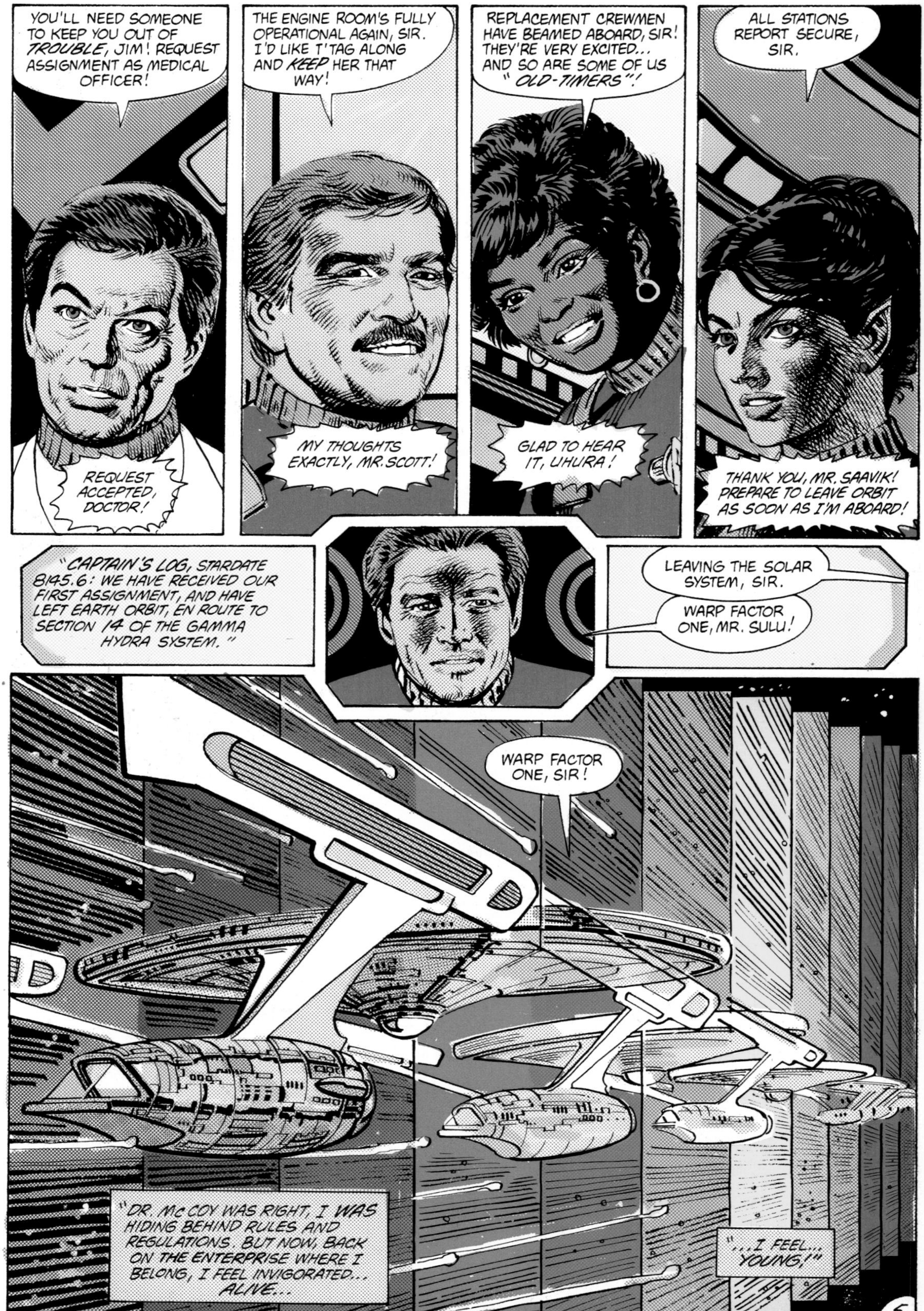
YOU'LL NEED SOMEONE TO KEEP YOU OUT OF TROUBLE, JIM! REQUEST ASSIGNMENT AS MEDICAL OFFICER!
REQUEST ACCEPTED, DOCTOR!
THE ENGINE ROOM'S FULLY OPERATIONAL AGAIN, SIR. I'D LIKE T'TAG ALONG AND KEEP HER THAT WAY!
MY THOUGHTS EXACTLY, MR. SCOTT!
REPLACEMENT CREWMEN HAVE BEAMED ABOARD, SIR! THEY'RE VERY EXCITED... AND SO ARE SOME OF US "OLD-TIMERS"!
GLAD TO HEAR IT, UHURA!
ALL STATIONS REPORT SECURE, SIR.
THANK YOU, MR. SAAVIK! PREPARE TO LEAVE ORBIT AS SOON AS I'M ABOARD!
"CAPTAIN'S LOG, STARDATE 8145.6: WE HAVE RECEIVED OUR FIRST ASSIGNMENT, AND HAVE LEFT EARTH ORBIT, EN ROUTE TO SECTION 14 OF THE GAMMA HYDRA SYSTEM."
LEAVING THE SOLAR SYSTEM, SIR.
WARP FACTOR ONE, MR. SULU!
WARP FACTOR ONE, SIR!
"DR. McCOY WAS RIGHT, I WAS HIDING BEHIND RULES AND REGULATIONS. BUT NOW, BACK ON THE ENTERPRISE WHERE I BELONG, I FEEL INVIGORATED... ALIVE...
"...I FEEL... YOUNG!"
5

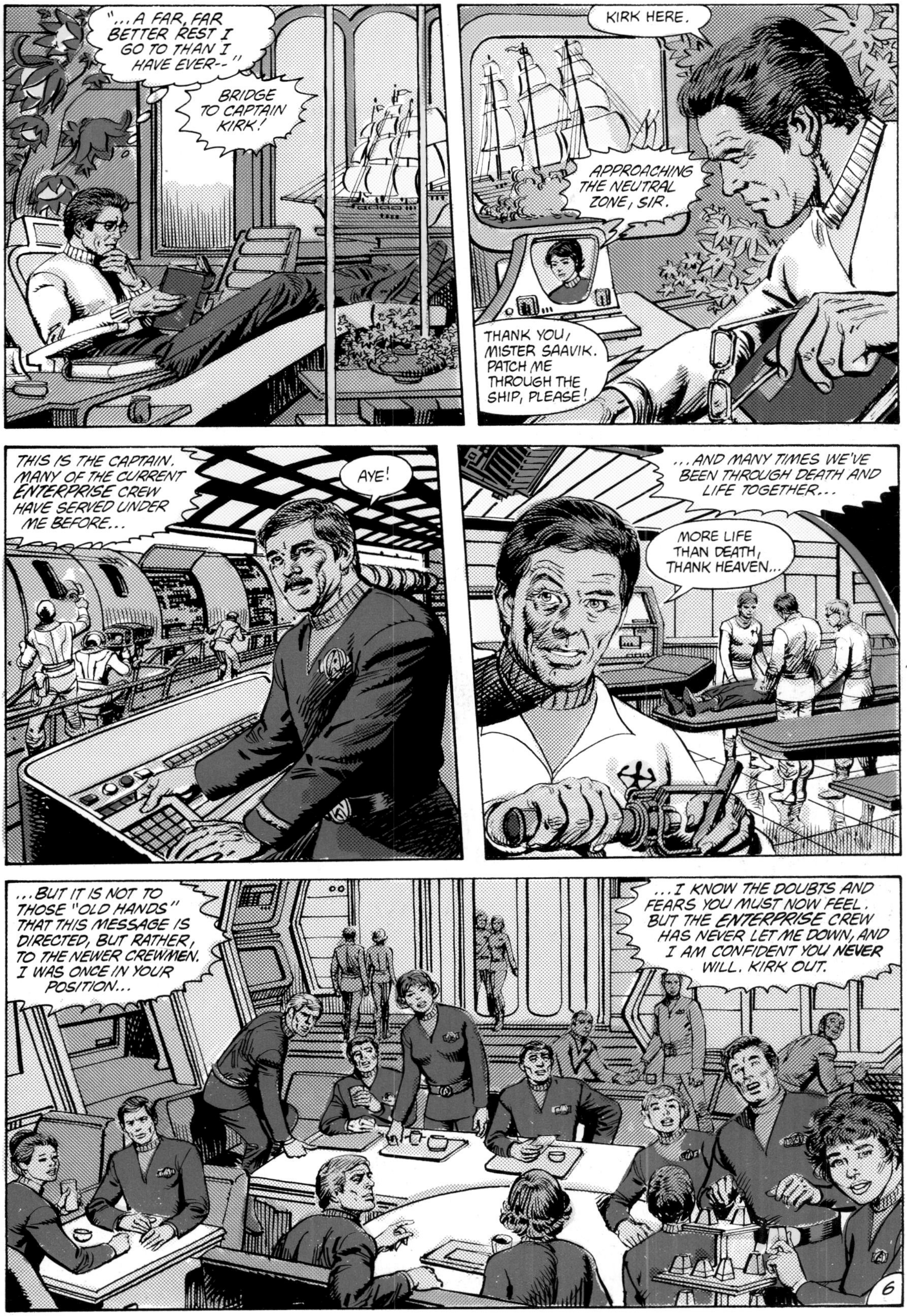
"...A FAR, FAR BETTER REST I GO TO THAN I HAVE EVER--"
BRIDGE TO CAPTAIN KIRK!
KIRK HERE.
APPROACHING THE NEUTRAL ZONE, SIR.
THANK YOU, MISTER SAAVIK. PATCH ME THROUGH THE SHIP, PLEASE!
THIS IS THE CAPTAIN. MANY OF THE CURRENT ENTERPRISE CREW HAVE SERVED UNDER ME BEFORE...
AYE!
...AND MANY TIMES WE'VE BEEN THROUGH DEATH AND LIFE TOGETHER...
MORE LIFE THAN DEATH, THANK HEAVEN...
...BUT IT IS NOT TO THOSE "OLD HANDS" THAT THIS MESSAGE IS DIRECTED, BUT RATHER, TO THE NEWER CREWMEN. I WAS ONCE IN YOUR POSITION...
...I KNOW THE DOUBTS AND FEARS YOU MUST NOW FEEL. BUT THE ENTERPRISE CREW HAS NEVER LET ME DOWN, AND I AM CONFIDENT YOU NEVER WILL. KIRK OUT.
6

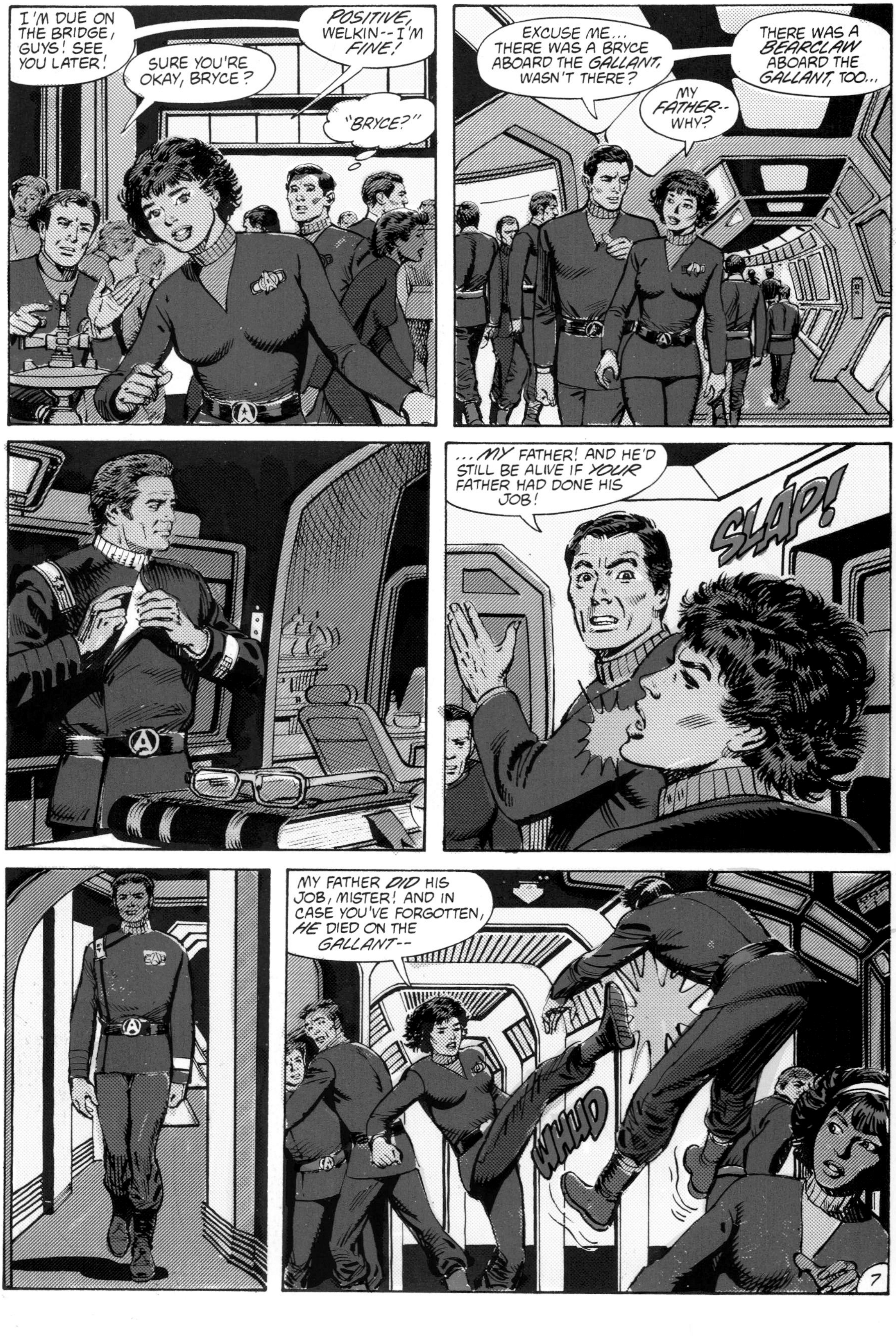
I'M DUE ON THE BRIDGE, GUYS! SEE YOU LATER!
SURE YOU'RE OKAY, BRYCE?
POSITIVE, WELKIN--I'M FINE!
"BRYCE?"
EXCUSE ME... THERE WAS A BRYCE ABOARD THE GALLANT, WASN'T THERE?
MY FATHER-- WHY?
THERE WAS A BEARCLAW ABOARD THE GALLANT, TOO...
...MY FATHER! AND HE'D STILL BE ALIVE IF YOUR FATHER HAD DONE HIS JOB!
SLAP!
MY FATHER DID HIS JOB, MISTER! AND IN CASE YOU'VE FORGOTTEN, HE DIED ON THE GALLANT--
WHUD

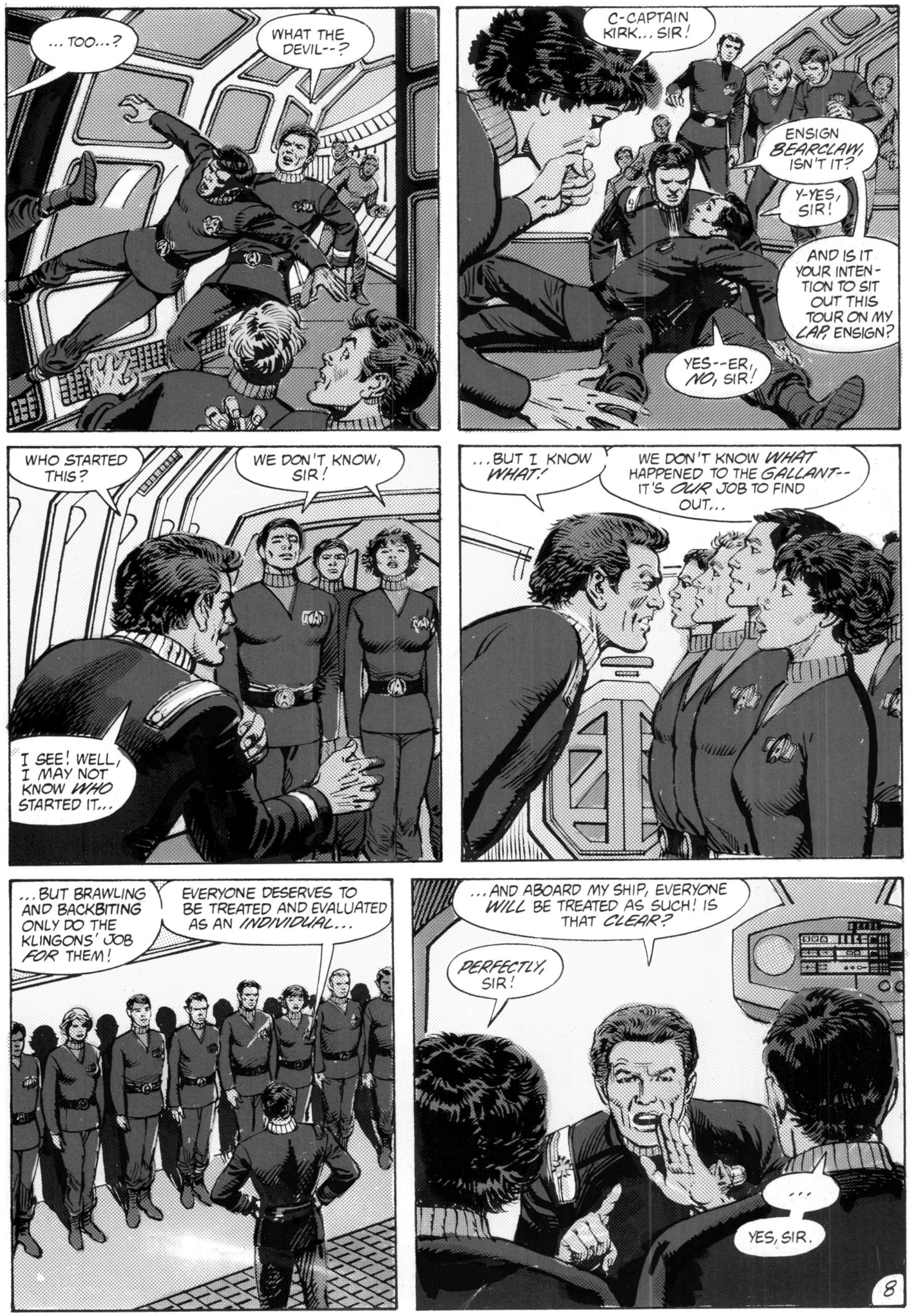

... TOO...?
WHAT THE DEVIL--?
C-CAPTAIN KIRK... SIR!
ENSIGN BEARCLAW, ISN'T IT?
Y-YES, SIR!
AND IS IT YOUR INTENTION TO SIT OUT THIS TOUR ON MY LAP, ENSIGN?
YES--ER, NO, SIR!
WHO STARTED THIS?
WE DON'T KNOW, SIR!
I SEE! WELL, I MAY NOT KNOW WHO STARTED IT...
...BUT I KNOW WHAT!
WE DON'T KNOW WHAT HAPPENED TO THE GALLANT--IT'S OUR JOB TO FIND OUT...
...BUT BRAWLING AND BACKBITING ONLY DO THE KLINGONS' JOB FOR THEM!
EVERYONE DESERVES TO BE TREATED AND EVALUATED AS AN INDIVIDUAL...
...AND ABOARD MY SHIP, EVERYONE WILL BE TREATED AS SUCH! IS THAT CLEAR?
PERFECTLY, SIR!
...
YES, SIR.

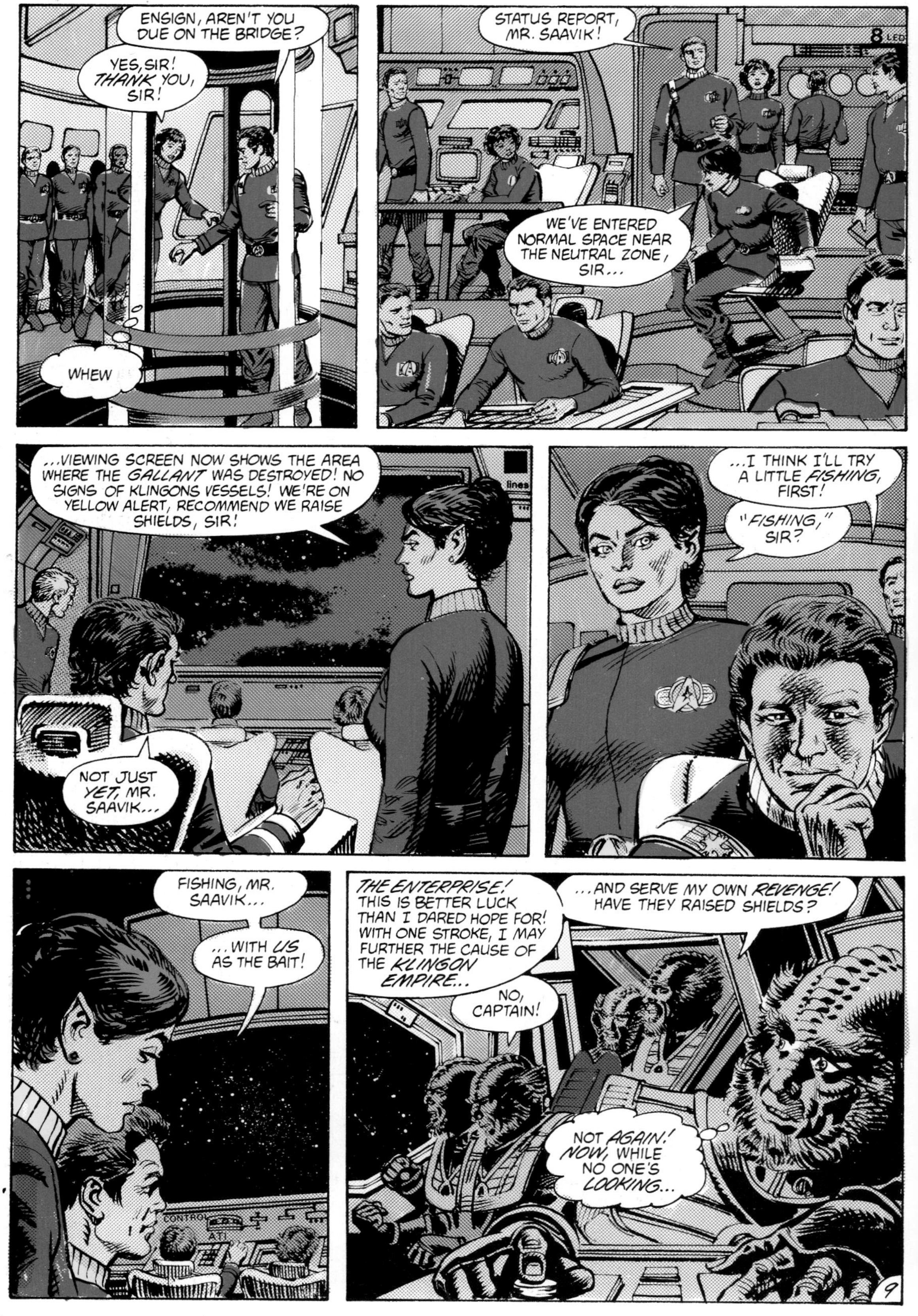

ENSIGN, AREN'T YOU DUE ON THE BRIDGE?
YES, SIR! THANK YOU, SIR!
WHEW
STATUS REPORT, MR. SAAVIK!
WE'VE ENTERED NORMAL SPACE NEAR THE NEUTRAL ZONE, SIR...
...VIEWING SCREEN NOW SHOWS THE AREA WHERE THE GALLANT WAS DESTROYED! NO SIGNS OF KLINGONS VESSELS! WE'RE ON YELLOW ALERT, RECOMMEND WE RAISE SHIELDS, SIR!
NOT JUST YET, MR. SAAVIK...
...I THINK I'LL TRY A LITTLE FISHING, FIRST!
"FISHING," SIR?
FISHING, MR. SAAVIK...
...WITH US AS THE BAIT!
THE ENTERPRISE! THIS IS BETTER LUCK THAN I DARED HOPE FOR! WITH ONE STROKE, I MAY FURTHER THE CAUSE OF THE KLINGON EMPIRE...
...AND SERVE MY OWN REVENGE! HAVE THEY RAISED SHIELDS?
NO, CAPTAIN!
NOT AGAIN! NOW, WHILE NO ONE'S LOOKING...
9

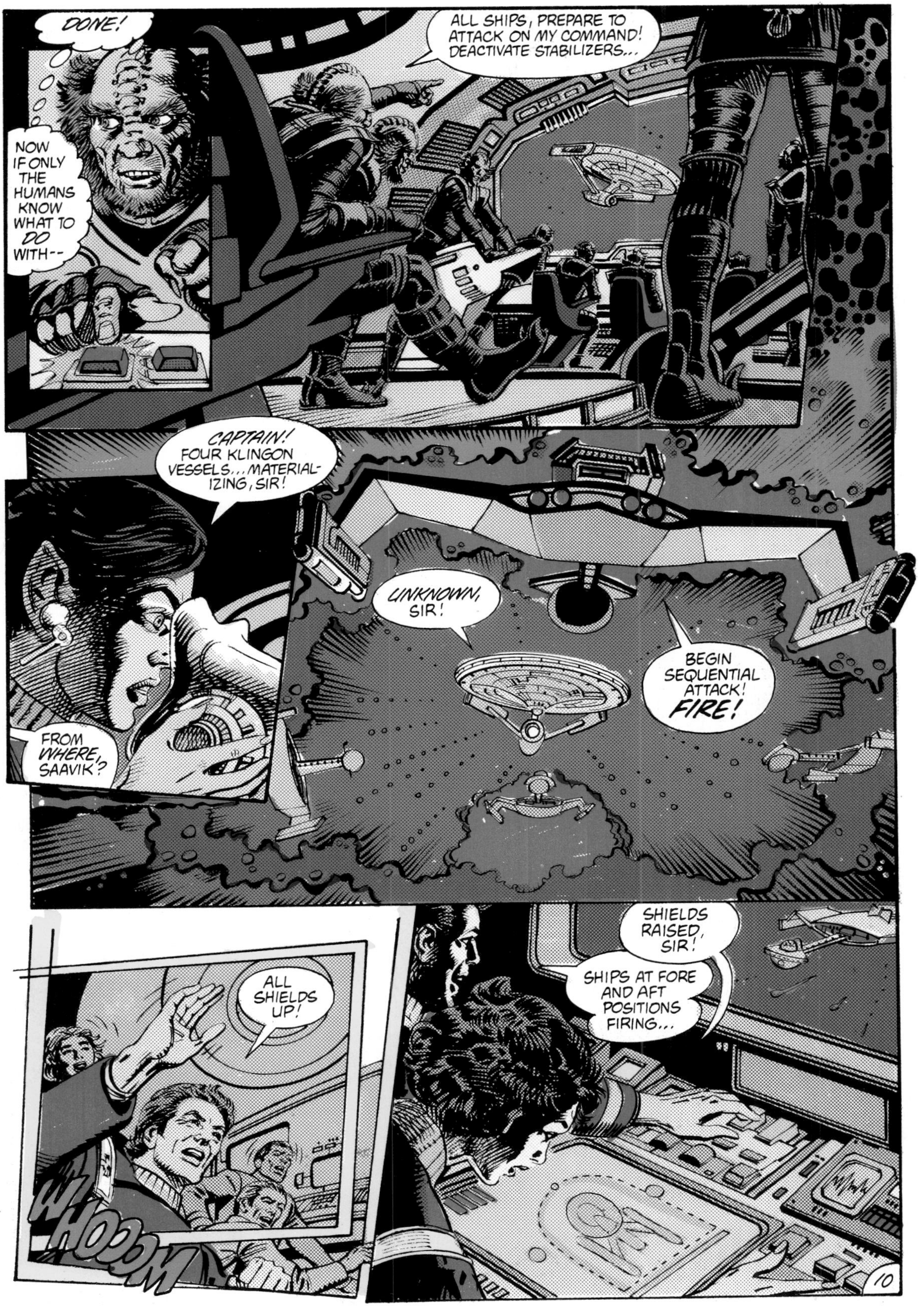
DONE!
NOW IF ONLY THE HUMANS KNOW WHAT TO DO WITH--
ALL SHIPS, PREPARE TO ATTACK ON MY COMMAND! DEACTIVATE STABILIZERS...
CAPTAIN! FOUR KLINGON VESSELS... MATERIAL-IZING, SIR!
FROM WHERE, SAAVIK?
UNKNOWN, SIR!
BEGIN SEQUENTIAL ATTACK! FIRE!
ALL SHIELDS UP!
WHOOOM
SHIELDS RAISED, SIR!
SHIPS AT FORE AND AFT POSITIONS FIRING...

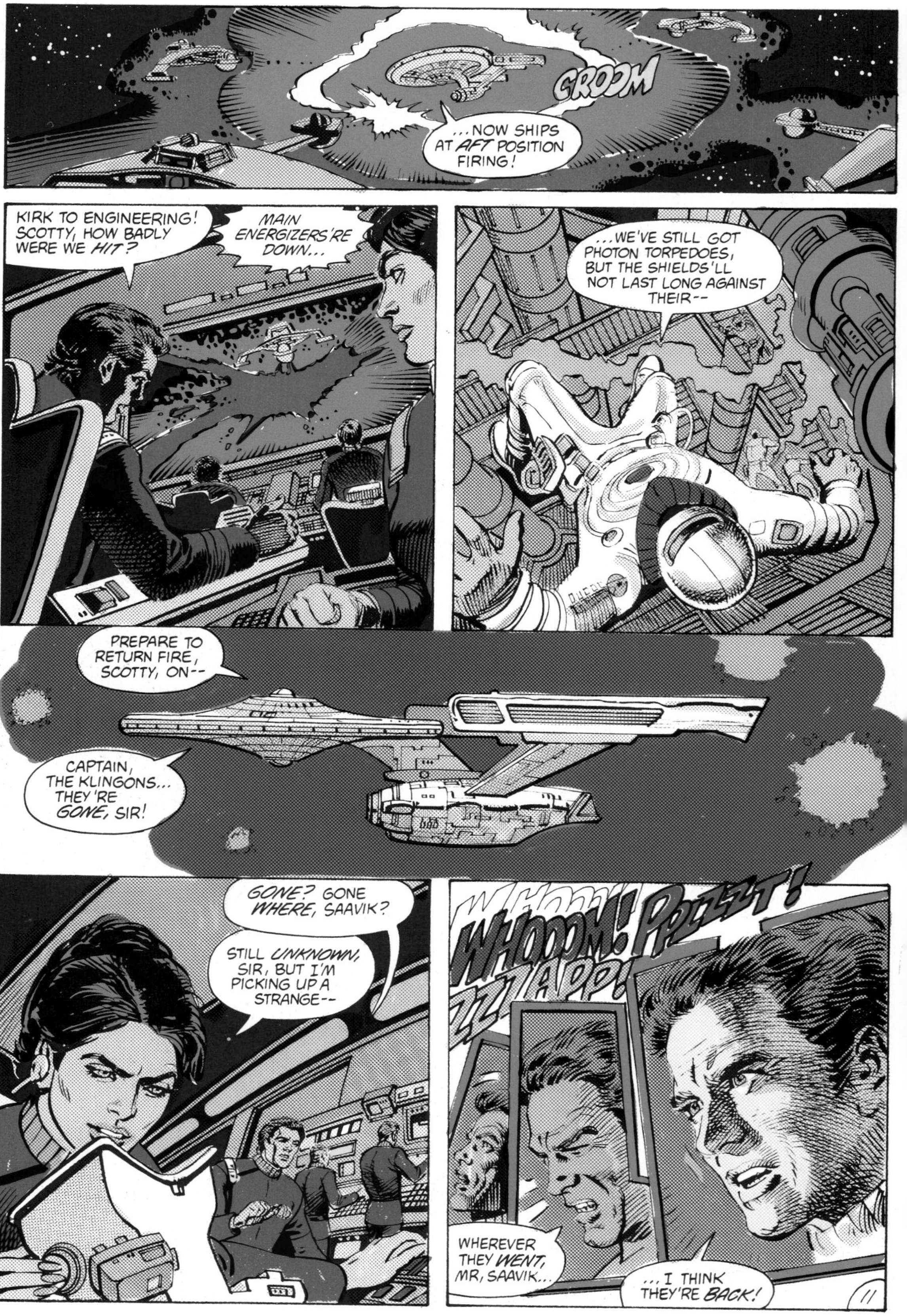
CROOM
...NOW SHIPS AT AFT POSITION FIRING!
KIRK TO ENGINEERING! SCOTTY, HOW BADLY WERE WE HIT?
MAIN ENERGIZERS'RE DOWN...
...WE'VE STILL GOT PHOTON TORPEDOES, BUT THE SHIELDS'LL NOT LAST LONG AGAINST THEIR--
PREPARE TO RETURN FIRE, SCOTTY, ON--
CAPTAIN, THE KLINGONS... THEY'RE GONE, SIR!
GONE? GONE WHERE, SAAVIK?
STILL UNKNOWN, SIR, BUT I'M PICKING UP A STRANGE--
WHOOOM! PPZZZT!
ZZZAPP!
WHEREVER THEY WENT, MR. SAAVIK...
...I THINK THEY'RE BACK!
11

THAT SALVO WAS TO OUR *TAIL*, SIR--KLINGONS *AHEAD* OF US FIRING NOW!

WHOOM

ENGINEERING, *ALL POWER* TO SHIELDS!

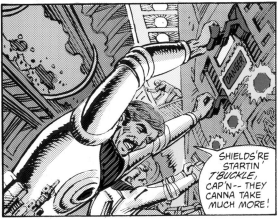

DANGER

SHIELDS'RE STARTIN' *T'BUCKLE*, CAP'N-- THEY CANNA TAKE MUCH MORE!

AFT SHIPS FIRING AGAIN, SIR!

THEY'RE ONE-TWOING US, MR. SULU...

...MAYBE WE CAN *USE* THAT...!

MR. SULU-- ON MY COMMAND, *DROP* AFT SHIELDS!

?

Y-YES, SIR!

...AND, MR. CHEKOV, PREPARE TO FIRE *AFT PHOTON TORPEDOES!*

AYE, KEPTIN!

CAPTAIN, DO YOU THINK--

WHEN I NEED A COMMENT FROM *YOU*, MR. SAAVIK, I'LL *ASK* FOR IT! IS THAT CLEAR?

YES... SIR.

12

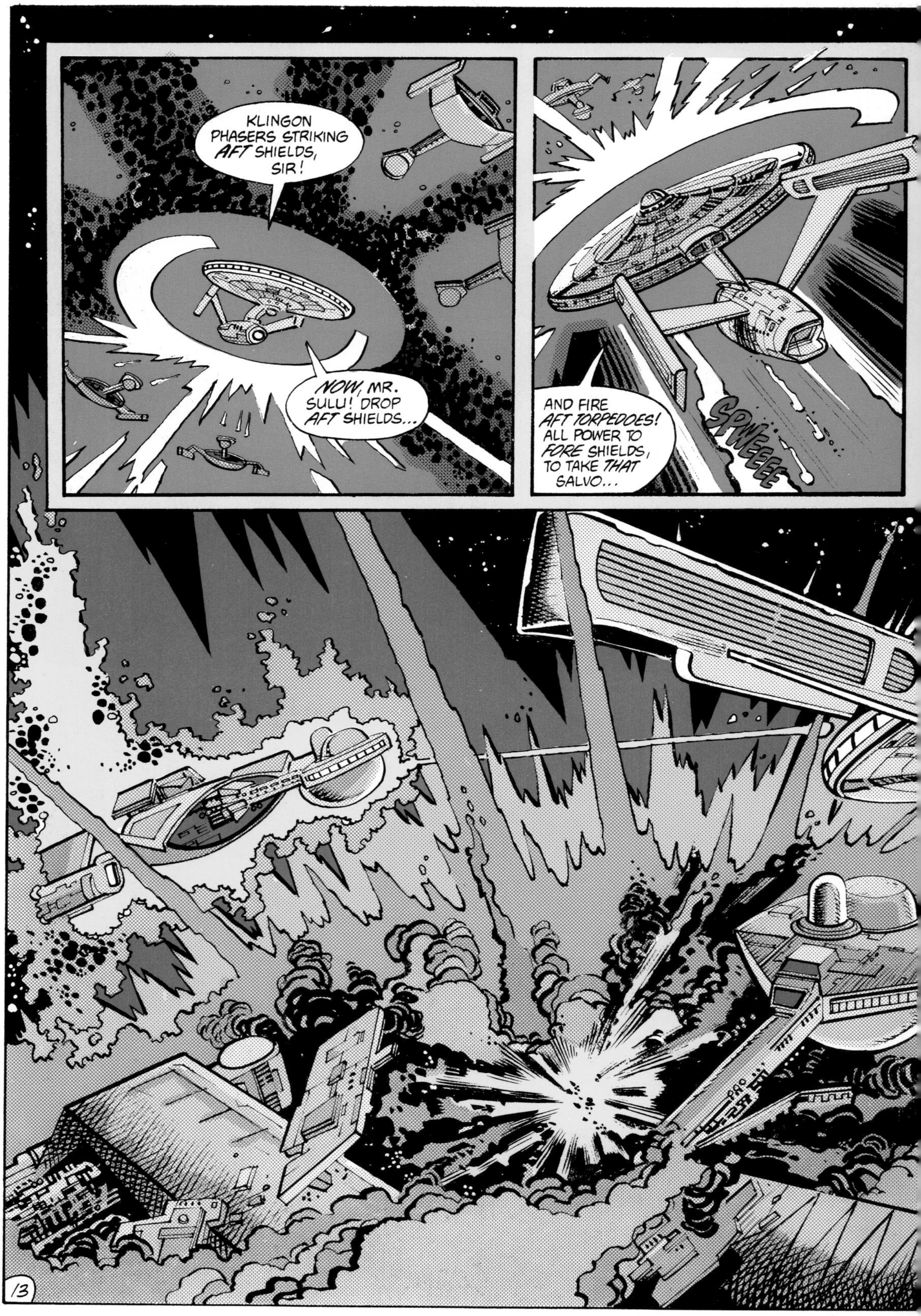
KLINGON PHASERS STRIKING AFT SHIELDS, SIR!
NOW, MR. SULU! DROP AFT SHIELDS...
AND FIRE AFT TORPEDOES! ALL POWER TO FORE SHIELDS, TO TAKE THAT SALVO...
SPWEEEEE
13

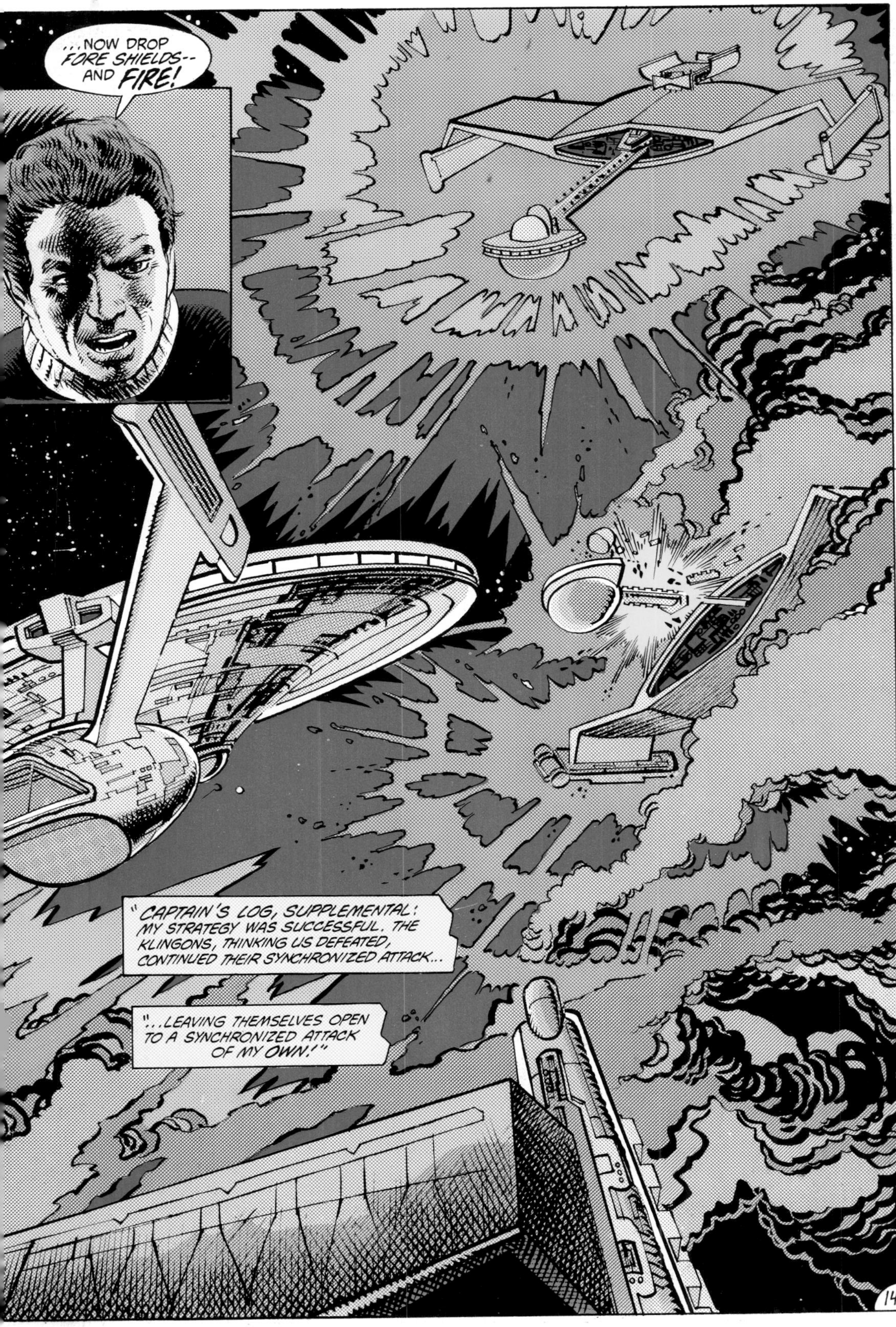
...NOW DROP FORE SHIELDS-- AND FIRE!
"CAPTAIN'S LOG, SUPPLEMENTAL: MY STRATEGY WAS SUCCESSFUL. THE KLINGONS, THINKING US DEFEATED, CONTINUED THEIR SYNCHRONIZED ATTACK...
"...LEAVING THEMSELVES OPEN TO A SYNCHRONIZED ATTACK OF MY OWN!"
14

DAMN THAT KIRK! HE IS A *SORCERER!* HELMSMAN KONOM, GET US *OUT* OF HERE!

YES, CAPTAIN KOLOTH!

IF ONLY THEY REALIZED WHAT I WAS TRYING TO *TELL* THEM...!

TWO SHIPS HAVE SELF-DESTRUCTED, TWO SHIPS *VANISHING,* SIR!

BUT *HOW* DO THEY APPEAR AND DISAPPEAR, MR. SAAVIK?

UNKNOWN, SIR, BUT I'M TRYING--

I'M INTERESTED IN *RESULTS,* SAAVIK, NOT EXCUSES FOR YOUR *LACK* OF THEM!

UHURA, THERE WILL BE A MEETING OF ALL DEPARTMENT HEADS IN THE BRIEFING ROOM, IN 15 MINUTES!

YES, CAPTAIN!

DON'T MAKE ME--OR YOUR *TEACHER*--SORRY YOU WERE ASSIGNED TO YOUR POST, SAAVIK.

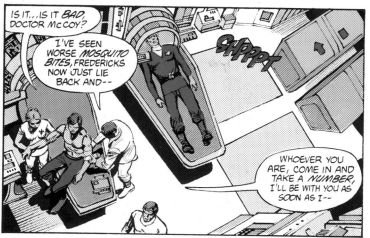

IS IT...IS IT *BAD,* DOCTOR McCOY?

I'VE SEEN WORSE *MOSQUITO BITES,* FREDERICKS. NOW JUST LIE BACK AND--

SHPPPT

WHOEVER YOU ARE, COME IN AND TAKE A *NUMBER,* I'LL BE WITH YOU AS SOON AS I--

WELL, THIS *IS* A SURPRISE!

15

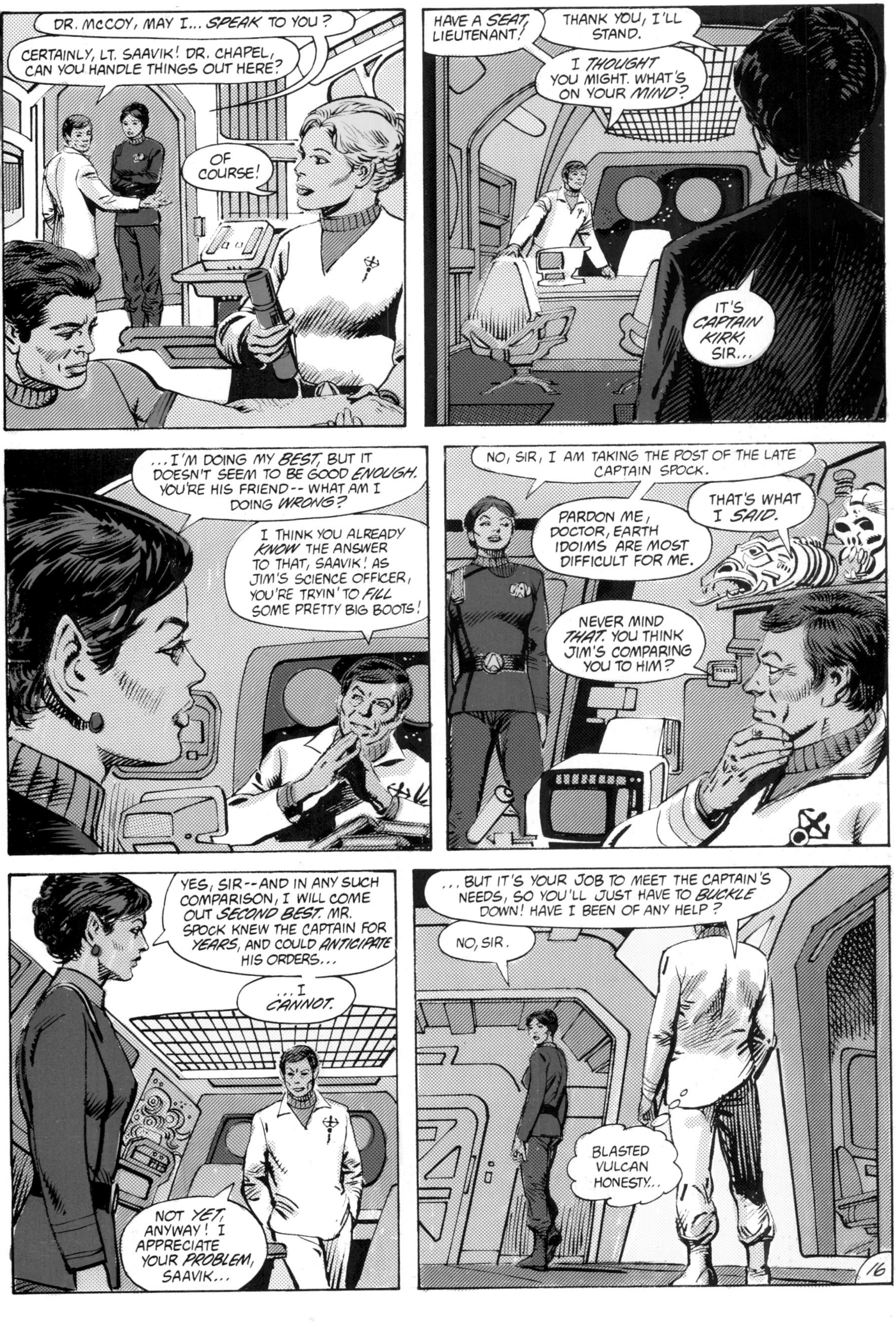
DR. McCOY, MAY I... SPEAK TO YOU?
CERTAINLY, LT. SAAVIK! DR. CHAPEL, CAN YOU HANDLE THINGS OUT HERE?
OF COURSE!
HAVE A SEAT, LIEUTENANT!
THANK YOU, I'LL STAND.
I THOUGHT YOU MIGHT. WHAT'S ON YOUR MIND?
IT'S CAPTAIN KIRK, SIR...
...I'M DOING MY BEST, BUT IT DOESN'T SEEM TO BE GOOD ENOUGH. YOU'RE HIS FRIEND-- WHAT AM I DOING WRONG?
I THINK YOU ALREADY KNOW THE ANSWER TO THAT, SAAVIK! AS JIM'S SCIENCE OFFICER, YOU'RE TRYIN' TO FILL SOME PRETTY BIG BOOTS!
NO, SIR, I AM TAKING THE POST OF THE LATE CAPTAIN SPOCK.
THAT'S WHAT I SAID.
PARDON ME, DOCTOR, EARTH IDOIMS ARE MOST DIFFICULT FOR ME.
NEVER MIND THAT. YOU THINK JIM'S COMPARING YOU TO HIM?
YES, SIR--AND IN ANY SUCH COMPARISON, I WILL COME OUT SECOND BEST. MR. SPOCK KNEW THE CAPTAIN FOR YEARS, AND COULD ANTICIPATE HIS ORDERS...
...I CANNOT.
NOT YET, ANYWAY! I APPRECIATE YOUR PROBLEM, SAAVIK...
...BUT IT'S YOUR JOB TO MEET THE CAPTAIN'S NEEDS, SO YOU'LL JUST HAVE TO BUCKLE DOWN! HAVE I BEEN OF ANY HELP?
NO, SIR.
BLASTED VULCAN HONESTY...
16

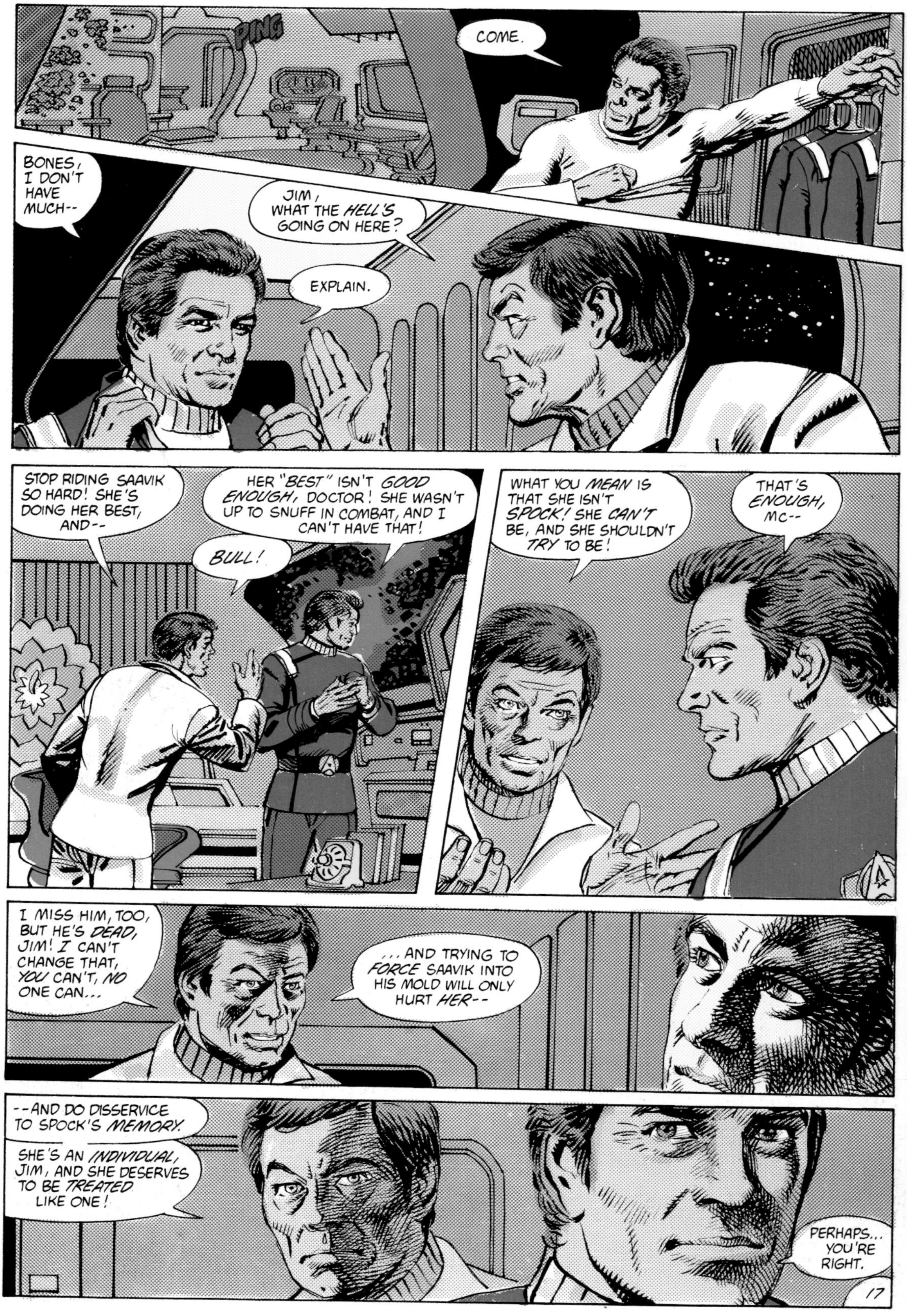
PING
COME.
BONES, I DON'T HAVE MUCH--
JIM, WHAT THE HELL'S GOING ON HERE?
EXPLAIN.
STOP RIDING SAAVIK SO HARD! SHE'S DOING HER BEST, AND--
HER "BEST" ISN'T GOOD ENOUGH, DOCTOR! SHE WASN'T UP TO SNUFF IN COMBAT, AND I CAN'T HAVE THAT!
BULL!
WHAT YOU MEAN IS THAT SHE ISN'T SPOCK! SHE CAN'T BE, AND SHE SHOULDN'T TRY TO BE!
THAT'S ENOUGH, MC--
I MISS HIM, TOO, BUT HE'S DEAD, JIM! I CAN'T CHANGE THAT, YOU CAN'T, NO ONE CAN...
...AND TRYING TO FORCE SAAVIK INTO HIS MOLD WILL ONLY HURT HER--
--AND DO DISSERVICE TO SPOCK'S MEMORY.
SHE'S AN INDIVIDUAL, JIM, AND SHE DESERVES TO BE TREATED LIKE ONE!
PERHAPS... YOU'RE RIGHT.
17

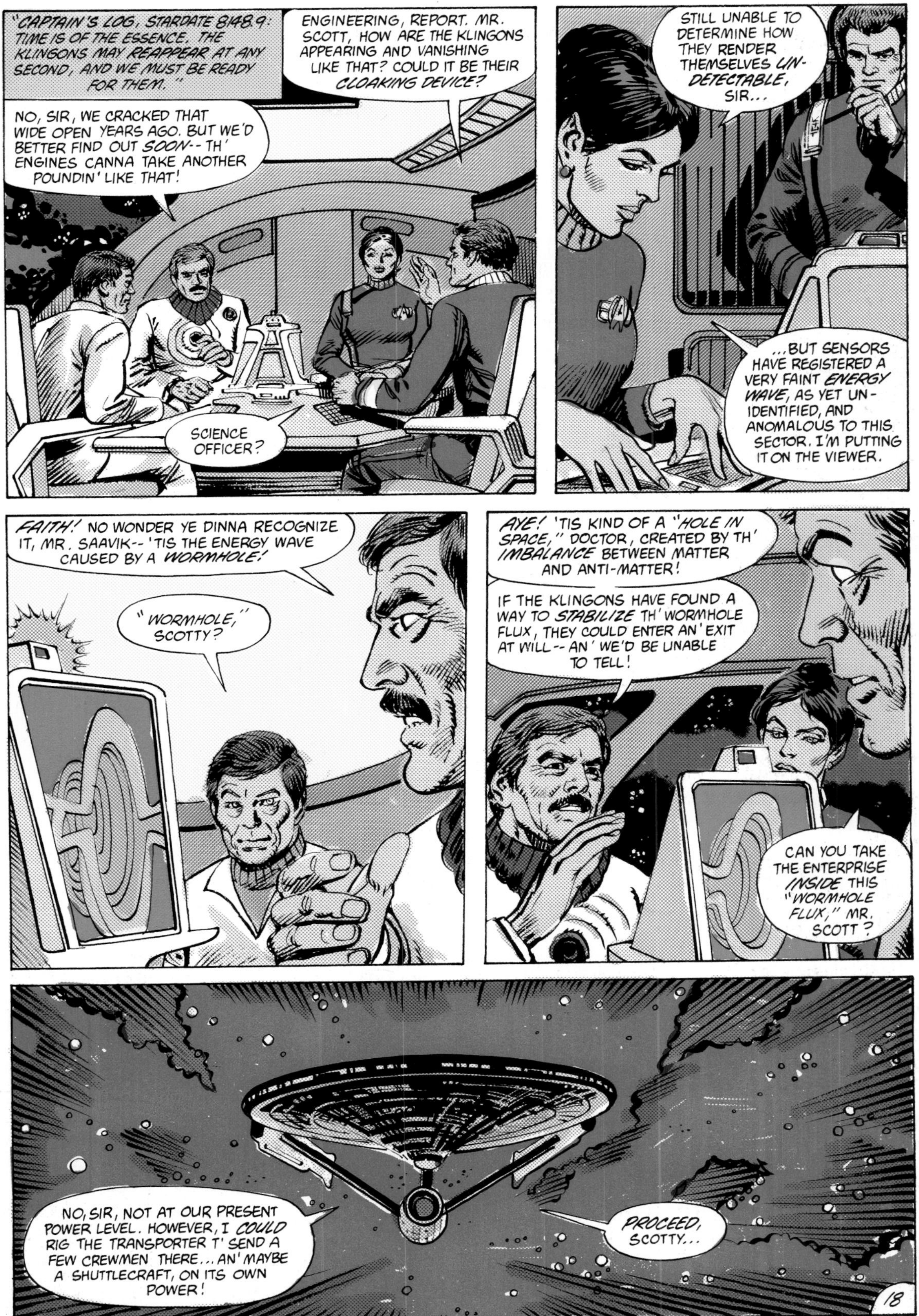

"CAPTAIN'S LOG, STARDATE 8148.9: TIME IS OF THE ESSENCE. THE KLINGONS MAY REAPPEAR AT ANY SECOND, AND WE MUST BE READY FOR THEM."
ENGINEERING, REPORT. MR. SCOTT, HOW ARE THE KLINGONS APPEARING AND VANISHING LIKE THAT? COULD IT BE THEIR CLOAKING DEVICE?
NO, SIR, WE CRACKED THAT WIDE OPEN YEARS AGO. BUT WE'D BETTER FIND OUT SOON-- TH' ENGINES CANNA TAKE ANOTHER POUNDIN' LIKE THAT!
SCIENCE OFFICER?
STILL UNABLE TO DETERMINE HOW THEY RENDER THEMSELVES UN-DETECTABLE, SIR...
...BUT SENSORS HAVE REGISTERED A VERY FAINT ENERGY WAVE, AS YET UN-IDENTIFIED, AND ANOMALOUS TO THIS SECTOR. I'M PUTTING IT ON THE VIEWER.
FAITH! NO WONDER YE DINNA RECOGNIZE IT, MR. SAAVIK-- 'TIS THE ENERGY WAVE CAUSED BY A WORMHOLE!
"WORMHOLE," SCOTTY?
AYE! 'TIS KIND OF A "HOLE IN SPACE," DOCTOR, CREATED BY TH' IMBALANCE BETWEEN MATTER AND ANTI-MATTER!
IF THE KLINGONS HAVE FOUND A WAY TO STABILIZE TH' WORMHOLE FLUX, THEY COULD ENTER AN' EXIT AT WILL-- AN' WE'D BE UNABLE TO TELL!
CAN YOU TAKE THE ENTERPRISE INSIDE THIS "WORMHOLE FLUX," MR. SCOTT?
NO, SIR, NOT AT OUR PRESENT POWER LEVEL. HOWEVER, I COULD RIG THE TRANSPORTER T' SEND A FEW CREWMEN THERE... AN' MAYBE A SHUTTLECRAFT, ON ITS OWN POWER!
PROCEED, SCOTTY...

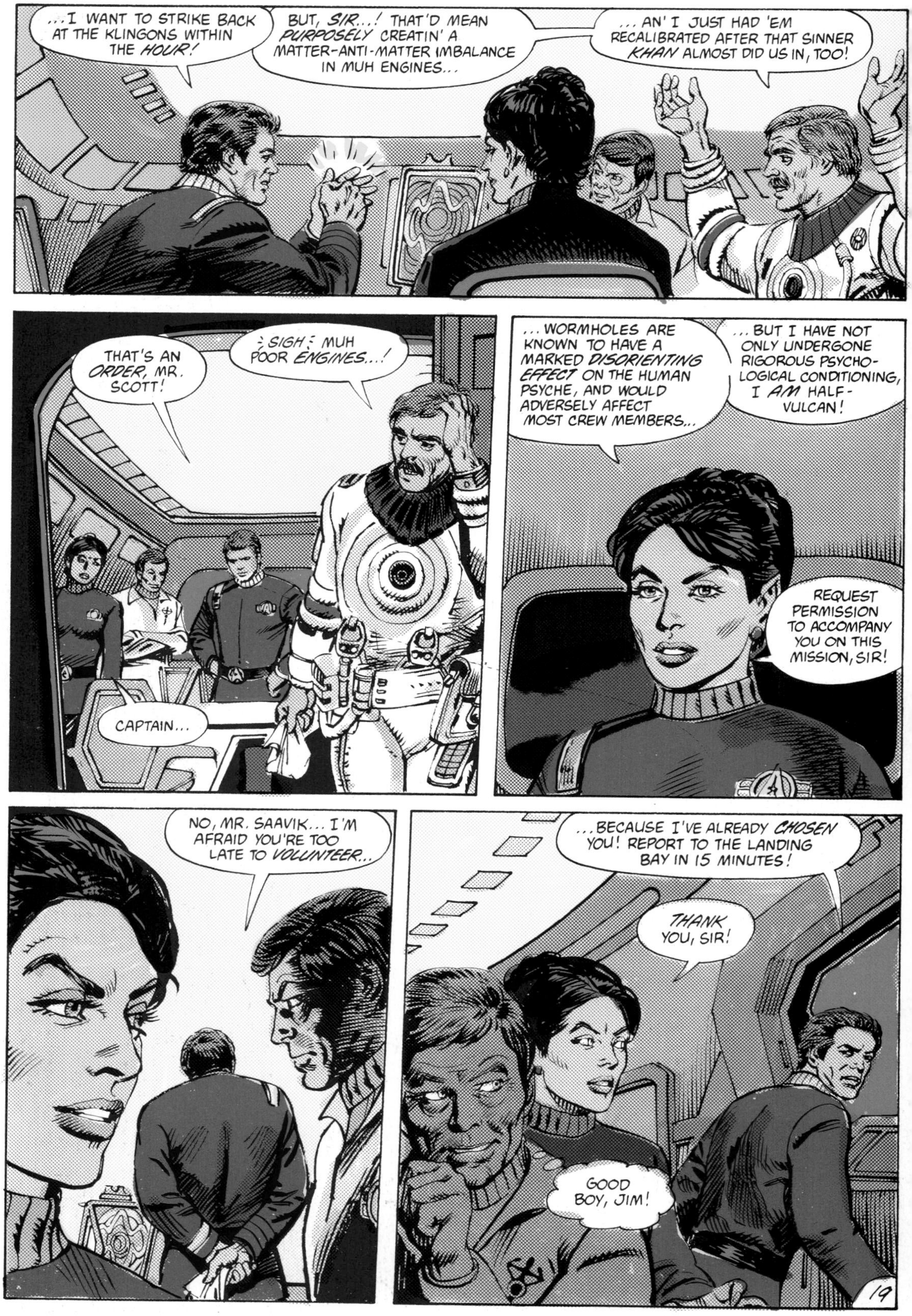
...I WANT TO STRIKE BACK AT THE KLINGONS WITHIN THE HOUR!
BUT, SIR...! THAT'D MEAN PURPOSELY CREATIN' A MATTER-ANTI-MATTER IMBALANCE IN MUH ENGINES...
...AN' I JUST HAD 'EM RECALIBRATED AFTER THAT SINNER KHAN ALMOST DID US IN, TOO!
THAT'S AN ORDER, MR. SCOTT!
SIGH MUH POOR ENGINES...!
CAPTAIN...
...WORMHOLES ARE KNOWN TO HAVE A MARKED DISORIENTING EFFECT ON THE HUMAN PSYCHE, AND WOULD ADVERSELY AFFECT MOST CREW MEMBERS...
...BUT I HAVE NOT ONLY UNDERGONE RIGOROUS PSYCHOLOGICAL CONDITIONING, I AM HALF-VULCAN!
REQUEST PERMISSION TO ACCOMPANY YOU ON THIS MISSION, SIR!
NO, MR. SAAVIK... I'M AFRAID YOU'RE TOO LATE TO VOLUNTEER...
...BECAUSE I'VE ALREADY CHOSEN YOU! REPORT TO THE LANDING BAY IN 15 MINUTES!
THANK YOU, SIR!
GOOD BOY, JIM!

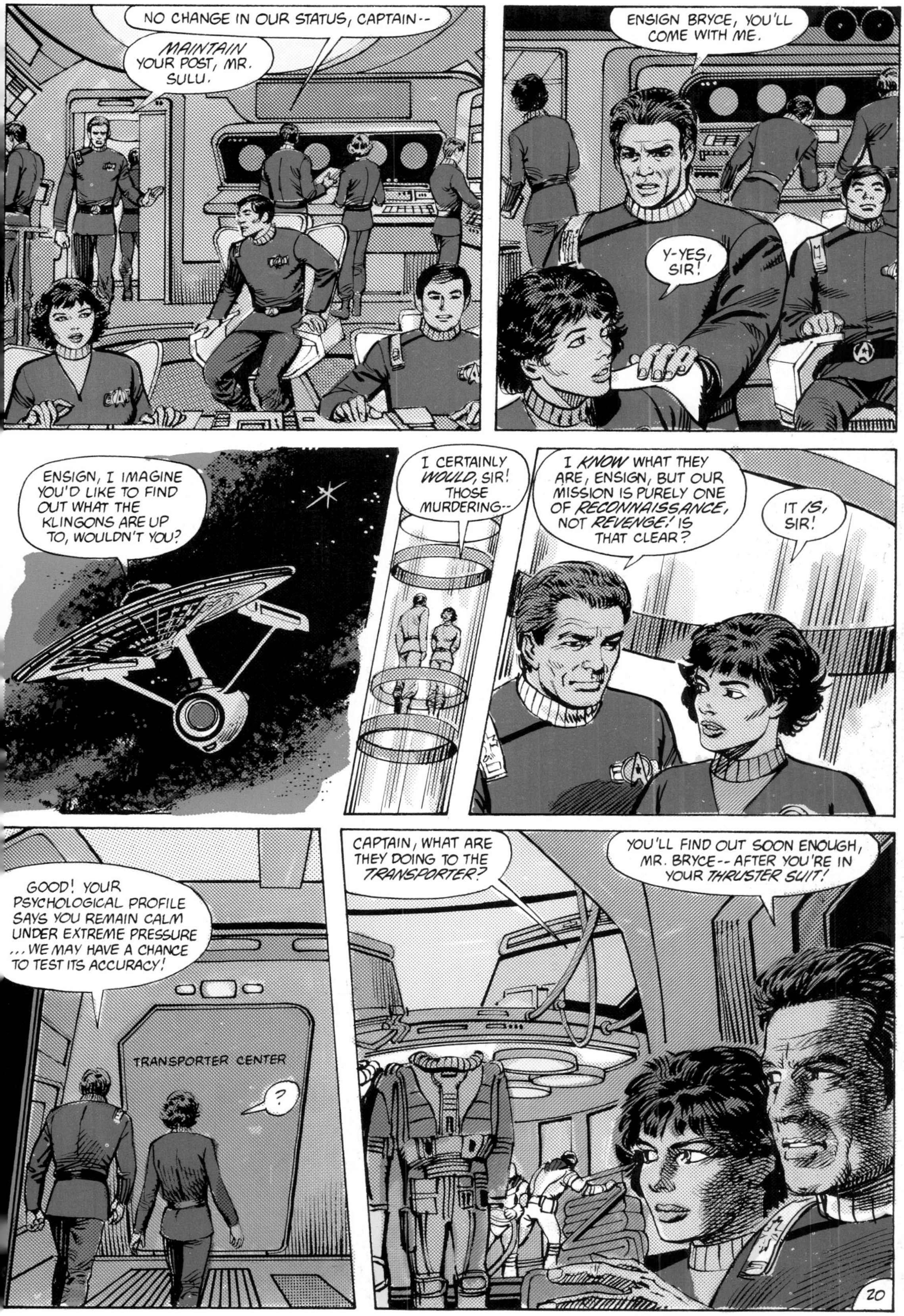

NO CHANGE IN OUR STATUS, CAPTAIN--
MAINTAIN YOUR POST, MR. SULU.
ENSIGN BRYCE, YOU'LL COME WITH ME.
Y-YES, SIR!
ENSIGN, I IMAGINE YOU'D LIKE TO FIND OUT WHAT THE KLINGONS ARE UP TO, WOULDN'T YOU?
I CERTAINLY WOULD, SIR! THOSE MURDERING--
I KNOW WHAT THEY ARE, ENSIGN, BUT OUR MISSION IS PURELY ONE OF RECONNAISSANCE, NOT REVENGE! IS THAT CLEAR?
IT IS, SIR!
GOOD! YOUR PSYCHOLOGICAL PROFILE SAYS YOU REMAIN CALM UNDER EXTREME PRESSURE ... WE MAY HAVE A CHANCE TO TEST ITS ACCURACY!
TRANSPORTER CENTER
?
CAPTAIN, WHAT ARE THEY DOING TO THE TRANSPORTER?
YOU'LL FIND OUT SOON ENOUGH, MR. BRYCE-- AFTER YOU'RE IN YOUR THRUSTER SUIT!
20

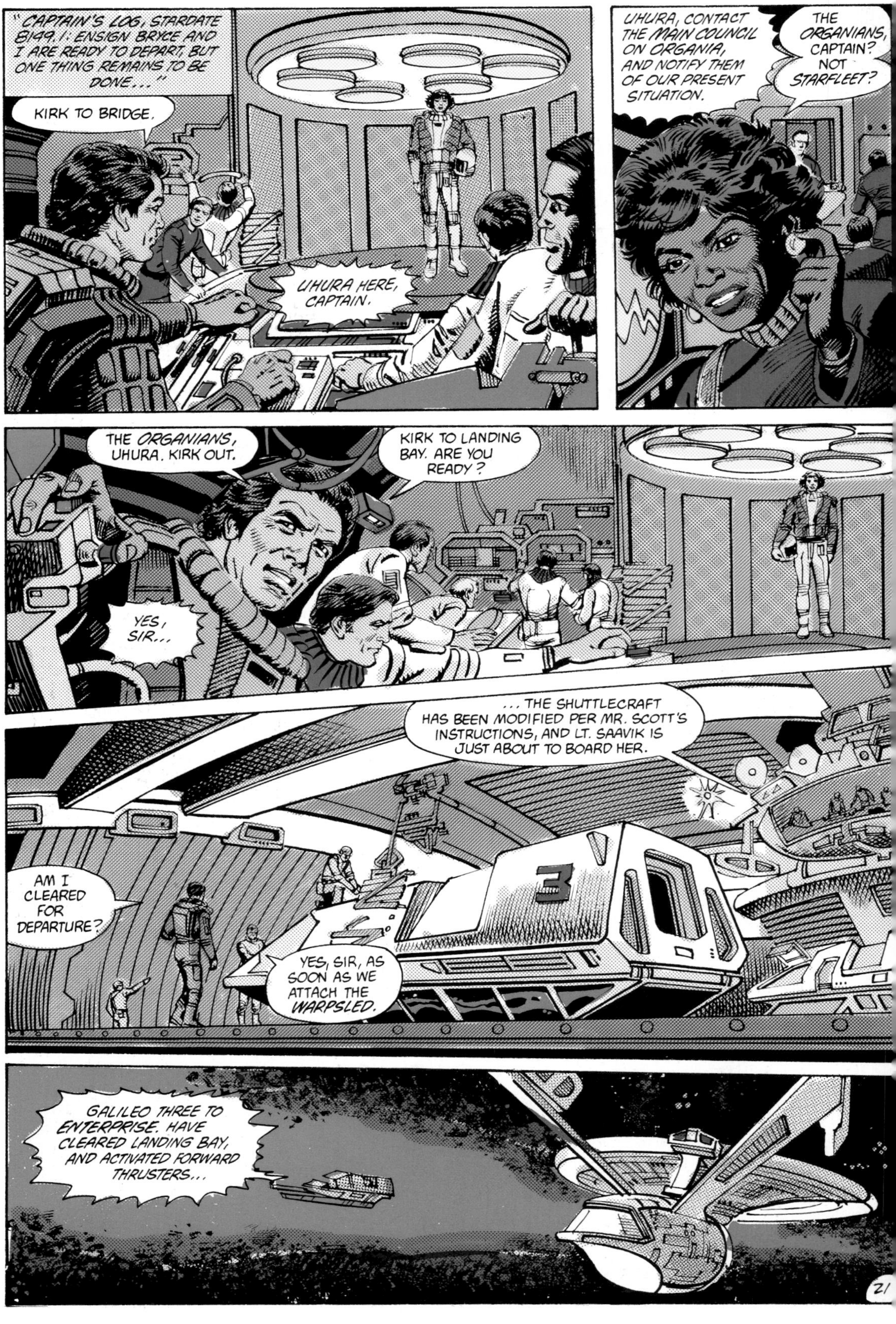
"CAPTAIN'S LOG, STARDATE 8149.1: ENSIGN BRYCE AND I ARE READY TO DEPART, BUT ONE THING REMAINS TO BE DONE..."
KIRK TO BRIDGE.
UHURA HERE, CAPTAIN.
UHURA, CONTACT THE MAIN COUNCIL ON ORGANIA, AND NOTIFY THEM OF OUR PRESENT SITUATION.
THE ORGANIANS, CAPTAIN? NOT STARFLEET?
THE ORGANIANS, UHURA. KIRK OUT.
KIRK TO LANDING BAY. ARE YOU READY?
YES, SIR...
... THE SHUTTLECRAFT HAS BEEN MODIFIED PER MR. SCOTT'S INSTRUCTIONS, AND LT. SAAVIK IS JUST ABOUT TO BOARD HER.
AM I CLEARED FOR DEPARTURE?
YES, SIR, AS SOON AS WE ATTACH THE WARPSLED.
GALILEO THREE TO ENTERPRISE. HAVE CLEARED LANDING BAY, AND ACTIVATED FORWARD THRUSTERS...

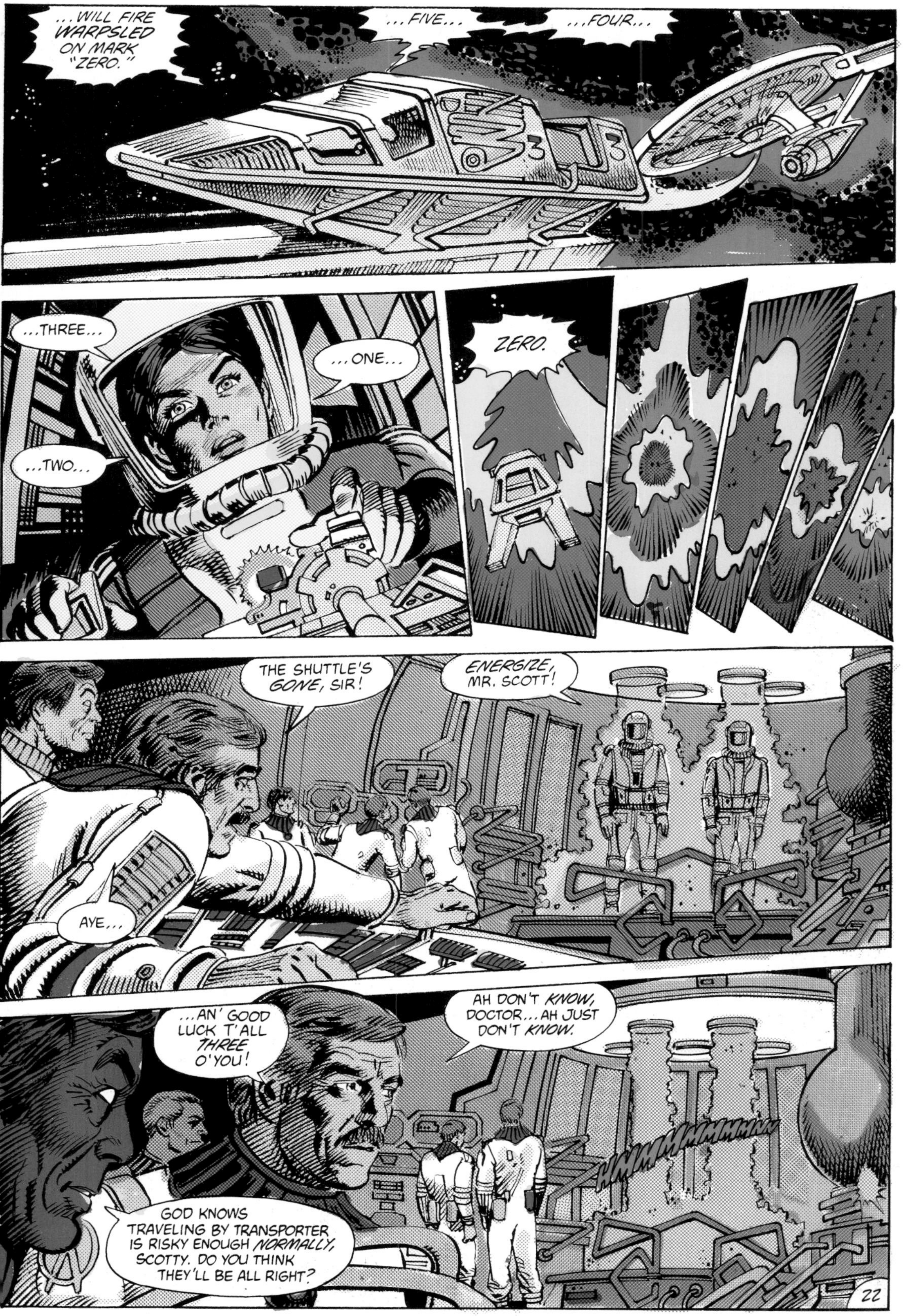
...WILL FIRE WARPSLED ON MARK "ZERO."
...FIVE...
...FOUR...
...THREE...
...TWO...
...ONE...
ZERO.
THE SHUTTLE'S GONE, SIR!
ENERGIZE, MR. SCOTT!
AYE...
...AN' GOOD LUCK T'ALL THREE O'YOU!
AH DON'T KNOW, DOCTOR... AH JUST DON'T KNOW.
HMMMMMMMMMMMM
GOD KNOWS TRAVELING BY TRANSPORTER IS RISKY ENOUGH NORMALLY, SCOTTY. DO YOU THINK THEY'LL BE ALL RIGHT?
22

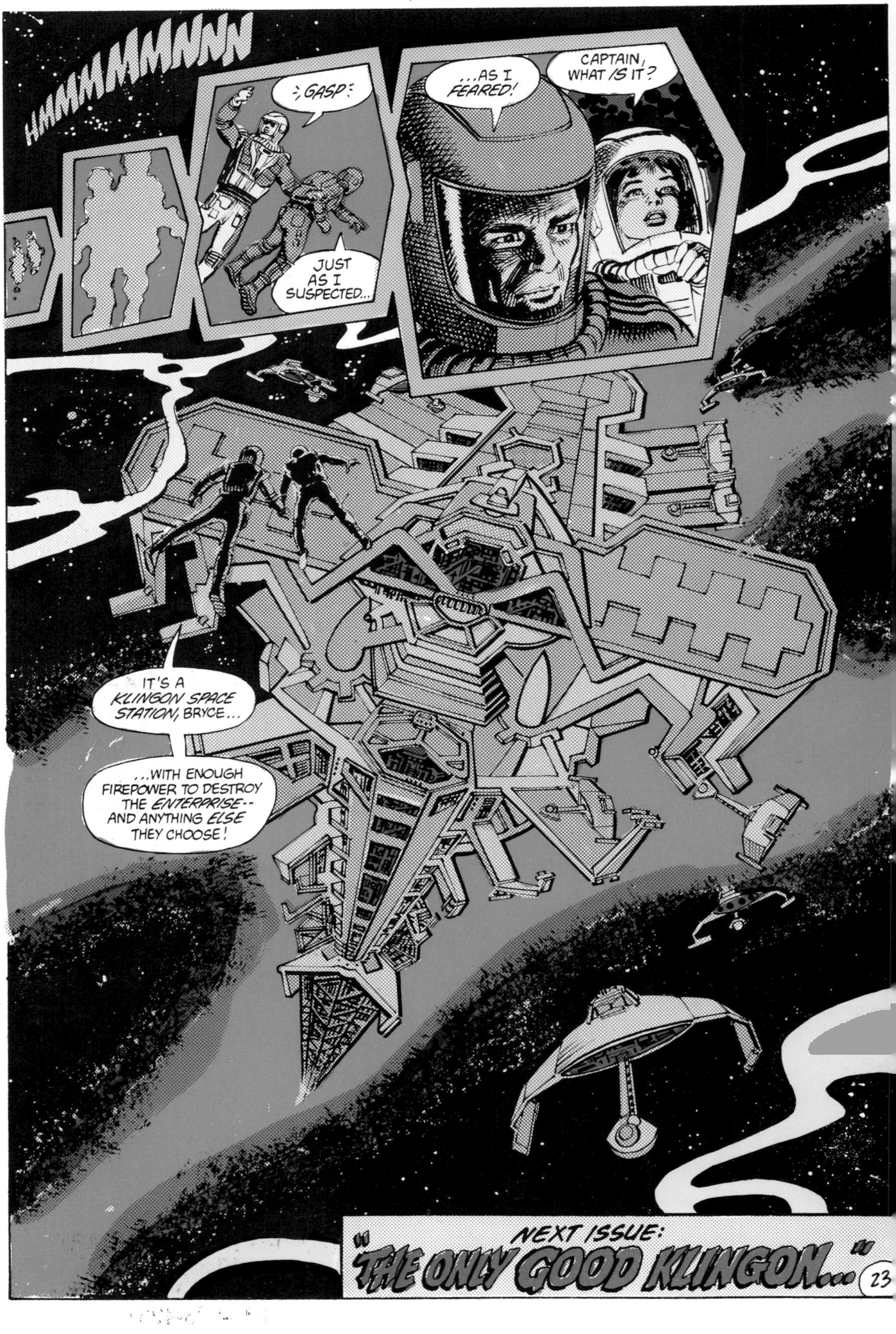
HMMMMMNNN
GASP
JUST AS I SUSPECTED...
...AS I FEARED!
CAPTAIN, WHAT IS IT?
IT'S A KLINGON SPACE STATION, BRYCE...
...WITH ENOUGH FIREPOWER TO DESTROY THE ENTERPRISE-- AND ANYTHING ELSE THEY CHOOSE!
NEXT ISSUE:
"THE ONLY GOOD KLINGON..."

STAR TREK™

Based on the series created by **Gene Roddenberry**

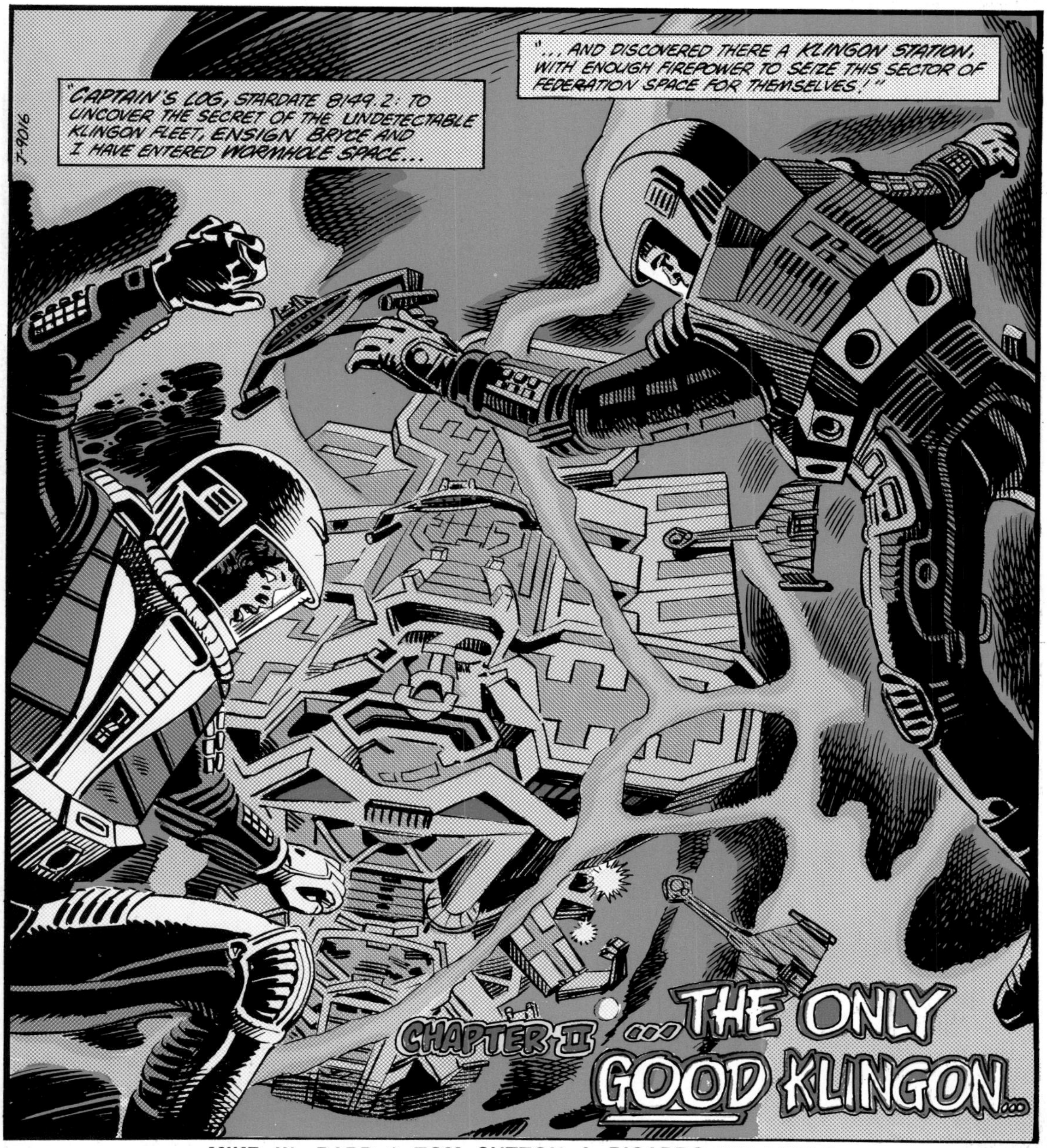
J-9016
"CAPTAIN'S LOG, STARDATE 8149.2: TO UNCOVER THE SECRET OF THE UNDETECTABLE KLINGON FLEET, ENSIGN BRYCE AND I HAVE ENTERED WORMHOLE SPACE...
"...AND DISCOVERED THERE A KLINGON STATION, WITH ENOUGH FIREPOWER TO SEIZE THIS SECTOR OF FEDERATION SPACE FOR THEMSELVES!"
CHAPTER II ...THE ONLY GOOD KLINGON...

MIKE W. BARR * **TOM SUTTON & RICARDO VILLAGRAN**
Writer — Artists

JOHN COSTANZA * **MICHELE WOLFMAN** * **MARV WOLFMAN**
Letterer — Colorist — Editor

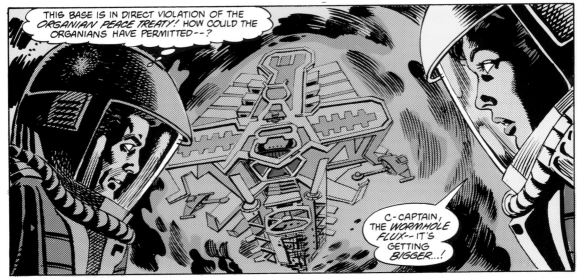

THIS BASE IS IN DIRECT VIOLATION OF THE *ORGANIAN PEACE TREATY!* HOW COULD THE ORGANIANS HAVE PERMITTED--?

C-CAPTAIN, THE *WORMHOLE FLUX*--IT'S GETTING *BIGGER...!*

...GOING TO *SWALLOW* US...

BRYCE, *NO!*

IT'S THE DISORIENTING EFFECT THE WORMHOLE HAS ON THE HUMAN MIND! BUT YOU CAN *FIGHT* IT! USE YOUR *MIND!*

I'LL *TRY*, CAPTAIN...

I'M *SORRY*, SIR! IT WON'T HAPPEN *AGAIN!*

I'M *CONFIDENT* OF THAT, MR. BRYCE...

...LET'S GO! THRUSTERS ON FULL!

YES, SIR!

SHOOSH

SHOOSH

2

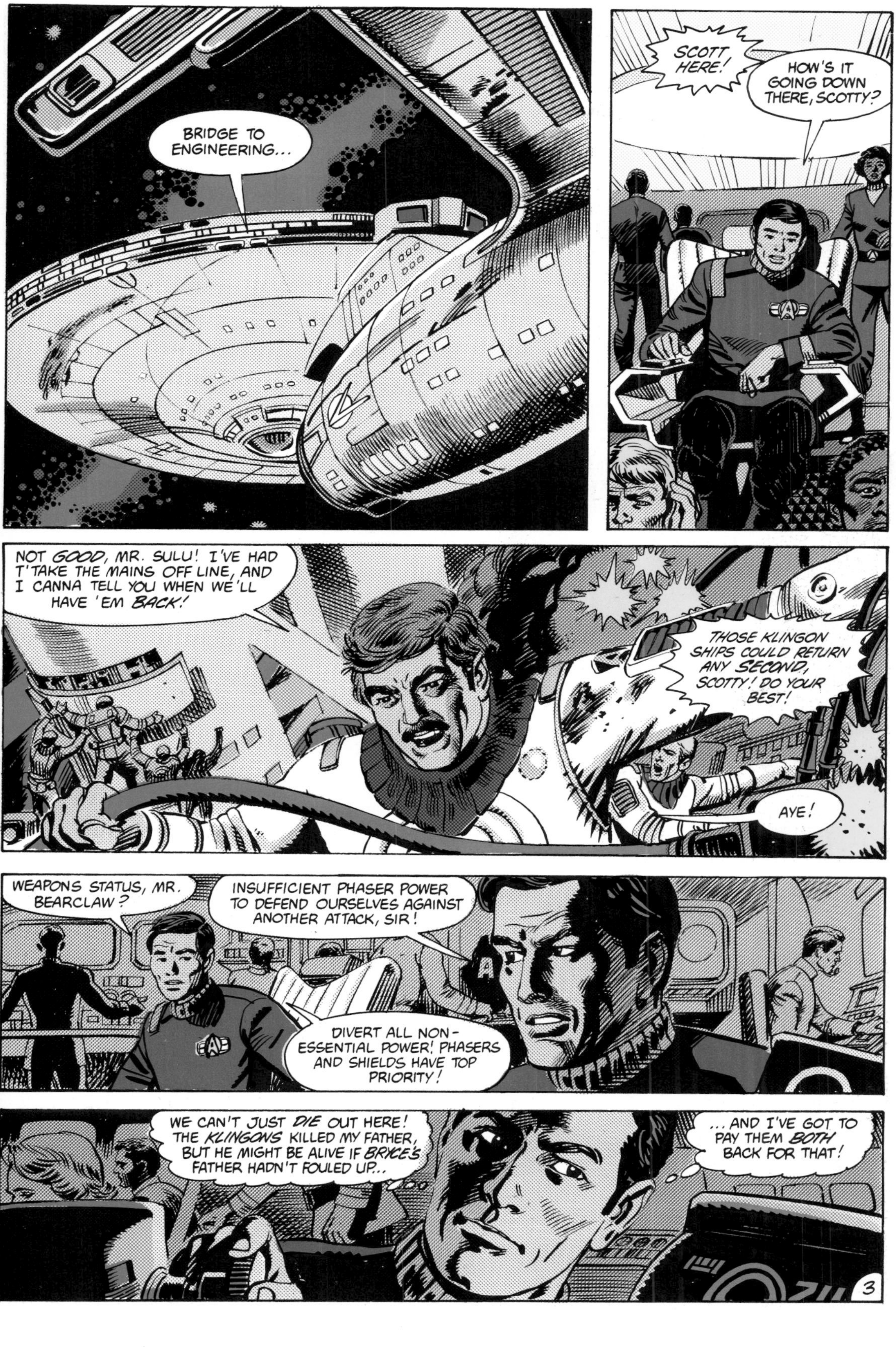

BRIDGE TO ENGINEERING...
SCOTT HERE!
HOW'S IT GOING DOWN THERE, SCOTTY?
NOT GOOD, MR. SULU! I'VE HAD T'TAKE THE MAINS OFF LINE, AND I CANNA TELL YOU WHEN WE'LL HAVE 'EM BACK!
THOSE KLINGON SHIPS COULD RETURN ANY SECOND, SCOTTY! DO YOUR BEST!
AYE!
WEAPONS STATUS, MR. BEARCLAW?
INSUFFICIENT PHASER POWER TO DEFEND OURSELVES AGAINST ANOTHER ATTACK, SIR!
DIVERT ALL NON-ESSENTIAL POWER! PHASERS AND SHIELDS HAVE TOP PRIORITY!
WE CAN'T JUST DIE OUT HERE! THE KLINGONS KILLED MY FATHER, BUT HE MIGHT BE ALIVE IF BRYCE'S FATHER HADN'T FOULED UP...
...AND I'VE GOT TO PAY THEM BOTH BACK FOR THAT!

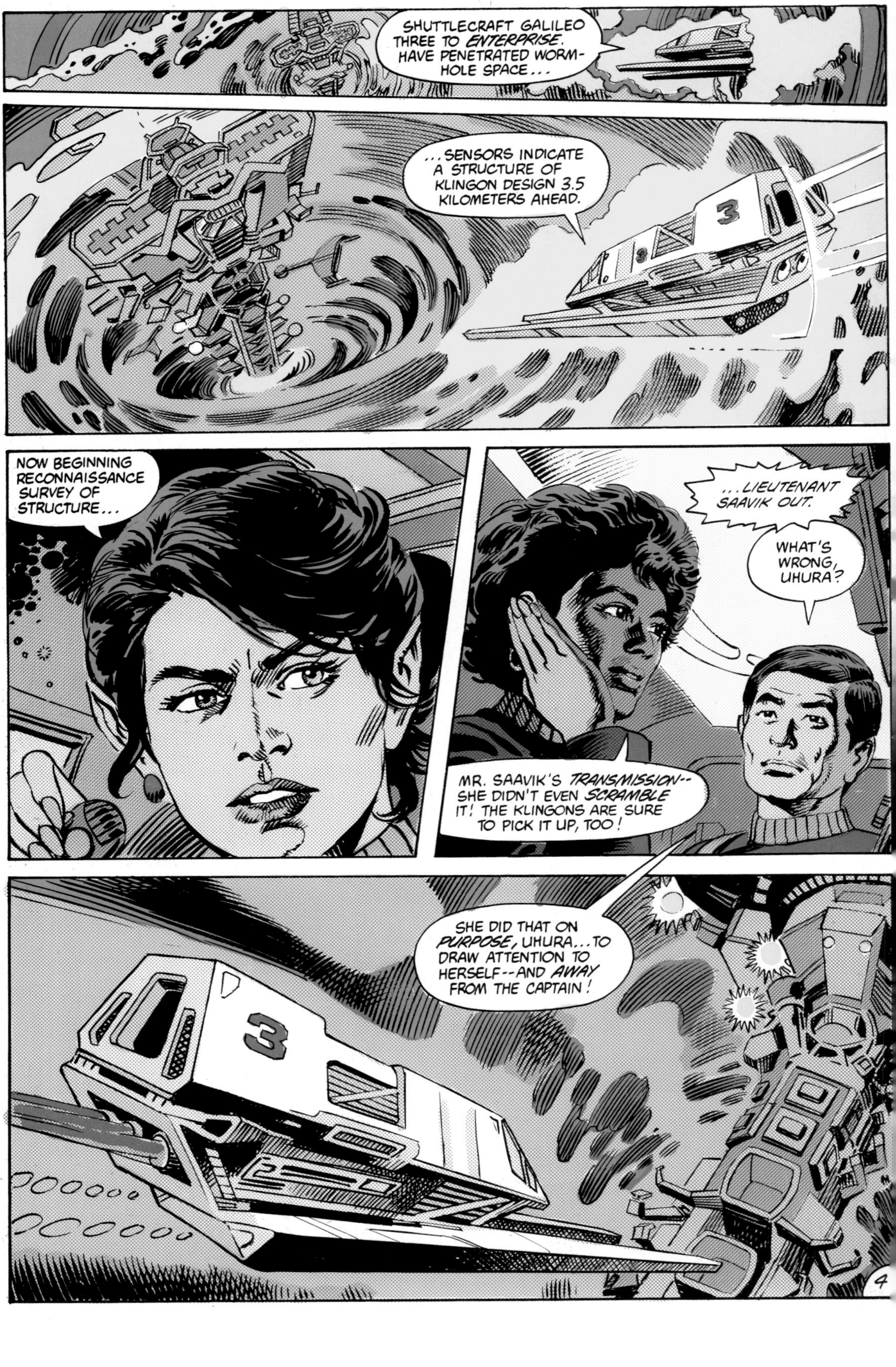
SHUTTLECRAFT GALILEO THREE TO ENTERPRISE. HAVE PENETRATED WORM-HOLE SPACE...
...SENSORS INDICATE A STRUCTURE OF KLINGON DESIGN 3.5 KILOMETERS AHEAD.
NOW BEGINNING RECONNAISSANCE SURVEY OF STRUCTURE...
...LIEUTENANT SAAVIK OUT.
WHAT'S WRONG, UHURA?
MR. SAAVIK'S TRANSMISSION-- SHE DIDN'T EVEN SCRAMBLE IT! THE KLINGONS ARE SURE TO PICK IT UP, TOO!
SHE DID THAT ON PURPOSE, UHURA... TO DRAW ATTENTION TO HERSELF--AND AWAY FROM THE CAPTAIN!
4

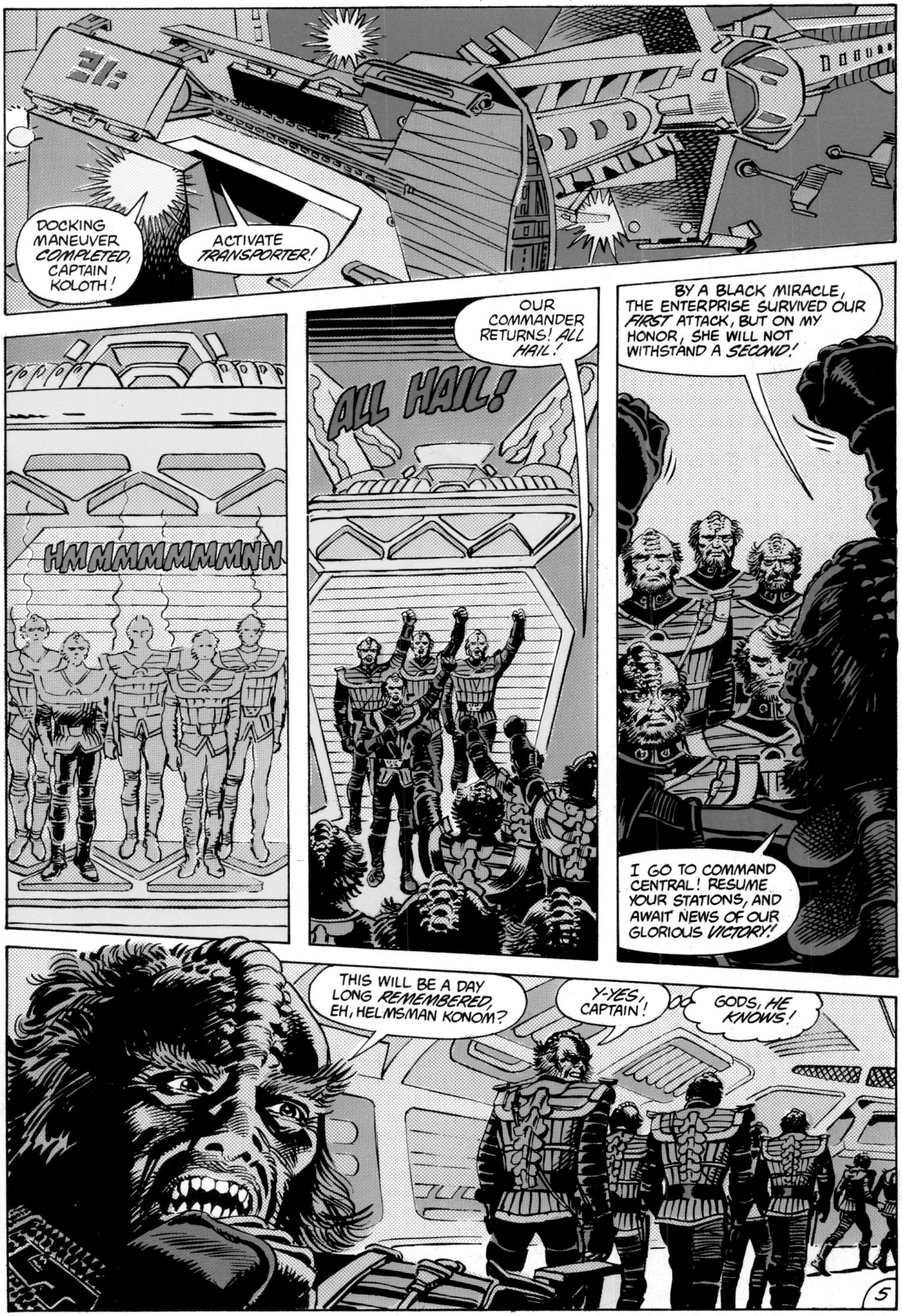
DOCKING MANEUVER COMPLETED, CAPTAIN KOLOTH!
ACTIVATE TRANSPORTER!
HMMMMMMMMNN
OUR COMMANDER RETURNS! ALL HAIL!
ALL HAIL!
BY A BLACK MIRACLE, THE ENTERPRISE SURVIVED OUR FIRST ATTACK, BUT ON MY HONOR, SHE WILL NOT WITHSTAND A SECOND!
I GO TO COMMAND CENTRAL! RESUME YOUR STATIONS, AND AWAIT NEWS OF OUR GLORIOUS VICTORY!
THIS WILL BE A DAY LONG REMEMBERED, EH, HELMSMAN KONOM?
Y-YES, CAPTAIN!
GODS, HE KNOWS!
5

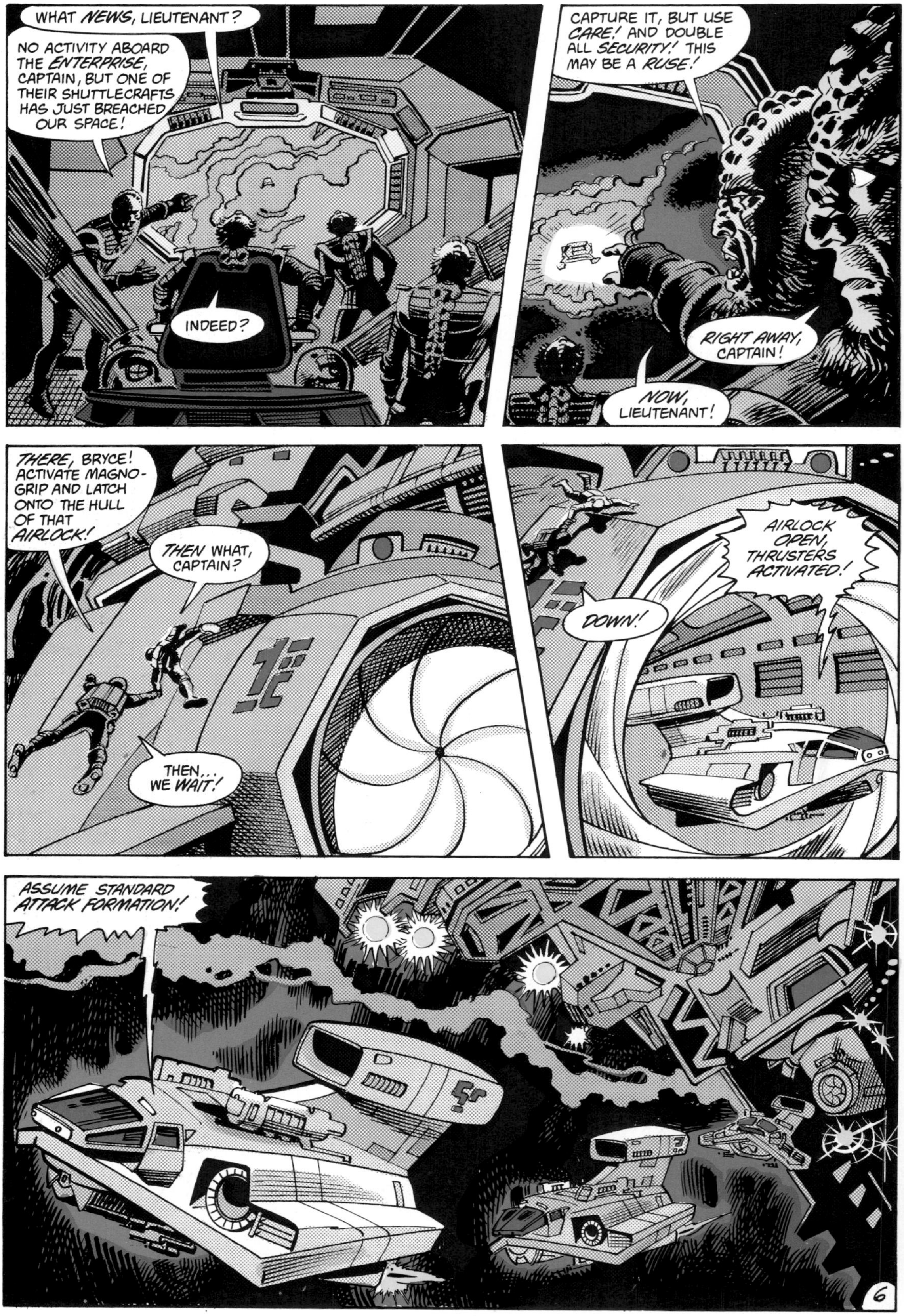
WHAT NEWS, LIEUTENANT?
NO ACTIVITY ABOARD THE ENTERPRISE, CAPTAIN, BUT ONE OF THEIR SHUTTLECRAFTS HAS JUST BREACHED OUR SPACE!
INDEED?
CAPTURE IT, BUT USE CARE! AND DOUBLE ALL SECURITY! THIS MAY BE A RUSE!
RIGHT AWAY, CAPTAIN!
NOW, LIEUTENANT!
THERE, BRYCE! ACTIVATE MAGNO-GRIP AND LATCH ONTO THE HULL OF THAT AIRLOCK!
THEN WHAT, CAPTAIN?
THEN... WE WAIT!
AIRLOCK OPEN, THRUSTERS ACTIVATED!
DOWN!
ASSUME STANDARD ATTACK FORMATION!
6

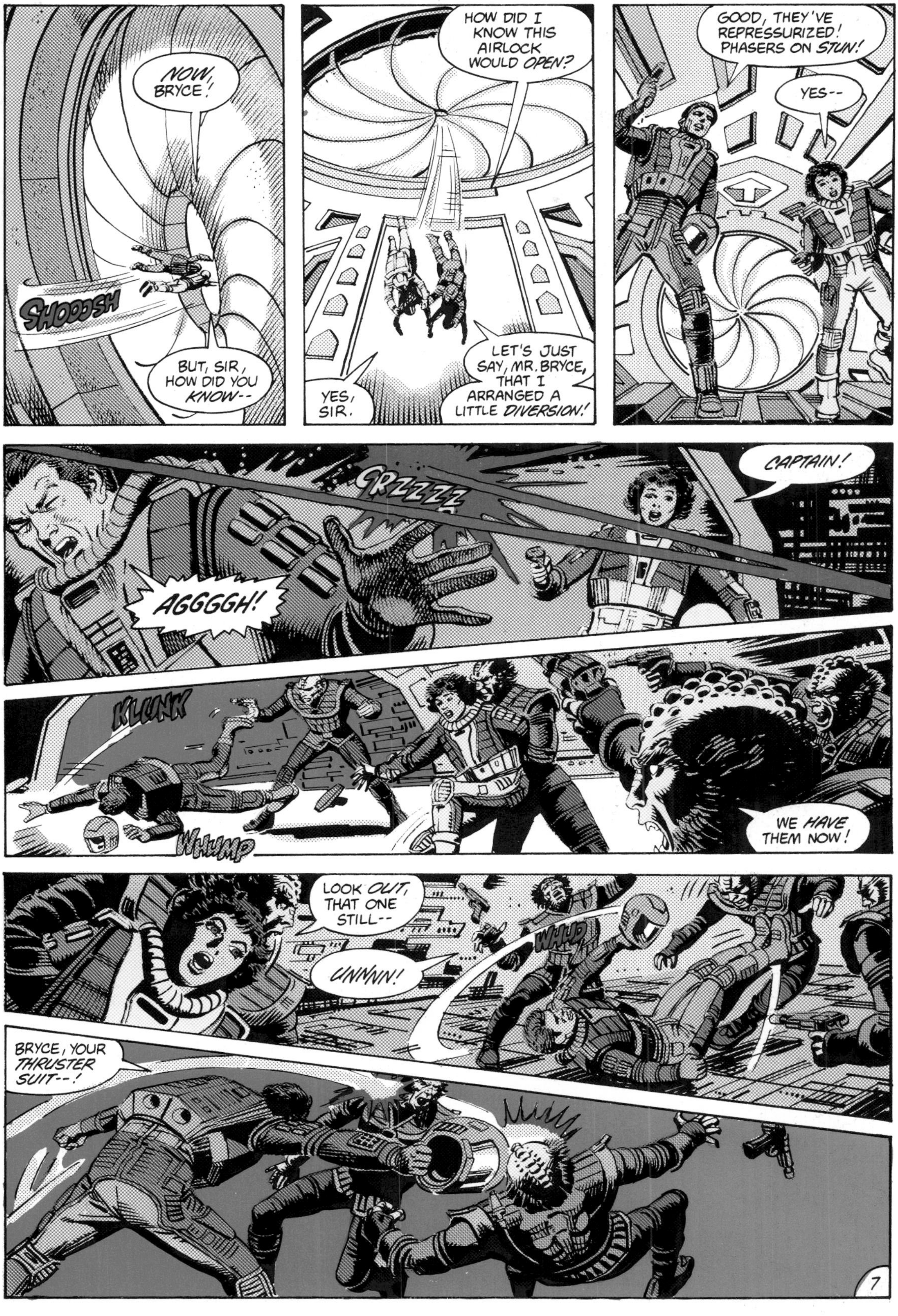
NOW, BRYCE!
SHOOOSH
BUT, SIR, HOW DID YOU KNOW--
HOW DID I KNOW THIS AIRLOCK WOULD OPEN?
LET'S JUST SAY, MR. BRYCE, THAT I ARRANGED A LITTLE DIVERSION!
YES, SIR.
GOOD, THEY'VE REPRESSURIZED! PHASERS ON STUN!
YES--
CAPTAIN!
GRZZZZ
AGGGGH!
KLUNK
WHUMP
WE HAVE THEM NOW!
LOOK OUT, THAT ONE STILL--
UNNNN!
WHUD
BRYCE, YOUR THRUSTER SUIT--!

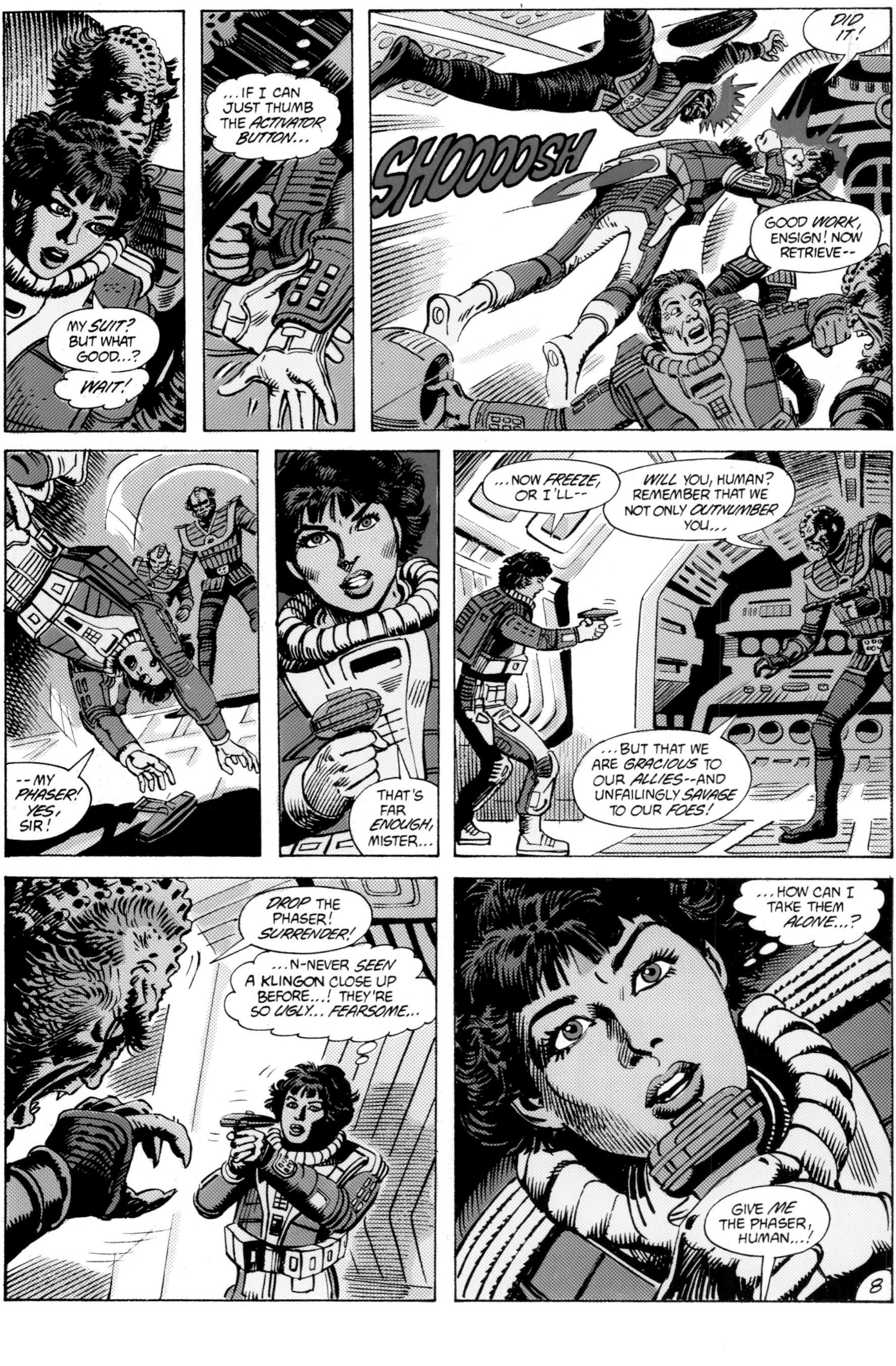
MY SUIT? BUT WHAT GOOD...?
WAIT!
...IF I CAN JUST THUMB THE ACTIVATOR BUTTON...
SHOOOOSH
DID IT!
GOOD WORK, ENSIGN! NOW RETRIEVE--
--MY PHASER! YES, SIR!
THAT'S FAR ENOUGH, MISTER...
...NOW FREEZE, OR I'LL--
WILL YOU, HUMAN? REMEMBER THAT WE NOT ONLY OUTNUMBER YOU...
...BUT THAT WE ARE GRACIOUS TO OUR ALLIES--AND UNFAILINGLY SAVAGE TO OUR FOES!
DROP THE PHASER! SURRENDER!
...N-NEVER SEEN A KLINGON CLOSE UP BEFORE...! THEY'RE SO UGLY... FEARSOME...
...HOW CAN I TAKE THEM ALONE...?
GIVE ME THE PHASER, HUMAN...!
8

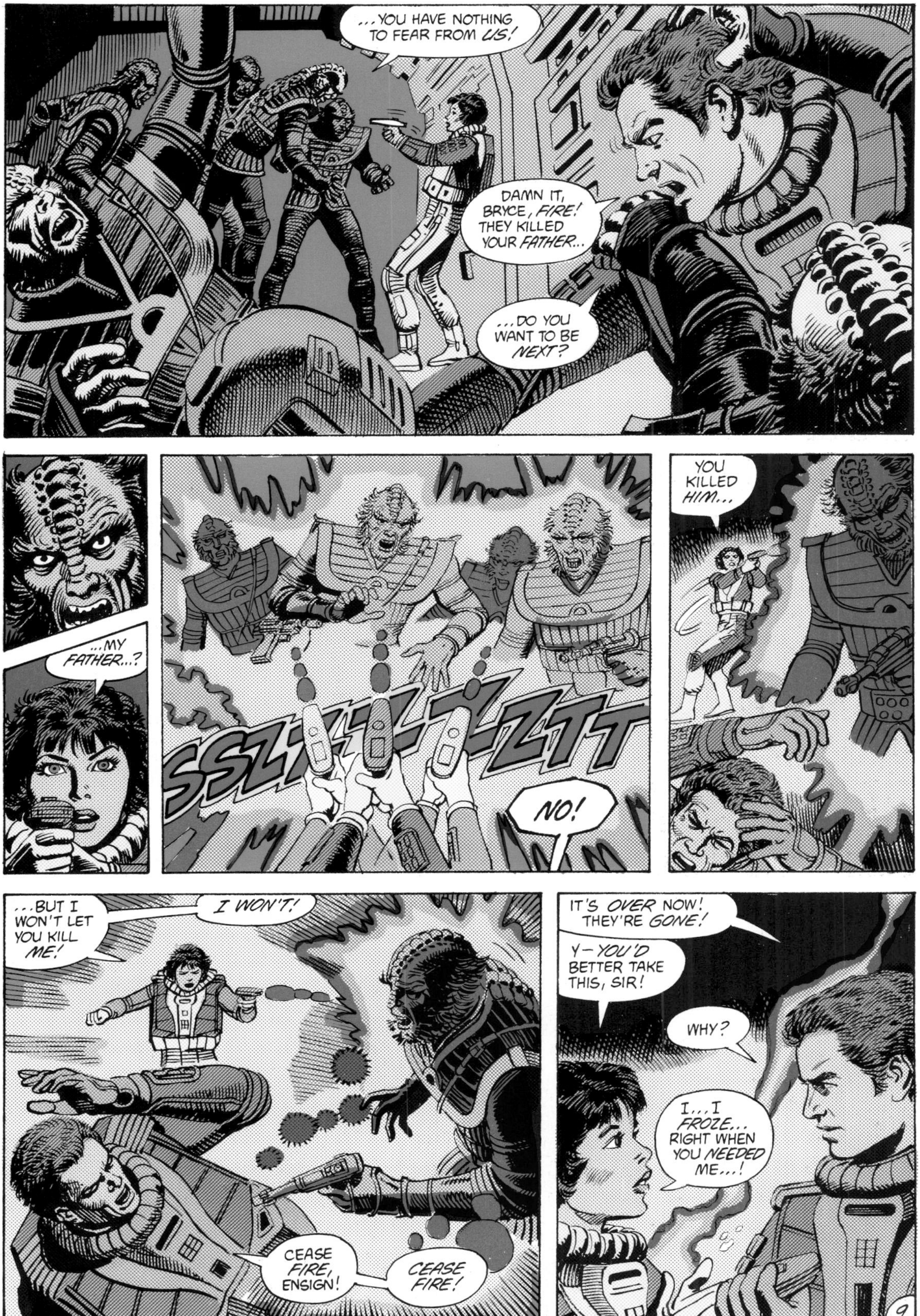
...YOU HAVE NOTHING TO FEAR FROM US!
DAMN IT, BRYCE, FIRE! THEY KILLED YOUR FATHER...
...DO YOU WANT TO BE NEXT?
...MY FATHER...?
SSZZZZZTT
NO!
YOU KILLED HIM...
...BUT I WON'T LET YOU KILL ME!
I WON'T!
CEASE FIRE, ENSIGN!
CEASE FIRE!
IT'S OVER NOW! THEY'RE GONE!
Y-YOU'D BETTER TAKE THIS, SIR!
WHY?
I...I FROZE... RIGHT WHEN YOU NEEDED ME...!
9

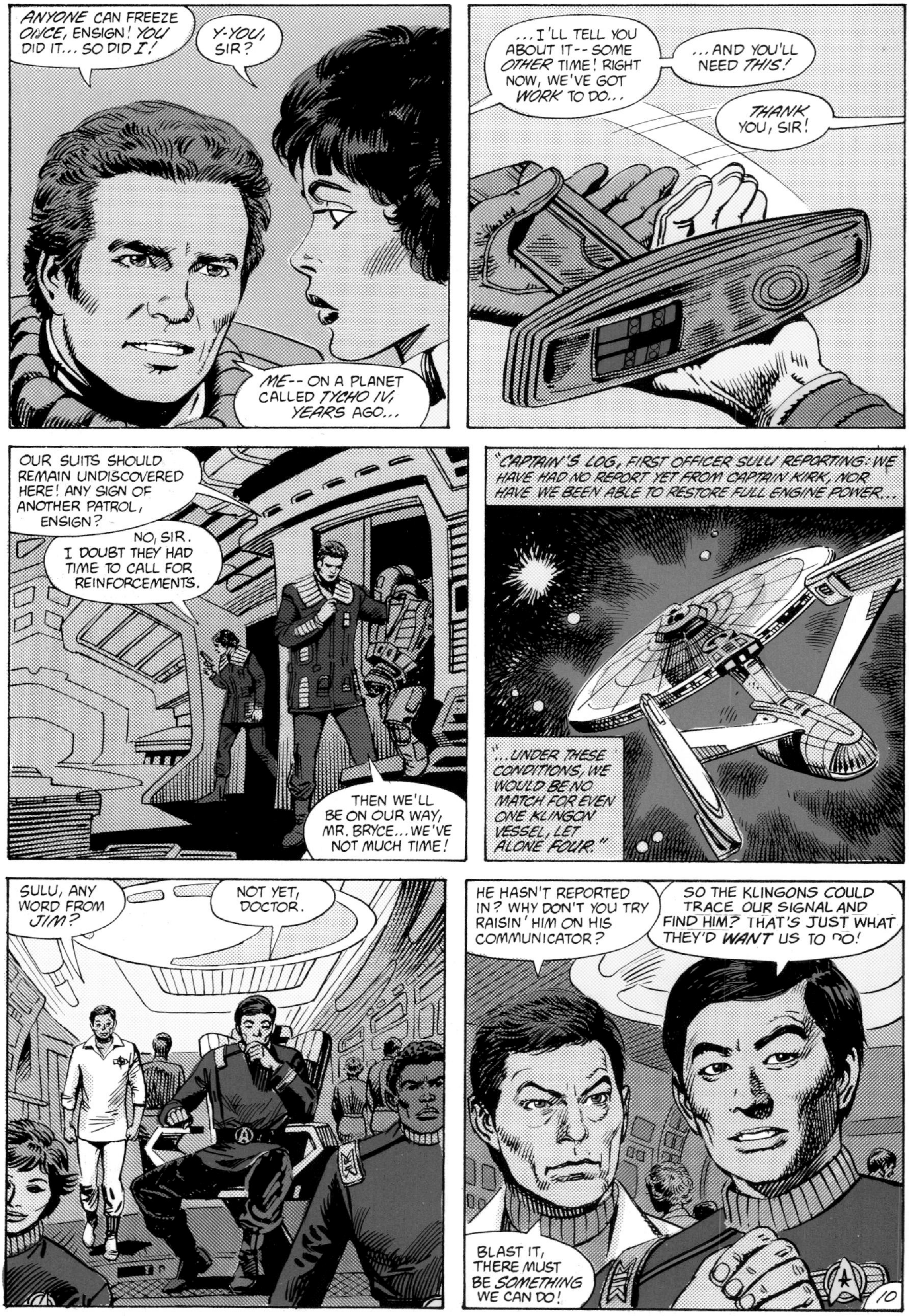

ANYONE CAN FREEZE ONCE, ENSIGN! YOU DID IT... SO DID I!
Y-YOU, SIR?
ME-- ON A PLANET CALLED TYCHO IV, YEARS AGO...
...I'LL TELL YOU ABOUT IT-- SOME OTHER TIME! RIGHT NOW, WE'VE GOT WORK TO DO...
...AND YOU'LL NEED THIS!
THANK YOU, SIR!
OUR SUITS SHOULD REMAIN UNDISCOVERED HERE! ANY SIGN OF ANOTHER PATROL, ENSIGN?
NO, SIR. I DOUBT THEY HAD TIME TO CALL FOR REINFORCEMENTS.
THEN WE'LL BE ON OUR WAY, MR. BRYCE... WE'VE NOT MUCH TIME!
"CAPTAIN'S LOG, FIRST OFFICER SULU REPORTING: WE HAVE HAD NO REPORT YET FROM CAPTAIN KIRK, NOR HAVE WE BEEN ABLE TO RESTORE FULL ENGINE POWER...
"...UNDER THESE CONDITIONS, WE WOULD BE NO MATCH FOR EVEN ONE KLINGON VESSEL, LET ALONE FOUR."
SULU, ANY WORD FROM JIM?
NOT YET, DOCTOR.
HE HASN'T REPORTED IN? WHY DON'T YOU TRY RAISIN' HIM ON HIS COMMUNICATOR?
SO THE KLINGONS COULD TRACE OUR SIGNAL AND FIND HIM? THAT'S JUST WHAT THEY'D WANT US TO DO!
BLAST IT, THERE MUST BE SOMETHING WE CAN DO!
10

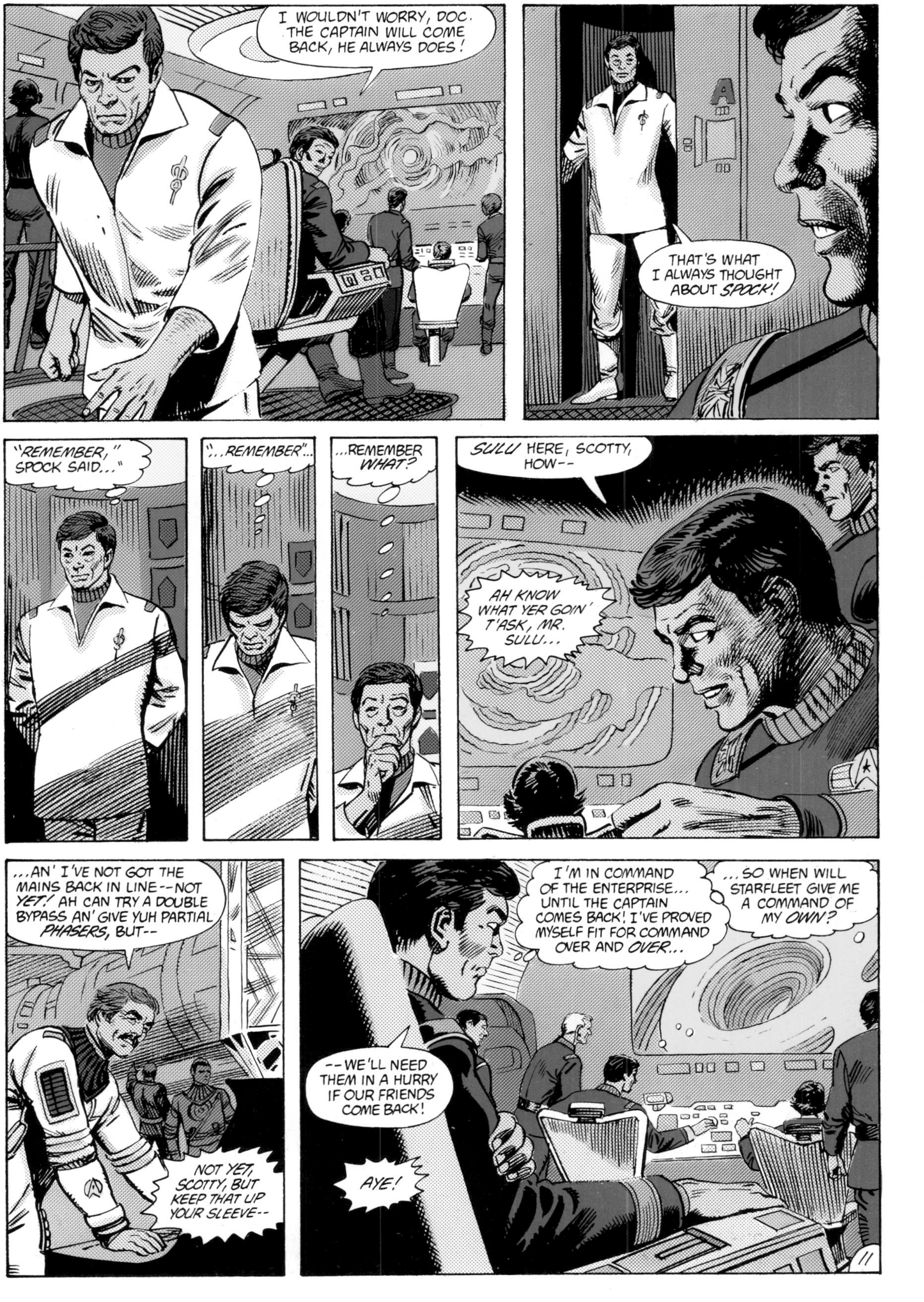
I WOULDN'T WORRY, DOC. THE CAPTAIN WILL COME BACK, HE ALWAYS DOES!
THAT'S WHAT I ALWAYS THOUGHT ABOUT SPOCK!
"REMEMBER," SPOCK SAID..."
"...REMEMBER"...
...REMEMBER WHAT?
SULU HERE, SCOTTY, HOW--
AH KNOW WHAT YER GOIN' T'ASK, MR. SULU...
...AN' I'VE NOT GOT THE MAINS BACK IN LINE--NOT YET! AH CAN TRY A DOUBLE BYPASS AN' GIVE YUH PARTIAL PHASERS, BUT--
NOT YET, SCOTTY, BUT KEEP THAT UP YOUR SLEEVE--
--WE'LL NEED THEM IN A HURRY IF OUR FRIENDS COME BACK!
AYE!
I'M IN COMMAND OF THE ENTERPRISE... UNTIL THE CAPTAIN COMES BACK! I'VE PROVED MYSELF FIT FOR COMMAND OVER AND OVER...
...SO WHEN WILL STARFLEET GIVE ME A COMMAND OF MY OWN?
11

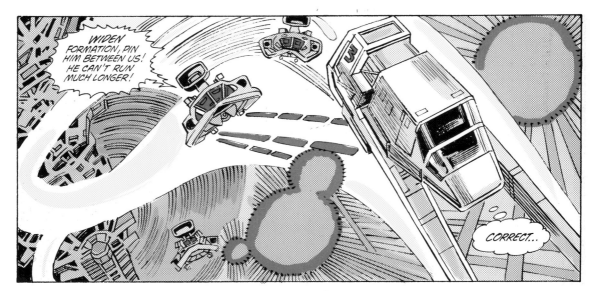

WIDEN FORMATION, PIN HIM BETWEEN US! HE CAN'T RUN MUCH LONGER!

CORRECT...

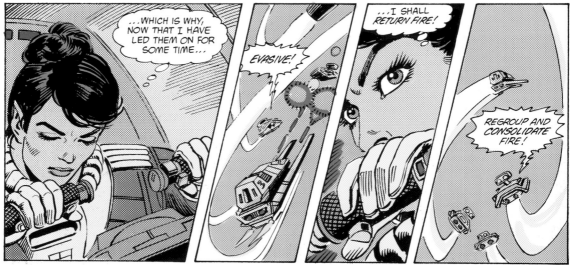

...WHICH IS WHY, NOW THAT I HAVE LED THEM ON FOR SOME TIME...

EVASIVE!

...I SHALL RETURN FIRE!

REGROUP AND CONSOLIDATE FIRE!

WE HAVE HIM NOW! ON MY COMM--

? GROUP LEADER, THE CRAFT HAS VANISHED!

DO NOT DISPERSE...

12

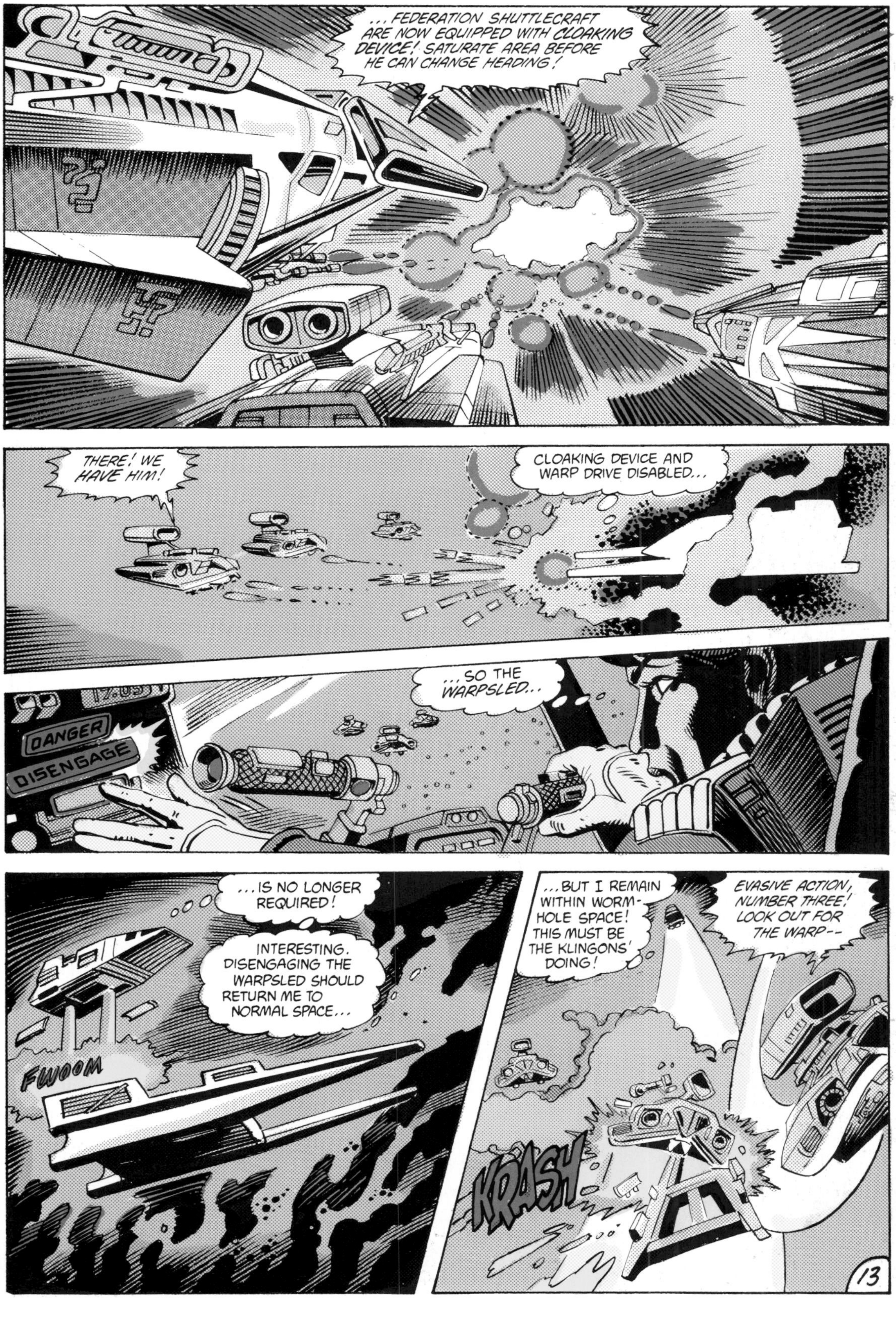
...FEDERATION SHUTTLECRAFT ARE NOW EQUIPPED WITH CLOAKING DEVICE! SATURATE AREA BEFORE HE CAN CHANGE HEADING!
THERE! WE HAVE HIM!
CLOAKING DEVICE AND WARP DRIVE DISABLED...
...SO THE WARPSLED...
DANGER
DISENGAGE
...IS NO LONGER REQUIRED!
INTERESTING. DISENGAGING THE WARPSLED SHOULD RETURN ME TO NORMAL SPACE...
FWOOM
...BUT I REMAIN WITHIN WORM-HOLE SPACE! THIS MUST BE THE KLINGONS' DOING!
EVASIVE ACTION, NUMBER THREE! LOOK OUT FOR THE WARP--
KRASH

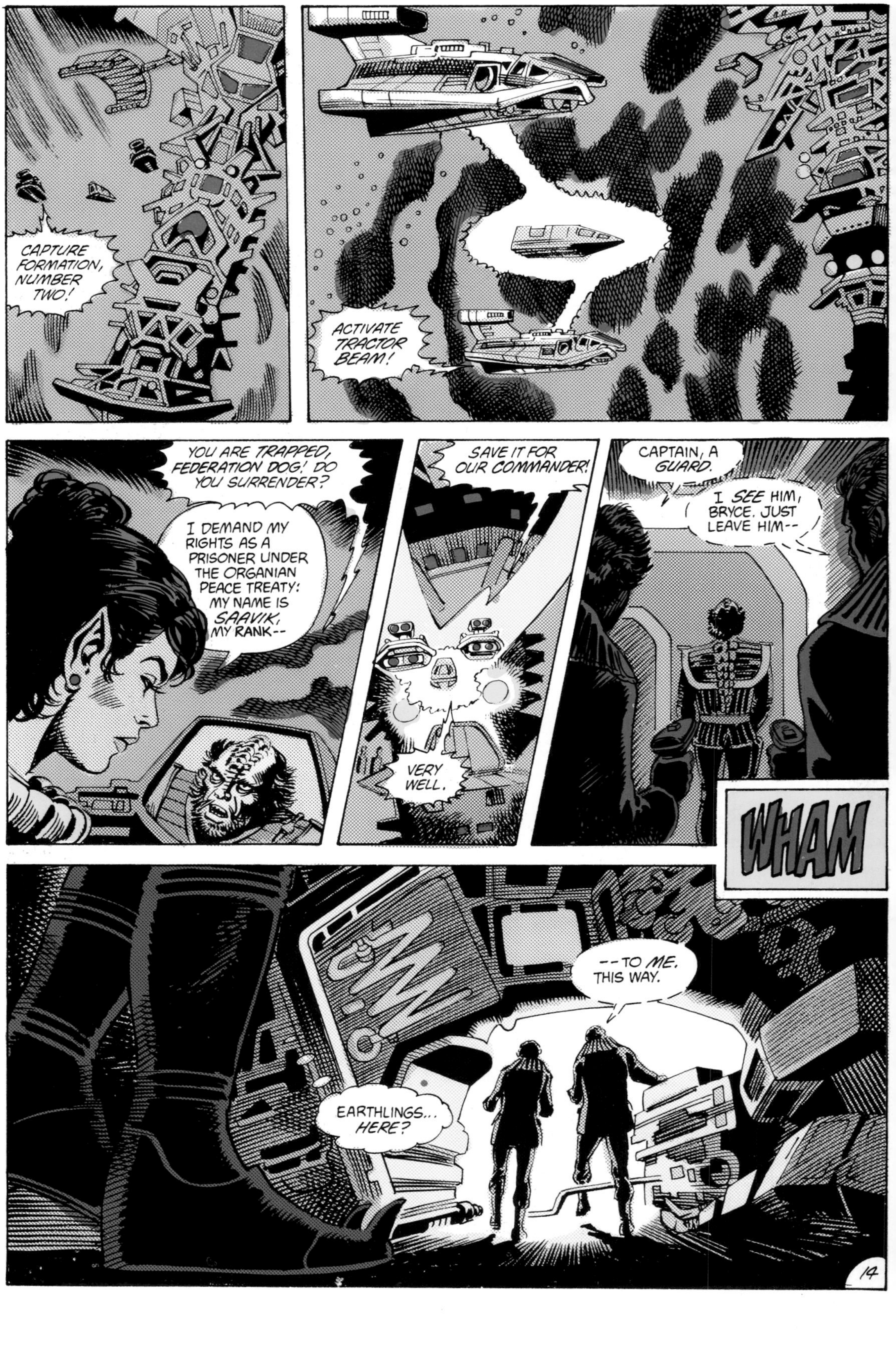
CAPTURE FORMATION, NUMBER TWO!
ACTIVATE TRACTOR BEAM!
YOU ARE TRAPPED, FEDERATION DOG! DO YOU SURRENDER?
I DEMAND MY RIGHTS AS A PRISONER UNDER THE ORGANIAN PEACE TREATY: MY NAME IS SAAVIK, MY RANK--
SAVE IT FOR OUR COMMANDER!
VERY WELL.
CAPTAIN, A GUARD.
I SEE HIM, BRYCE. JUST LEAVE HIM--
WHAM
--TO ME. THIS WAY.
EARTHLINGS... HERE?

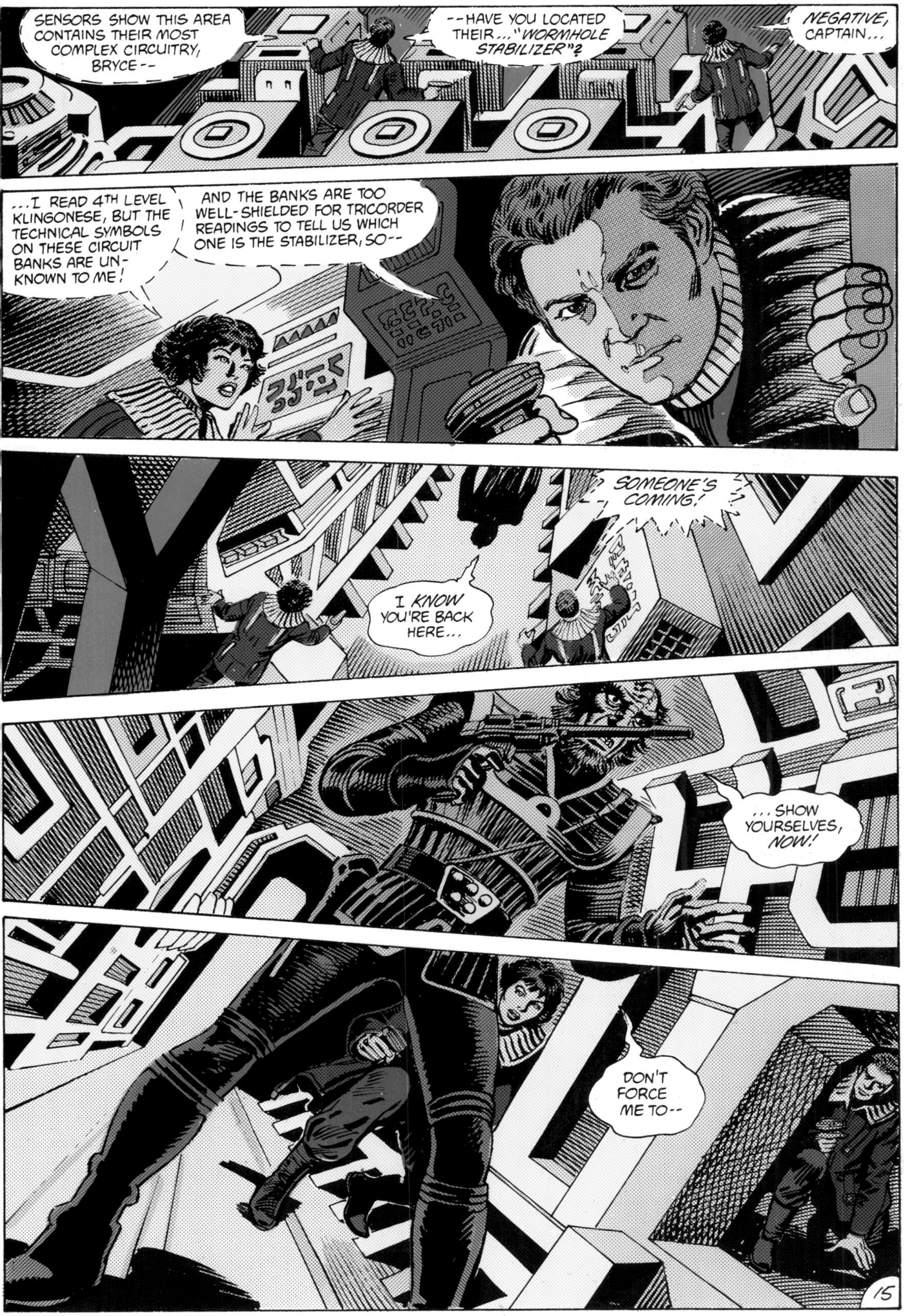
SENSORS SHOW THIS AREA CONTAINS THEIR MOST COMPLEX CIRCUITRY, BRYCE--
--HAVE YOU LOCATED THEIR..."WORMHOLE STABILIZER"?
NEGATIVE, CAPTAIN...
...I READ 4TH LEVEL KLINGONESE, BUT THE TECHNICAL SYMBOLS ON THESE CIRCUIT BANKS ARE UNKNOWN TO ME!
AND THE BANKS ARE TOO WELL-SHIELDED FOR TRICORDER READINGS TO TELL US WHICH ONE IS THE STABILIZER, SO--
SOMEONE'S COMING!
I KNOW YOU'RE BACK HERE...
...SHOW YOURSELVES, NOW!
DON'T FORCE ME TO--
15

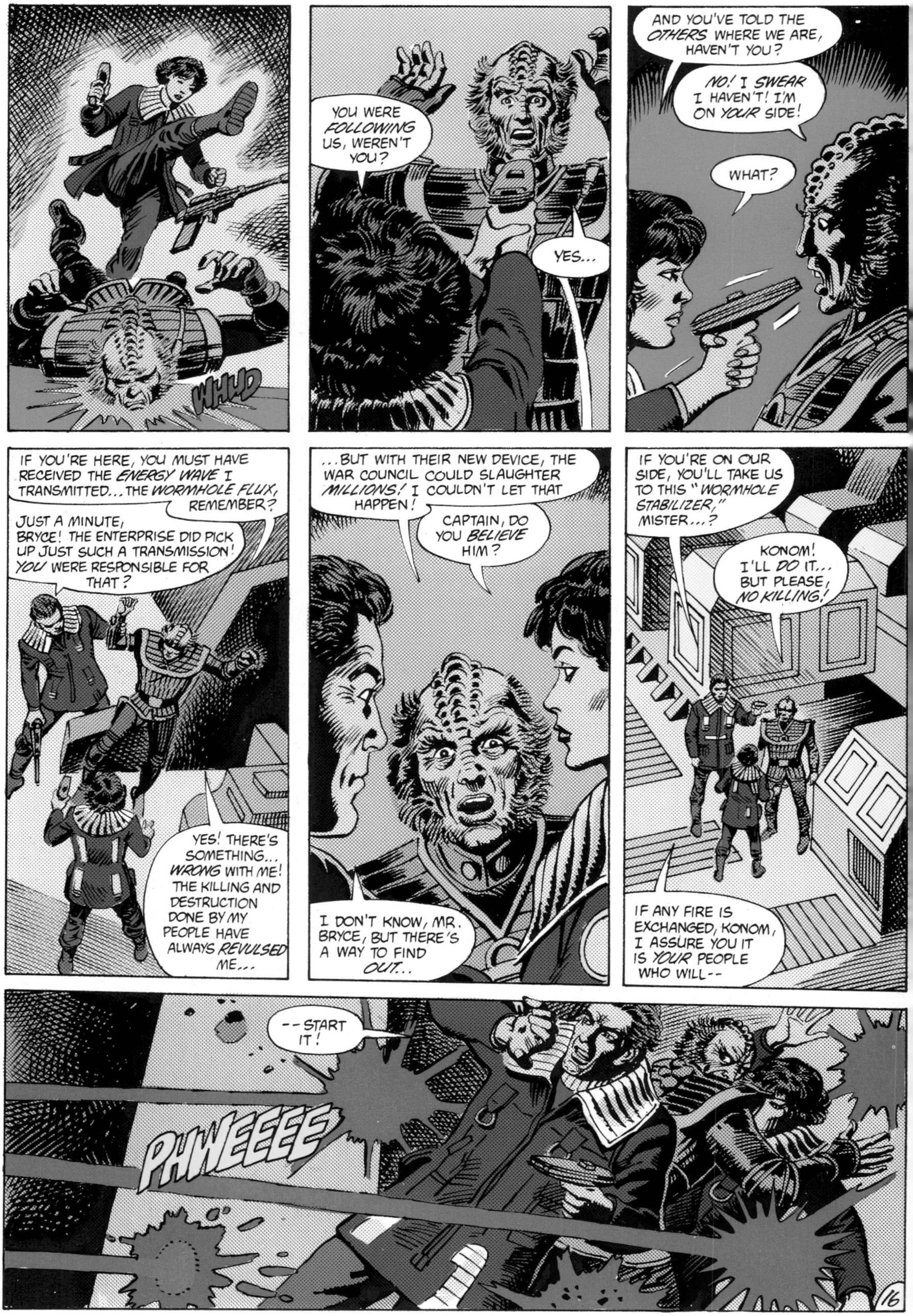

WHUD
YOU WERE FOLLOWING US, WEREN'T YOU?
YES...
AND YOU'VE TOLD THE OTHERS WHERE WE ARE, HAVEN'T YOU?
NO! I SWEAR I HAVEN'T! I'M ON YOUR SIDE!
WHAT?
IF YOU'RE HERE, YOU MUST HAVE RECEIVED THE ENERGY WAVE I TRANSMITTED... THE WORMHOLE FLUX, REMEMBER?
JUST A MINUTE, BRYCE! THE ENTERPRISE DID PICK UP JUST SUCH A TRANSMISSION! YOU WERE RESPONSIBLE FOR THAT?
YES! THERE'S SOMETHING... WRONG WITH ME! THE KILLING AND DESTRUCTION DONE BY MY PEOPLE HAVE ALWAYS REVULSED ME...
...BUT WITH THEIR NEW DEVICE, THE WAR COUNCIL COULD SLAUGHTER MILLIONS! I COULDN'T LET THAT HAPPEN!
CAPTAIN, DO YOU BELIEVE HIM?
I DON'T KNOW, MR. BRYCE, BUT THERE'S A WAY TO FIND OUT...
IF YOU'RE ON OUR SIDE, YOU'LL TAKE US TO THIS "WORMHOLE STABILIZER," MISTER...?
KONOM! I'LL DO IT... BUT PLEASE, NO KILLING!
IF ANY FIRE IS EXCHANGED, KONOM, I ASSURE YOU IT IS YOUR PEOPLE WHO WILL--
--START IT!
PHWEEEE

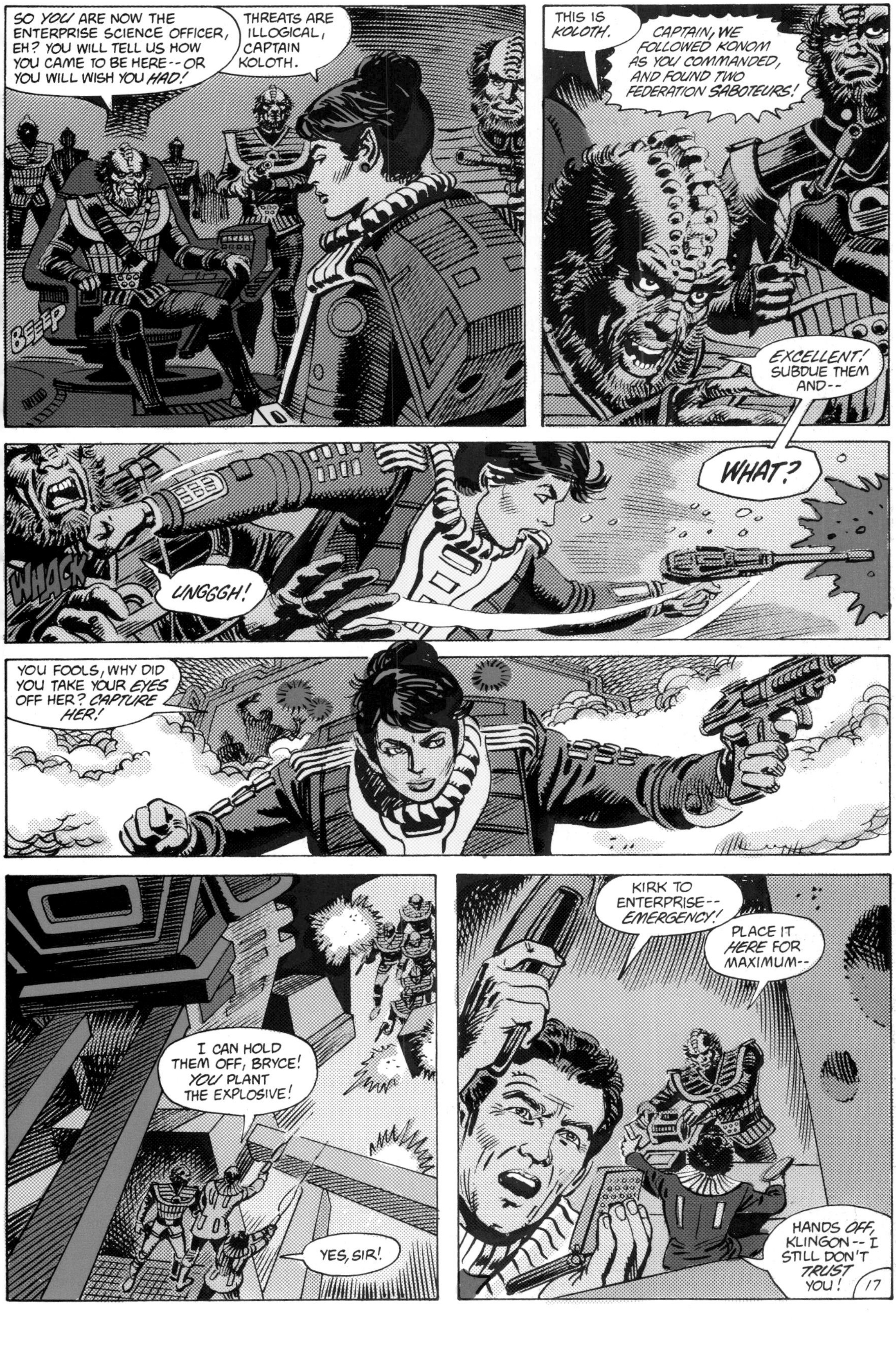
SO YOU ARE NOW THE ENTERPRISE SCIENCE OFFICER, EH? YOU WILL TELL US HOW YOU CAME TO BE HERE--OR YOU WILL WISH YOU HAD!
THREATS ARE ILLOGICAL, CAPTAIN KOLOTH.
BEEEP
THIS IS KOLOTH.
CAPTAIN, WE FOLLOWED KONOM AS YOU COMMANDED, AND FOUND TWO FEDERATION SABOTEURS!
EXCELLENT! SUBDUE THEM AND--
WHAT?
WHACK
UNGGGH!
YOU FOOLS, WHY DID YOU TAKE YOUR EYES OFF HER? CAPTURE HER!
I CAN HOLD THEM OFF, BRYCE! YOU PLANT THE EXPLOSIVE!
YES, SIR!
KIRK TO ENTERPRISE--EMERGENCY!
PLACE IT HERE FOR MAXIMUM--
HANDS OFF, KLINGON--I STILL DON'T TRUST YOU!
17

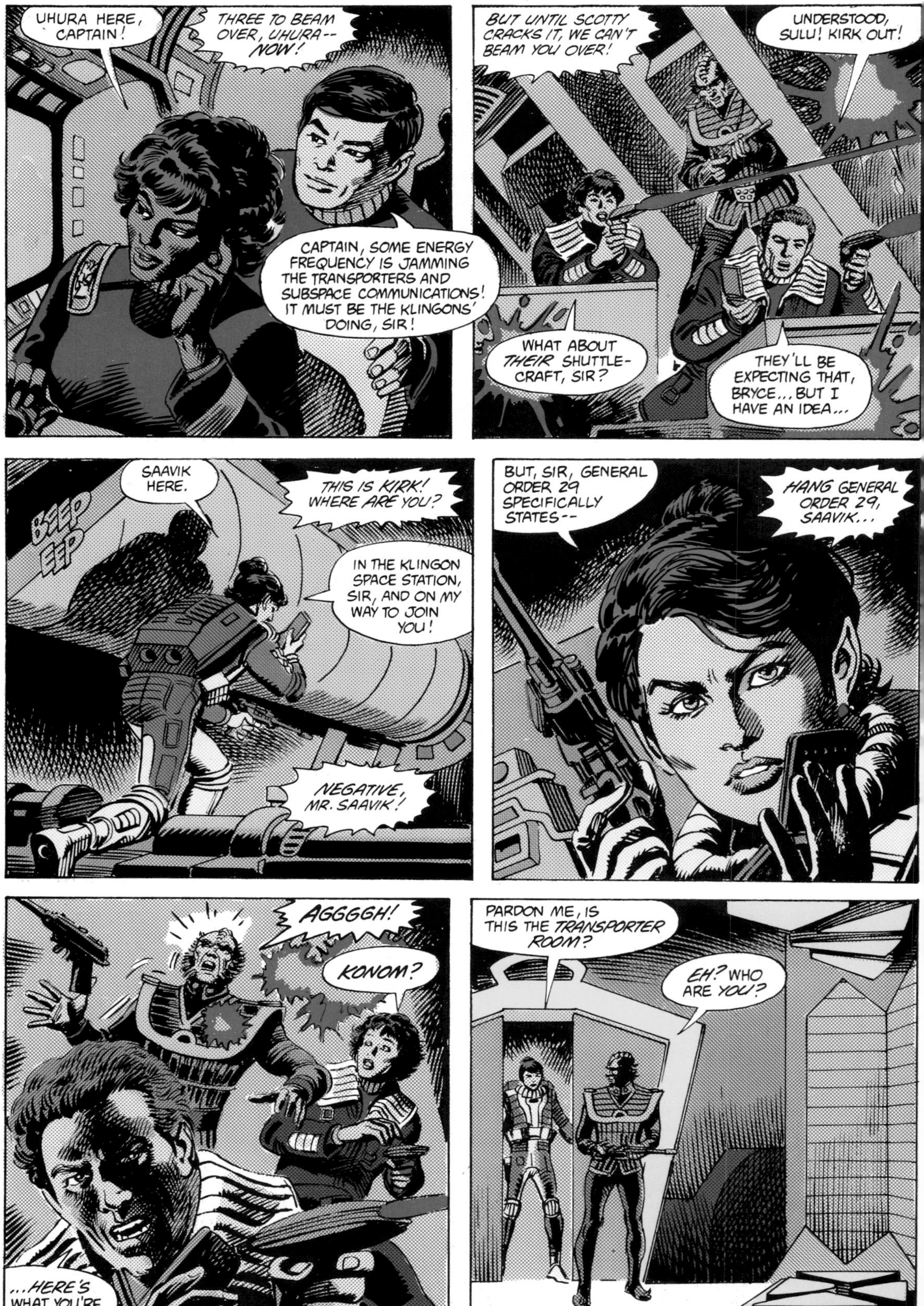
UHURA HERE, CAPTAIN!
THREE TO BEAM OVER, UHURA-- NOW!
CAPTAIN, SOME ENERGY FREQUENCY IS JAMMING THE TRANSPORTERS AND SUBSPACE COMMUNICATIONS! IT MUST BE THE KLINGONS' DOING, SIR!
BUT UNTIL SCOTTY CRACKS IT, WE CAN'T BEAM YOU OVER!
UNDERSTOOD, SULU! KIRK OUT!
WHAT ABOUT THEIR SHUTTLE-CRAFT, SIR?
THEY'LL BE EXPECTING THAT, BRYCE... BUT I HAVE AN IDEA...
BEEP EEP
SAAVIK HERE.
THIS IS KIRK! WHERE ARE YOU?
IN THE KLINGON SPACE STATION, SIR, AND ON MY WAY TO JOIN YOU!
NEGATIVE, MR. SAAVIK!
BUT, SIR, GENERAL ORDER 29 SPECIFICALLY STATES--
HANG GENERAL ORDER 29, SAAVIK...
AGGGGH!
KONOM?
...HERE'S WHAT YOU'RE TO DO...
PARDON ME, IS THIS THE TRANSPORTER ROOM?
EH? WHO ARE YOU?
18

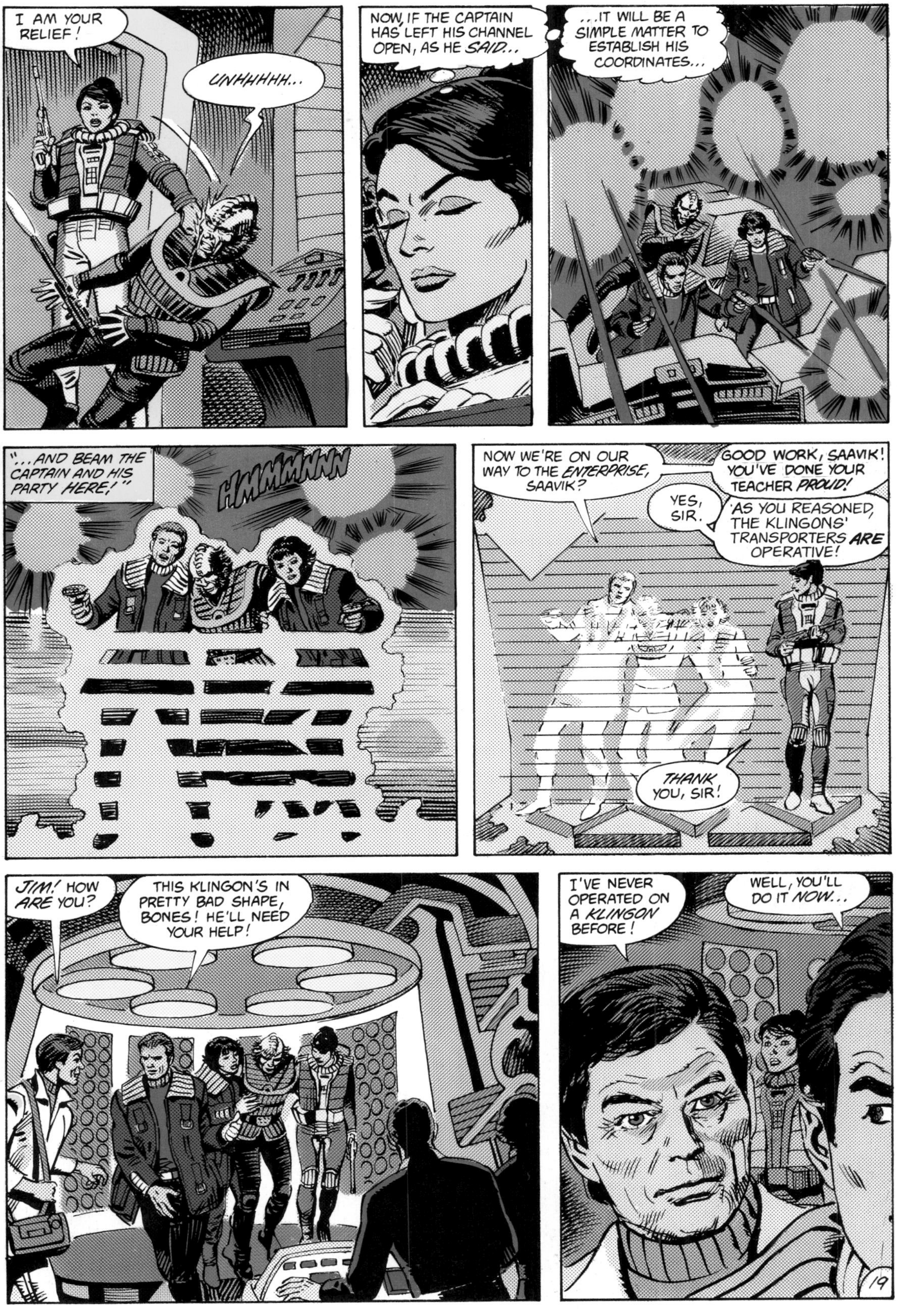
I AM YOUR RELIEF!
UNHHHHH...
NOW, IF THE CAPTAIN HAS LEFT HIS CHANNEL OPEN, AS HE SAID...
...IT WILL BE A SIMPLE MATTER TO ESTABLISH HIS COORDINATES...
"...AND BEAM THE CAPTAIN AND HIS PARTY HERE!"
HMMMNNN
NOW WE'RE ON OUR WAY TO THE ENTERPRISE, SAAVIK?
YES, SIR.
GOOD WORK, SAAVIK! YOU'VE DONE YOUR TEACHER PROUD!
AS YOU REASONED, THE KLINGONS' TRANSPORTERS ARE OPERATIVE!
THANK YOU, SIR!
JIM! HOW ARE YOU?
THIS KLINGON'S IN PRETTY BAD SHAPE, BONES! HE'LL NEED YOUR HELP!
I'VE NEVER OPERATED ON A KLINGON BEFORE!
WELL, YOU'LL DO IT NOW...

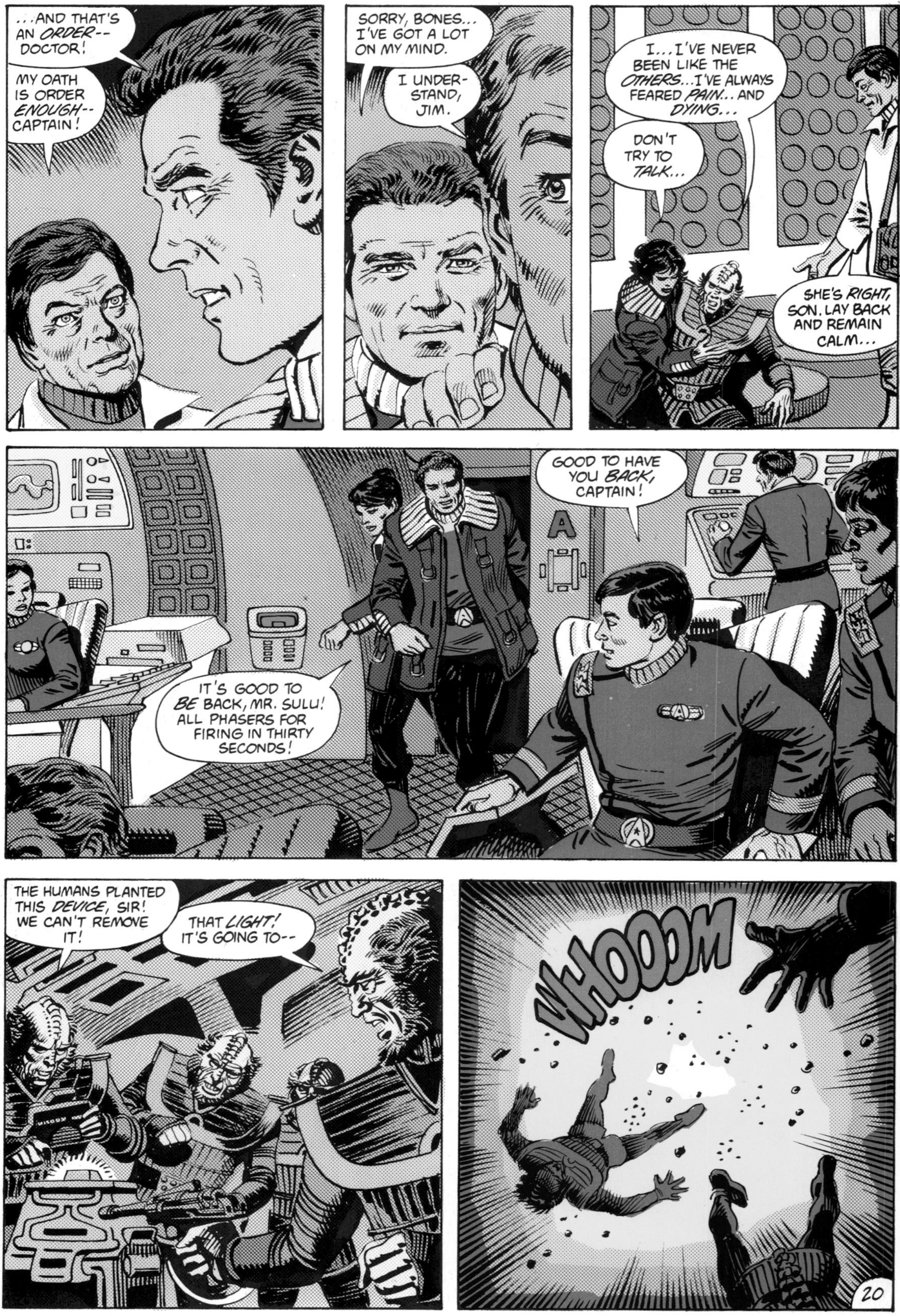
...AND THAT'S AN ORDER-- DOCTOR!
MY OATH IS ORDER ENOUGH-- CAPTAIN!
SORRY, BONES... I'VE GOT A LOT ON MY MIND.
I UNDERSTAND, JIM.
I... I'VE NEVER BEEN LIKE THE OTHERS... I'VE ALWAYS FEARED PAIN... AND DYING...
DON'T TRY TO TALK...
SHE'S RIGHT, SON. LAY BACK AND REMAIN CALM...
GOOD TO HAVE YOU BACK, CAPTAIN!
IT'S GOOD TO BE BACK, MR. SULU! ALL PHASERS FOR FIRING IN THIRTY SECONDS!
THE HUMANS PLANTED THIS DEVICE, SIR! WE CAN'T REMOVE IT!
THAT LIGHT! IT'S GOING TO--
WHOOOM
20

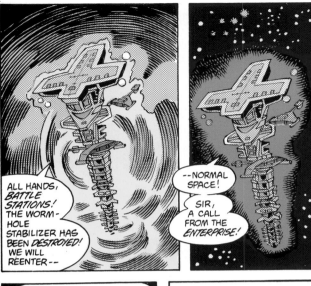

ALL HANDS, *BATTLE STATIONS!* THE WORM-HOLE STABILIZER HAS BEEN *DESTROYED!* WE WILL REENTER--

--NORMAL SPACE!

SIR, A CALL FROM THE *ENTERPRISE!*

THIS IS *CAPTAIN JAMES T. KIRK,* KOLOTH! GIVE IT UP, IT'S *OVER!*

OVER?

I THINK *NOT,* CAPTAIN... AS YOU AND YOUR ACCURSED *FEDERATION* WILL SOON FIND OUT!

FOR AS YOU KNOW, WE KLINGONS *LIVE* BY OUR OWN RULES...

...AND *DIE* BY THEM, AS WELL!

KLIK

FWOOOOOM

21

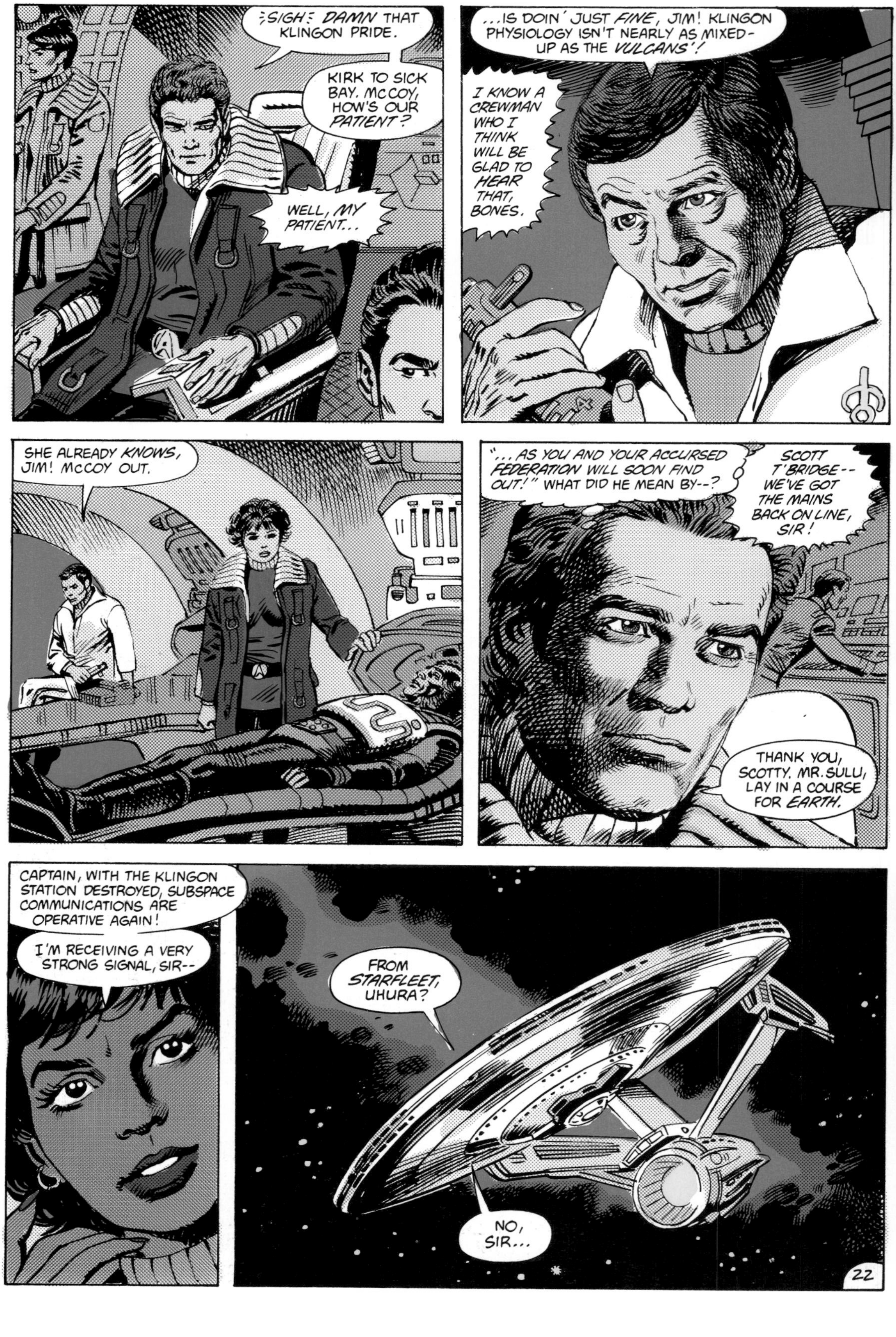

:SIGH: DAMN THAT KLINGON PRIDE.
KIRK TO SICK BAY. McCOY, HOW'S OUR PATIENT?
WELL, MY PATIENT...
...IS DOIN' JUST FINE, JIM! KLINGON PHYSIOLOGY ISN'T NEARLY AS MIXED-UP AS THE VULCANS'!
I KNOW A CREWMAN WHO I THINK WILL BE GLAD TO HEAR THAT, BONES.
SHE ALREADY KNOWS, JIM! McCOY OUT.
"...AS YOU AND YOUR ACCURSED FEDERATION WILL SOON FIND OUT!" WHAT DID HE MEAN BY--?
SCOTT T'BRIDGE--WE'VE GOT THE MAINS BACK ON LINE, SIR!
THANK YOU, SCOTTY. MR. SULU, LAY IN A COURSE FOR EARTH.
CAPTAIN, WITH THE KLINGON STATION DESTROYED, SUBSPACE COMMUNICATIONS ARE OPERATIVE AGAIN!
I'M RECEIVING A VERY STRONG SIGNAL, SIR--
FROM STARFLEET, UHURA?
NO, SIR...
22

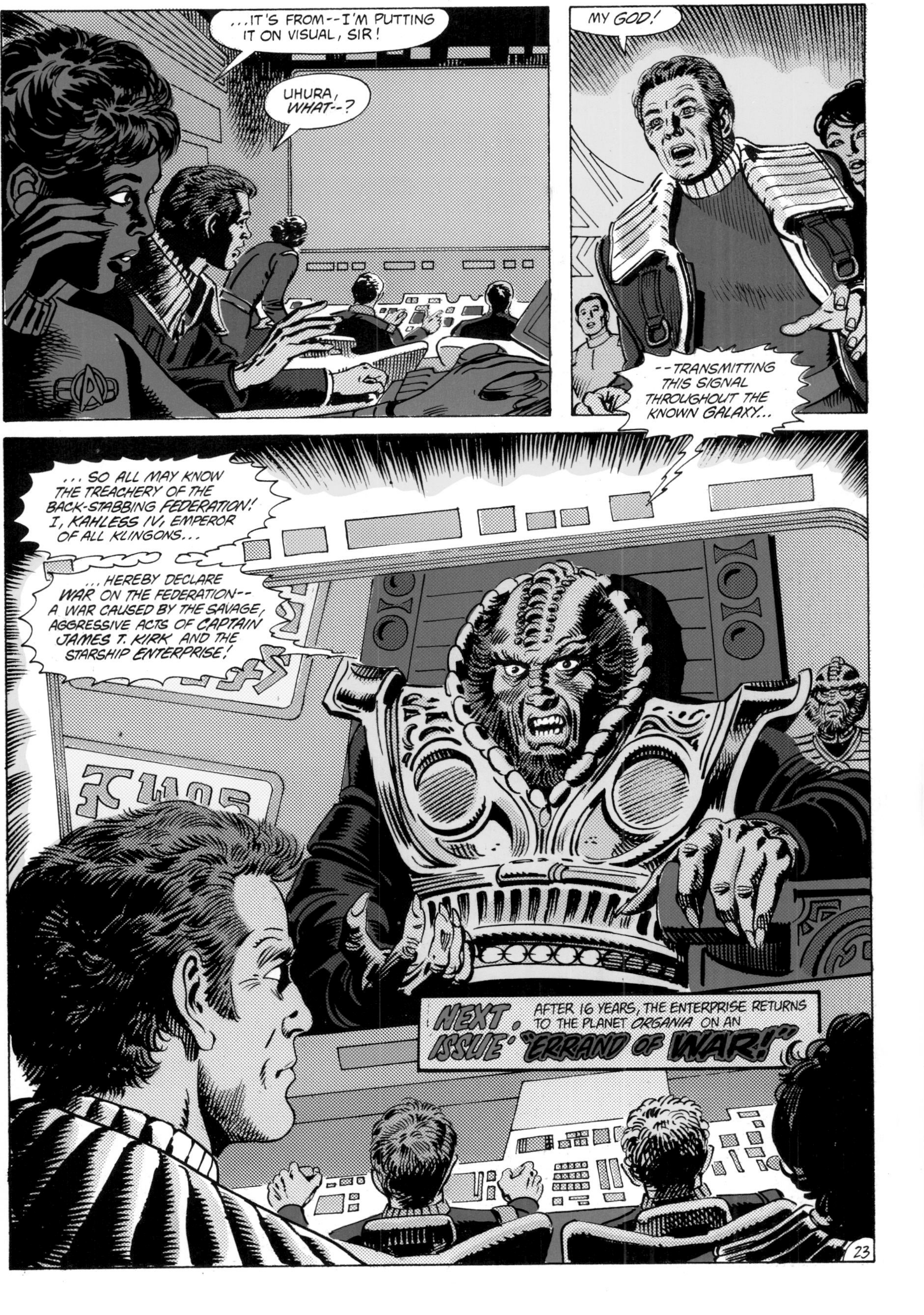
...IT'S FROM--I'M PUTTING IT ON VISUAL, SIR!
UHURA, WHAT--?
MY GOD!
--TRANSMITTING THIS SIGNAL THROUGHOUT THE KNOWN GALAXY...
...SO ALL MAY KNOW THE TREACHERY OF THE BACK-STABBING FEDERATION! I, KAHLESS IV, EMPEROR OF ALL KLINGONS...
...HEREBY DECLARE WAR ON THE FEDERATION--A WAR CAUSED BY THE SAVAGE, AGGRESSIVE ACTS OF CAPTAIN JAMES T. KIRK AND THE STARSHIP ENTERPRISE!
NEXT ISSUE: AFTER 16 YEARS, THE ENTERPRISE RETURNS TO THE PLANET ORGANIA ON AN "ERRAND OF WAR!"
23

STAR TREK

Based on the series created by **Gene Roddenberry**

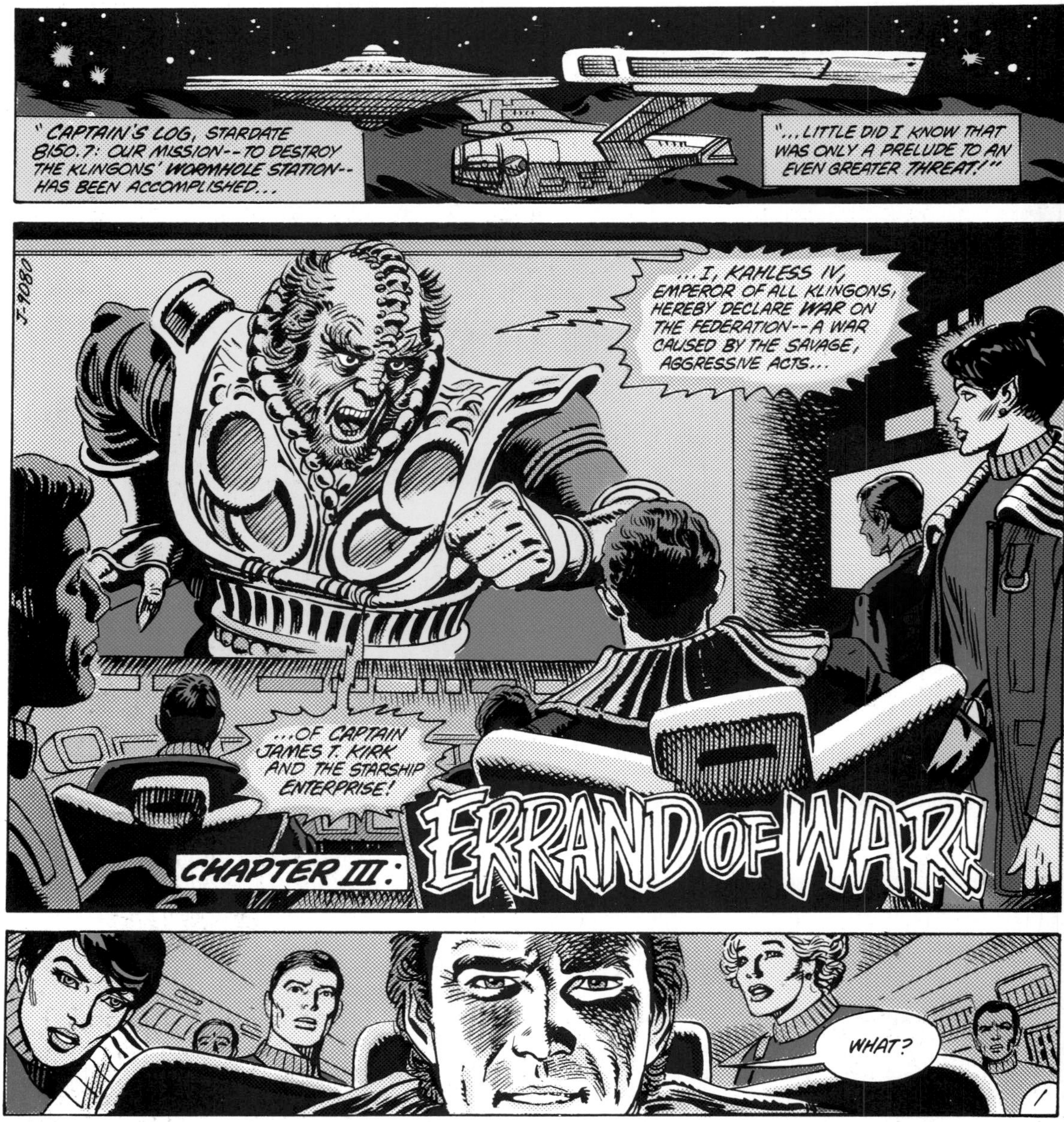
"CAPTAIN'S LOG, STARDATE 8150.7: OUR MISSION--TO DESTROY THE KLINGONS' WORMHOLE STATION--HAS BEEN ACCOMPLISHED...
"...LITTLE DID I KNOW THAT WAS ONLY A PRELUDE TO AN EVEN GREATER THREAT!"
...I, KAHLESS IV, EMPEROR OF ALL KLINGONS, HEREBY DECLARE WAR ON THE FEDERATION--A WAR CAUSED BY THE SAVAGE, AGGRESSIVE ACTS...
...OF CAPTAIN JAMES T. KIRK AND THE STARSHIP ENTERPRISE!
CHAPTER III: ERRAND OF WAR!
WHAT?

MIKE W. BARR * **TOM SUTTON & RICARDO VILLAGRAN**
Writer — Artists

JOHN COSTANZA * **MICHELE WOLFMAN** * **MARV WOLFMAN**
Letterer — Colorist — Editor

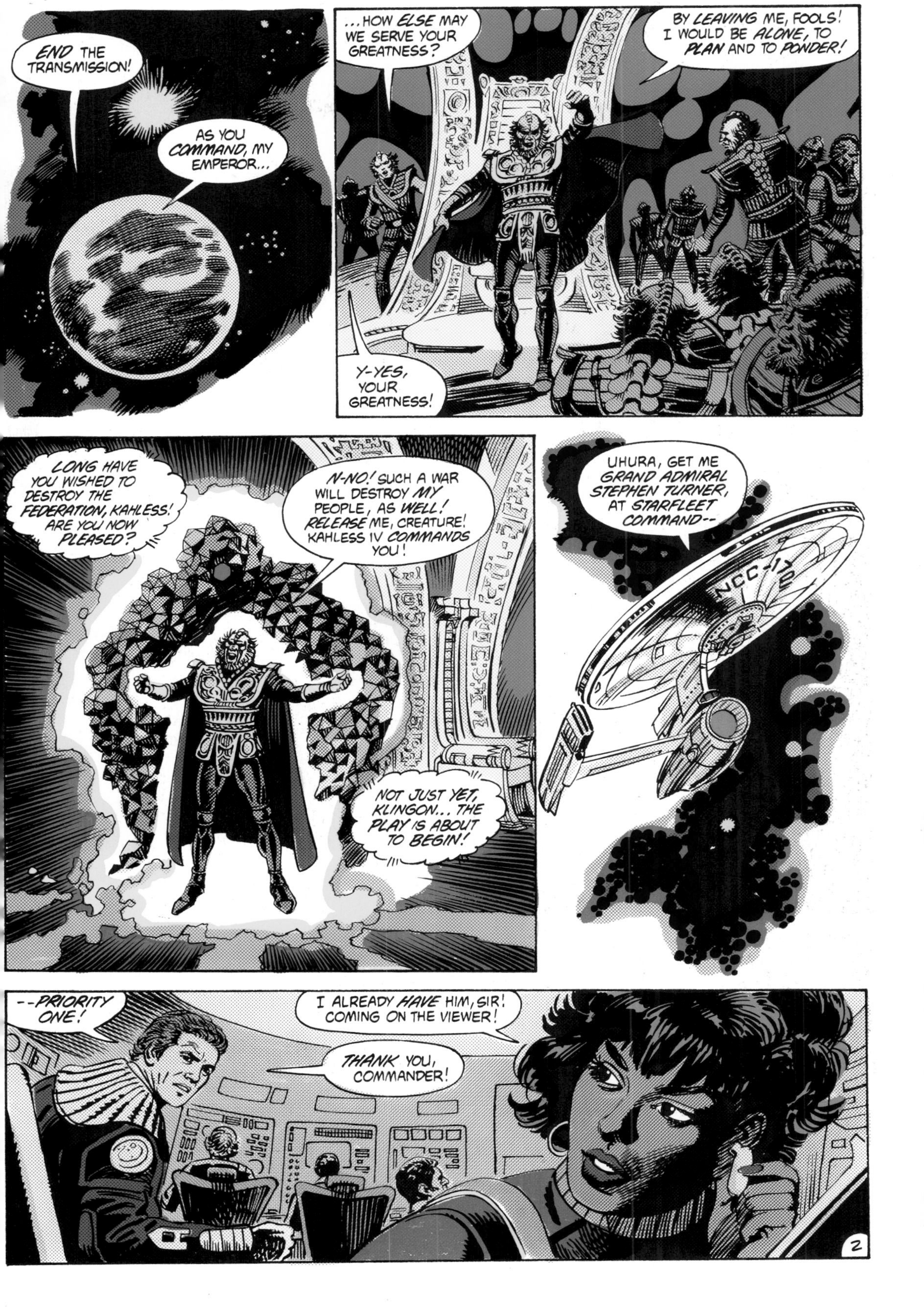

END THE TRANSMISSION!
AS YOU COMMAND, MY EMPEROR...
...HOW ELSE MAY WE SERVE YOUR GREATNESS?
BY LEAVING ME, FOOLS! I WOULD BE ALONE, TO PLAN AND TO PONDER!
Y-YES, YOUR GREATNESS!
LONG HAVE YOU WISHED TO DESTROY THE FEDERATION, KAHLESS! ARE YOU NOW PLEASED?
N-NO! SUCH A WAR WILL DESTROY MY PEOPLE, AS WELL! RELEASE ME, CREATURE! KAHLESS IV COMMANDS YOU!
NOT JUST YET, KLINGON... THE PLAY IS ABOUT TO BEGIN!
UHURA, GET ME GRAND ADMIRAL STEPHEN TURNER, AT STARFLEET COMMAND--
NCC-1702
--PRIORITY ONE!
I ALREADY HAVE HIM, SIR! COMING ON THE VIEWER!
THANK YOU, COMMANDER!
2

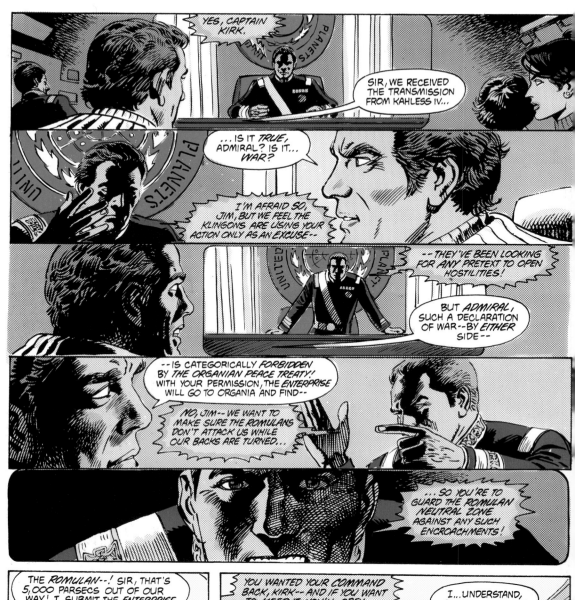

YES, CAPTAIN KIRK.

SIR, WE RECEIVED THE TRANSMISSION FROM KAHLESS IV...

...IS IT *TRUE*, ADMIRAL? IS IT... *WAR?*

I'M AFRAID SO, JIM, BUT WE FEEL THE *KLINGONS* ARE USING YOUR ACTION ONLY AS AN EXCUSE--

--THEY'VE BEEN LOOKING FOR ANY PRETEXT TO OPEN HOSTILITIES!

BUT *ADMIRAL*, SUCH A DECLARATION OF WAR--BY *EITHER* SIDE--

--IS CATEGORICALLY *FORBIDDEN* BY *THE ORGANIAN PEACE TREATY!* WITH YOUR PERMISSION, THE *ENTERPRISE* WILL GO TO ORGANIA AND FIND--

NO, JIM--WE WANT TO MAKE SURE THE *ROMULANS* DON'T ATTACK US WHILE OUR BACKS ARE TURNED...

...SO YOU'RE TO GUARD THE *ROMULAN NEUTRAL ZONE* AGAINST ANY SUCH ENCROACHMENTS!

THE *ROMULAN*--! SIR, THAT'S 5,000 PARSECS OUT OF OUR WAY! I SUBMIT THE *ENTERPRISE* WOULD BE BETTER USED--

YOU WANTED YOUR *COMMAND* BACK, KIRK-- AND IF YOU WANT TO *KEEP* IT, YOU'LL OBEY ORDERS... *CAPTAIN!*

I... UNDERSTAND, ADMIRAL. KIRK OUT.

;WHEW;

3

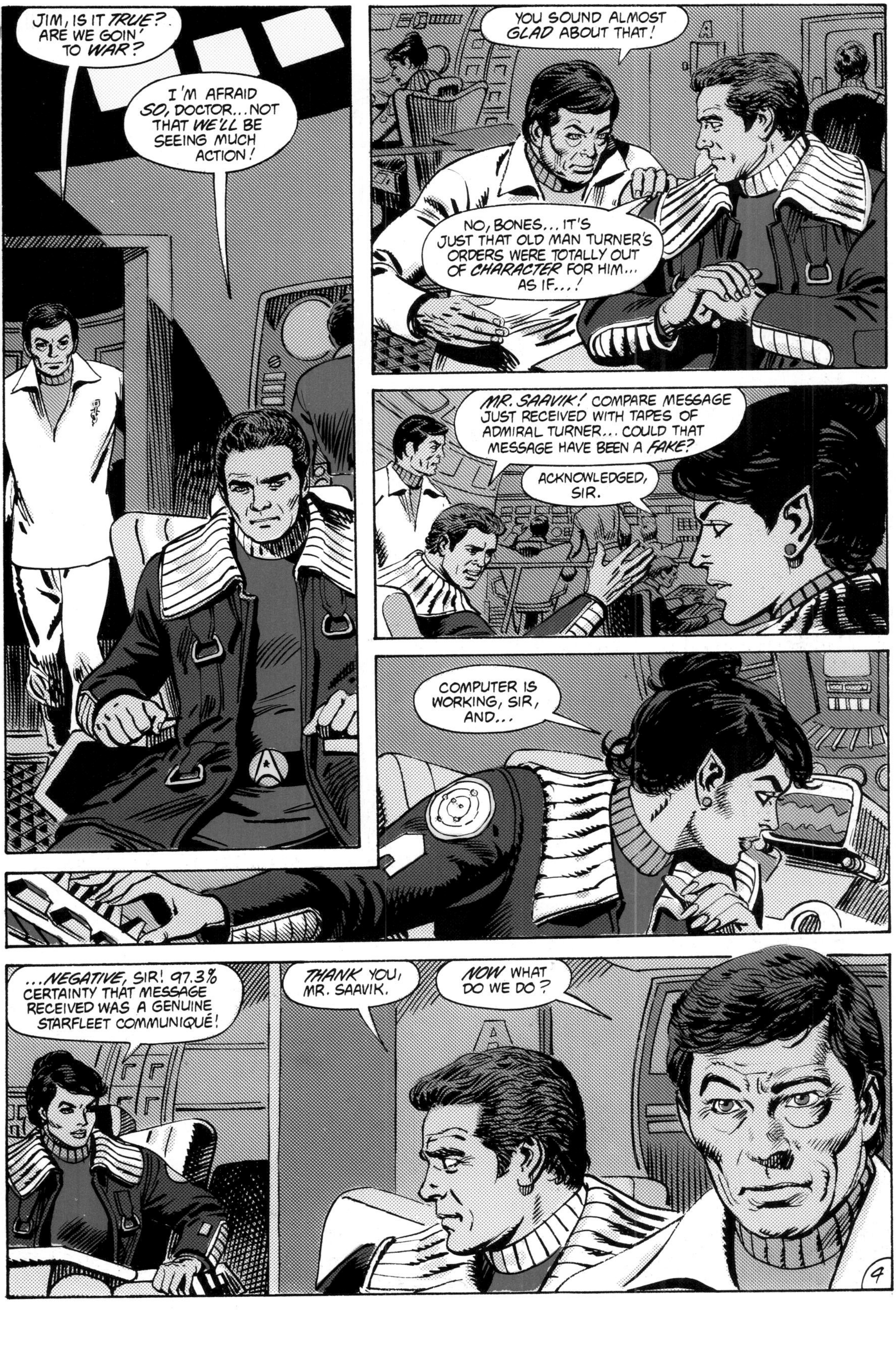

JIM, IS IT TRUE? ARE WE GOIN' TO WAR?
I'M AFRAID SO, DOCTOR... NOT THAT WE'LL BE SEEING MUCH ACTION!
YOU SOUND ALMOST GLAD ABOUT THAT!
NO, BONES... IT'S JUST THAT OLD MAN TURNER'S ORDERS WERE TOTALLY OUT OF CHARACTER FOR HIM... AS IF...!
MR. SAAVIK! COMPARE MESSAGE JUST RECEIVED WITH TAPES OF ADMIRAL TURNER... COULD THAT MESSAGE HAVE BEEN A FAKE?
ACKNOWLEDGED, SIR.
COMPUTER IS WORKING, SIR, AND...
...NEGATIVE, SIR! 97.3% CERTAINTY THAT MESSAGE RECEIVED WAS A GENUINE STARFLEET COMMUNIQUÉ!
THANK YOU, MR. SAAVIK.
NOW WHAT DO WE DO?

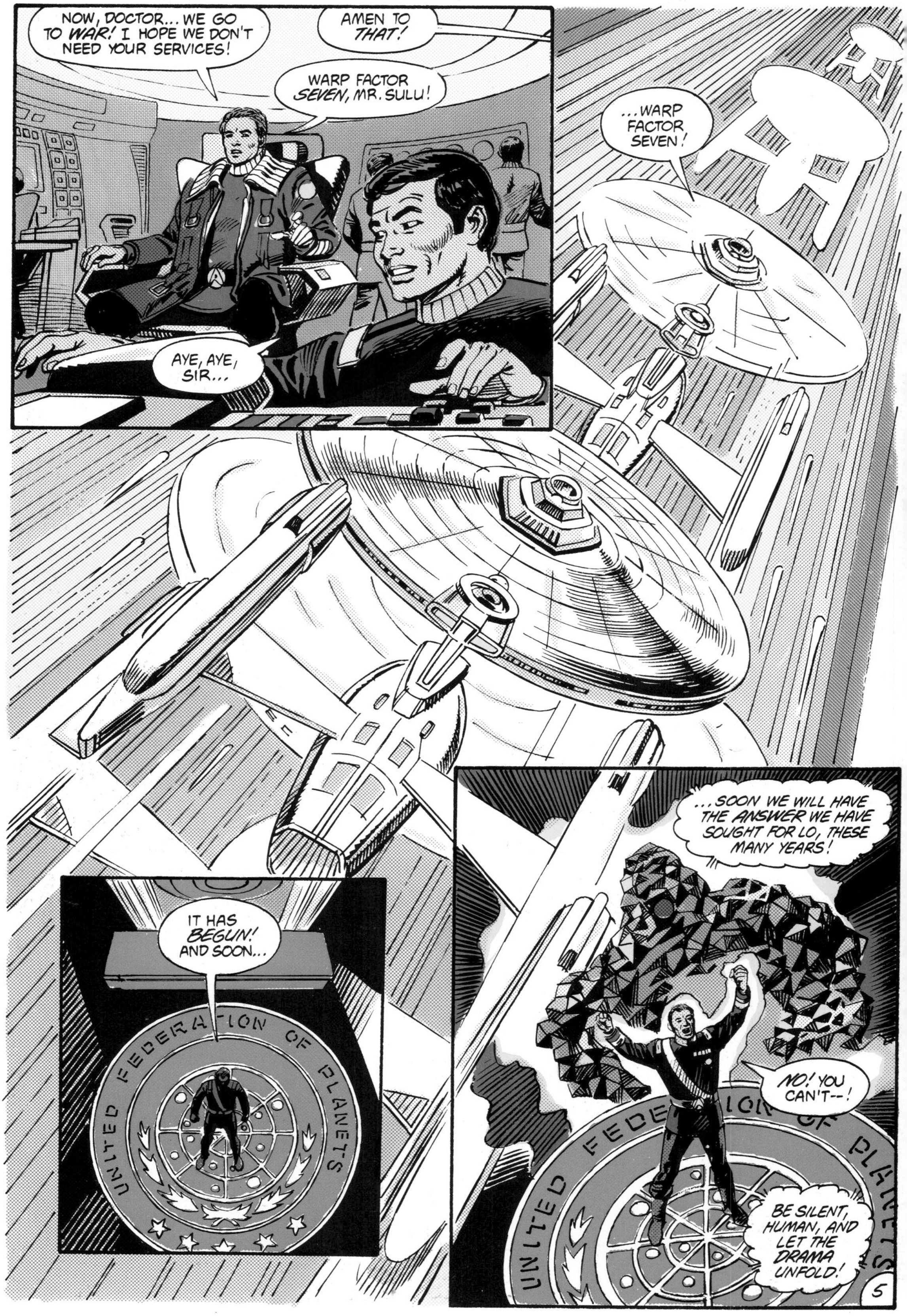
NOW, DOCTOR... WE GO TO WAR! I HOPE WE DON'T NEED YOUR SERVICES!
AMEN TO THAT!
WARP FACTOR SEVEN, MR. SULU!
AYE, AYE, SIR...
...WARP FACTOR SEVEN!
IT HAS BEGUN! AND SOON...
UNITED FEDERATION OF PLANETS
...SOON WE WILL HAVE THE ANSWER WE HAVE SOUGHT FOR LO, THESE MANY YEARS!
NO! YOU CAN'T--!
BE SILENT, HUMAN, AND LET THE DRAMA UNFOLD!

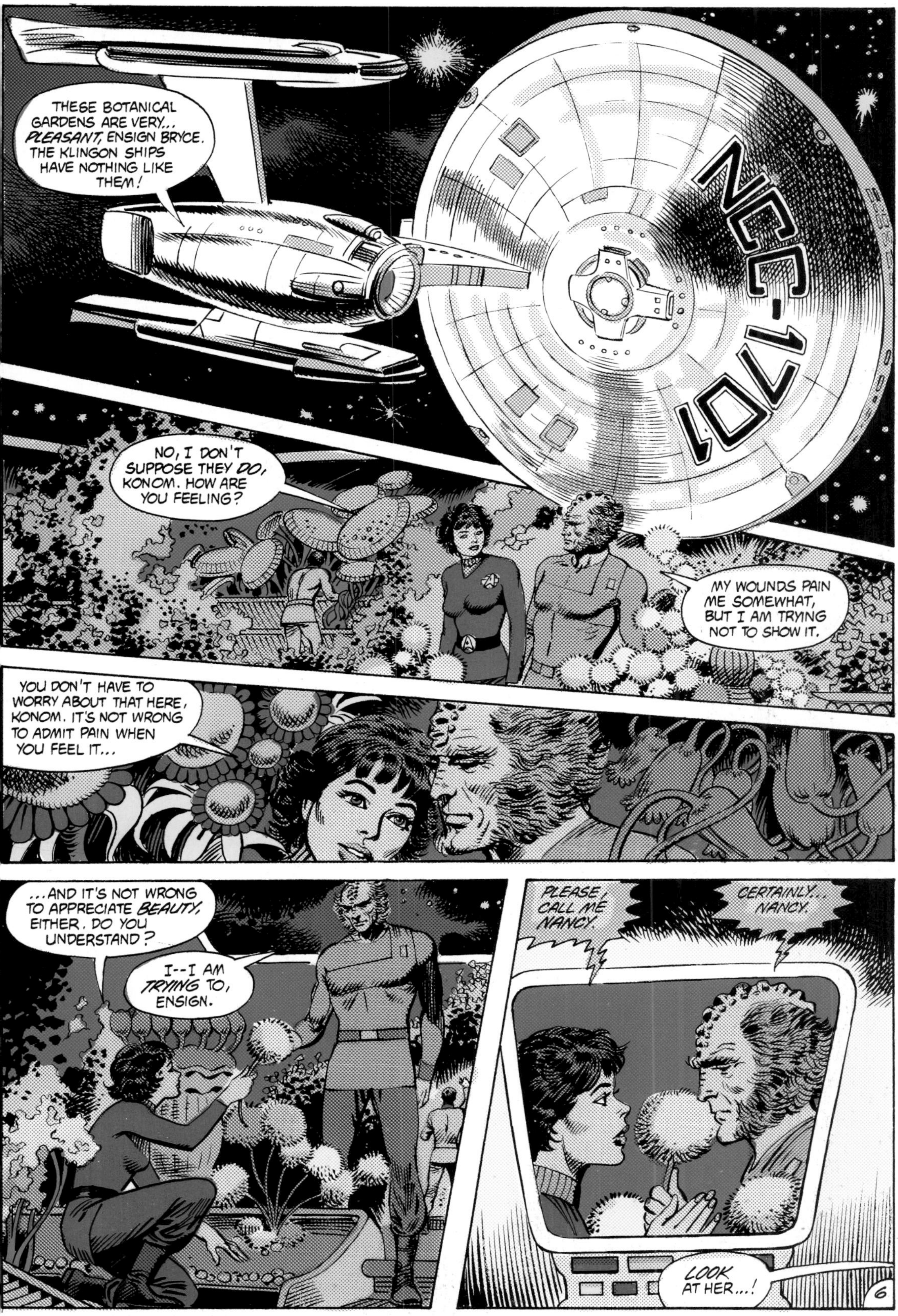

THESE BOTANICAL GARDENS ARE VERY... PLEASANT, ENSIGN BRYCE. THE KLINGON SHIPS HAVE NOTHING LIKE THEM!
NCC-1701
NO, I DON'T SUPPOSE THEY DO, KONOM. HOW ARE YOU FEELING?
MY WOUNDS PAIN ME SOMEWHAT, BUT I AM TRYING NOT TO SHOW IT.
YOU DON'T HAVE TO WORRY ABOUT THAT HERE, KONOM. IT'S NOT WRONG TO ADMIT PAIN WHEN YOU FEEL IT...
...AND IT'S NOT WRONG TO APPRECIATE BEAUTY, EITHER. DO YOU UNDERSTAND?
I--I AM TRYING TO, ENSIGN.
PLEASE, CALL ME NANCY.
CERTAINLY... NANCY.
LOOK AT HER...!
6

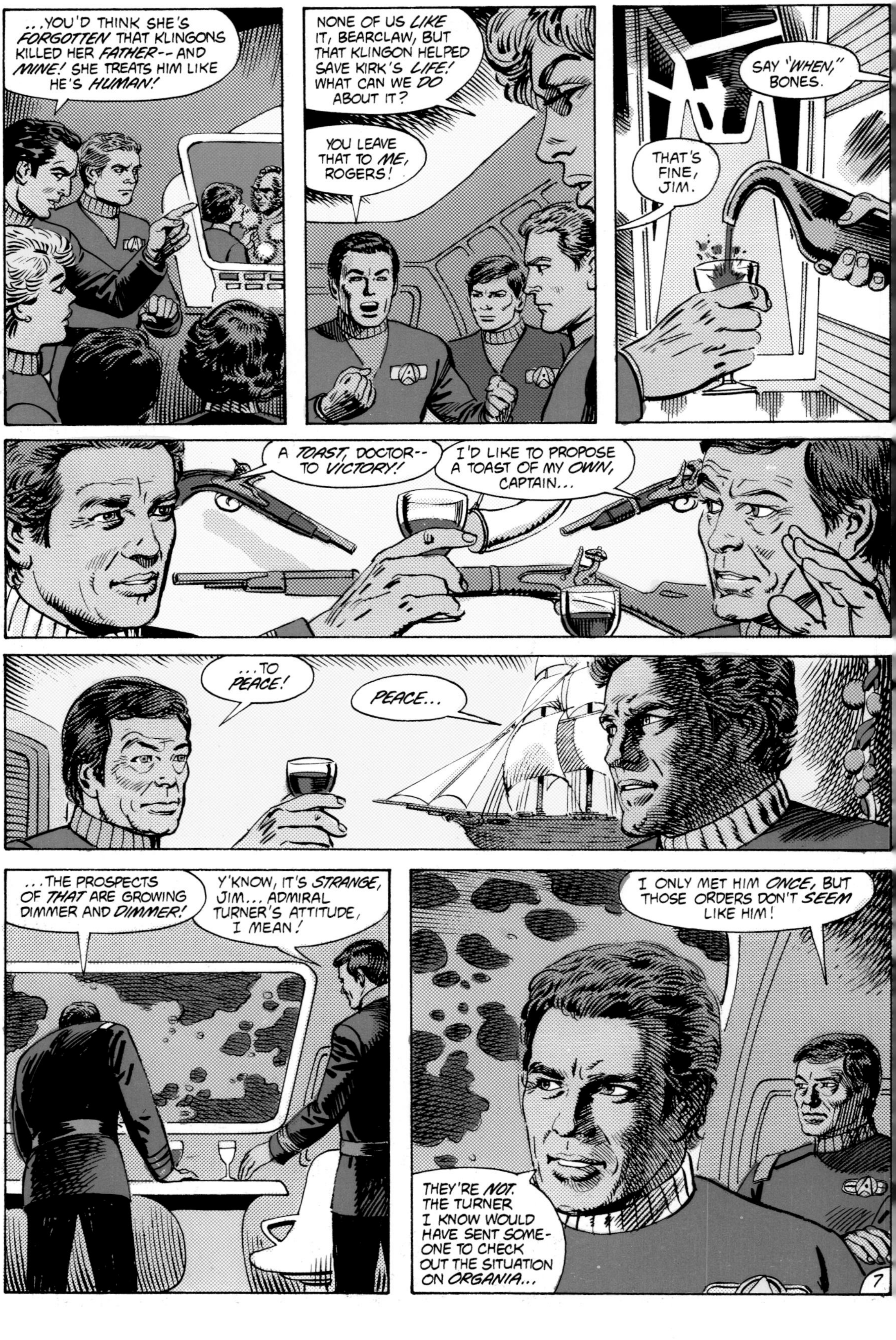
...YOU'D THINK SHE'S FORGOTTEN THAT KLINGONS KILLED HER FATHER-- AND MINE! SHE TREATS HIM LIKE HE'S HUMAN!
NONE OF US LIKE IT, BEARCLAW, BUT THAT KLINGON HELPED SAVE KIRK'S LIFE! WHAT CAN WE DO ABOUT IT?
YOU LEAVE THAT TO ME, ROGERS!
SAY "WHEN," BONES.
THAT'S FINE, JIM.
A TOAST, DOCTOR-- TO VICTORY!
I'D LIKE TO PROPOSE A TOAST OF MY OWN, CAPTAIN...
...TO PEACE!
PEACE...
...THE PROSPECTS OF THAT ARE GROWING DIMMER AND DIMMER!
Y'KNOW, IT'S STRANGE, JIM... ADMIRAL TURNER'S ATTITUDE, I MEAN!
I ONLY MET HIM ONCE, BUT THOSE ORDERS DON'T SEEM LIKE HIM!
THEY'RE NOT. THE TURNER I KNOW WOULD HAVE SENT SOME-ONE TO CHECK OUT THE SITUATION ON ORGANIA...
7

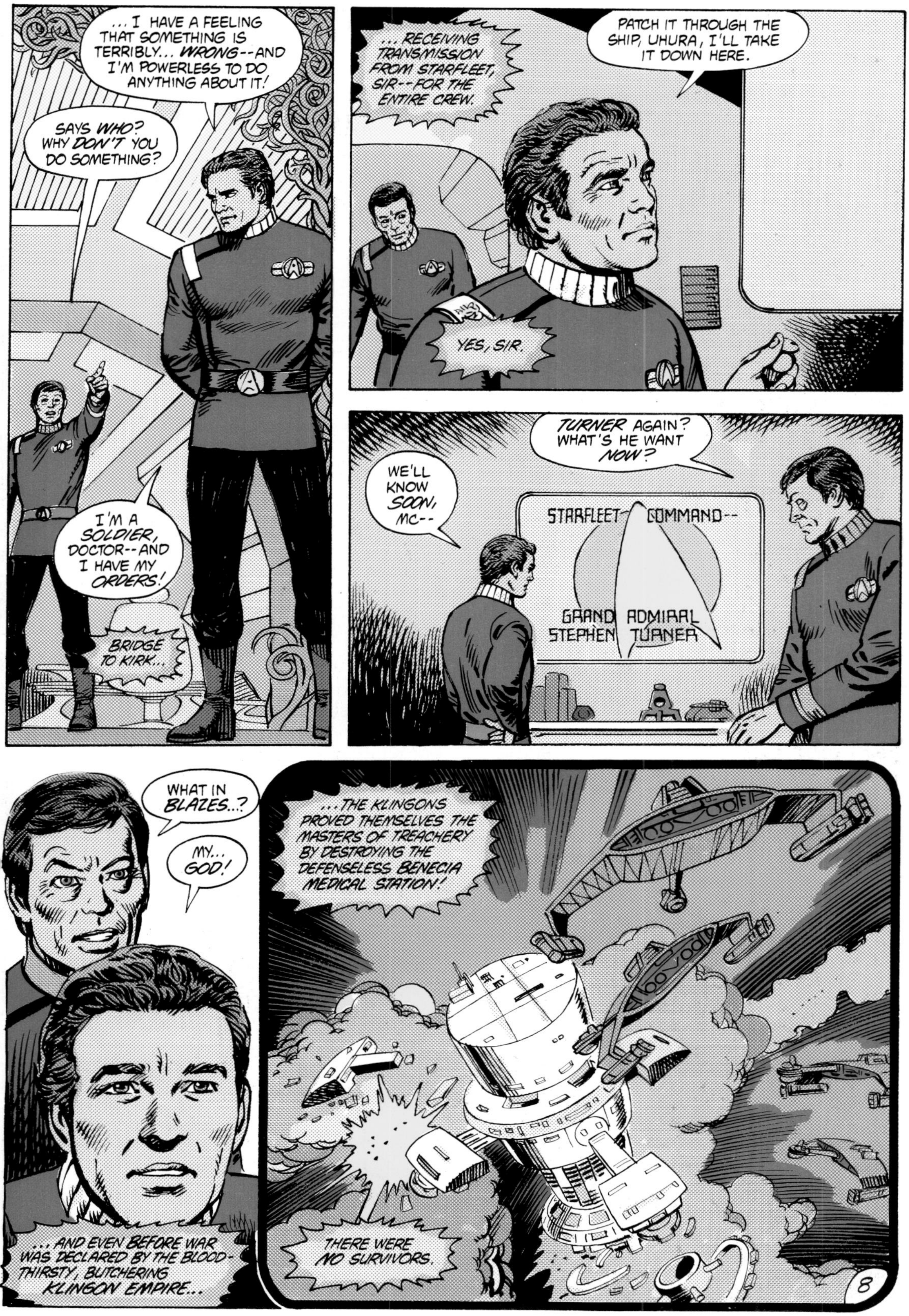

...I HAVE A FEELING THAT SOMETHING IS TERRIBLY... WRONG--AND I'M POWERLESS TO DO ANYTHING ABOUT IT!
SAYS WHO? WHY DON'T YOU DO SOMETHING?
I'M A SOLDIER, DOCTOR--AND I HAVE MY ORDERS!
BRIDGE TO KIRK...
...RECEIVING TRANSMISSION FROM STARFLEET, SIR--FOR THE ENTIRE CREW.
PATCH IT THROUGH THE SHIP, UHURA, I'LL TAKE IT DOWN HERE.
YES, SIR.
TURNER AGAIN? WHAT'S HE WANT NOW?
WE'LL KNOW SOON, MC--
STARFLEET COMMAND--
GRAND ADMIRAL STEPHEN TURNER
WHAT IN BLAZES...?
MY... GOD!
...AND EVEN BEFORE WAR WAS DECLARED BY THE BLOOD-THIRSTY, BUTCHERING KLINGON EMPIRE...
...THE KLINGONS PROVED THEMSELVES THE MASTERS OF TREACHERY BY DESTROYING THE DEFENSELESS BENECIA MEDICAL STATION!
THERE WERE NO SURVIVORS.
8

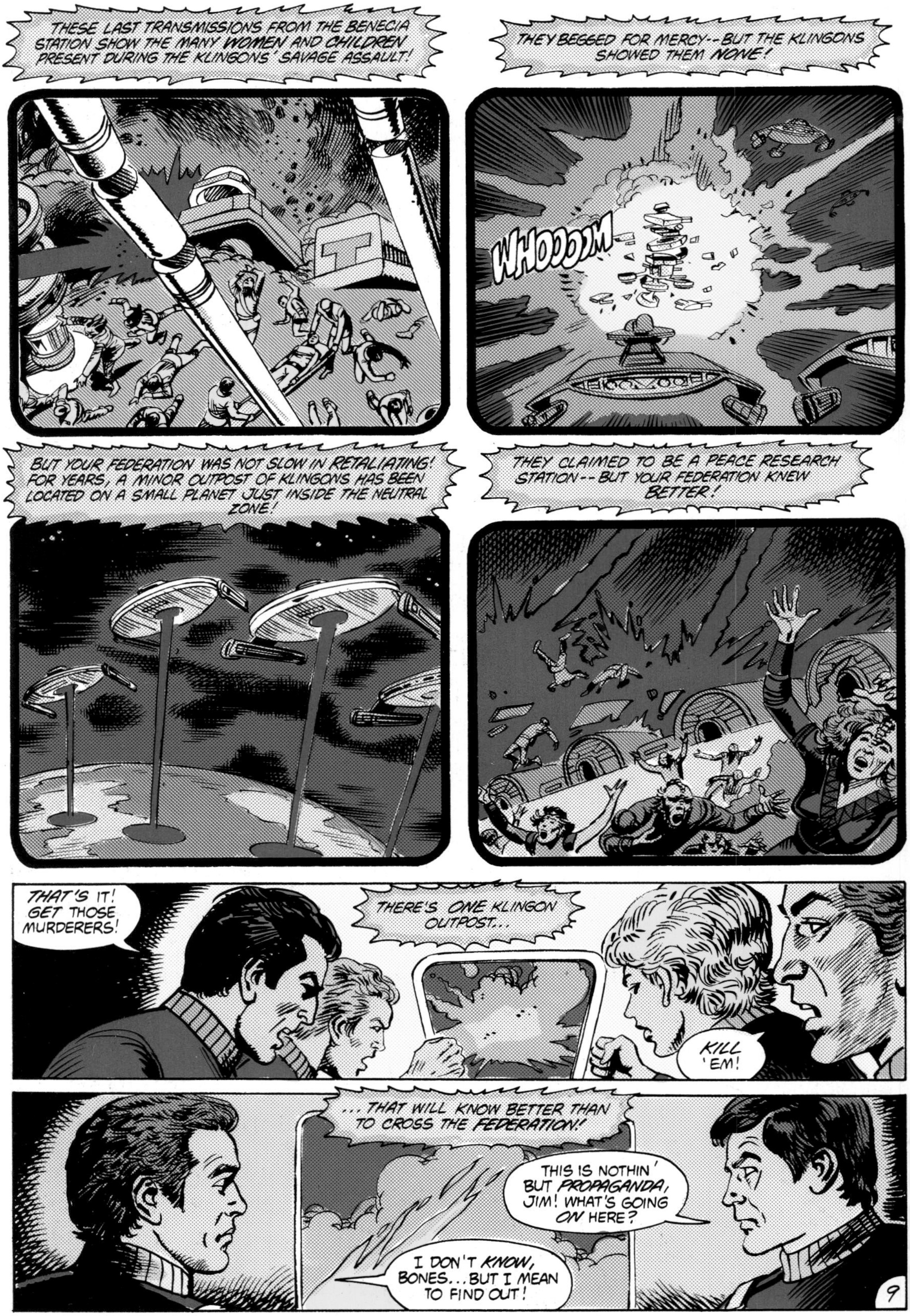
THESE LAST TRANSMISSIONS FROM THE BENECIA STATION SHOW THE MANY WOMEN AND CHILDREN PRESENT DURING THE KLINGONS' SAVAGE ASSAULT!
THEY BEGGED FOR MERCY--BUT THE KLINGONS SHOWED THEM NONE!
WHOOOOOM
BUT YOUR FEDERATION WAS NOT SLOW IN RETALIATING! FOR YEARS, A MINOR OUTPOST OF KLINGONS HAS BEEN LOCATED ON A SMALL PLANET JUST INSIDE THE NEUTRAL ZONE!
THEY CLAIMED TO BE A PEACE RESEARCH STATION--BUT YOUR FEDERATION KNEW BETTER!
THAT'S IT! GET THOSE MURDERERS!
THERE'S ONE KLINGON OUTPOST...
KILL 'EM!
...THAT WILL KNOW BETTER THAN TO CROSS THE FEDERATION!
THIS IS NOTHIN' BUT PROPAGANDA, JIM! WHAT'S GOING ON HERE?
I DON'T KNOW, BONES... BUT I MEAN TO FIND OUT!
9

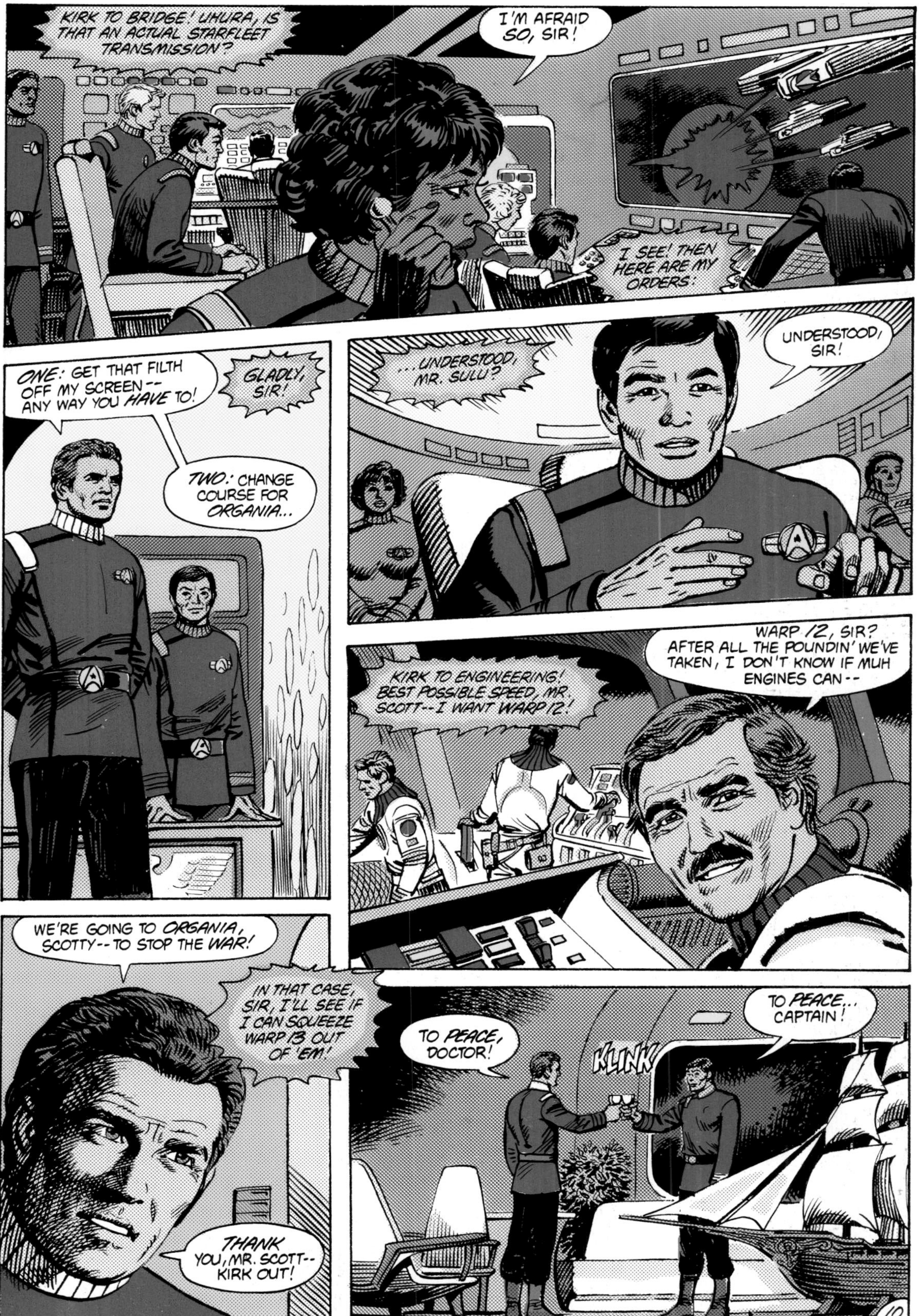
KIRK TO BRIDGE! UHURA, IS THAT AN ACTUAL STARFLEET TRANSMISSION?
I'M AFRAID SO, SIR!
I SEE! THEN HERE ARE MY ORDERS:
ONE: GET THAT FILTH OFF MY SCREEN-- ANY WAY YOU HAVE TO!
GLADLY, SIR!
TWO: CHANGE COURSE FOR ORGANIA...
...UNDERSTOOD, MR. SULU?
UNDERSTOOD, SIR!
KIRK TO ENGINEERING! BEST POSSIBLE SPEED, MR. SCOTT--I WANT WARP 12!
WARP 12, SIR? AFTER ALL THE POUNDIN' WE'VE TAKEN, I DON'T KNOW IF MUH ENGINES CAN--
WE'RE GOING TO ORGANIA, SCOTTY--TO STOP THE WAR!
IN THAT CASE, SIR, I'LL SEE IF I CAN SQUEEZE WARP 13 OUT OF 'EM!
THANK YOU, MR. SCOTT-- KIRK OUT!
TO PEACE, DOCTOR!
KLINK
TO PEACE... CAPTAIN!
10

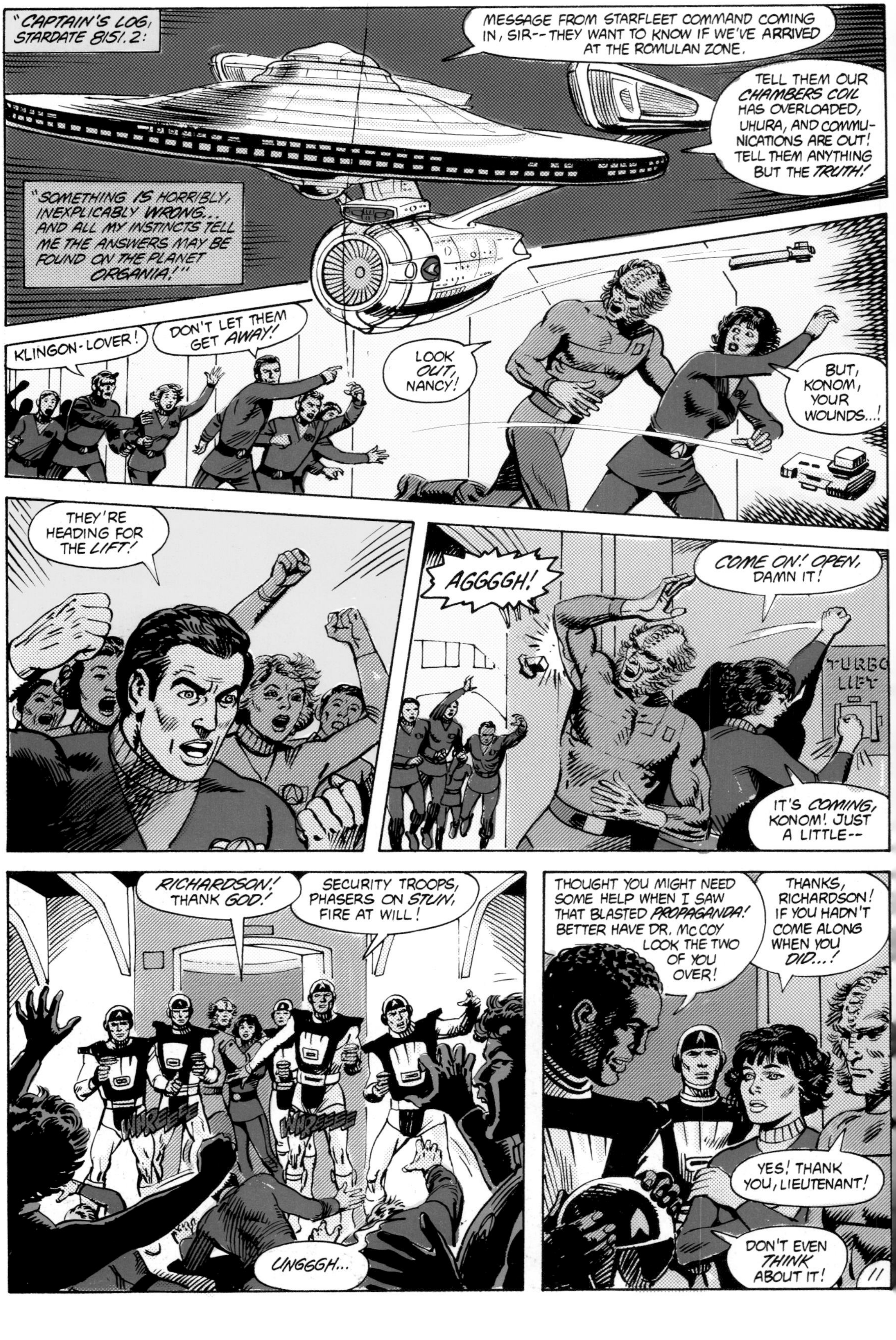
"CAPTAIN'S LOG, STARDATE 8151.2:
MESSAGE FROM STARFLEET COMMAND COMING IN, SIR--THEY WANT TO KNOW IF WE'VE ARRIVED AT THE ROMULAN ZONE.
TELL THEM OUR CHAMBERS COIL HAS OVERLOADED, UHURA, AND COMMUNICATIONS ARE OUT! TELL THEM ANYTHING BUT THE TRUTH!
"SOMETHING IS HORRIBLY, INEXPLICABLY WRONG.. AND ALL MY INSTINCTS TELL ME THE ANSWERS MAY BE FOUND ON THE PLANET ORGANIA!"
KLINGON-LOVER!
DON'T LET THEM GET AWAY!
LOOK OUT, NANCY!
BUT, KONOM, YOUR WOUNDS...!
THEY'RE HEADING FOR THE LIFT!
AGGGGH!
COME ON! OPEN, DAMN IT!
TURBO LIFT
IT'S COMING, KONOM! JUST A LITTLE--
RICHARDSON! THANK GOD!
SECURITY TROOPS, PHASERS ON STUN, FIRE AT WILL!
UNGGGH...
THOUGHT YOU MIGHT NEED SOME HELP WHEN I SAW THAT BLASTED PROPAGANDA! BETTER HAVE DR. McCOY LOOK THE TWO OF YOU OVER!
THANKS, RICHARDSON! IF YOU HADN'T COME ALONG WHEN YOU DID...!
YES! THANK YOU, LIEUTENANT!
DON'T EVEN THINK ABOUT IT!

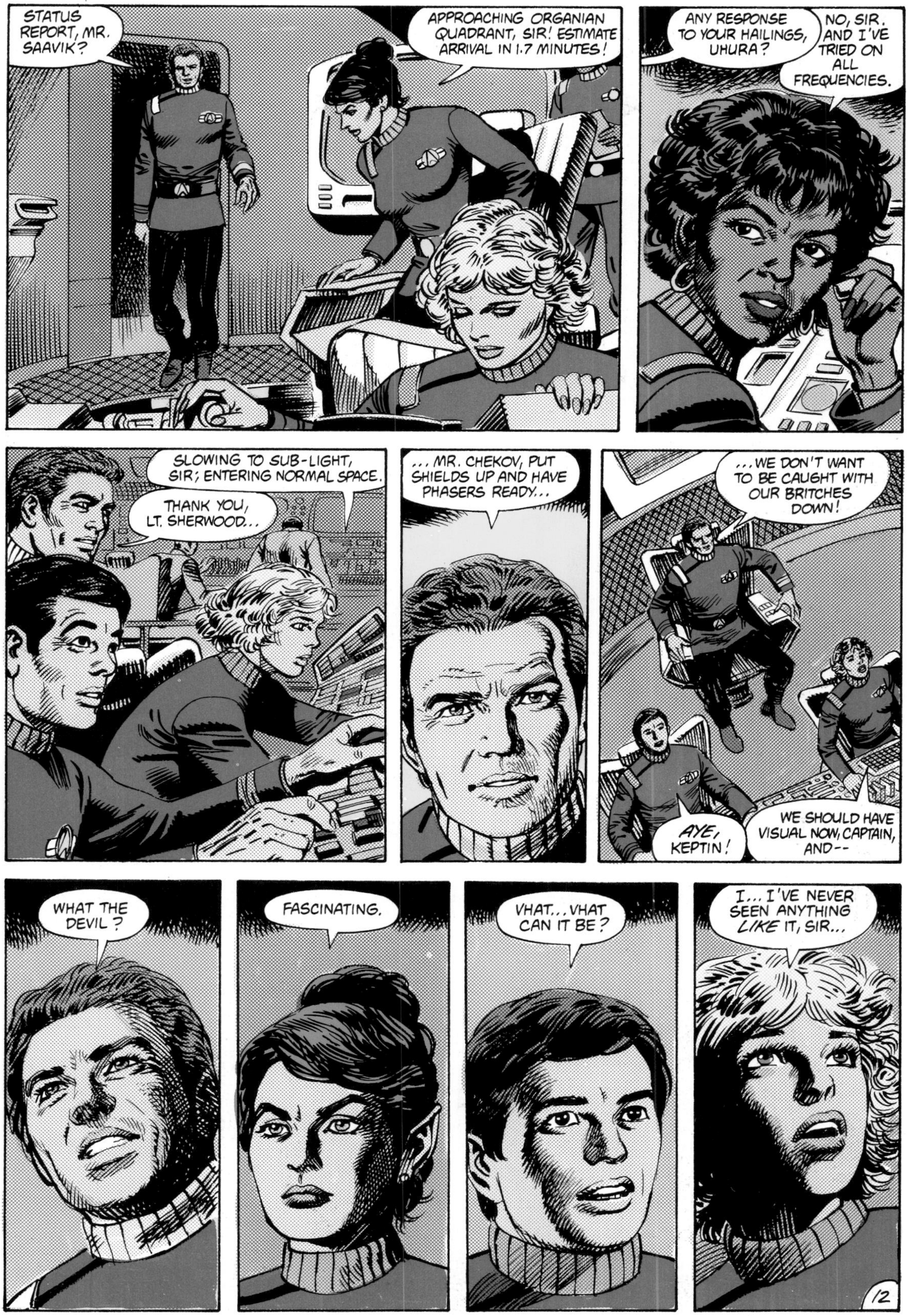
STATUS REPORT, MR. SAAVIK?
APPROACHING ORGANIAN QUADRANT, SIR! ESTIMATE ARRIVAL IN 1.7 MINUTES!
ANY RESPONSE TO YOUR HAILINGS, UHURA?
NO, SIR. AND I'VE TRIED ON ALL FREQUENCIES.
SLOWING TO SUB-LIGHT, SIR; ENTERING NORMAL SPACE.
THANK YOU, LT. SHERWOOD...
...MR. CHEKOV, PUT SHIELDS UP AND HAVE PHASERS READY...
...WE DON'T WANT TO BE CAUGHT WITH OUR BRITCHES DOWN!
AYE, KEPTIN!
WE SHOULD HAVE VISUAL NOW, CAPTAIN, AND--
WHAT THE DEVIL?
FASCINATING.
VHAT...VHAT CAN IT BE?
I... I'VE NEVER SEEN ANYTHING LIKE IT, SIR...
12

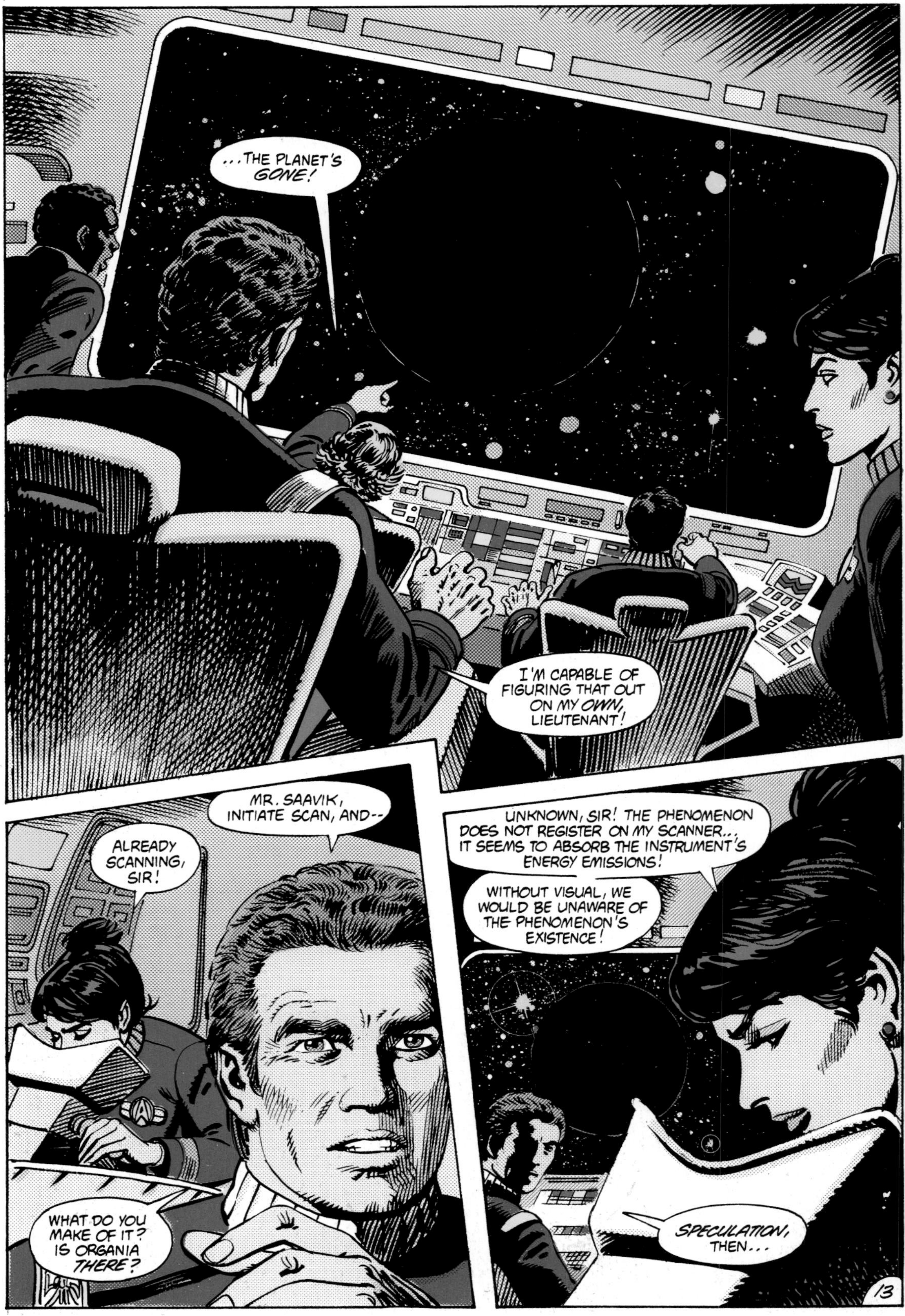
...THE PLANET'S GONE!
I'M CAPABLE OF FIGURING THAT OUT ON MY OWN, LIEUTENANT!
MR. SAAVIK, INITIATE SCAN, AND--
ALREADY SCANNING, SIR!
WHAT DO YOU MAKE OF IT? IS ORGANIA THERE?
UNKNOWN, SIR! THE PHENOMENON DOES NOT REGISTER ON MY SCANNER... IT SEEMS TO ABSORB THE INSTRUMENT'S ENERGY EMISSIONS!
WITHOUT VISUAL, WE WOULD BE UNAWARE OF THE PHENOMENON'S EXISTENCE!
SPECULATION, THEN...

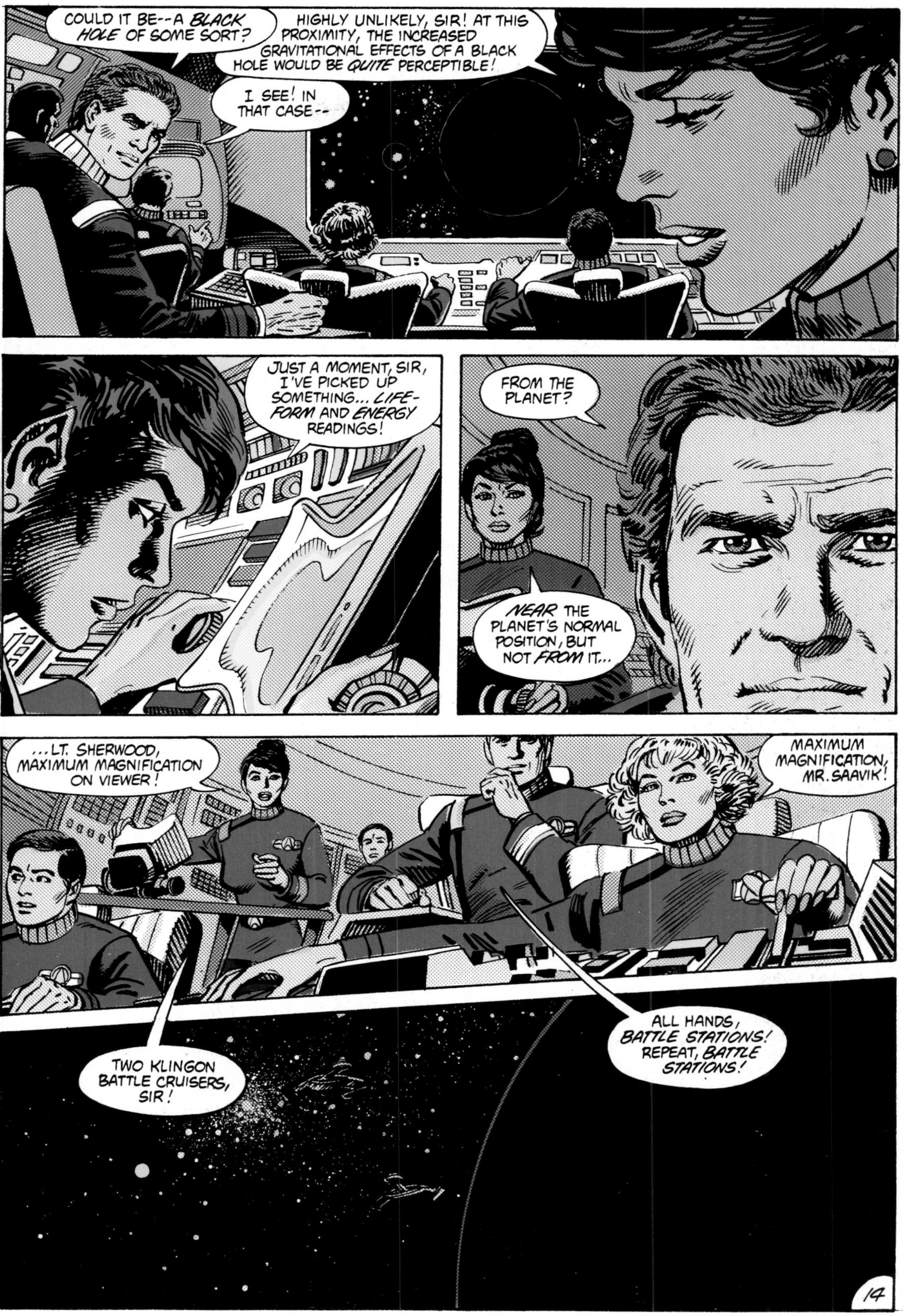
COULD IT BE--A BLACK HOLE OF SOME SORT?
HIGHLY UNLIKELY, SIR! AT THIS PROXIMITY, THE INCREASED GRAVITATIONAL EFFECTS OF A BLACK HOLE WOULD BE QUITE PERCEPTIBLE!
I SEE! IN THAT CASE--
JUST A MOMENT, SIR, I'VE PICKED UP SOMETHING... LIFE-FORM AND ENERGY READINGS!
FROM THE PLANET?
NEAR THE PLANET'S NORMAL POSITION, BUT NOT FROM IT...
...LT. SHERWOOD, MAXIMUM MAGNIFICATION ON VIEWER!
MAXIMUM MAGNIFICATION, MR. SAAVIK!
TWO KLINGON BATTLE CRUISERS, SIR!
ALL HANDS, BATTLE STATIONS! REPEAT, BATTLE STATIONS!
14

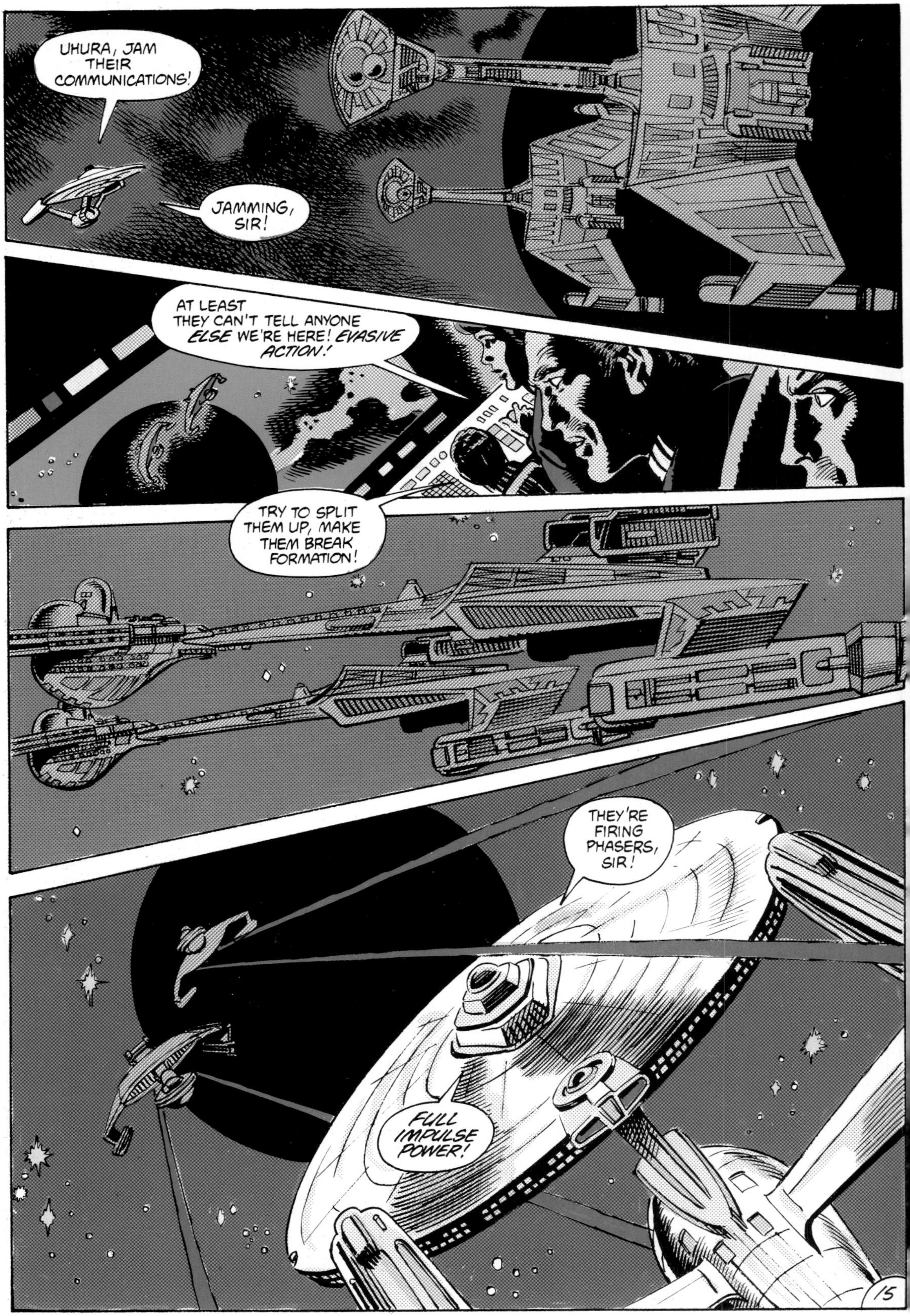
UHURA, JAM THEIR COMMUNICATIONS!
JAMMING, SIR!
AT LEAST THEY CAN'T TELL ANYONE ELSE WE'RE HERE! EVASIVE ACTION!
TRY TO SPLIT THEM UP, MAKE THEM BREAK FORMATION!
THEY'RE FIRING PHASERS, SIR!
FULL IMPULSE POWER!
15

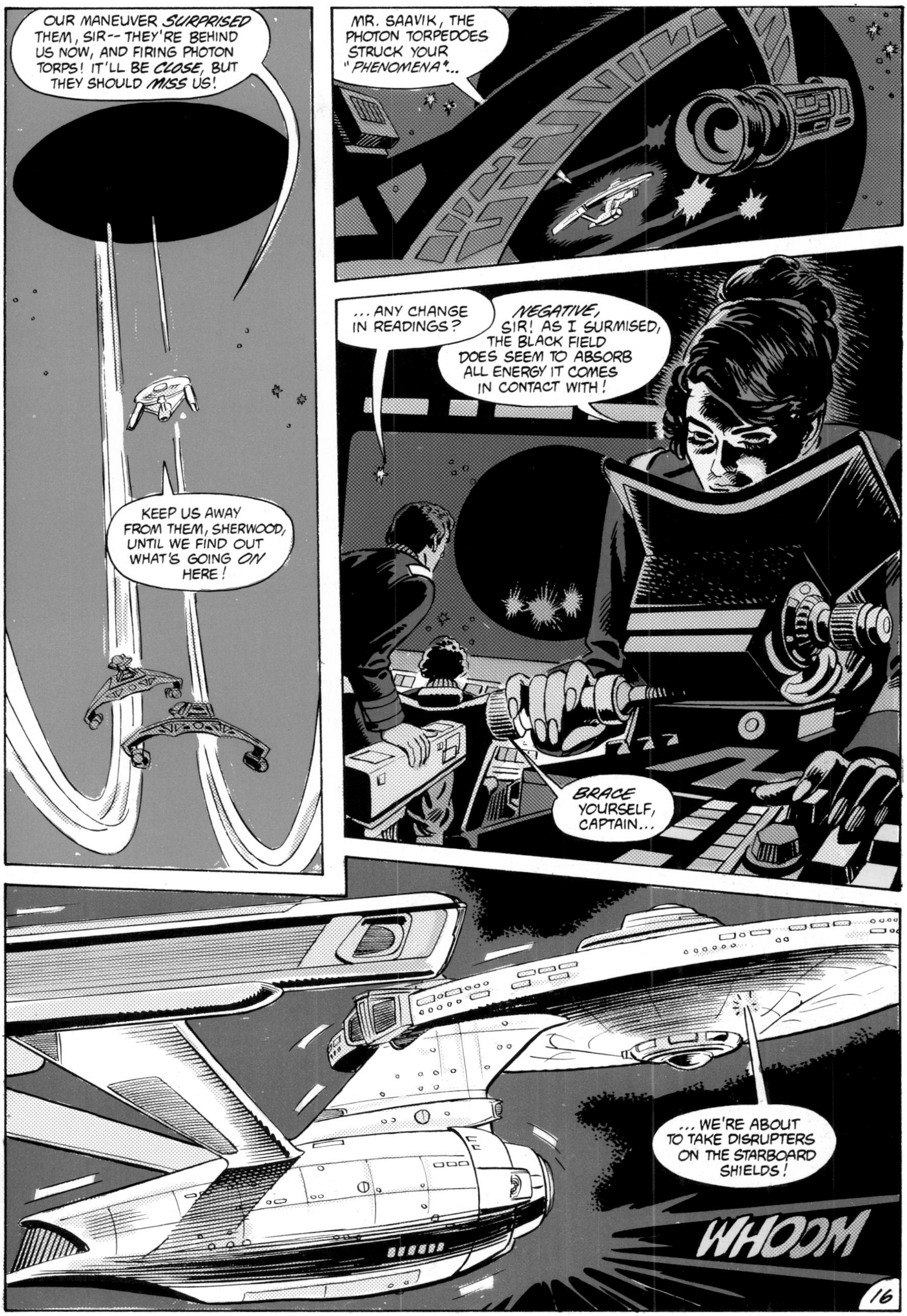
OUR MANEUVER SURPRISED THEM, SIR-- THEY'RE BEHIND US NOW, AND FIRING PHOTON TORPS! IT'LL BE CLOSE, BUT THEY SHOULD MISS US!
KEEP US AWAY FROM THEM, SHERWOOD, UNTIL WE FIND OUT WHAT'S GOING ON HERE!
MR. SAAVIK, THE PHOTON TORPEDOES STRUCK YOUR "PHENOMENA"...
... ANY CHANGE IN READINGS?
NEGATIVE, SIR! AS I SURMISED, THE BLACK FIELD DOES SEEM TO ABSORB ALL ENERGY IT COMES IN CONTACT WITH!
BRACE YOURSELF, CAPTAIN...
... WE'RE ABOUT TO TAKE DISRUPTERS ON THE STARBOARD SHIELDS!
WHOOM

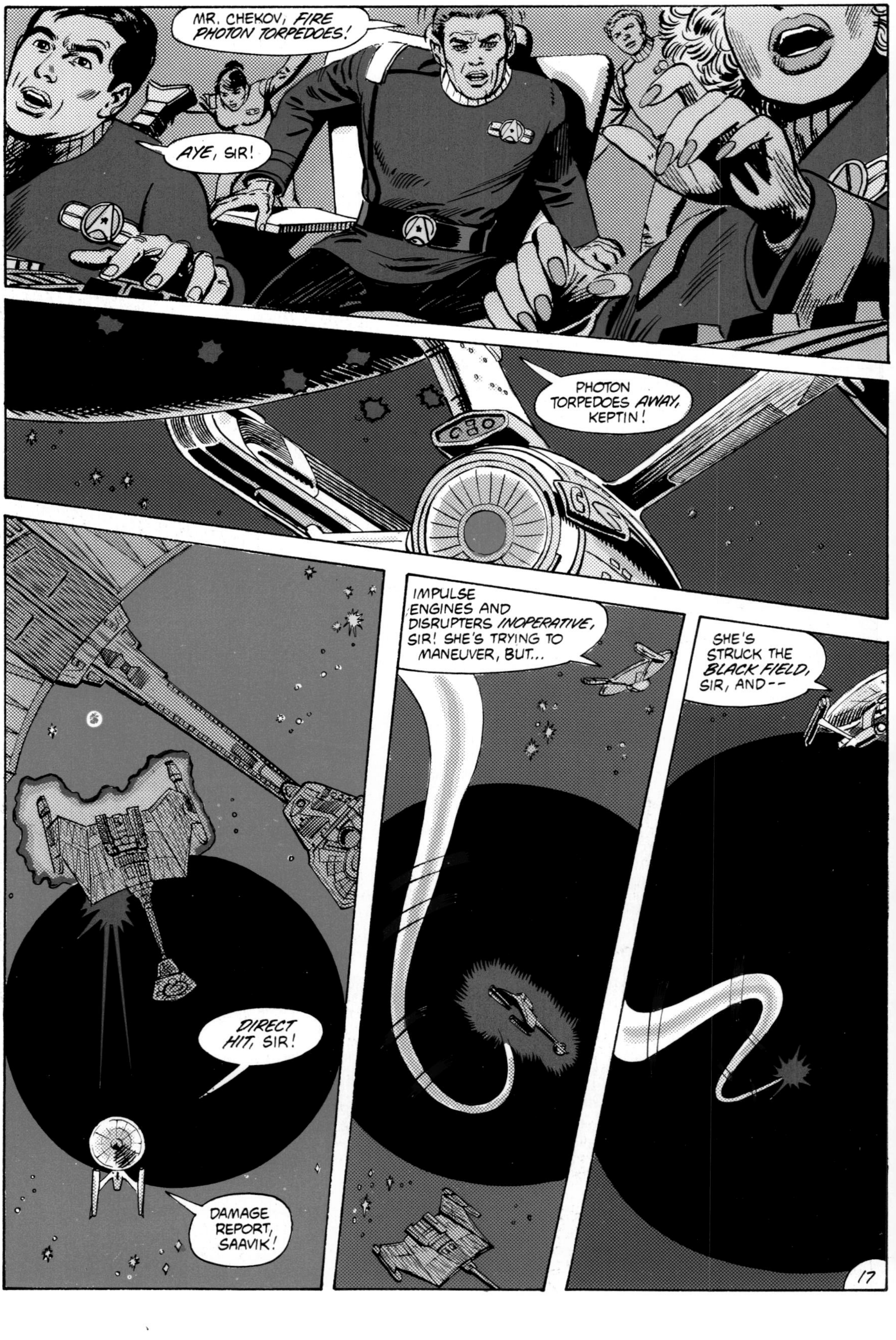
MR. CHEKOV, FIRE PHOTON TORPEDOES!
AYE, SIR!
PHOTON TORPEDOES AWAY, KEPTIN!
DIRECT HIT, SIR!
DAMAGE REPORT, SAAVIK!
IMPULSE ENGINES AND DISRUPTERS INOPERATIVE, SIR! SHE'S TRYING TO MANEUVER, BUT...
SHE'S STRUCK THE BLACK FIELD, SIR, AND--

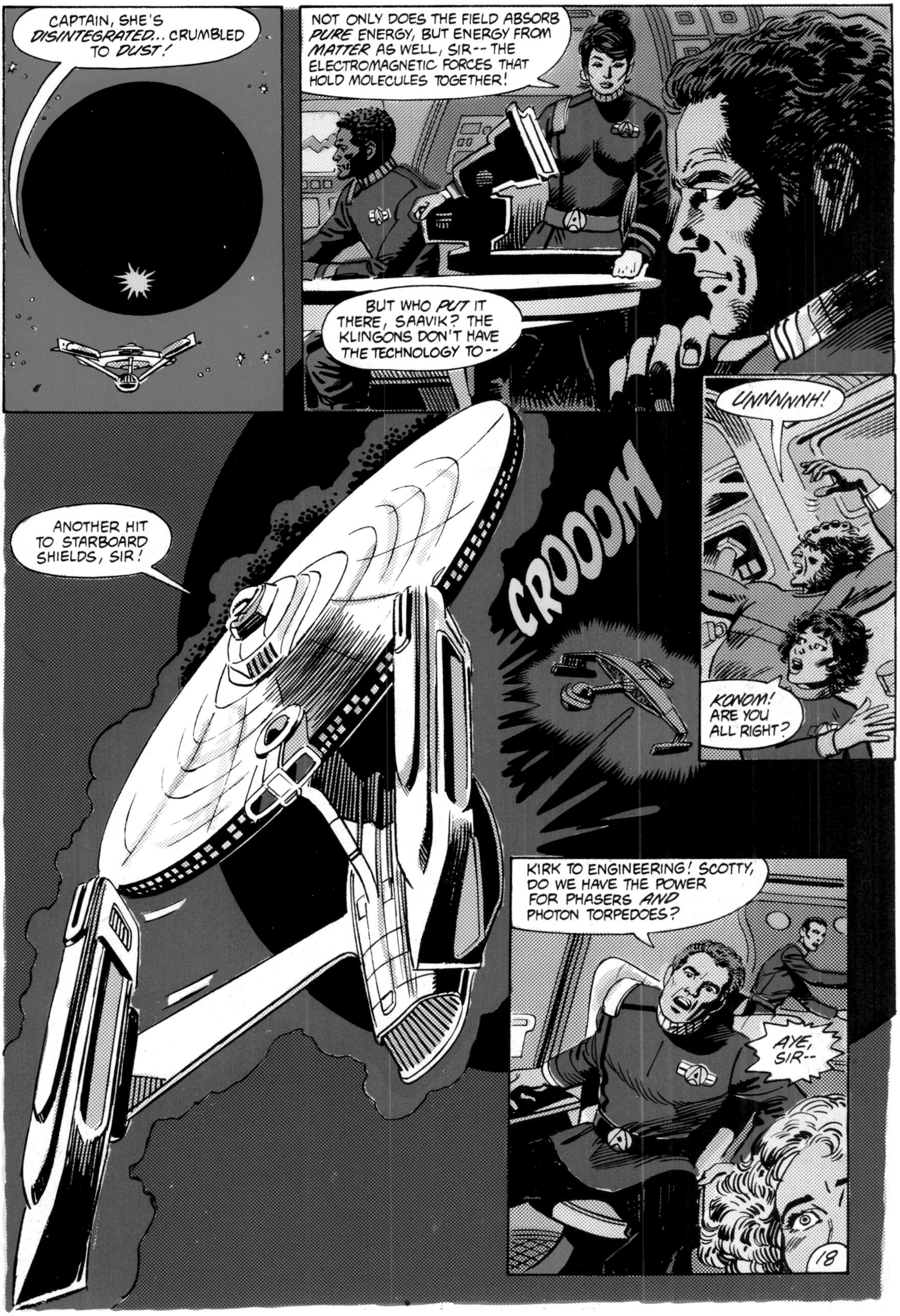

CAPTAIN, SHE'S DISINTEGRATED... CRUMBLED TO DUST!
NOT ONLY DOES THE FIELD ABSORB PURE ENERGY, BUT ENERGY FROM MATTER AS WELL, SIR-- THE ELECTROMAGNETIC FORCES THAT HOLD MOLECULES TOGETHER!
BUT WHO PUT IT THERE, SAAVIK? THE KLINGONS DON'T HAVE THE TECHNOLOGY TO--
ANOTHER HIT TO STARBOARD SHIELDS, SIR!
CROOOM
UNNNNNH!
KONOM! ARE YOU ALL RIGHT?
KIRK TO ENGINEERING! SCOTTY, DO WE HAVE THE POWER FOR PHASERS AND PHOTON TORPEDOES?
AYE, SIR--
18

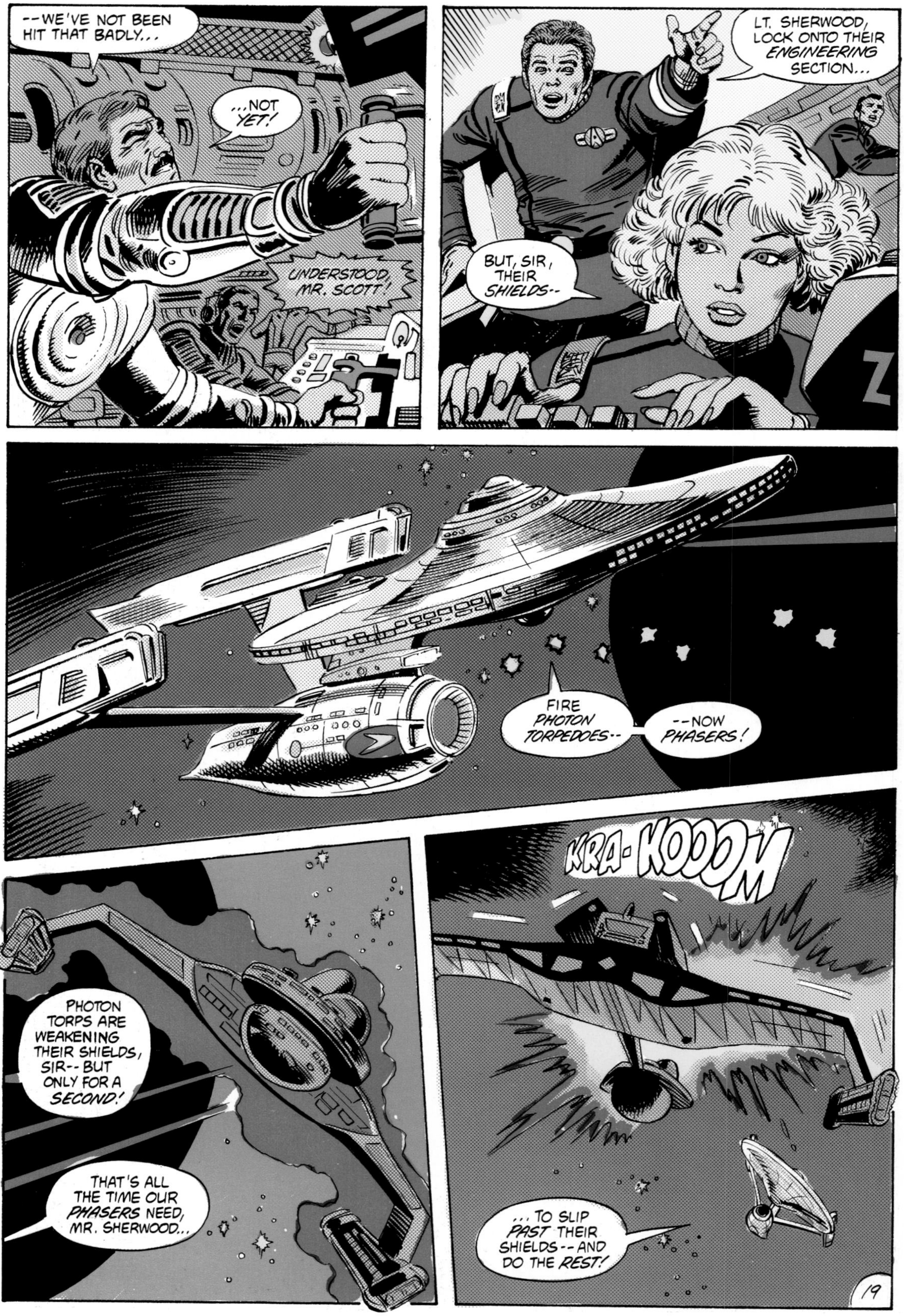
--WE'VE NOT BEEN HIT THAT BADLY...
...NOT YET!
UNDERSTOOD, MR. SCOTT!
LT. SHERWOOD, LOCK ONTO THEIR ENGINEERING SECTION...
BUT, SIR, THEIR SHIELDS--
FIRE PHOTON TORPEDOES--
--NOW PHASERS!
PHOTON TORPS ARE WEAKENING THEIR SHIELDS, SIR--BUT ONLY FOR A SECOND!
THAT'S ALL THE TIME OUR PHASERS NEED, MR. SHERWOOD...
KRA-KOOOM
...TO SLIP PAST THEIR SHIELDS--AND DO THE REST!
19

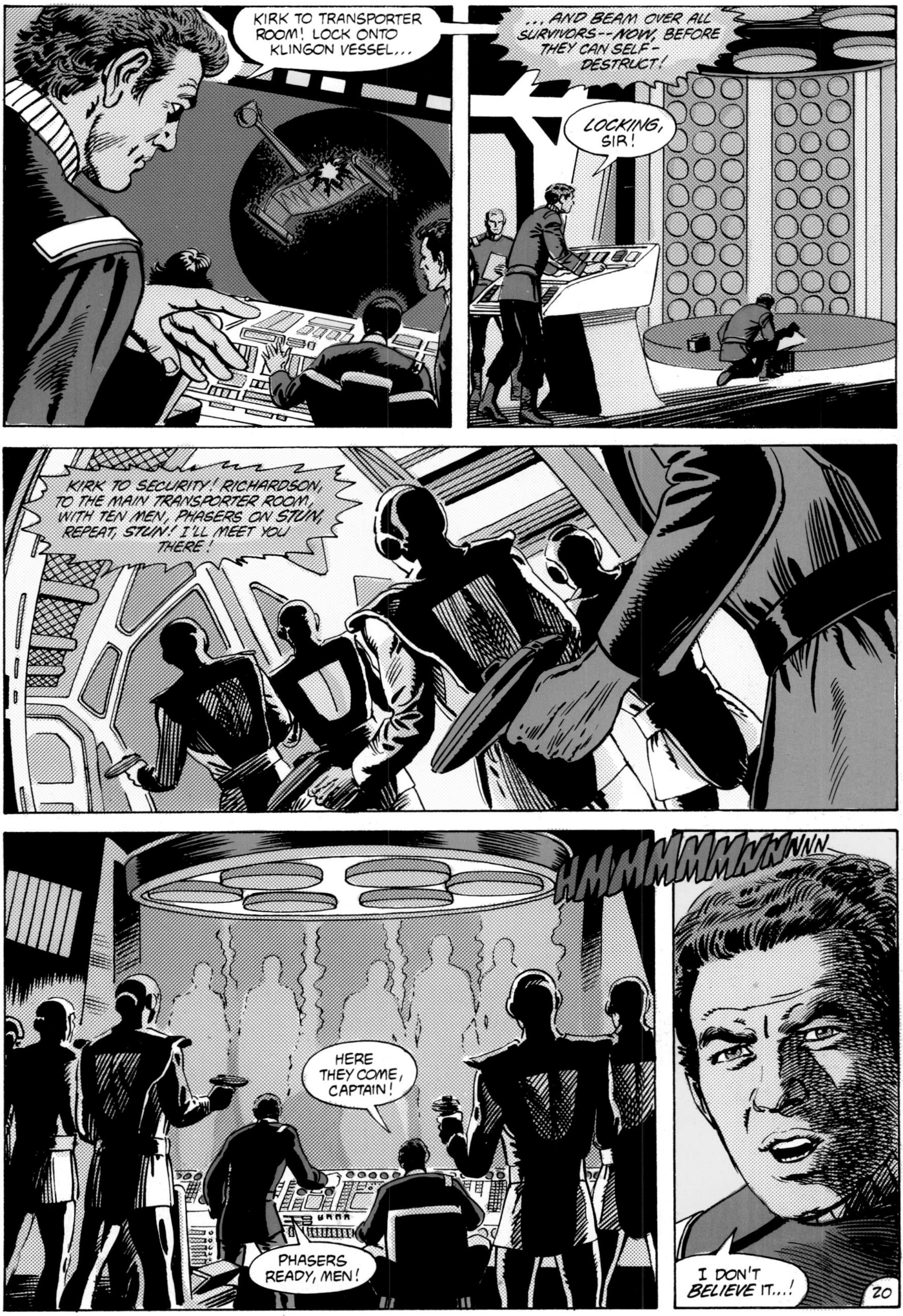
KIRK TO TRANSPORTER ROOM! LOCK ONTO KLINGON VESSEL...
...AND BEAM OVER ALL SURVIVORS--NOW, BEFORE THEY CAN SELF-DESTRUCT!
LOCKING, SIR!
KIRK TO SECURITY! RICHARDSON, TO THE MAIN TRANSPORTER ROOM, WITH TEN MEN, PHASERS ON STUN, REPEAT, STUN! I'LL MEET YOU THERE!
HMMMMMMNNNN
HERE THEY COME, CAPTAIN!
PHASERS READY, MEN!
I DON'T BELIEVE IT...!
20

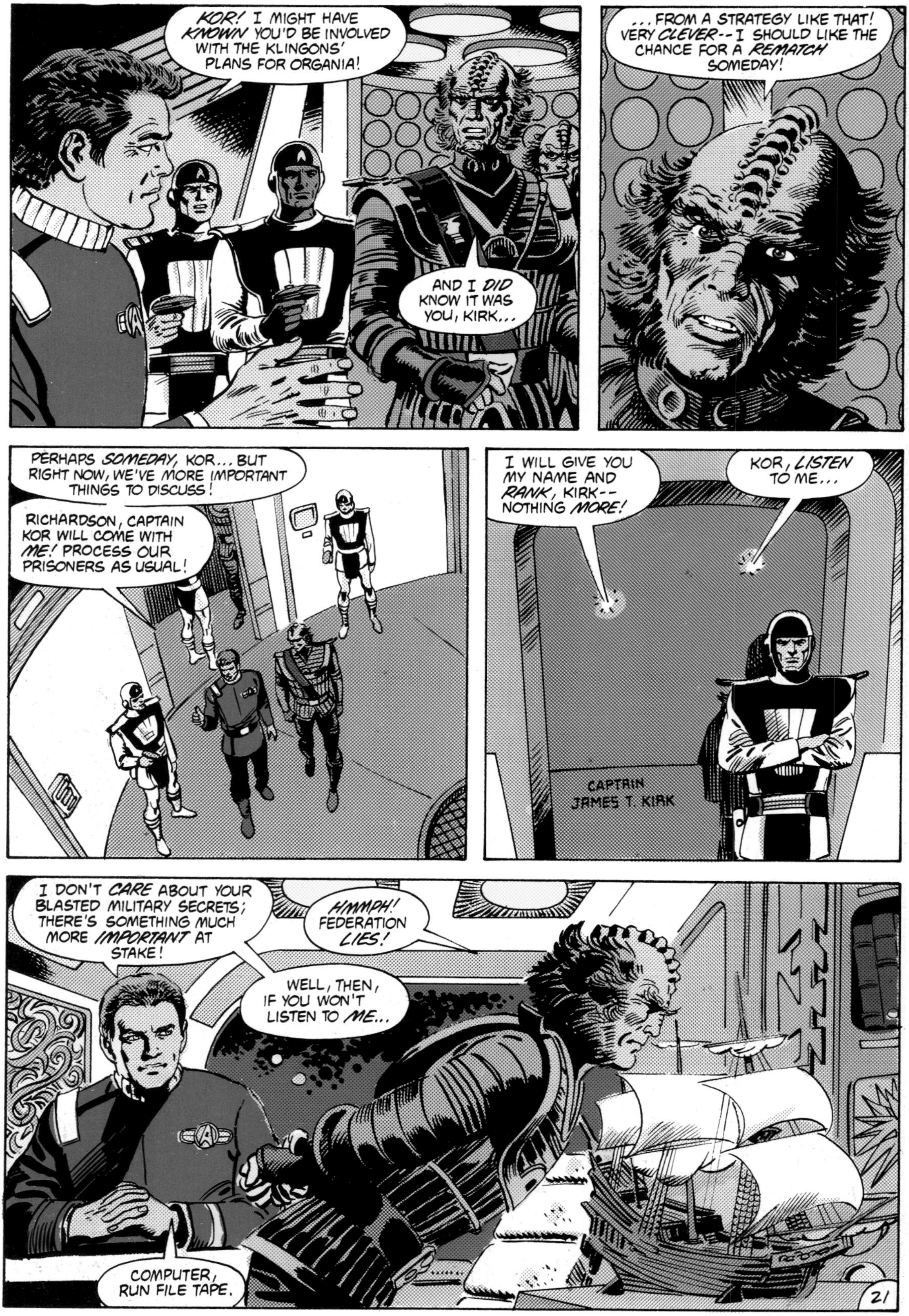
KOR! I MIGHT HAVE KNOWN YOU'D BE INVOLVED WITH THE KLINGONS' PLANS FOR ORGANIA!
AND I DID KNOW IT WAS YOU, KIRK...
...FROM A STRATEGY LIKE THAT! VERY CLEVER--I SHOULD LIKE THE CHANCE FOR A REMATCH SOMEDAY!
PERHAPS SOMEDAY, KOR... BUT RIGHT NOW, WE'VE MORE IMPORTANT THINGS TO DISCUSS!
RICHARDSON, CAPTAIN KOR WILL COME WITH ME! PROCESS OUR PRISONERS AS USUAL!
I WILL GIVE YOU MY NAME AND RANK, KIRK-- NOTHING MORE!
KOR, LISTEN TO ME...
CAPTAIN
JAMES T. KIRK
I DON'T CARE ABOUT YOUR BLASTED MILITARY SECRETS; THERE'S SOMETHING MUCH MORE IMPORTANT AT STAKE!
HMMPH! FEDERATION LIES!
WELL, THEN, IF YOU WON'T LISTEN TO ME...
COMPUTER, RUN FILE TAPE.

...AT LEAST TAKE A LOOK AT *THIS*!

OUR *RESEARCH BASE*--! DESTROYED BY *YOUR SHIPS*!

THERE WERE *WOMEN* AND *CHILDREN* ON THAT BASE, KIRK! AND YOU CALL *US* BARBARIANS?

AND WHAT ABOUT THE *BENECIA MEDICAL CENTER*, KOR? *KLINGON* SHIPS DESTROYED THAT! AN *UNARMED HOSPITAL*!

THAT'S NOT WARFARE, THAT'S *BUTCHERY*! KOR, WE'VE GOT TO *STOP* THIS, AND I THINK ORGANIA IS THE *KEY*!

IS THAT BLACK FIELD A *KLINGON* WEAPON?

I DO NOT *KNOW*, KIRK...

...I KNOW ONLY THAT I WAS TAKEN FROM BEHIND MY ADMIRAL'S DESK, AND GIVEN MY COMMAND BACK-- BY THE ORDER OF *KAHLESS IV*, HIMSELF!

YOU WERE SENT *HERE*...?

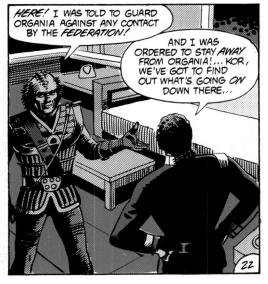

HERE! I WAS TOLD TO GUARD ORGANIA AGAINST ANY CONTACT BY THE *FEDERATION*!

AND I WAS ORDERED TO STAY *AWAY* FROM ORGANIA!...KOR, WE'VE GOT TO FIND OUT WHAT'S GOING *ON* DOWN THERE...

22

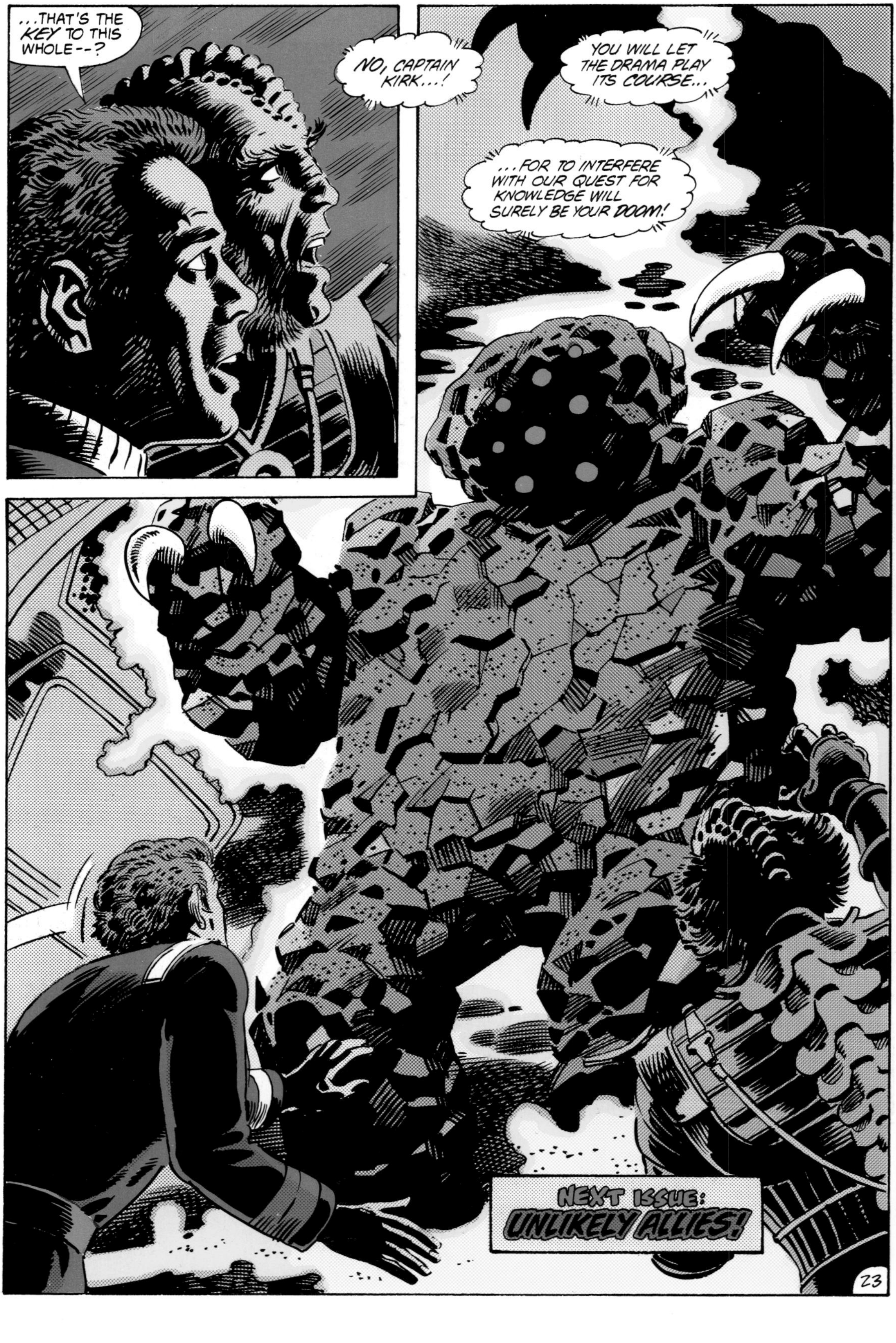
...THAT'S THE KEY TO THIS WHOLE--?
NO, CAPTAIN KIRK...!
YOU WILL LET THE DRAMA PLAY ITS COURSE...
...FOR TO INTERFERE WITH OUR QUEST FOR KNOWLEDGE WILL SURELY BE YOUR DOOM!
NEXT ISSUE: UNLIKELY ALLIES!

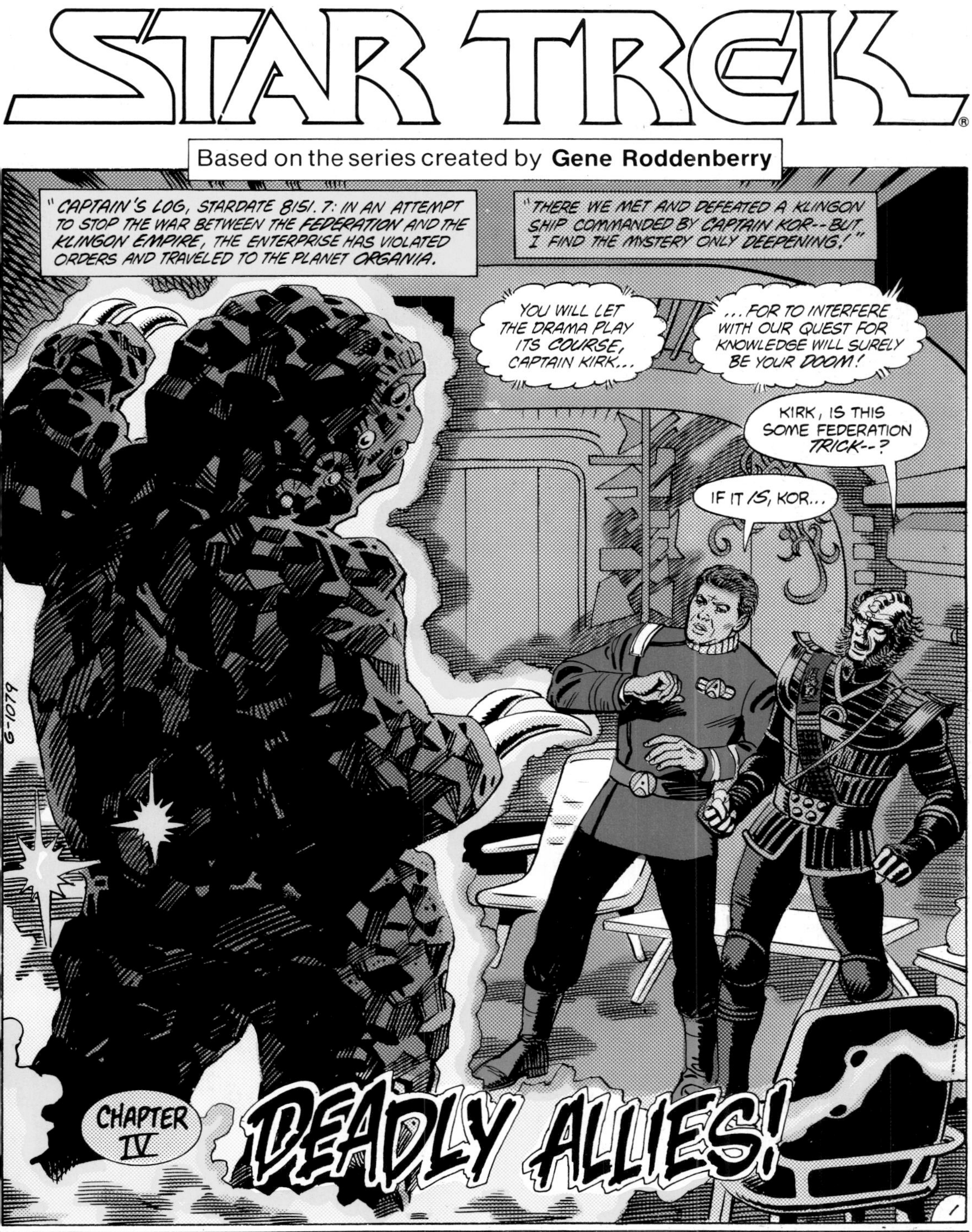
STAR TREK®
Based on the series created by Gene Roddenberry
"CAPTAIN'S LOG, STARDATE 8151.7: IN AN ATTEMPT TO STOP THE WAR BETWEEN THE FEDERATION AND THE KLINGON EMPIRE, THE ENTERPRISE HAS VIOLATED ORDERS AND TRAVELED TO THE PLANET ORGANIA.
"THERE WE MET AND DEFEATED A KLINGON SHIP COMMANDED BY CAPTAIN KOR--BUT I FIND THE MYSTERY ONLY DEEPENING!"
YOU WILL LET THE DRAMA PLAY ITS COURSE, CAPTAIN KIRK...
...FOR TO INTERFERE WITH OUR QUEST FOR KNOWLEDGE WILL SURELY BE YOUR DOOM!
KIRK, IS THIS SOME FEDERATION TRICK--?
IF IT IS, KOR...
CHAPTER IV
DEADLY ALLIES!
G-1079
1

MIKE W. BARR * **TOM SUTTON** & **RICARDO VILLAGRAN**
Writer — Artists

JOHN COSTANZA * **MICHELE WOLFMAN** * **MARV WOLFMAN**
Letterer — Colorist — Editor

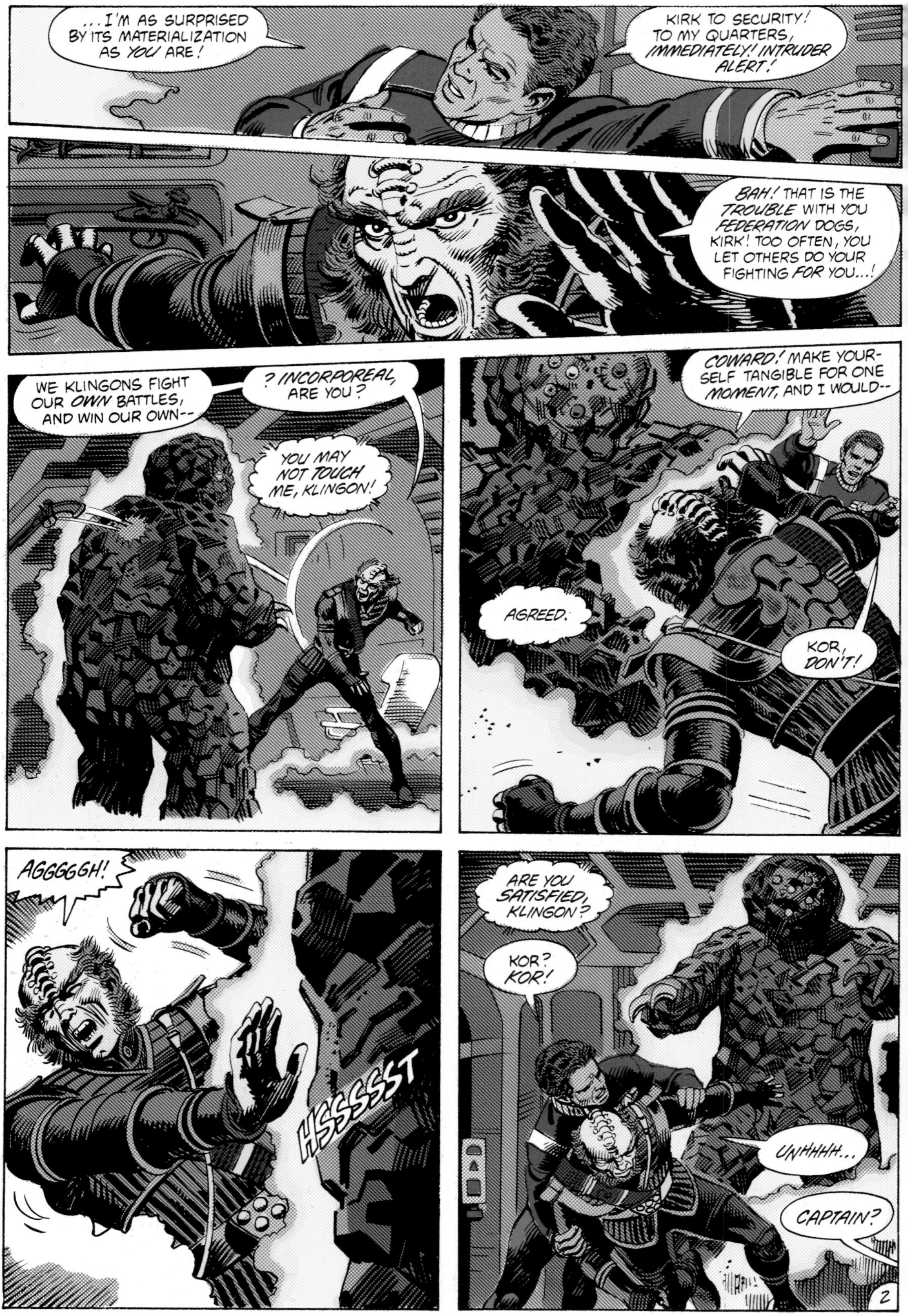
...I'M AS SURPRISED BY ITS MATERIALIZATION AS YOU ARE!
KIRK TO SECURITY! TO MY QUARTERS, IMMEDIATELY! INTRUDER ALERT!
BAH! THAT IS THE TROUBLE WITH YOU FEDERATION DOGS, KIRK! TOO OFTEN, YOU LET OTHERS DO YOUR FIGHTING FOR YOU...!
WE KLINGONS FIGHT OUR OWN BATTLES, AND WIN OUR OWN--
? INCORPOREAL, ARE YOU?
YOU MAY NOT TOUCH ME, KLINGON!
COWARD! MAKE YOURSELF TANGIBLE FOR ONE MOMENT, AND I WOULD--
AGREED.
KOR, DON'T!
AGGGGGH!
HSSSSST
ARE YOU SATISFIED, KLINGON?
KOR? KOR!
UNHHHH...
CAPTAIN?

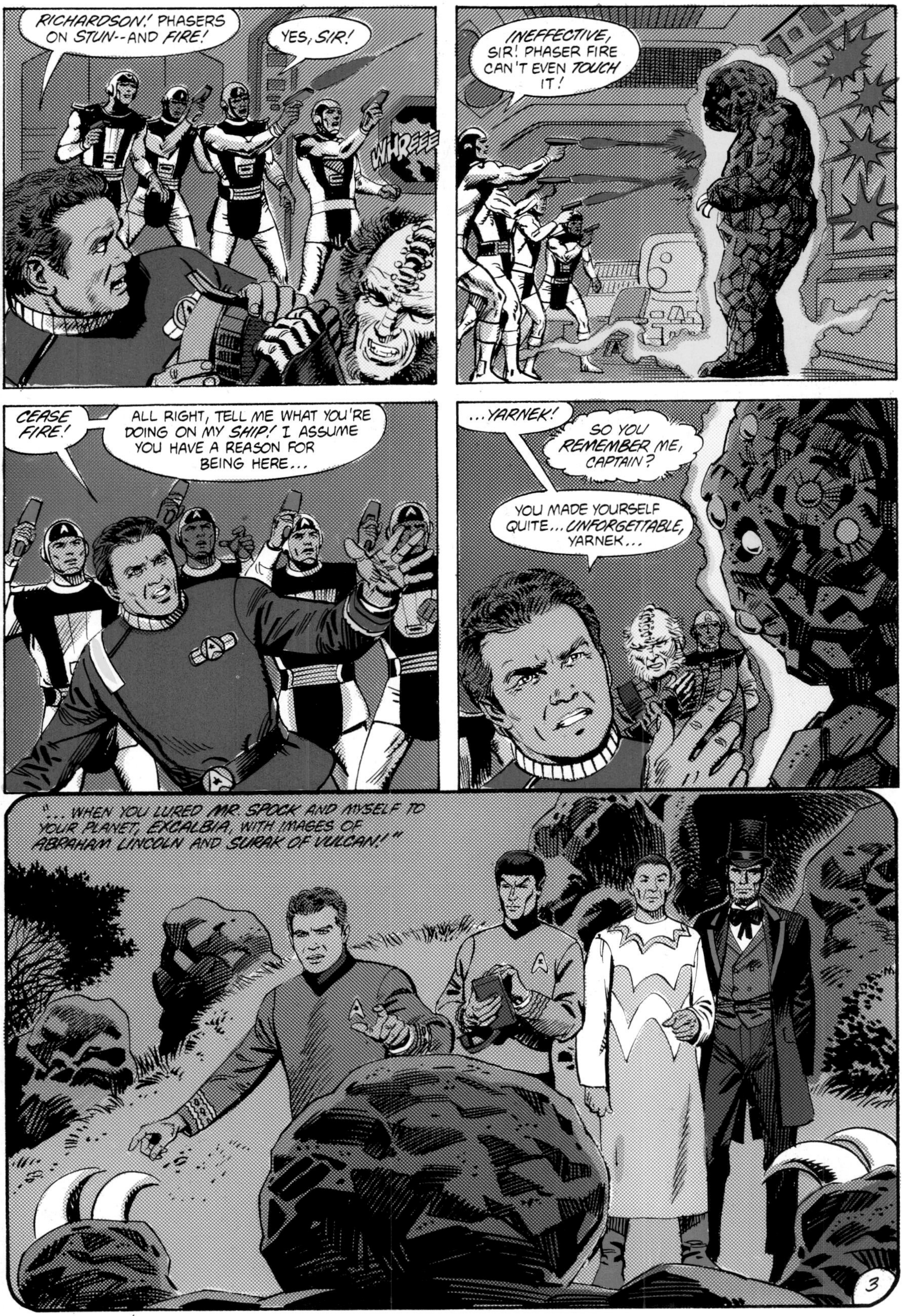
RICHARDSON! PHASERS ON STUN--AND FIRE!
YES, SIR!
WHREEE
INEFFECTIVE, SIR! PHASER FIRE CAN'T EVEN TOUCH IT!
CEASE FIRE!
ALL RIGHT, TELL ME WHAT YOU'RE DOING ON MY SHIP! I ASSUME YOU HAVE A REASON FOR BEING HERE...
...YARNEK!
SO YOU REMEMBER ME, CAPTAIN?
YOU MADE YOURSELF QUITE... UNFORGETTABLE, YARNEK...
"...WHEN YOU LURED MR. SPOCK AND MYSELF TO YOUR PLANET, EXCALBIA, WITH IMAGES OF ABRAHAM LINCOLN AND SURAK OF VULCAN!"
3

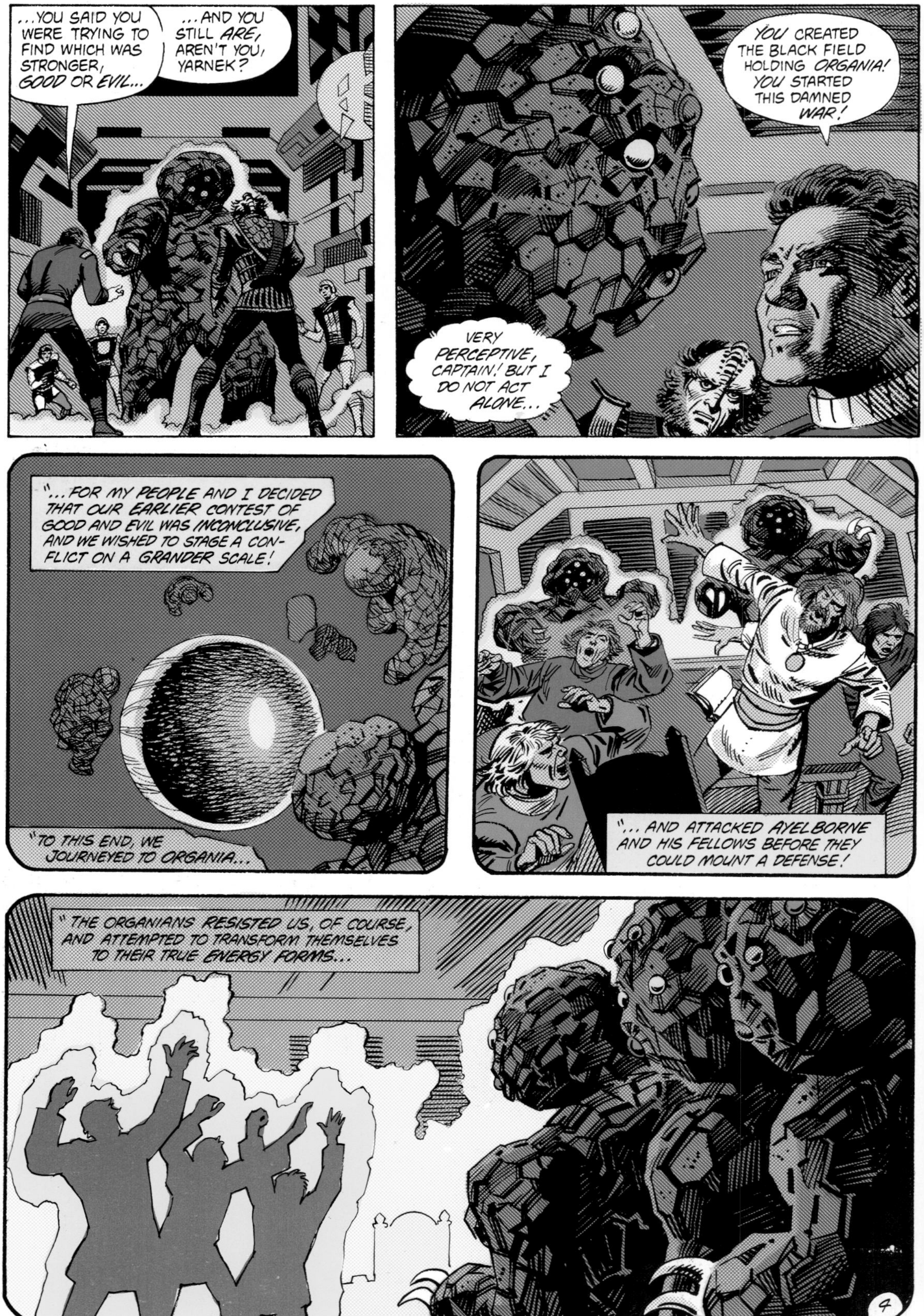
...YOU SAID YOU WERE TRYING TO FIND WHICH WAS STRONGER, GOOD OR EVIL...
...AND YOU STILL ARE, AREN'T YOU, YARNEK?
YOU CREATED THE BLACK FIELD HOLDING ORGANIA! YOU STARTED THIS DAMNED WAR!
VERY PERCEPTIVE, CAPTAIN! BUT I DO NOT ACT ALONE...
"...FOR MY PEOPLE AND I DECIDED THAT OUR EARLIER CONTEST OF GOOD AND EVIL WAS INCONCLUSIVE, AND WE WISHED TO STAGE A CON-FLICT ON A GRANDER SCALE!
"TO THIS END, WE JOURNEYED TO ORGANIA...
"...AND ATTACKED AYELBORNE AND HIS FELLOWS BEFORE THEY COULD MOUNT A DEFENSE!
"THE ORGANIANS RESISTED US, OF COURSE, AND ATTEMPTED TO TRANSFORM THEMSELVES TO THEIR TRUE ENERGY FORMS...
4

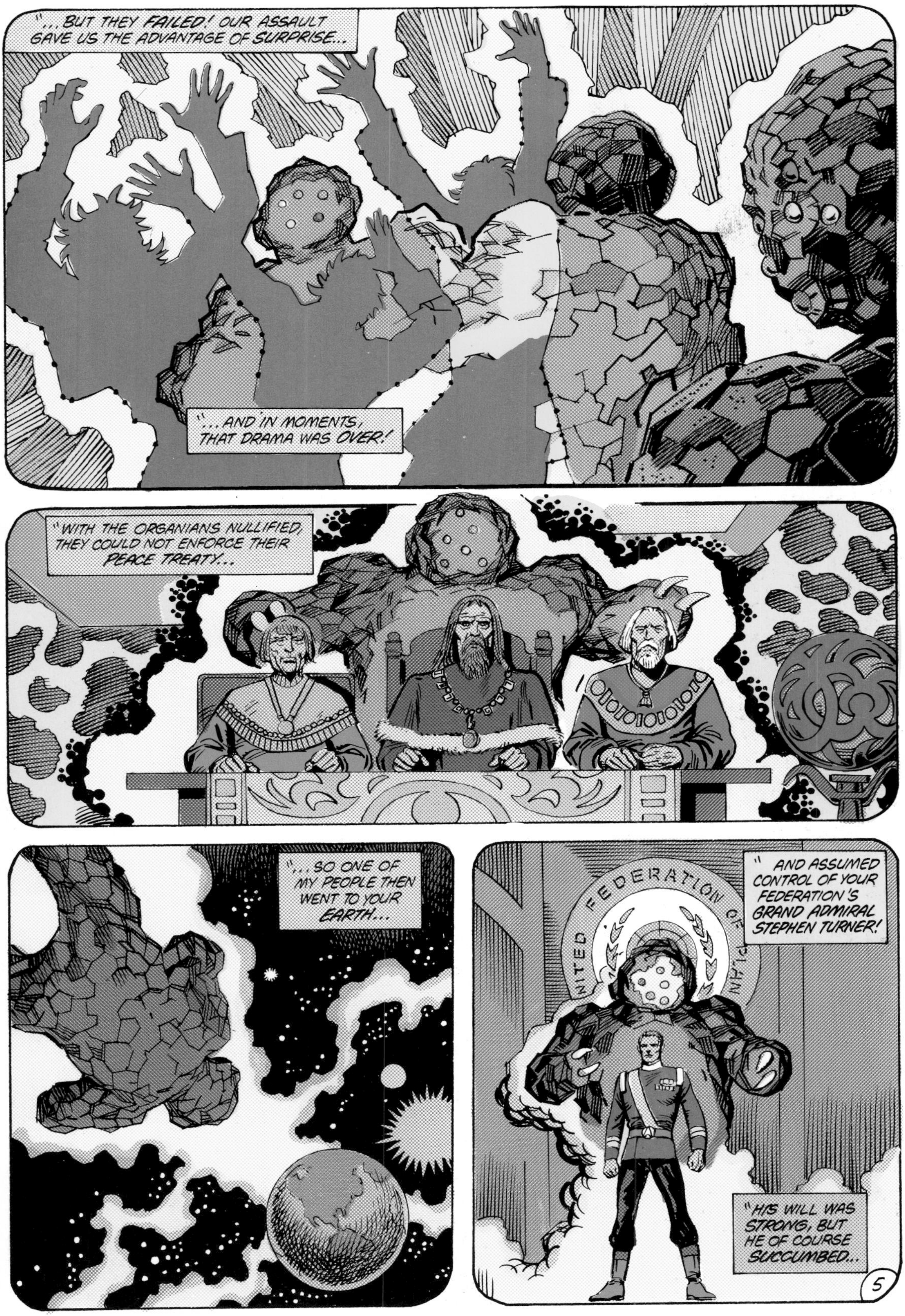
"...BUT THEY FAILED! OUR ASSAULT GAVE US THE ADVANTAGE OF SURPRISE...
"...AND IN MOMENTS, THAT DRAMA WAS OVER!
"WITH THE ORGANIANS NULLIFIED, THEY COULD NOT ENFORCE THEIR PEACE TREATY...
"...SO ONE OF MY PEOPLE THEN WENT TO YOUR EARTH...
" AND ASSUMED CONTROL OF YOUR FEDERATION'S GRAND ADMIRAL STEPHEN TURNER!
UNITED FEDERATION OF PLAN
"HIS WILL WAS STRONG, BUT HE OF COURSE SUCCUMBED...

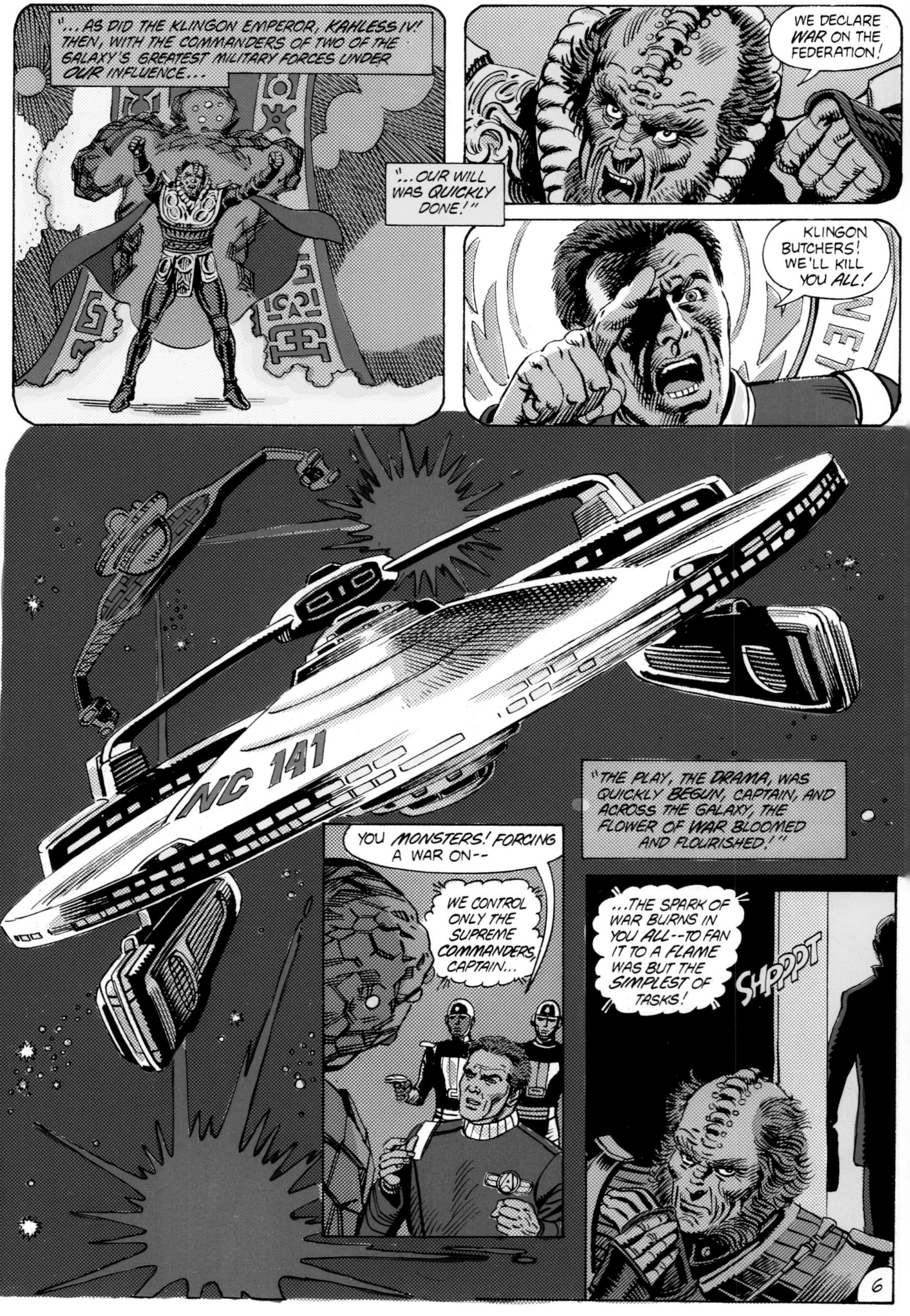
"...AS DID THE KLINGON EMPEROR, KAHLESS IV! THEN, WITH THE COMMANDERS OF TWO OF THE GALAXY'S GREATEST MILITARY FORCES UNDER OUR INFLUENCE...
"...OUR WILL WAS QUICKLY DONE!"
WE DECLARE WAR ON THE FEDERATION!
KLINGON BUTCHERS! WE'LL KILL YOU ALL!
NC 141
"THE PLAY, THE DRAMA, WAS QUICKLY BEGUN, CAPTAIN, AND ACROSS THE GALAXY, THE FLOWER OF WAR BLOOMED AND FLOURISHED!"
YOU MONSTERS! FORCING A WAR ON--
WE CONTROL ONLY THE SUPREME COMMANDERS, CAPTAIN...
...THE SPARK OF WAR BURNS IN YOU ALL--TO FAN IT TO A FLAME WAS BUT THE SIMPLEST OF TASKS!
SHPPPT

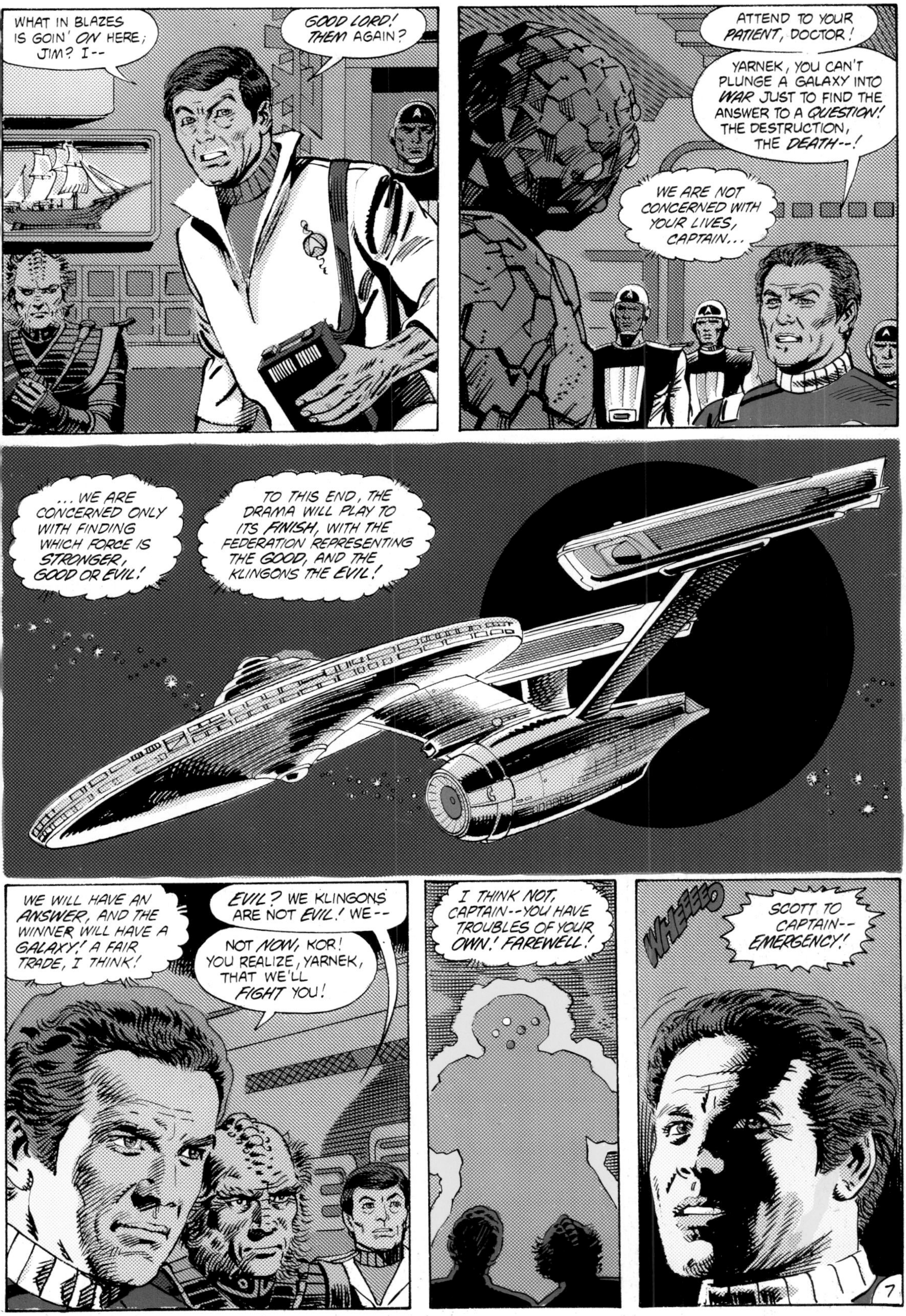
WHAT IN BLAZES IS GOIN' ON HERE, JIM? I--
GOOD LORD! THEM AGAIN?
ATTEND TO YOUR PATIENT, DOCTOR!
YARNEK, YOU CAN'T PLUNGE A GALAXY INTO WAR JUST TO FIND THE ANSWER TO A QUESTION! THE DESTRUCTION, THE DEATH--!
WE ARE NOT CONCERNED WITH YOUR LIVES, CAPTAIN...
...WE ARE CONCERNED ONLY WITH FINDING WHICH FORCE IS STRONGER, GOOD OR EVIL!
TO THIS END, THE DRAMA WILL PLAY TO ITS FINISH, WITH THE FEDERATION REPRESENTING THE GOOD, AND THE KLINGONS THE EVIL!
WE WILL HAVE AN ANSWER, AND THE WINNER WILL HAVE A GALAXY! A FAIR TRADE, I THINK!
EVIL? WE KLINGONS ARE NOT EVIL! WE--
NOT NOW, KOR! YOU REALIZE, YARNEK, THAT WE'LL FIGHT YOU!
I THINK NOT, CAPTAIN--YOU HAVE TROUBLES OF YOUR OWN! FAREWELL!
WHEEEEEO
SCOTT TO CAPTAIN--EMERGENCY!

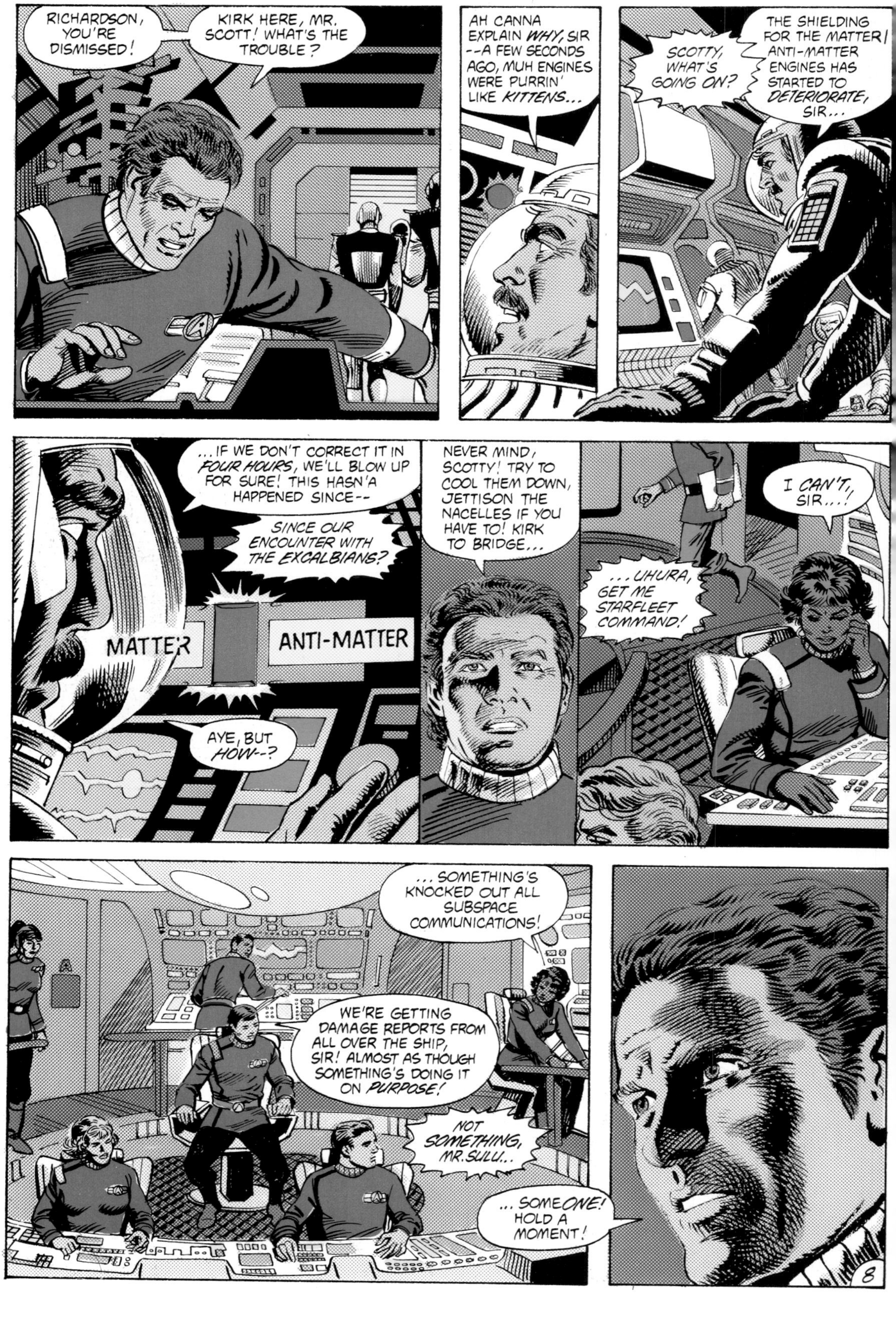
RICHARDSON, YOU'RE DISMISSED!
KIRK HERE, MR. SCOTT! WHAT'S THE TROUBLE?
AH CANNA EXPLAIN WHY, SIR --A FEW SECONDS AGO, MUH ENGINES WERE PURRIN' LIKE KITTENS...
SCOTTY, WHAT'S GOING ON?
THE SHIELDING FOR THE MATTER/ANTI-MATTER ENGINES HAS STARTED TO DETERIORATE, SIR...
...IF WE DON'T CORRECT IT IN FOUR HOURS, WE'LL BLOW UP FOR SURE! THIS HASN'A HAPPENED SINCE--
SINCE OUR ENCOUNTER WITH THE EXCALBIANS?
MATTER
ANTI-MATTER
AYE, BUT HOW--?
NEVER MIND, SCOTTY! TRY TO COOL THEM DOWN, JETTISON THE NACELLES IF YOU HAVE TO! KIRK TO BRIDGE...
I CAN'T, SIR...!
...UHURA, GET ME STARFLEET COMMAND!
...SOMETHING'S KNOCKED OUT ALL SUBSPACE COMMUNICATIONS!
WE'RE GETTING DAMAGE REPORTS FROM ALL OVER THE SHIP, SIR! ALMOST AS THOUGH SOMETHING'S DOING IT ON PURPOSE!
NOT SOMETHING, MR. SULU...
...SOMEONE! HOLD A MOMENT!
8

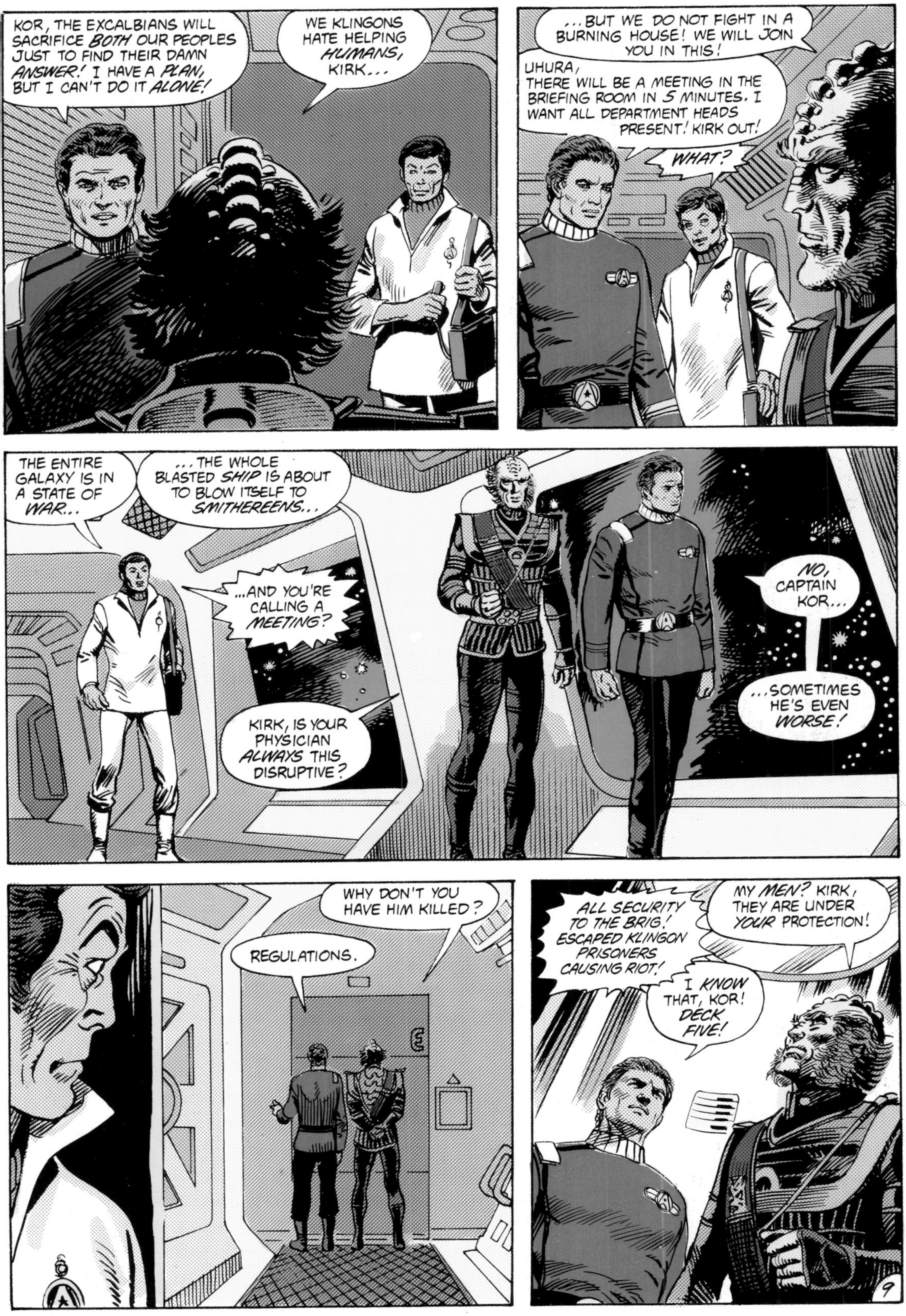
KOR, THE EXCALBIANS WILL SACRIFICE BOTH OUR PEOPLES JUST TO FIND THEIR DAMN ANSWER! I HAVE A PLAN, BUT I CAN'T DO IT ALONE!
WE KLINGONS HATE HELPING HUMANS, KIRK...
...BUT WE DO NOT FIGHT IN A BURNING HOUSE! WE WILL JOIN YOU IN THIS!
UHURA, THERE WILL BE A MEETING IN THE BRIEFING ROOM IN 5 MINUTES. I WANT ALL DEPARTMENT HEADS PRESENT! KIRK OUT!
WHAT?
THE ENTIRE GALAXY IS IN A STATE OF WAR...
...THE WHOLE BLASTED SHIP IS ABOUT TO BLOW ITSELF TO SMITHEREENS...
...AND YOU'RE CALLING A MEETING?
KIRK, IS YOUR PHYSICIAN ALWAYS THIS DISRUPTIVE?
NO, CAPTAIN KOR...
...SOMETIMES HE'S EVEN WORSE!
WHY DON'T YOU HAVE HIM KILLED?
REGULATIONS.
ALL SECURITY TO THE BRIG! ESCAPED KLINGON PRISONERS CAUSING RIOT!
MY MEN? KIRK, THEY ARE UNDER YOUR PROTECTION!
I KNOW THAT, KOR! DECK FIVE!
9

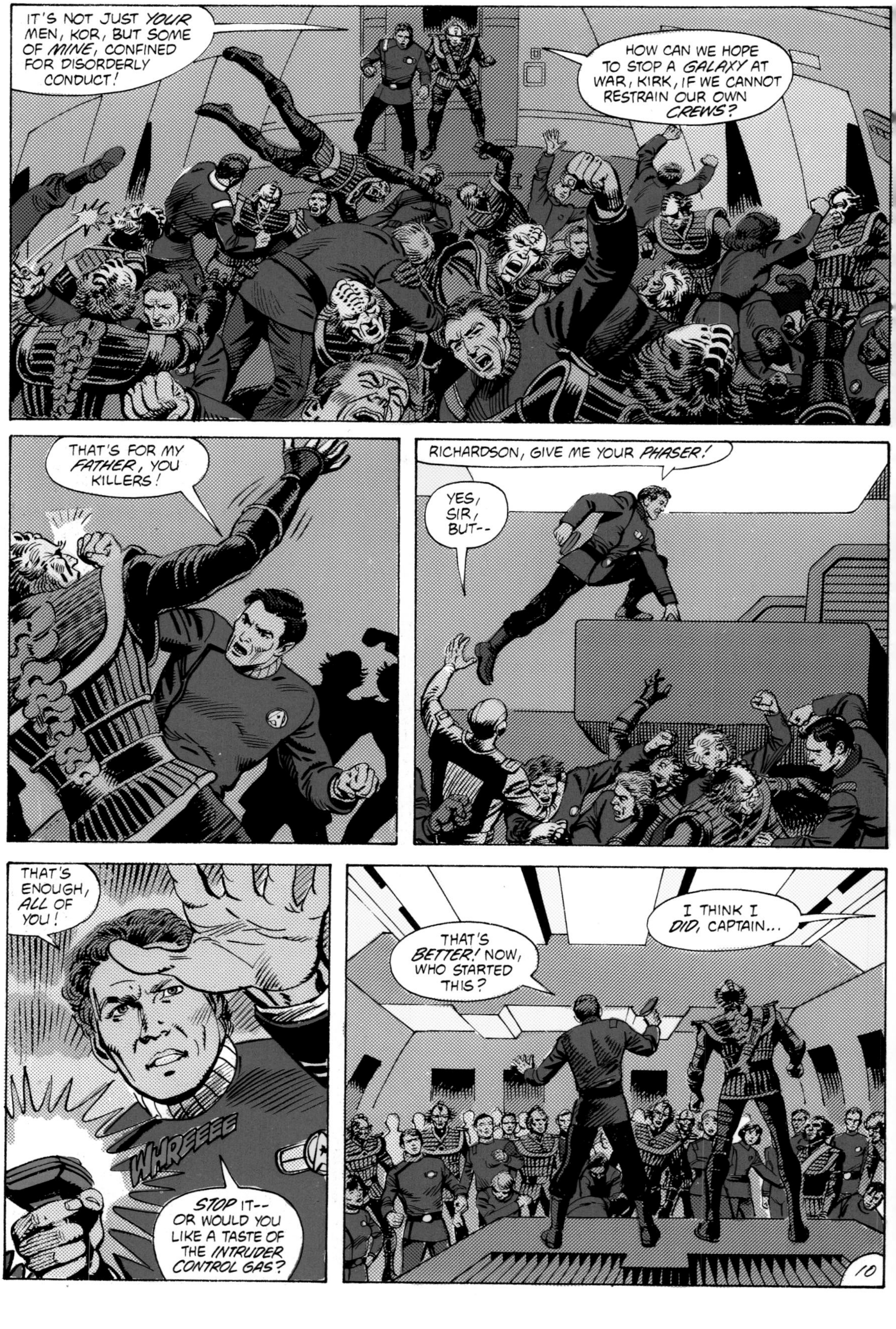
IT'S NOT JUST YOUR MEN, KOR, BUT SOME OF MINE, CONFINED FOR DISORDERLY CONDUCT!
HOW CAN WE HOPE TO STOP A GALAXY AT WAR, KIRK, IF WE CANNOT RESTRAIN OUR OWN CREWS?
THAT'S FOR MY FATHER, YOU KILLERS!
RICHARDSON, GIVE ME YOUR PHASER!
YES, SIR, BUT--
THAT'S ENOUGH, ALL OF YOU!
WHREEEE
STOP IT-- OR WOULD YOU LIKE A TASTE OF THE INTRUDER CONTROL GAS?
I THINK I DID, CAPTAIN...
THAT'S BETTER! NOW, WHO STARTED THIS?
10

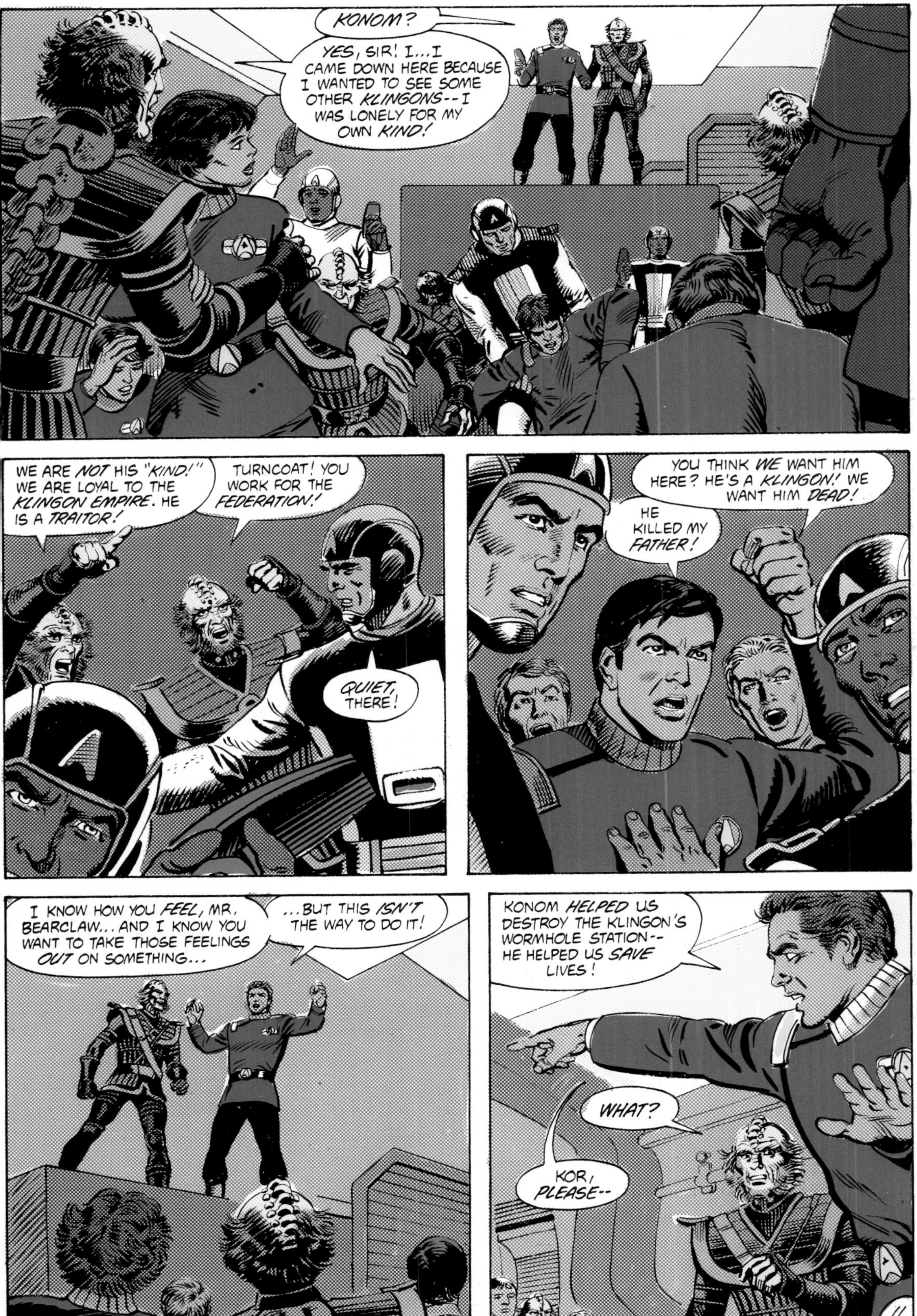
KONOM?
YES, SIR! I...I CAME DOWN HERE BECAUSE I WANTED TO SEE SOME OTHER KLINGONS--I WAS LONELY FOR MY OWN KIND!
WE ARE NOT HIS "KIND!" WE ARE LOYAL TO THE KLINGON EMPIRE. HE IS A TRAITOR!
TURNCOAT! YOU WORK FOR THE FEDERATION!
QUIET, THERE!
YOU THINK WE WANT HIM HERE? HE'S A KLINGON! WE WANT HIM DEAD!
HE KILLED MY FATHER!
I KNOW HOW YOU FEEL, MR. BEARCLAW... AND I KNOW YOU WANT TO TAKE THOSE FEELINGS OUT ON SOMETHING...
...BUT THIS ISN'T THE WAY TO DO IT!
KONOM HELPED US DESTROY THE KLINGON'S WORMHOLE STATION--HE HELPED US SAVE LIVES!
WHAT?
KOR, PLEASE--
11

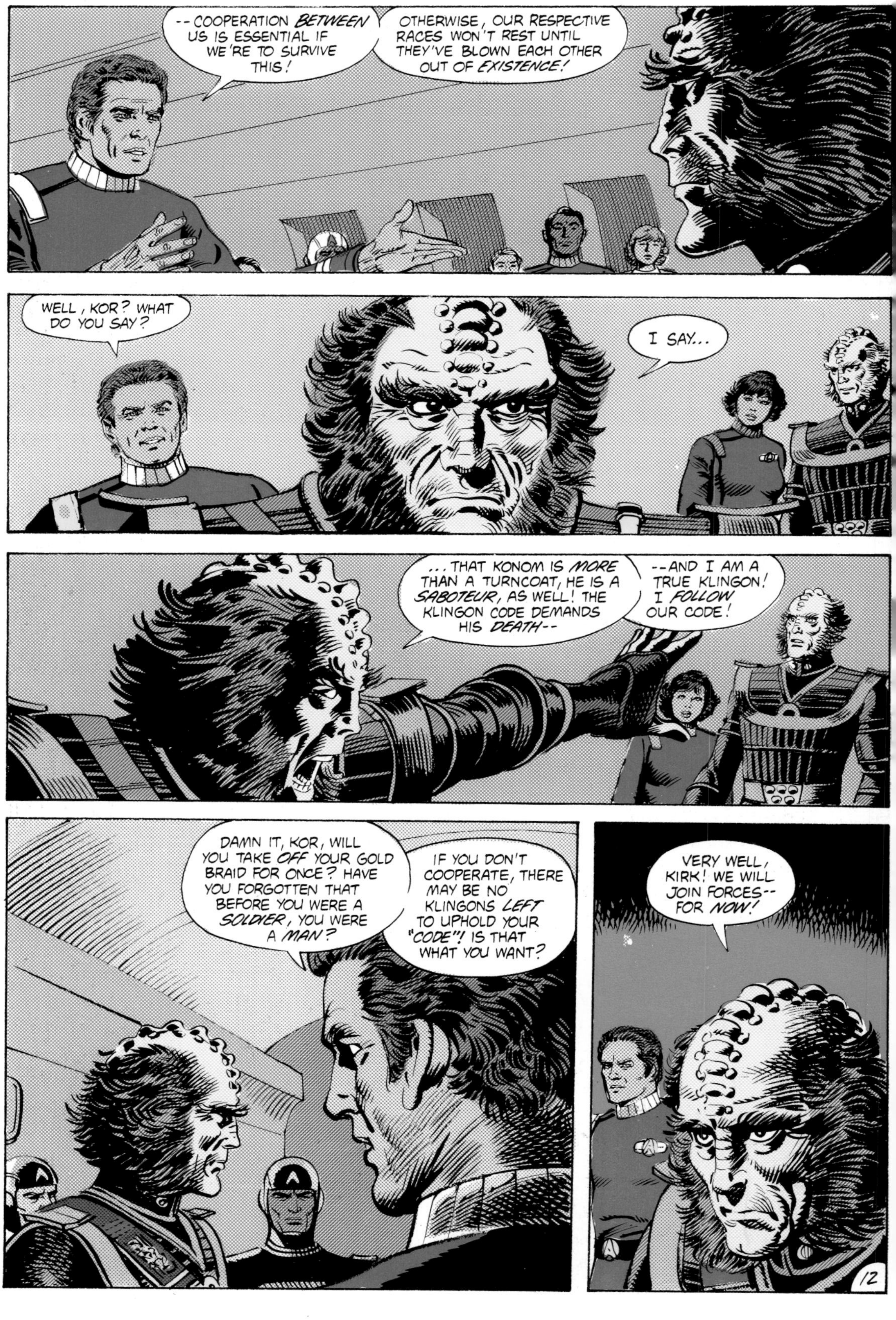
--COOPERATION BETWEEN US IS ESSENTIAL IF WE'RE TO SURVIVE THIS!
OTHERWISE, OUR RESPECTIVE RACES WON'T REST UNTIL THEY'VE BLOWN EACH OTHER OUT OF EXISTENCE!
WELL, KOR? WHAT DO YOU SAY?
I SAY...
...THAT KONOM IS MORE THAN A TURNCOAT, HE IS A SABOTEUR, AS WELL! THE KLINGON CODE DEMANDS HIS DEATH--
--AND I AM A TRUE KLINGON! I FOLLOW OUR CODE!
DAMN IT, KOR, WILL YOU TAKE OFF YOUR GOLD BRAID FOR ONCE? HAVE YOU FORGOTTEN THAT BEFORE YOU WERE A SOLDIER, YOU WERE A MAN?
IF YOU DON'T COOPERATE, THERE MAY BE NO KLINGONS LEFT TO UPHOLD YOUR "CODE"! IS THAT WHAT YOU WANT?
VERY WELL, KIRK! WE WILL JOIN FORCES--FOR NOW!
12

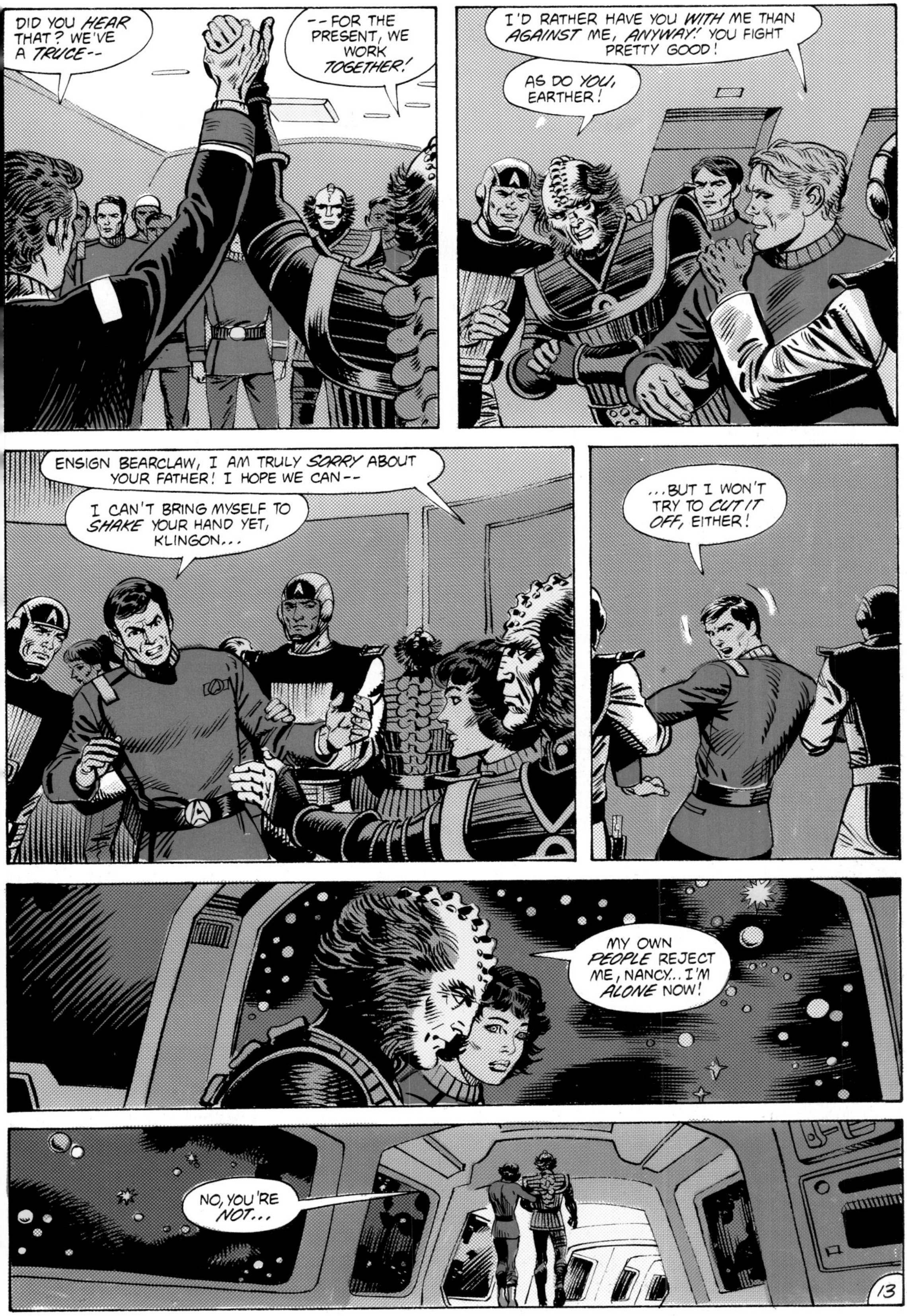
DID YOU HEAR THAT? WE'VE A TRUCE--
--FOR THE PRESENT, WE WORK TOGETHER!
I'D RATHER HAVE YOU WITH ME THAN AGAINST ME, ANYWAY! YOU FIGHT PRETTY GOOD!
AS DO YOU, EARTHER!
ENSIGN BEARCLAW, I AM TRULY SORRY ABOUT YOUR FATHER! I HOPE WE CAN--
I CAN'T BRING MYSELF TO SHAKE YOUR HAND YET, KLINGON...
...BUT I WON'T TRY TO CUT IT OFF, EITHER!
MY OWN PEOPLE REJECT ME, NANCY... I'M ALONE NOW!
NO, YOU'RE NOT...
13

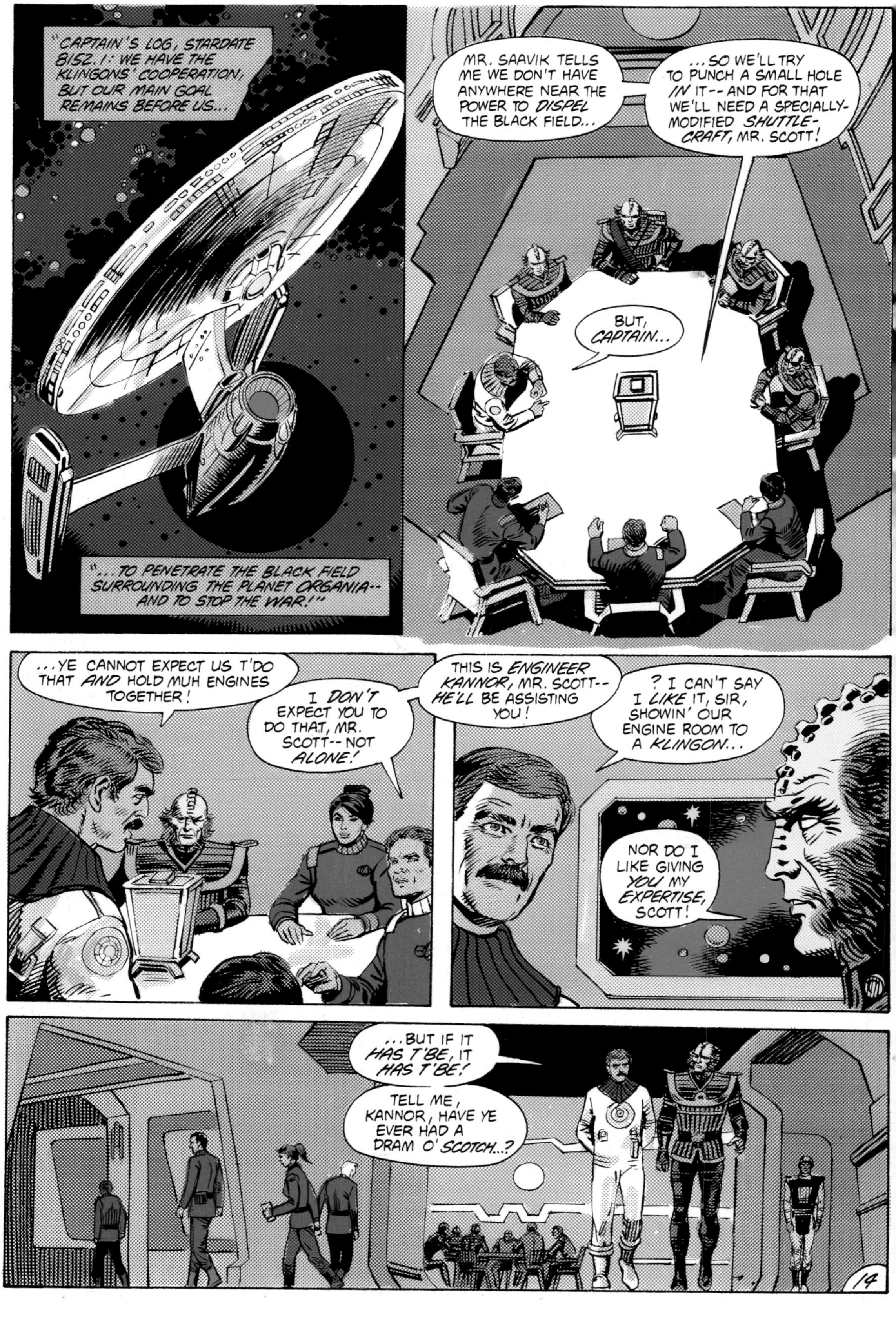
"CAPTAIN'S LOG, STARDATE 8152.1: WE HAVE THE KLINGONS' COOPERATION, BUT OUR MAIN GOAL REMAINS BEFORE US...
"...TO PENETRATE THE BLACK FIELD SURROUNDING THE PLANET ORGANIA-- AND TO STOP THE WAR!"
MR. SAAVIK TELLS ME WE DON'T HAVE ANYWHERE NEAR THE POWER TO DISPEL THE BLACK FIELD...
...SO WE'LL TRY TO PUNCH A SMALL HOLE IN IT-- AND FOR THAT WE'LL NEED A SPECIALLY-MODIFIED SHUTTLECRAFT, MR. SCOTT!
BUT, CAPTAIN...
...YE CANNOT EXPECT US T'DO THAT AND HOLD MUH ENGINES TOGETHER!
I DON'T EXPECT YOU TO DO THAT, MR. SCOTT-- NOT ALONE!
THIS IS ENGINEER KANNOR, MR. SCOTT-- HE'LL BE ASSISTING YOU!
? I CAN'T SAY I LIKE IT, SIR, SHOWIN' OUR ENGINE ROOM TO A KLINGON...
NOR DO I LIKE GIVING YOU MY EXPERTISE, SCOTT!
...BUT IF IT HAS T'BE, IT HAS T'BE!
TELL ME, KANNOR, HAVE YE EVER HAD A DRAM O' SCOTCH...?

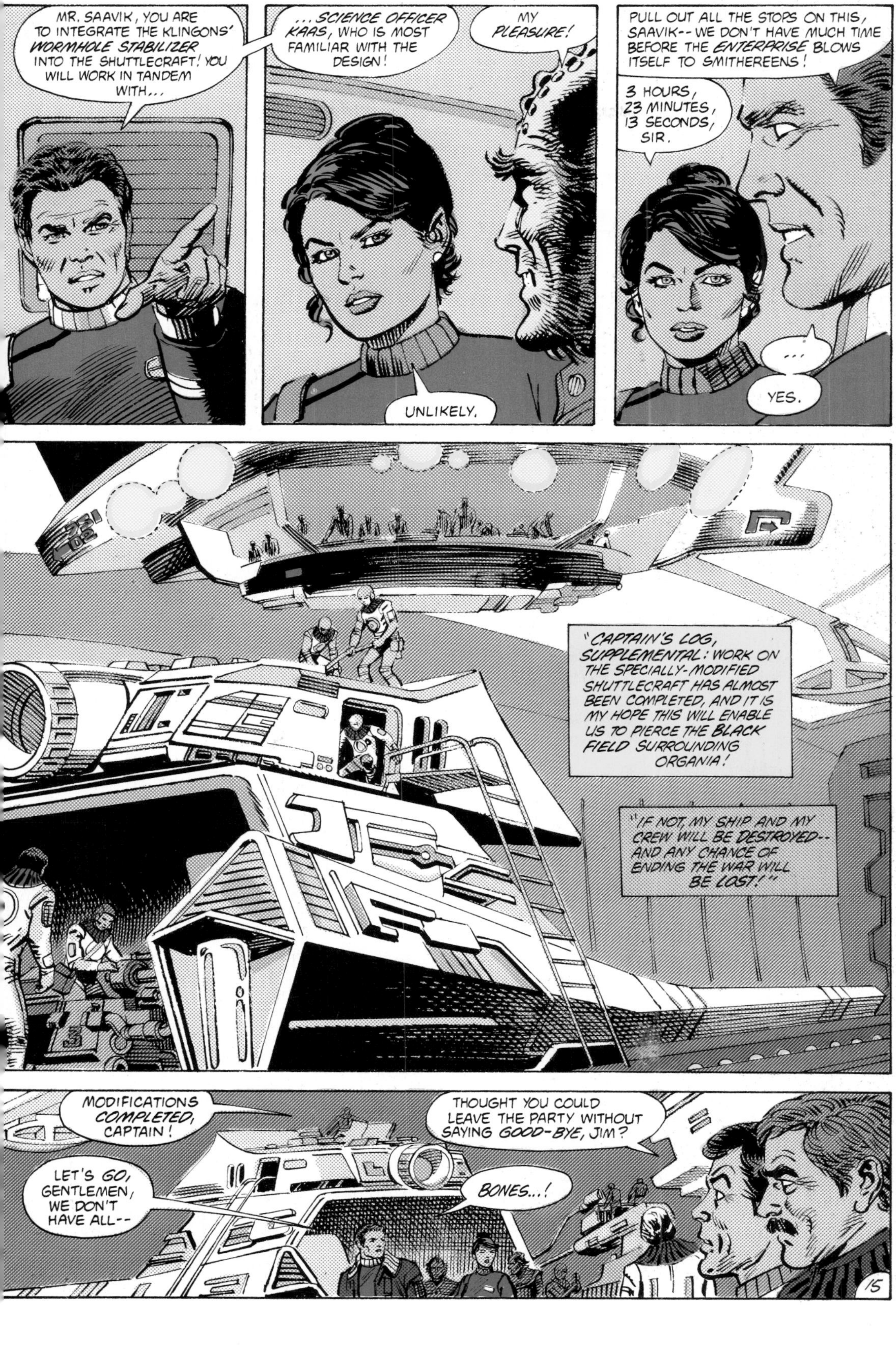
MR. SAAVIK, YOU ARE TO INTEGRATE THE KLINGONS' WORMHOLE STABILIZER INTO THE SHUTTLECRAFT! YOU WILL WORK IN TANDEM WITH...
...SCIENCE OFFICER KAAS, WHO IS MOST FAMILIAR WITH THE DESIGN!
MY PLEASURE!
UNLIKELY.
PULL OUT ALL THE STOPS ON THIS, SAAVIK--WE DON'T HAVE MUCH TIME BEFORE THE ENTERPRISE BLOWS ITSELF TO SMITHEREENS!
3 HOURS, 23 MINUTES, 13 SECONDS, SIR.
...
YES.
"CAPTAIN'S LOG, SUPPLEMENTAL: WORK ON THE SPECIALLY-MODIFIED SHUTTLECRAFT HAS ALMOST BEEN COMPLETED, AND IT IS MY HOPE THIS WILL ENABLE US TO PIERCE THE BLACK FIELD SURROUNDING ORGANIA!
"IF NOT, MY SHIP AND MY CREW WILL BE DESTROYED--AND ANY CHANCE OF ENDING THE WAR WILL BE LOST!"
MODIFICATIONS COMPLETED, CAPTAIN!
LET'S GO, GENTLEMEN, WE DON'T HAVE ALL--
THOUGHT YOU COULD LEAVE THE PARTY WITHOUT SAYING GOOD-BYE, JIM?
BONES...!

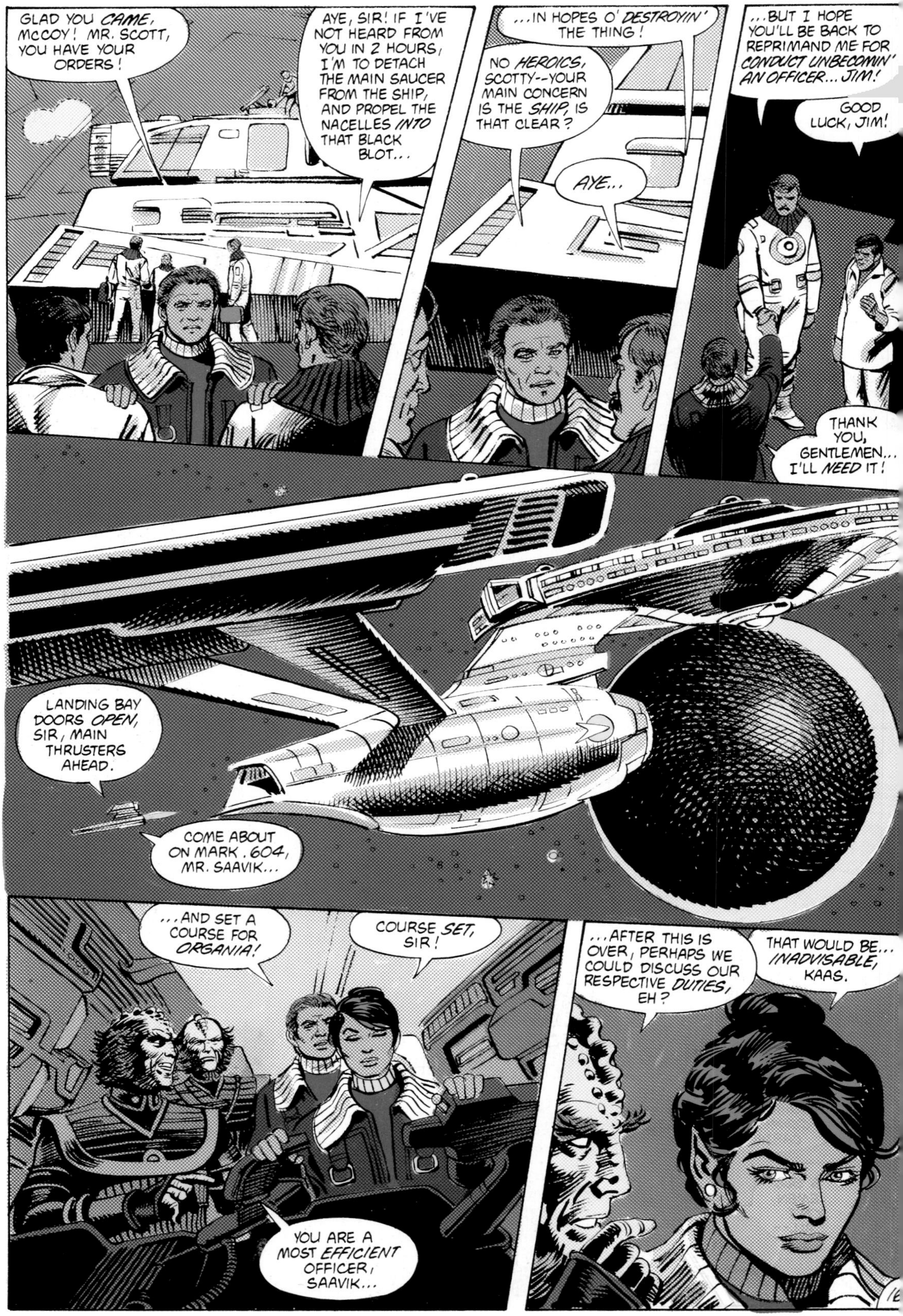
GLAD YOU CAME, McCOY! MR. SCOTT, YOU HAVE YOUR ORDERS!
AYE, SIR! IF I'VE NOT HEARD FROM YOU IN 2 HOURS, I'M TO DETACH THE MAIN SAUCER FROM THE SHIP, AND PROPEL THE NACELLES INTO THAT BLACK BLOT...
...IN HOPES O' DESTROYIN' THE THING!
NO HEROICS, SCOTTY--YOUR MAIN CONCERN IS THE SHIP, IS THAT CLEAR?
AYE...
...BUT I HOPE YOU'LL BE BACK TO REPRIMAND ME FOR CONDUCT UNBECOMIN' AN OFFICER... JIM!
GOOD LUCK, JIM!
THANK YOU, GENTLEMEN... I'LL NEED IT!
LANDING BAY DOORS OPEN, SIR, MAIN THRUSTERS AHEAD.
COME ABOUT ON MARK .604, MR. SAAVIK...
...AND SET A COURSE FOR ORGANIA!
COURSE SET, SIR!
YOU ARE A MOST EFFICIENT OFFICER, SAAVIK...
...AFTER THIS IS OVER, PERHAPS WE COULD DISCUSS OUR RESPECTIVE DUTIES, EH?
THAT WOULD BE... INADVISABLE, KAAS.
16

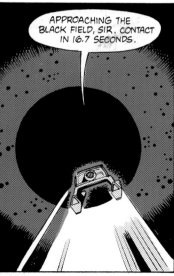

APPROACHING THE BLACK FIELD, SIR, CONTACT IN 16.7 SECONDS.

ACTIVATE *WORMHOLE STABILIZER*, MR. SAAVIK!

ACTIVATED, SIR, YOU REALIZE OUR CHANCES OF SUCCESS ARE ONLY--

PLEASE, MR. SAAVIK...

...IT'S A LITTLE *LATE* TO BE QUOTING THE ODDS! HERE WE GO!

STATUS REPORT?

OBVIOUSLY, WE DID *NOT* STRIKE THE BLACK FIELD, SIR. I READ AN *OXYGEN ATMOSPHERE* AHEAD. WE *MADE* IT, SIR!

GOOD WORK, MR. SAAVIK! BUT THAT'S ONLY THE FIRST STEP! PUT DOWN AT THE COORDINATES I GAVE YOU...

...AND WE'LL BEGIN STEP *TWO*!

ORGANIA! I HOPED NEVER TO SEE THIS MISERABLE PLANET AGAIN! I--

? KIRK, ON OUR *PREVIOUS* VISIT, THE DOORS *OPENED* ON OUR ARRIVAL!

SO THEY *DID*, KOR! BUT IT LOOKS LIKE *THIS* TIME...

17

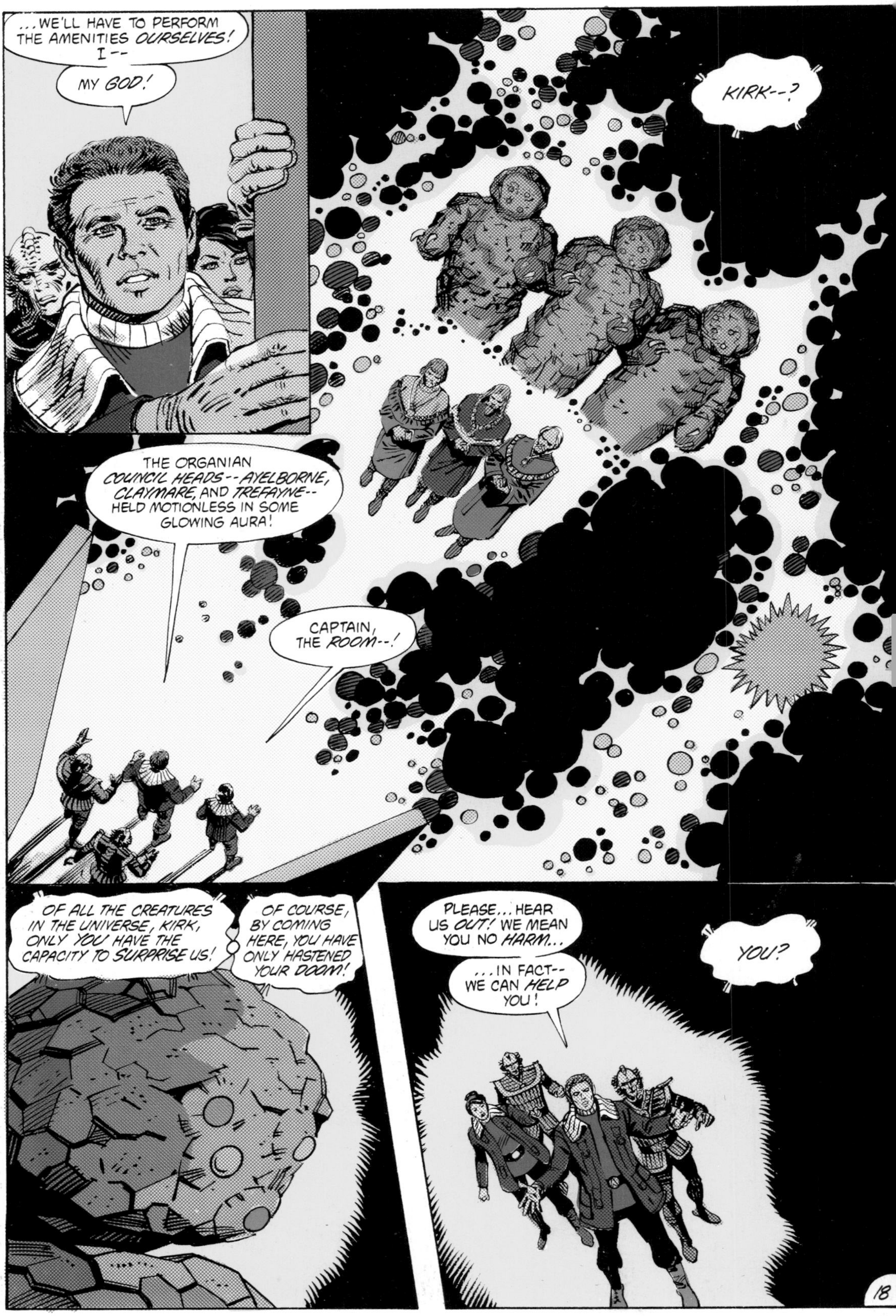
...WE'LL HAVE TO PERFORM THE AMENITIES OURSELVES! I--
MY GOD!
KIRK--?
THE ORGANIAN COUNCIL HEADS--AYELBORNE, CLAYMARE, AND TREFAYNE--HELD MOTIONLESS IN SOME GLOWING AURA!
CAPTAIN, THE ROOM--!
OF ALL THE CREATURES IN THE UNIVERSE, KIRK, ONLY YOU HAVE THE CAPACITY TO SURPRISE US!
OF COURSE, BY COMING HERE, YOU HAVE ONLY HASTENED YOUR DOOM!
PLEASE...HEAR US OUT! WE MEAN YOU NO HARM...
...IN FACT-- WE CAN HELP YOU!
YOU?

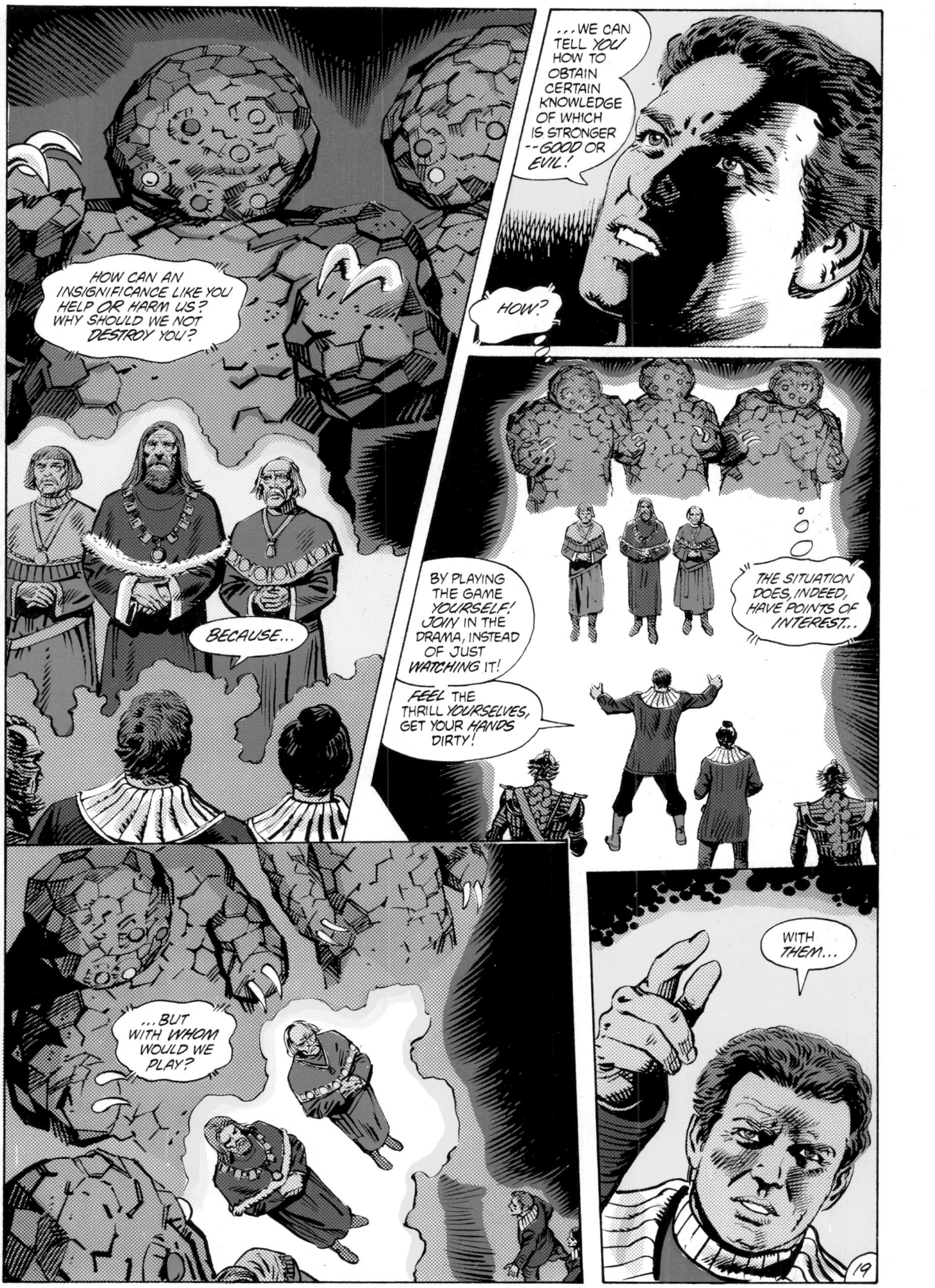
HOW CAN AN INSIGNIFICANCE LIKE YOU HELP OR HARM US? WHY SHOULD WE NOT DESTROY YOU?
BECAUSE...
...WE CAN TELL YOU HOW TO OBTAIN CERTAIN KNOWLEDGE OF WHICH IS STRONGER --GOOD OR EVIL!
HOW?
BY PLAYING THE GAME YOURSELF! JOIN IN THE DRAMA, INSTEAD OF JUST WATCHING IT!
FEEL THE THRILL YOURSELVES, GET YOUR HANDS DIRTY!
THE SITUATION DOES, INDEED, HAVE POINTS OF INTEREST...
...BUT WITH WHOM WOULD WE PLAY?
WITH THEM...
19

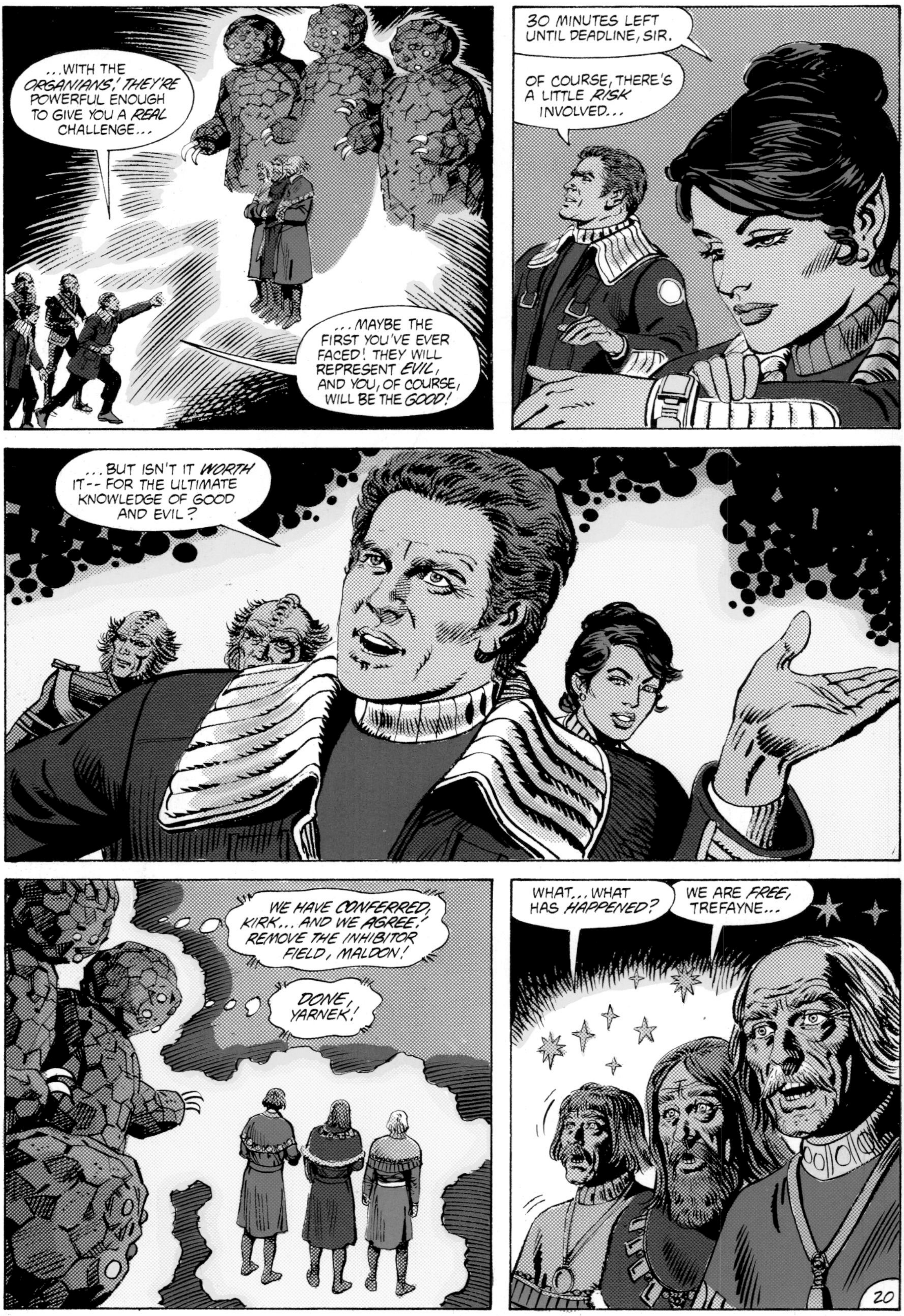
...WITH THE ORGANIANS! THEY'RE POWERFUL ENOUGH TO GIVE YOU A REAL CHALLENGE...
...MAYBE THE FIRST YOU'VE EVER FACED! THEY WILL REPRESENT EVIL, AND YOU, OF COURSE, WILL BE THE GOOD!
30 MINUTES LEFT UNTIL DEADLINE, SIR.
OF COURSE, THERE'S A LITTLE RISK INVOLVED...
...BUT ISN'T IT WORTH IT-- FOR THE ULTIMATE KNOWLEDGE OF GOOD AND EVIL?
WE HAVE CONFERRED, KIRK... AND WE AGREE! REMOVE THE INHIBITOR FIELD, MALDON!
DONE, YARNEK!
WHAT... WHAT HAS HAPPENED?
WE ARE FREE, TREFAYNE...
20

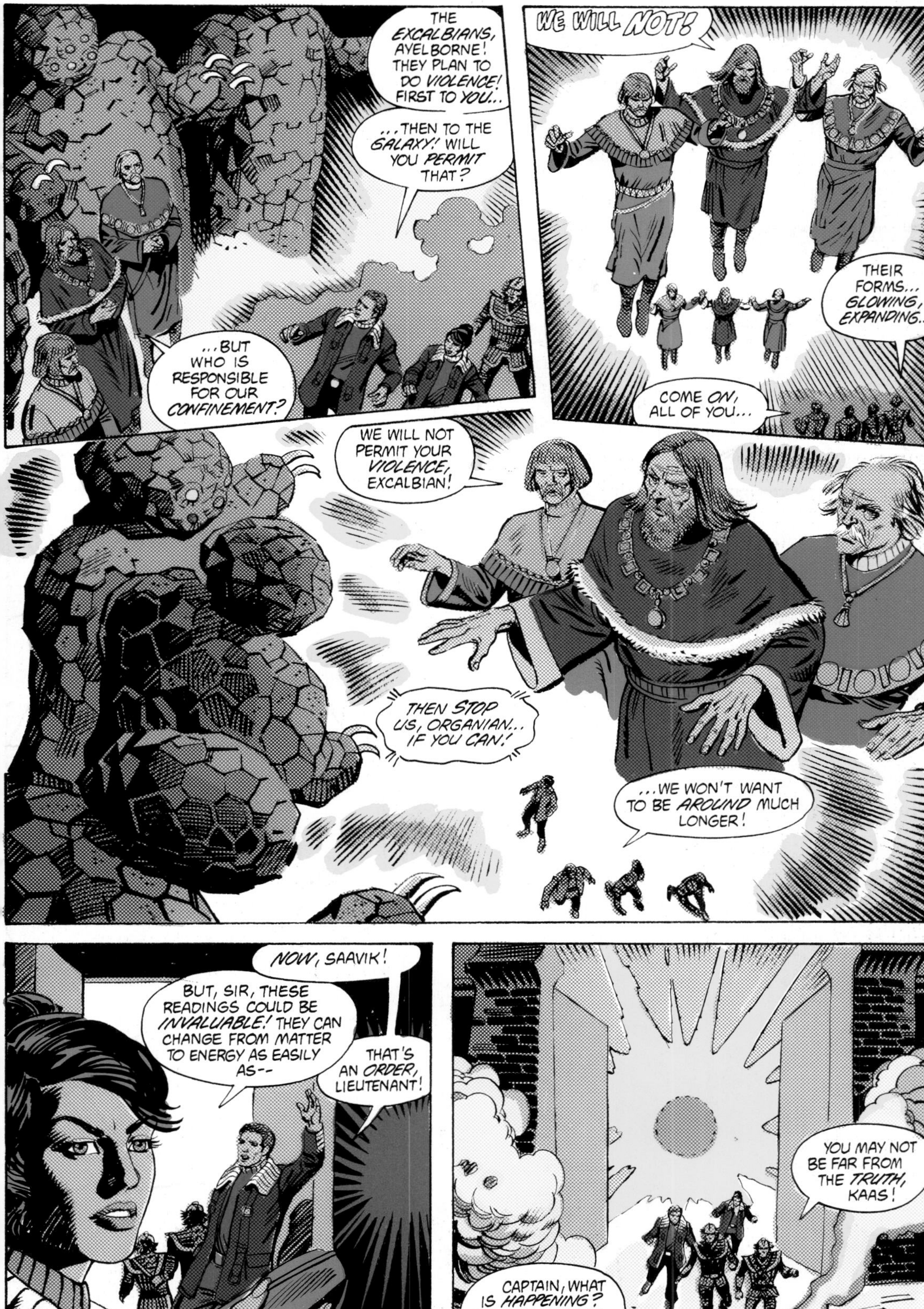
THE EXCALBIANS, AYELBORNE! THEY PLAN TO DO VIOLENCE! FIRST TO YOU...
...THEN TO THE GALAXY! WILL YOU PERMIT THAT?
...BUT WHO IS RESPONSIBLE FOR OUR CONFINEMENT?
WE WILL NOT!
THEIR FORMS... GLOWING, EXPANDING...
COME ON, ALL OF YOU...
WE WILL NOT PERMIT YOUR VIOLENCE, EXCALBIAN!
THEN STOP US, ORGANIAN... IF YOU CAN!
...WE WON'T WANT TO BE AROUND MUCH LONGER!
NOW, SAAVIK!
BUT, SIR, THESE READINGS COULD BE INVALUABLE! THEY CAN CHANGE FROM MATTER TO ENERGY AS EASILY AS--
THAT'S AN ORDER, LIEUTENANT!
YOU MAY NOT BE FAR FROM THE TRUTH, KAAS!
CAPTAIN, WHAT IS HAPPENING? THE VERY PLANET SEEMS TO BE BREAKING UP!
21

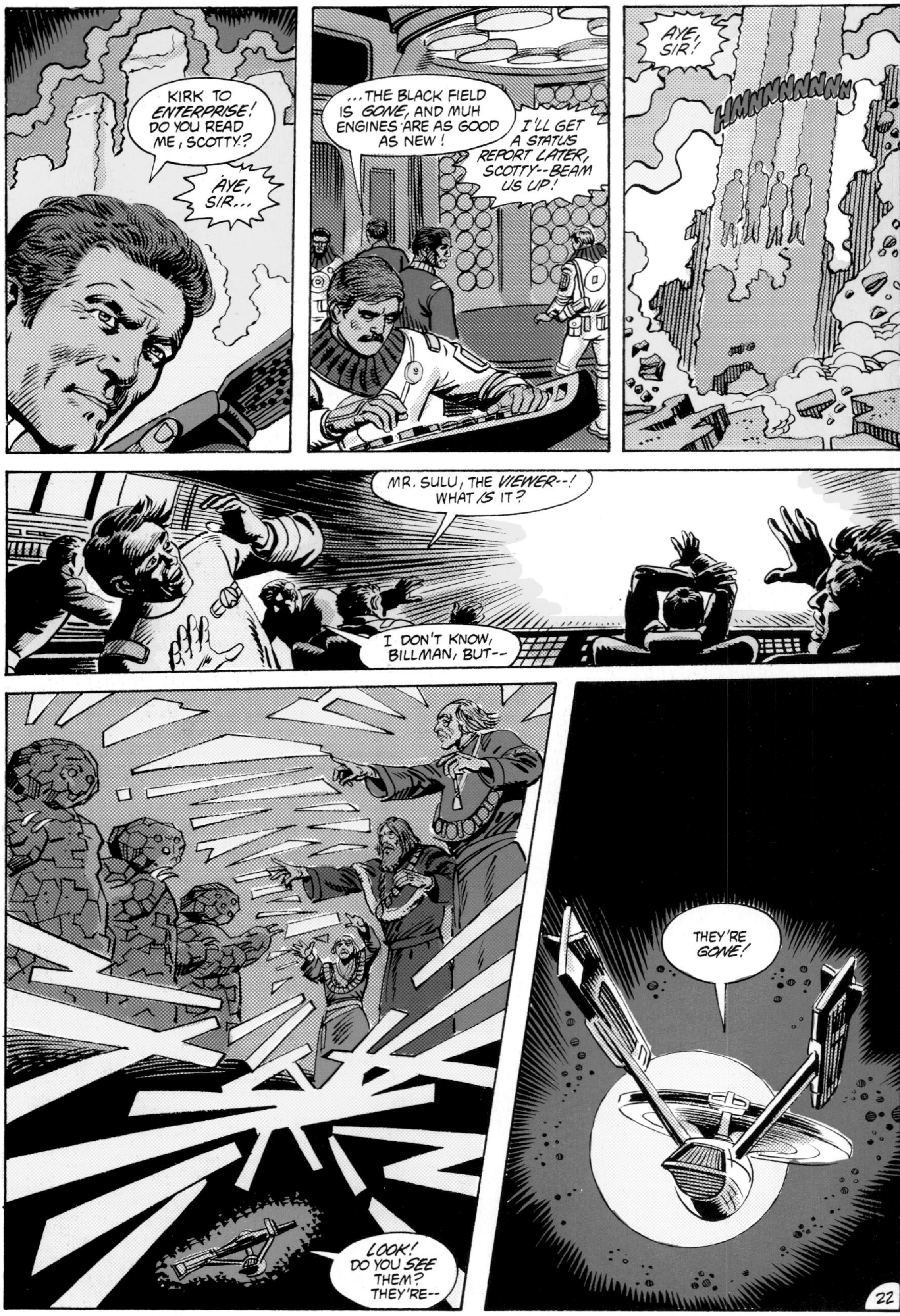
KIRK TO ENTERPRISE! DO YOU READ ME, SCOTTY?
AYE, SIR...
...THE BLACK FIELD IS GONE, AND MUH ENGINES ARE AS GOOD AS NEW!
I'LL GET A STATUS REPORT LATER, SCOTTY--BEAM US UP!
AYE, SIR!
HMNNNNNNNN
MR. SULU, THE VIEWER--! WHAT IS IT?
I DON'T KNOW, BILLMAN, BUT--
LOOK! DO YOU SEE THEM? THEY'RE--
THEY'RE GONE!

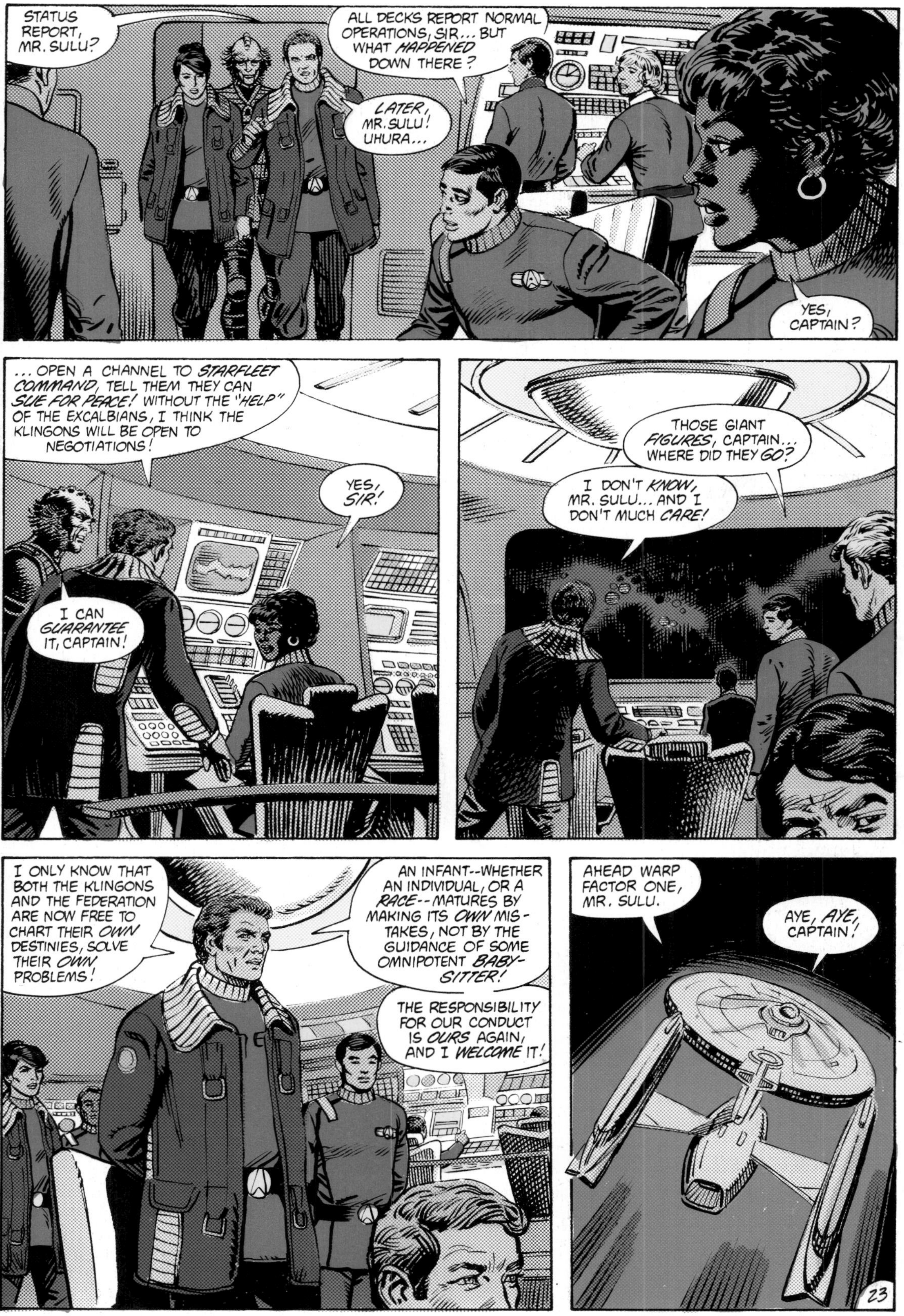
STATUS REPORT, MR. SULU?
ALL DECKS REPORT NORMAL OPERATIONS, SIR... BUT WHAT HAPPENED DOWN THERE?
LATER, MR. SULU! UHURA...
YES, CAPTAIN?
...OPEN A CHANNEL TO STARFLEET COMMAND, TELL THEM THEY CAN SUE FOR PEACE! WITHOUT THE "HELP" OF THE EXCALBIANS, I THINK THE KLINGONS WILL BE OPEN TO NEGOTIATIONS!
YES, SIR!
I CAN GUARANTEE IT, CAPTAIN!
THOSE GIANT FIGURES, CAPTAIN... WHERE DID THEY GO?
I DON'T KNOW, MR. SULU... AND I DON'T MUCH CARE!
I ONLY KNOW THAT BOTH THE KLINGONS AND THE FEDERATION ARE NOW FREE TO CHART THEIR OWN DESTINIES, SOLVE THEIR OWN PROBLEMS!
AN INFANT--WHETHER AN INDIVIDUAL, OR A RACE--MATURES BY MAKING ITS OWN MISTAKES, NOT BY THE GUIDANCE OF SOME OMNIPOTENT BABY-SITTER!
THE RESPONSIBILITY FOR OUR CONDUCT IS OURS AGAIN, AND I WELCOME IT!
AHEAD WARP FACTOR ONE, MR. SULU.
AYE, AYE, CAPTAIN!

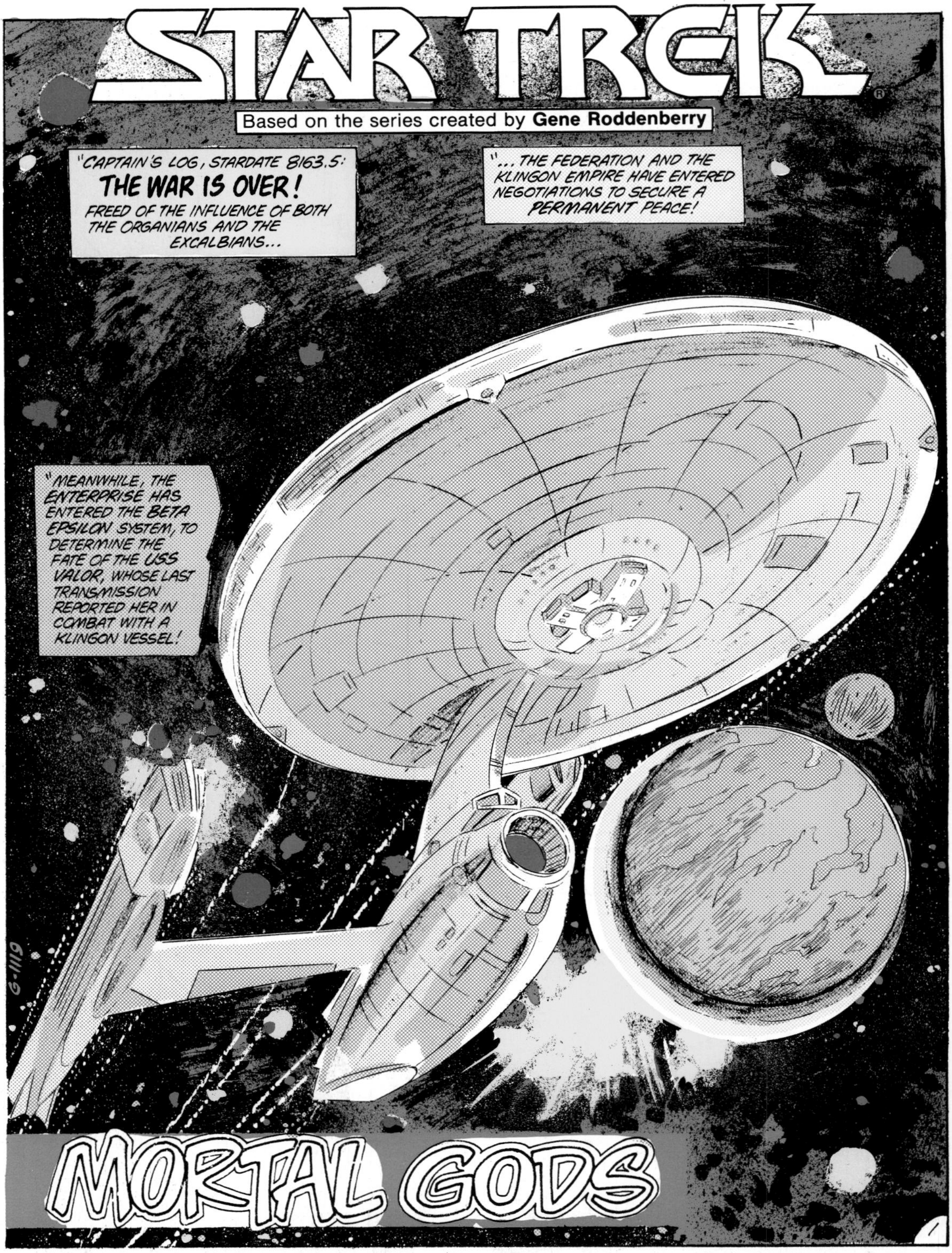
STAR TREK®
Based on the series created by Gene Roddenberry
"CAPTAIN'S LOG, STARDATE 8163.5: THE WAR IS OVER! FREED OF THE INFLUENCE OF BOTH THE ORGANIANS AND THE EXCALBIANS...
"...THE FEDERATION AND THE KLINGON EMPIRE HAVE ENTERED NEGOTIATIONS TO SECURE A PERMANENT PEACE!
"MEANWHILE, THE ENTERPRISE HAS ENTERED THE BETA EPSILON SYSTEM, TO DETERMINE THE FATE OF THE USS VALOR, WHOSE LAST TRANSMISSION REPORTED HER IN COMBAT WITH A KLINGON VESSEL!
MORTAL GODS
G-1119
1

Mike W. Barr * **Tom Sutton** & **Sal Amendola** ★ **John Costanza** * **Michele Wolfman** * **Marv Wolfman**

Writer — Artists — Letterer — Colorist — Editor

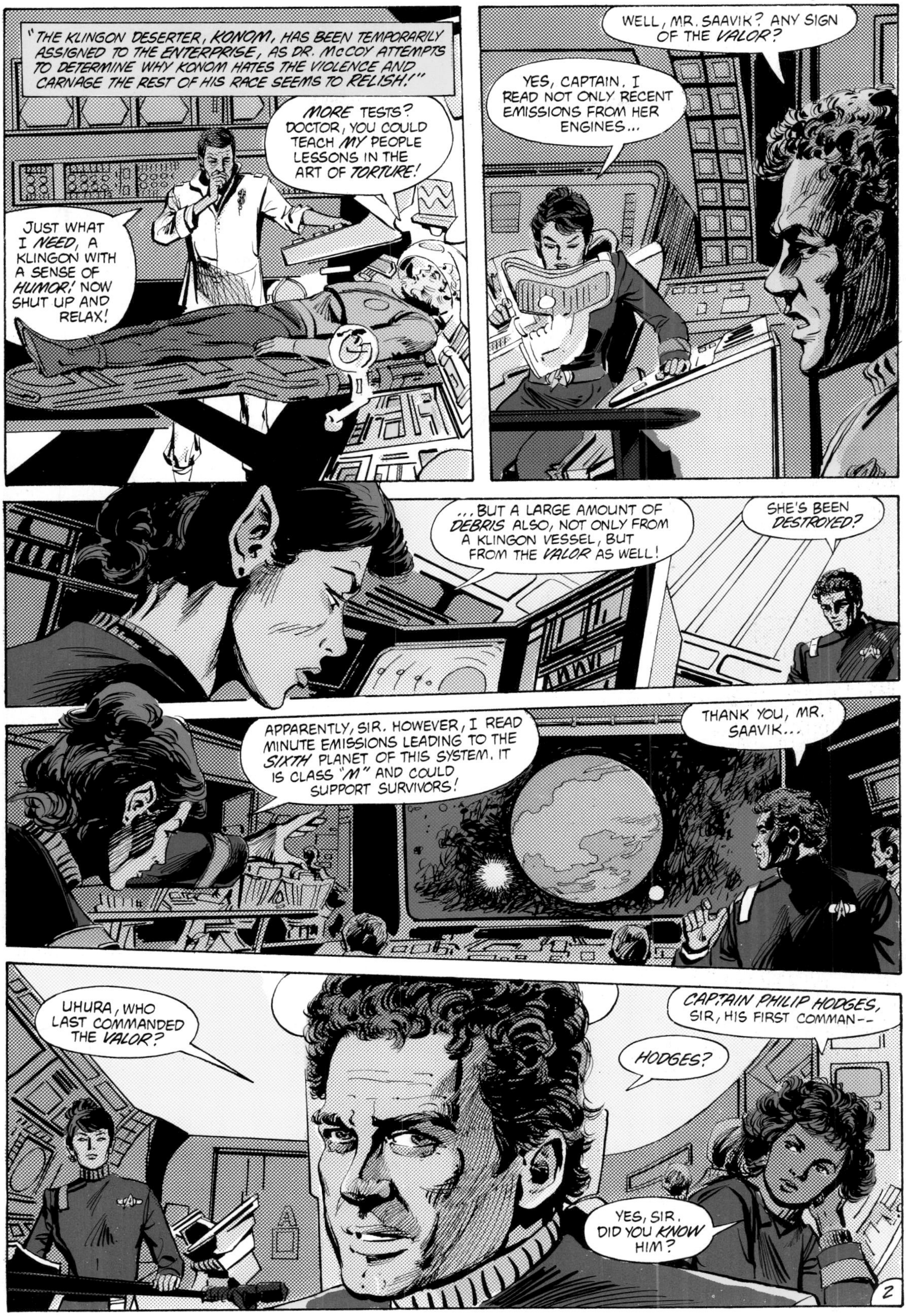
"THE KLINGON DESERTER, KONOM, HAS BEEN TEMPORARILY ASSIGNED TO THE ENTERPRISE, AS DR. McCOY ATTEMPTS TO DETERMINE WHY KONOM HATES THE VIOLENCE AND CARNAGE THE REST OF HIS RACE SEEMS TO RELISH!"
MORE TESTS? DOCTOR, YOU COULD TEACH MY PEOPLE LESSONS IN THE ART OF TORTURE!
JUST WHAT I NEED, A KLINGON WITH A SENSE OF HUMOR! NOW SHUT UP AND RELAX!
WELL, MR. SAAVIK? ANY SIGN OF THE VALOR?
YES, CAPTAIN. I READ NOT ONLY RECENT EMISSIONS FROM HER ENGINES...
...BUT A LARGE AMOUNT OF DEBRIS ALSO, NOT ONLY FROM A KLINGON VESSEL, BUT FROM THE VALOR AS WELL!
SHE'S BEEN DESTROYED?
APPARENTLY, SIR. HOWEVER, I READ MINUTE EMISSIONS LEADING TO THE SIXTH PLANET OF THIS SYSTEM. IT IS CLASS "M" AND COULD SUPPORT SURVIVORS!
THANK YOU, MR. SAAVIK...
UHURA, WHO LAST COMMANDED THE VALOR?
CAPTAIN PHILIP HODGES, SIR, HIS FIRST COMMAN--
HODGES?
YES, SIR. DID YOU KNOW HIM?
2

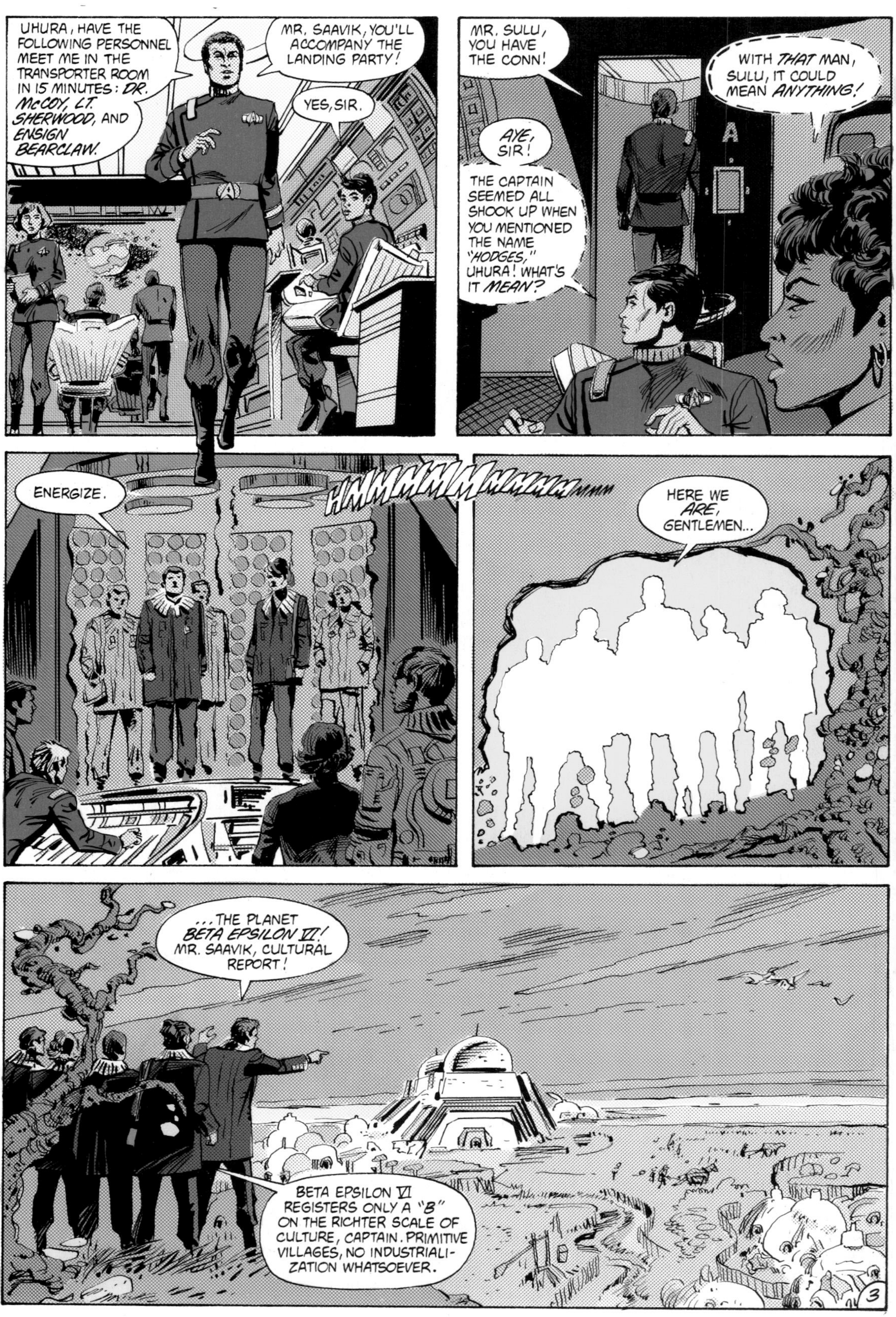
UHURA, HAVE THE FOLLOWING PERSONNEL MEET ME IN THE TRANSPORTER ROOM IN 15 MINUTES: DR. McCOY, LT. SHERWOOD, AND ENSIGN BEARCLAW.
MR. SAAVIK, YOU'LL ACCOMPANY THE LANDING PARTY!
YES, SIR.
MR. SULU, YOU HAVE THE CONN!
WITH THAT MAN, SULU, IT COULD MEAN ANYTHING!
AYE, SIR!
THE CAPTAIN SEEMED ALL SHOOK UP WHEN YOU MENTIONED THE NAME "HODGES," UHURA! WHAT'S IT MEAN?
ENERGIZE.
HMMMMMMMMMMMMMM
HERE WE ARE, GENTLEMEN...
...THE PLANET BETA EPSILON VI! MR. SAAVIK, CULTURAL REPORT!
BETA EPSILON VI REGISTERS ONLY A "B" ON THE RICHTER SCALE OF CULTURE, CAPTAIN. PRIMITIVE VILLAGES, NO INDUSTRIALIZATION WHATSOEVER.

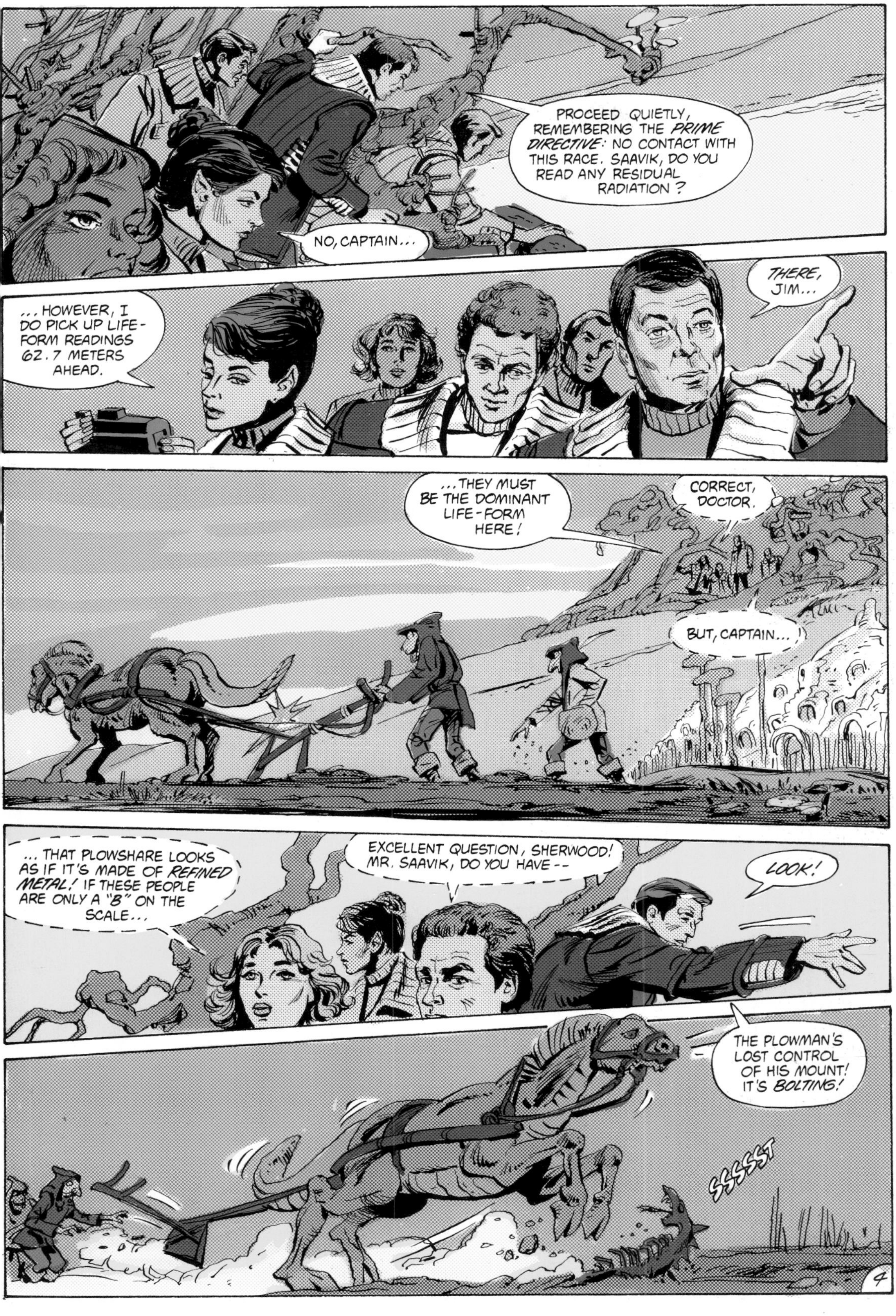
PROCEED QUIETLY, REMEMBERING THE PRIME DIRECTIVE: NO CONTACT WITH THIS RACE. SAAVIK, DO YOU READ ANY RESIDUAL RADIATION?
NO, CAPTAIN...
...HOWEVER, I DO PICK UP LIFE-FORM READINGS 62.7 METERS AHEAD.
THERE, JIM...
...THEY MUST BE THE DOMINANT LIFE-FORM HERE!
CORRECT, DOCTOR.
BUT, CAPTAIN...
...THAT PLOWSHARE LOOKS AS IF IT'S MADE OF REFINED METAL! IF THESE PEOPLE ARE ONLY A "B" ON THE SCALE...
EXCELLENT QUESTION, SHERWOOD! MR. SAAVIK, DO YOU HAVE --
LOOK!
THE PLOWMAN'S LOST CONTROL OF HIS MOUNT! IT'S BOLTING!
SSSSST
4

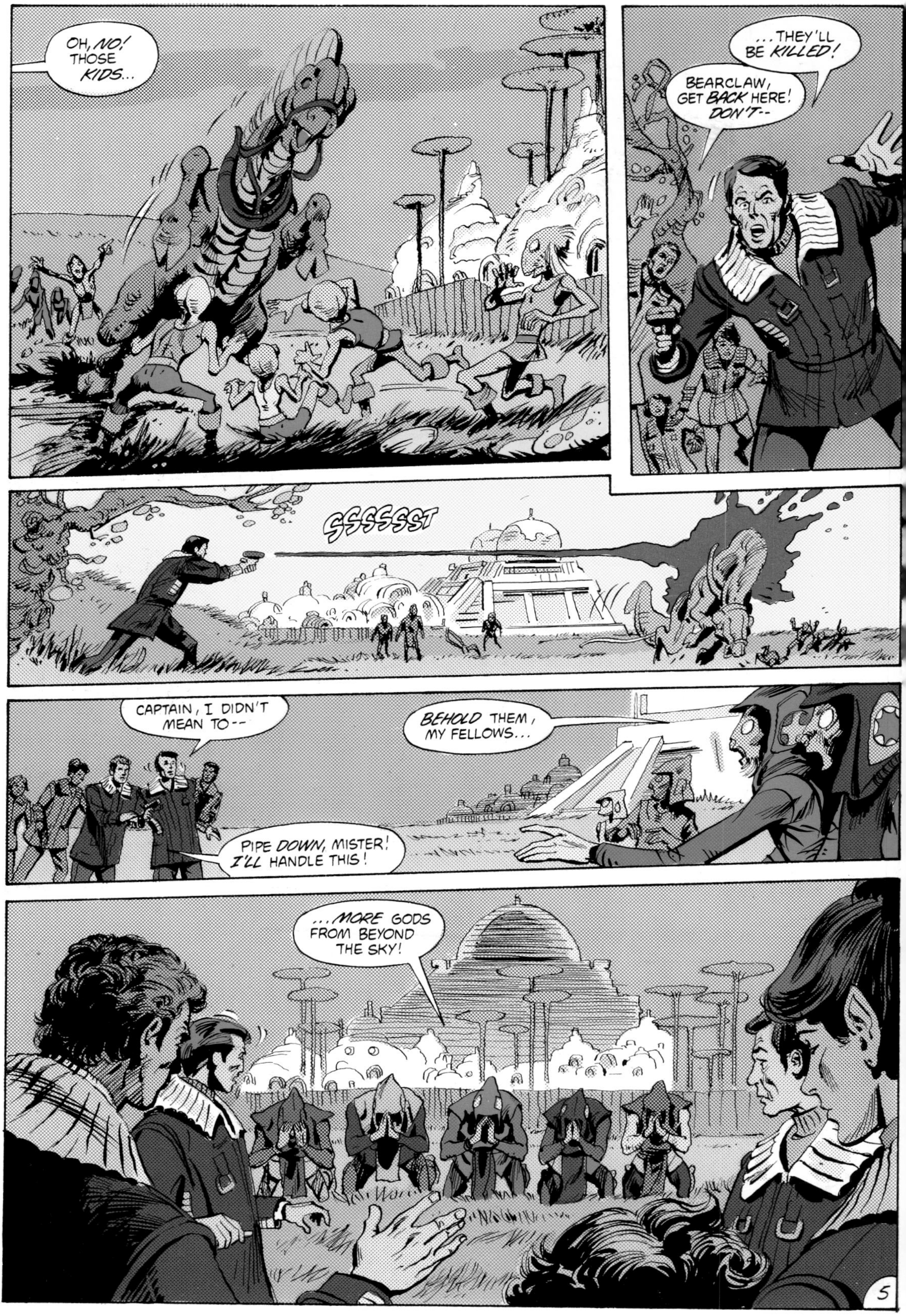
OH, NO! THOSE KIDS...
...THEY'LL BE KILLED!
BEARCLAW, GET BACK HERE! DON'T--
SSSSSST
CAPTAIN, I DIDN'T MEAN TO--
PIPE DOWN, MISTER! I'LL HANDLE THIS!
BEHOLD THEM, MY FELLOWS...
...MORE GODS FROM BEYOND THE SKY!
5

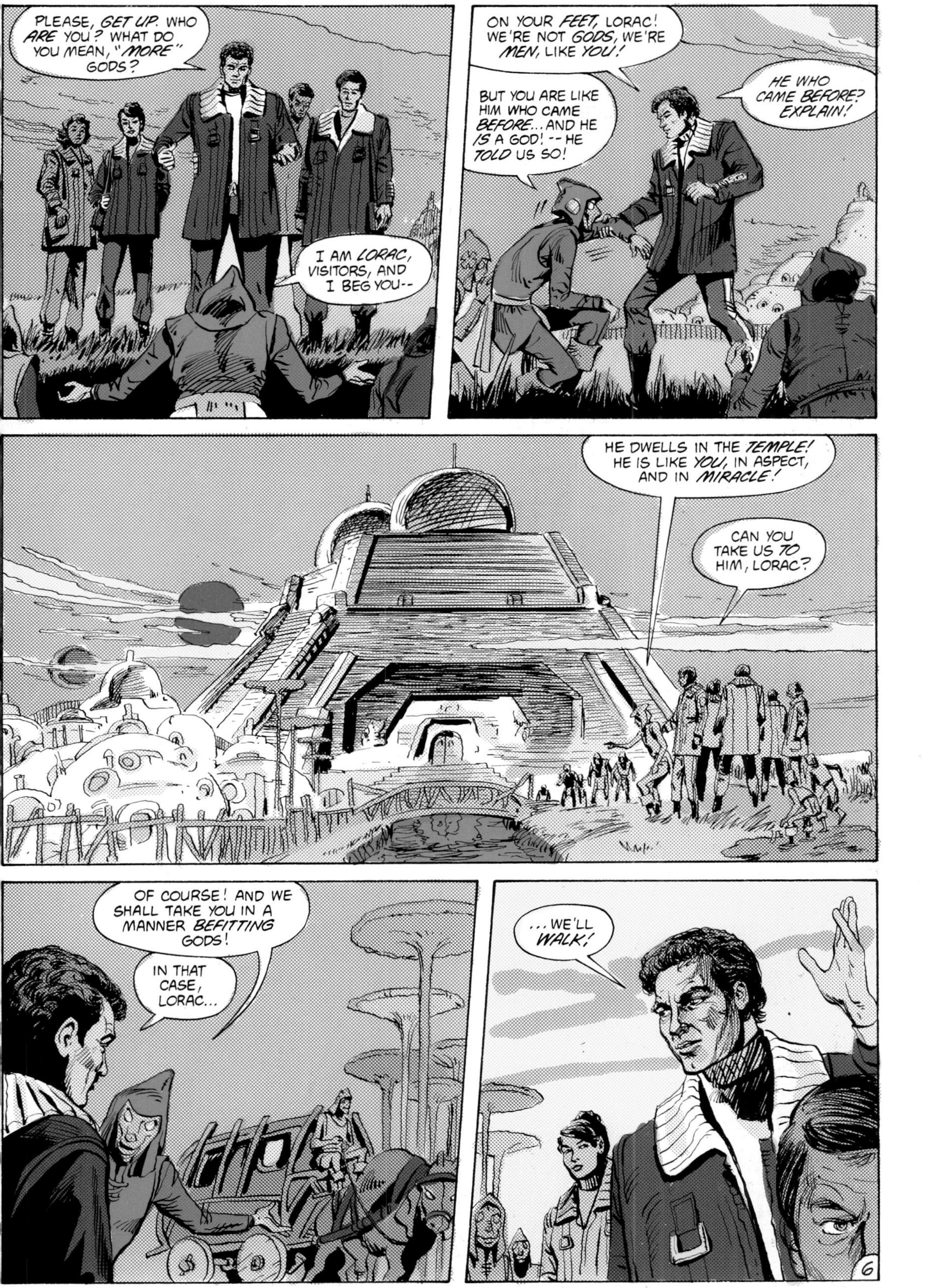

PLEASE, GET UP. WHO ARE YOU? WHAT DO YOU MEAN, "MORE" GODS?
I AM LORAC, VISITORS, AND I BEG YOU--
ON YOUR FEET, LORAC! WE'RE NOT GODS, WE'RE MEN, LIKE YOU!
BUT YOU ARE LIKE HIM WHO CAME BEFORE... AND HE IS A GOD! -- HE TOLD US SO!
HE WHO CAME BEFORE? EXPLAIN!
HE DWELLS IN THE TEMPLE! HE IS LIKE YOU, IN ASPECT, AND IN MIRACLE!
CAN YOU TAKE US TO HIM, LORAC?
OF COURSE! AND WE SHALL TAKE YOU IN A MANNER BEFITTING GODS!
IN THAT CASE, LORAC...
...WE'LL WALK!
6

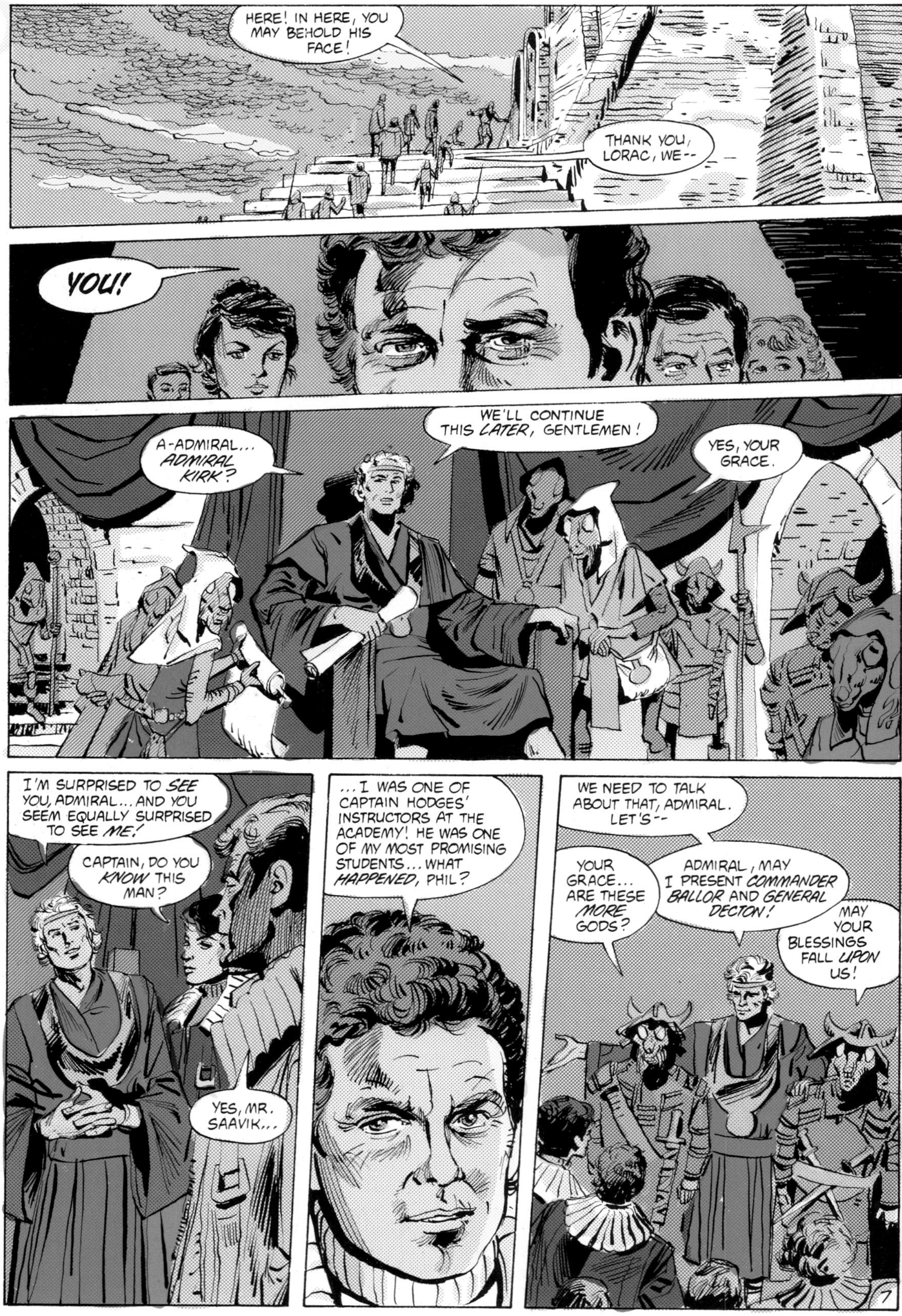
HERE! IN HERE, YOU MAY BEHOLD HIS FACE!
THANK YOU, LORAC, WE--
YOU!
A-ADMIRAL... ADMIRAL KIRK?
WE'LL CONTINUE THIS LATER, GENTLEMEN!
YES, YOUR GRACE.
I'M SURPRISED TO SEE YOU, ADMIRAL... AND YOU SEEM EQUALLY SURPRISED TO SEE ME!
CAPTAIN, DO YOU KNOW THIS MAN?
YES, MR. SAAVIK...
...I WAS ONE OF CAPTAIN HODGES' INSTRUCTORS AT THE ACADEMY! HE WAS ONE OF MY MOST PROMISING STUDENTS... WHAT HAPPENED, PHIL?
WE NEED TO TALK ABOUT THAT, ADMIRAL. LET'S--
YOUR GRACE... ARE THESE MORE GODS?
ADMIRAL, MAY I PRESENT COMMANDER BALLOR AND GENERAL DECTON!
MAY YOUR BLESSINGS FALL UPON US!
7

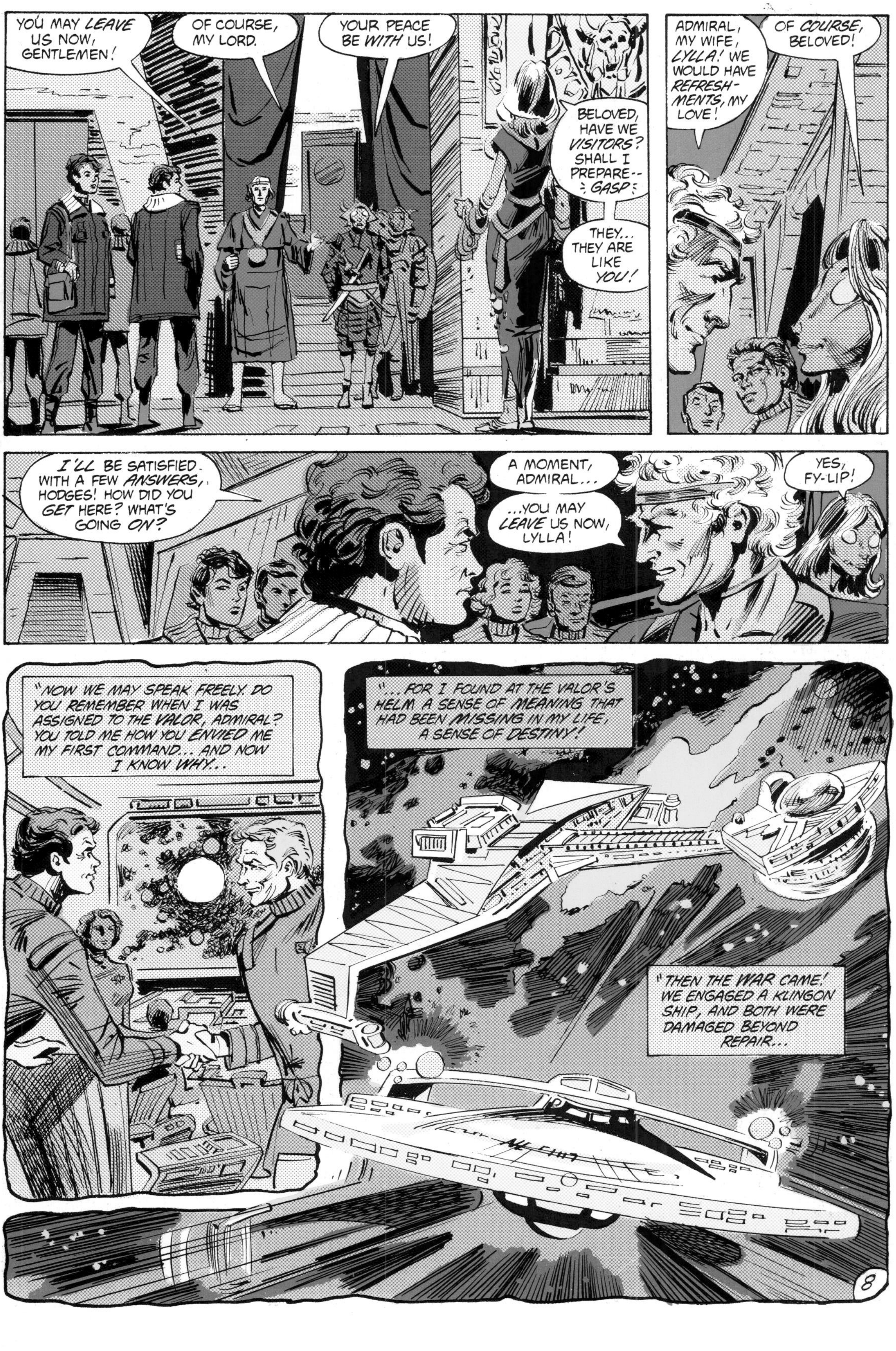
YOU MAY LEAVE US NOW, GENTLEMEN!
OF COURSE, MY LORD.
YOUR PEACE BE WITH US!
BELOVED, HAVE WE VISITORS? SHALL I PREPARE-- GASP!
THEY... THEY ARE LIKE YOU!
ADMIRAL, MY WIFE, LYLLA! WE WOULD HAVE REFRESHMENTS, MY LOVE!
OF COURSE, BELOVED!
I'LL BE SATISFIED WITH A FEW ANSWERS, HODGES! HOW DID YOU GET HERE? WHAT'S GOING ON?
A MOMENT, ADMIRAL...
...YOU MAY LEAVE US NOW, LYLLA!
YES, FY-LIP!
"NOW WE MAY SPEAK FREELY. DO YOU REMEMBER WHEN I WAS ASSIGNED TO THE VALOR, ADMIRAL? YOU TOLD ME HOW YOU ENVIED ME MY FIRST COMMAND... AND NOW I KNOW WHY...
"...FOR I FOUND AT THE VALOR'S HELM A SENSE OF MEANING THAT HAD BEEN MISSING IN MY LIFE, A SENSE OF DESTINY!
"THEN THE WAR CAME! WE ENGAGED A KLINGON SHIP, AND BOTH WERE DAMAGED BEYOND REPAIR...
8

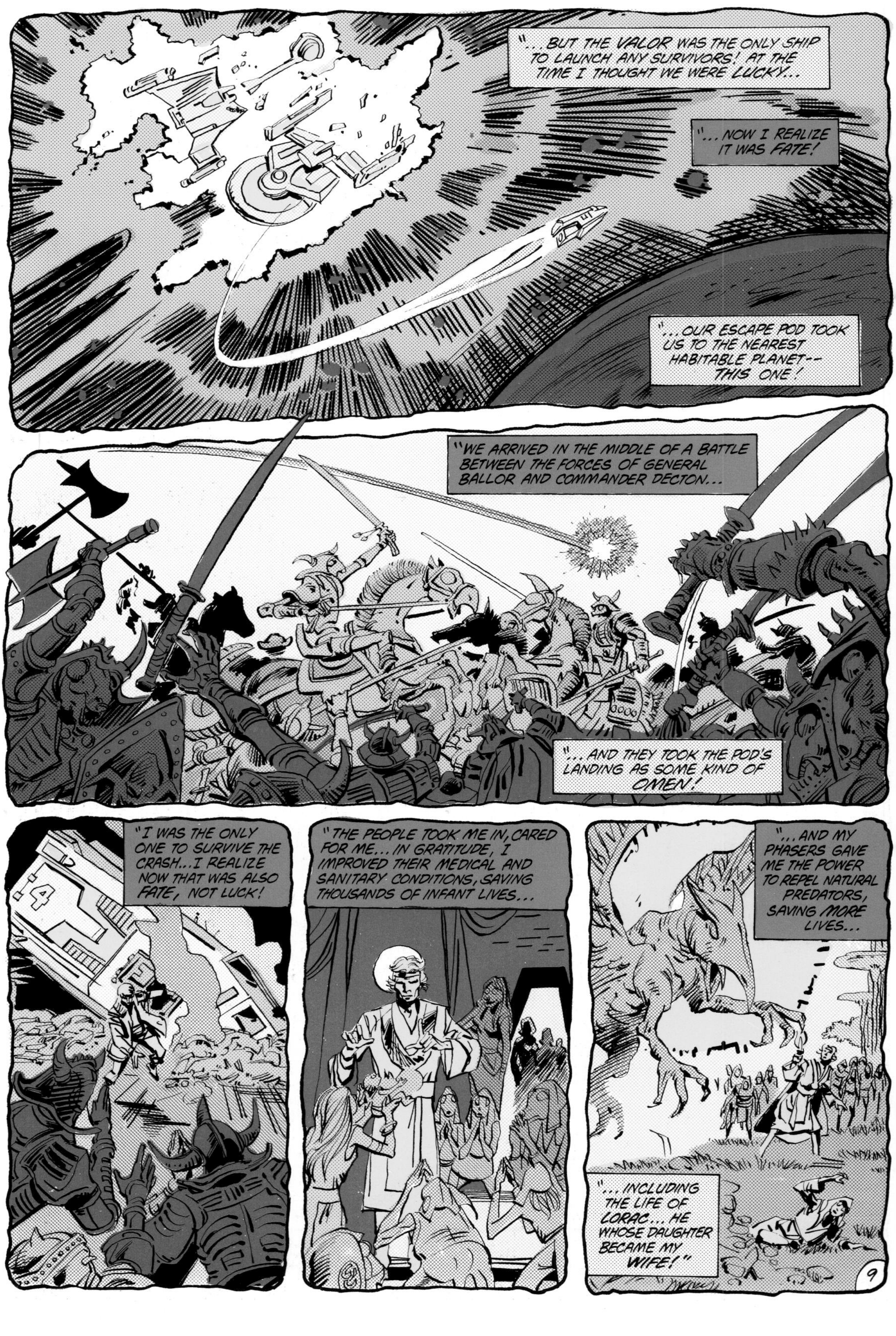
"...BUT THE VALOR WAS THE ONLY SHIP TO LAUNCH ANY SURVIVORS! AT THE TIME I THOUGHT WE WERE LUCKY...
"...NOW I REALIZE IT WAS FATE!
"...OUR ESCAPE POD TOOK US TO THE NEAREST HABITABLE PLANET-- THIS ONE!
"WE ARRIVED IN THE MIDDLE OF A BATTLE BETWEEN THE FORCES OF GENERAL BALLOR AND COMMANDER DECTON...
"...AND THEY TOOK THE POD'S LANDING AS SOME KIND OF OMEN!
"I WAS THE ONLY ONE TO SURVIVE THE CRASH...I REALIZE NOW THAT WAS ALSO FATE, NOT LUCK!
"THE PEOPLE TOOK ME IN, CARED FOR ME... IN GRATITUDE, I IMPROVED THEIR MEDICAL AND SANITARY CONDITIONS, SAVING THOUSANDS OF INFANT LIVES...
"...AND MY PHASERS GAVE ME THE POWER TO REPEL NATURAL PREDATORS, SAVING MORE LIVES...
"...INCLUDING THE LIFE OF LORAC... HE WHOSE DAUGHTER BECAME MY WIFE!"

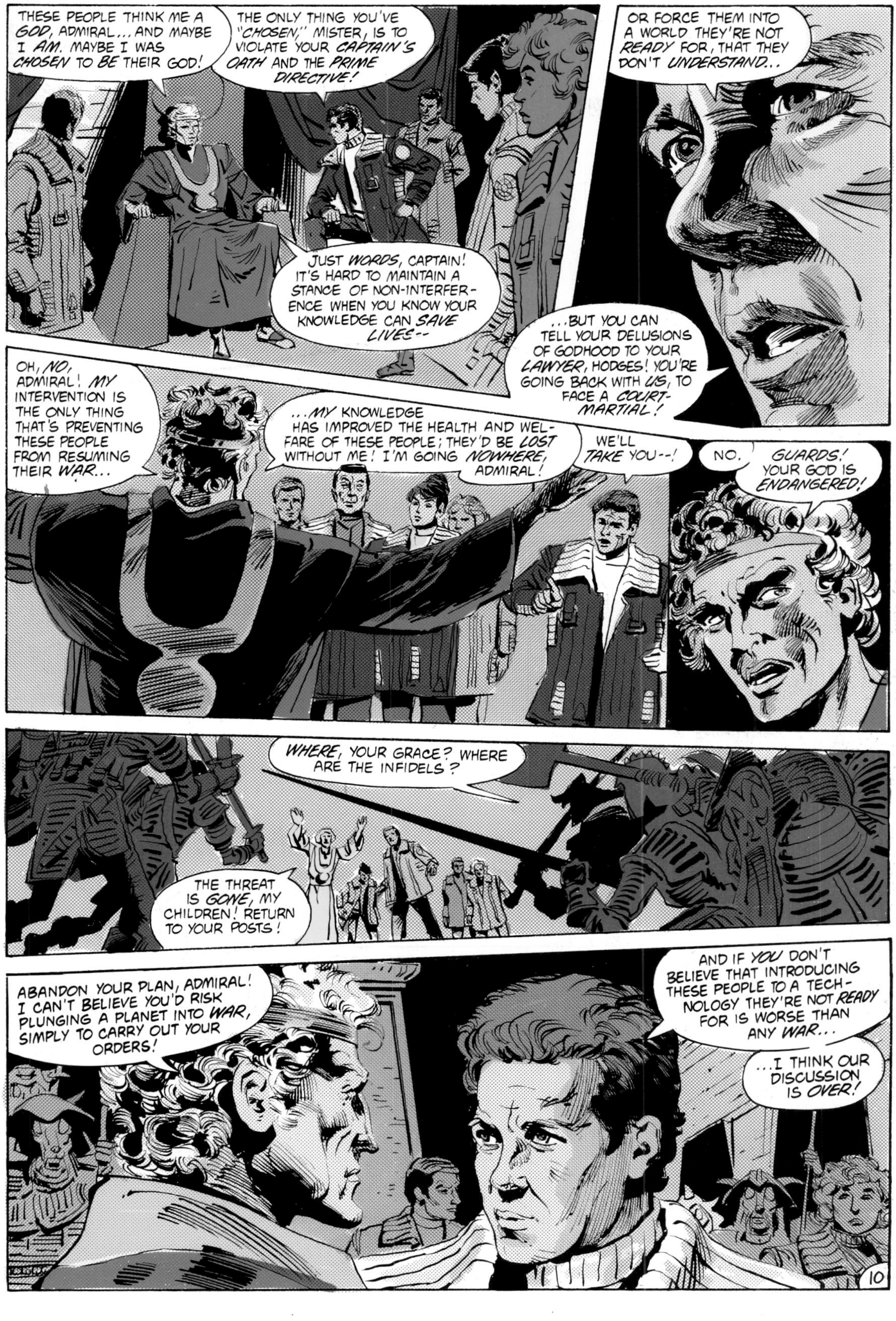
THESE PEOPLE THINK ME A GOD, ADMIRAL... AND MAYBE I AM. MAYBE I WAS CHOSEN TO BE THEIR GOD!
THE ONLY THING YOU'VE "CHOSEN," MISTER, IS TO VIOLATE YOUR CAPTAIN'S OATH AND THE PRIME DIRECTIVE!
OR FORCE THEM INTO A WORLD THEY'RE NOT READY FOR, THAT THEY DON'T UNDERSTAND...
JUST WORDS, CAPTAIN! IT'S HARD TO MAINTAIN A STANCE OF NON-INTERFERENCE WHEN YOU KNOW YOUR KNOWLEDGE CAN SAVE LIVES--
...BUT YOU CAN TELL YOUR DELUSIONS OF GODHOOD TO YOUR LAWYER, HODGES! YOU'RE GOING BACK WITH US, TO FACE A COURT-MARTIAL!
OH, NO, ADMIRAL! MY INTERVENTION IS THE ONLY THING THAT'S PREVENTING THESE PEOPLE FROM RESUMING THEIR WAR...
...MY KNOWLEDGE HAS IMPROVED THE HEALTH AND WELFARE OF THESE PEOPLE; THEY'D BE LOST WITHOUT ME! I'M GOING NOWHERE, ADMIRAL!
WE'LL TAKE YOU--!
NO.
GUARDS! YOUR GOD IS ENDANGERED!
WHERE, YOUR GRACE? WHERE ARE THE INFIDELS?
THE THREAT IS GONE, MY CHILDREN! RETURN TO YOUR POSTS!
ABANDON YOUR PLAN, ADMIRAL! I CAN'T BELIEVE YOU'D RISK PLUNGING A PLANET INTO WAR, SIMPLY TO CARRY OUT YOUR ORDERS!
AND IF YOU DON'T BELIEVE THAT INTRODUCING THESE PEOPLE TO A TECHNOLOGY THEY'RE NOT READY FOR IS WORSE THAN ANY WAR...
...I THINK OUR DISCUSSION IS OVER!
10

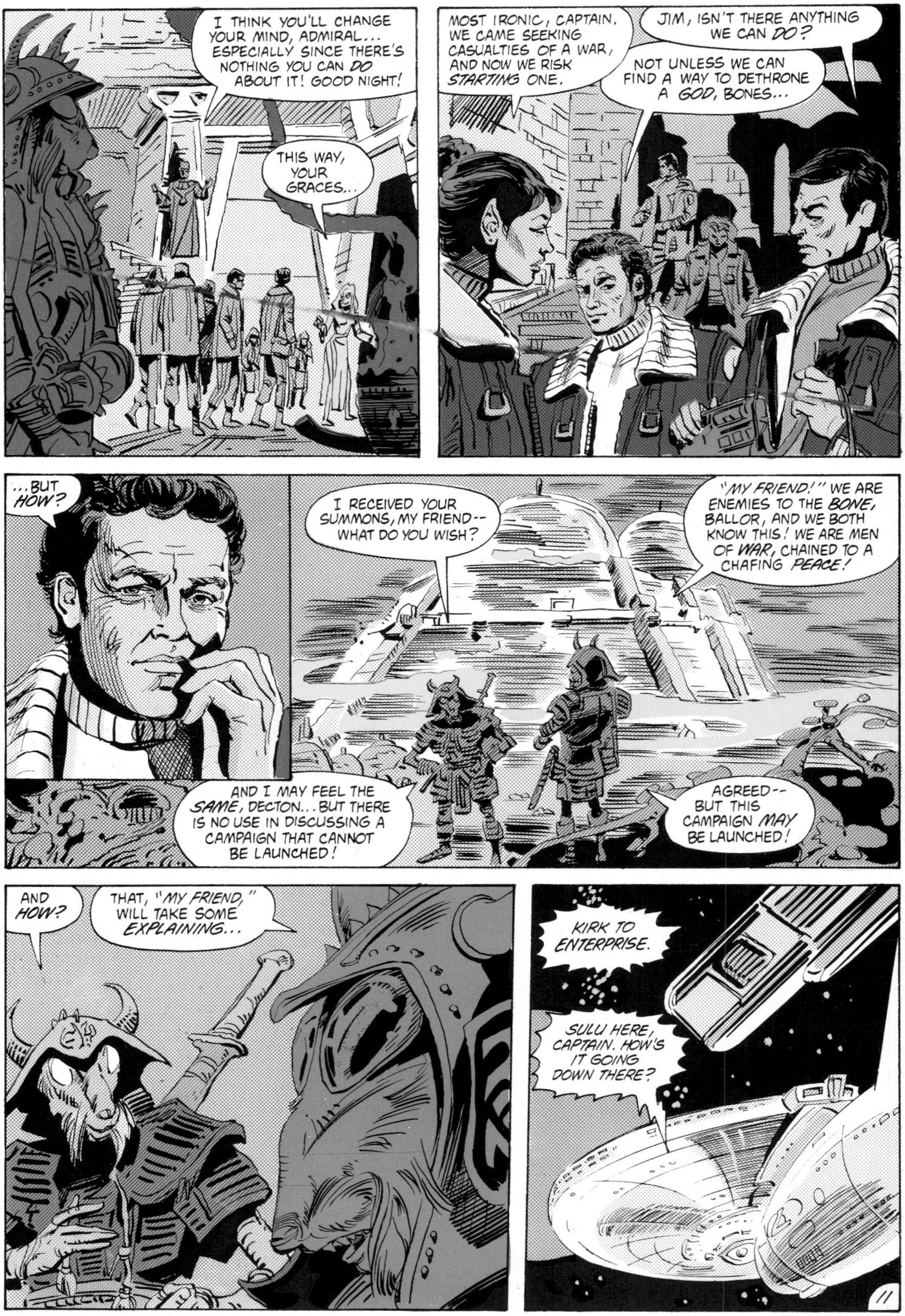
I THINK YOU'LL CHANGE YOUR MIND, ADMIRAL... ESPECIALLY SINCE THERE'S NOTHING YOU CAN DO ABOUT IT! GOOD NIGHT!
THIS WAY, YOUR GRACES...
MOST IRONIC, CAPTAIN. WE CAME SEEKING CASUALTIES OF A WAR, AND NOW WE RISK STARTING ONE.
JIM, ISN'T THERE ANYTHING WE CAN DO?
NOT UNLESS WE CAN FIND A WAY TO DETHRONE A GOD, BONES...
...BUT HOW?
I RECEIVED YOUR SUMMONS, MY FRIEND-- WHAT DO YOU WISH?
"MY FRIEND!" WE ARE ENEMIES TO THE BONE, BALLOR, AND WE BOTH KNOW THIS! WE ARE MEN OF WAR, CHAINED TO A CHAFING PEACE!
AND I MAY FEEL THE SAME, DECTON... BUT THERE IS NO USE IN DISCUSSING A CAMPAIGN THAT CANNOT BE LAUNCHED!
AGREED-- BUT THIS CAMPAIGN MAY BE LAUNCHED!
AND HOW?
THAT, "MY FRIEND," WILL TAKE SOME EXPLAINING...
KIRK TO ENTERPRISE.
SULU HERE, CAPTAIN. HOW'S IT GOING DOWN THERE?
11

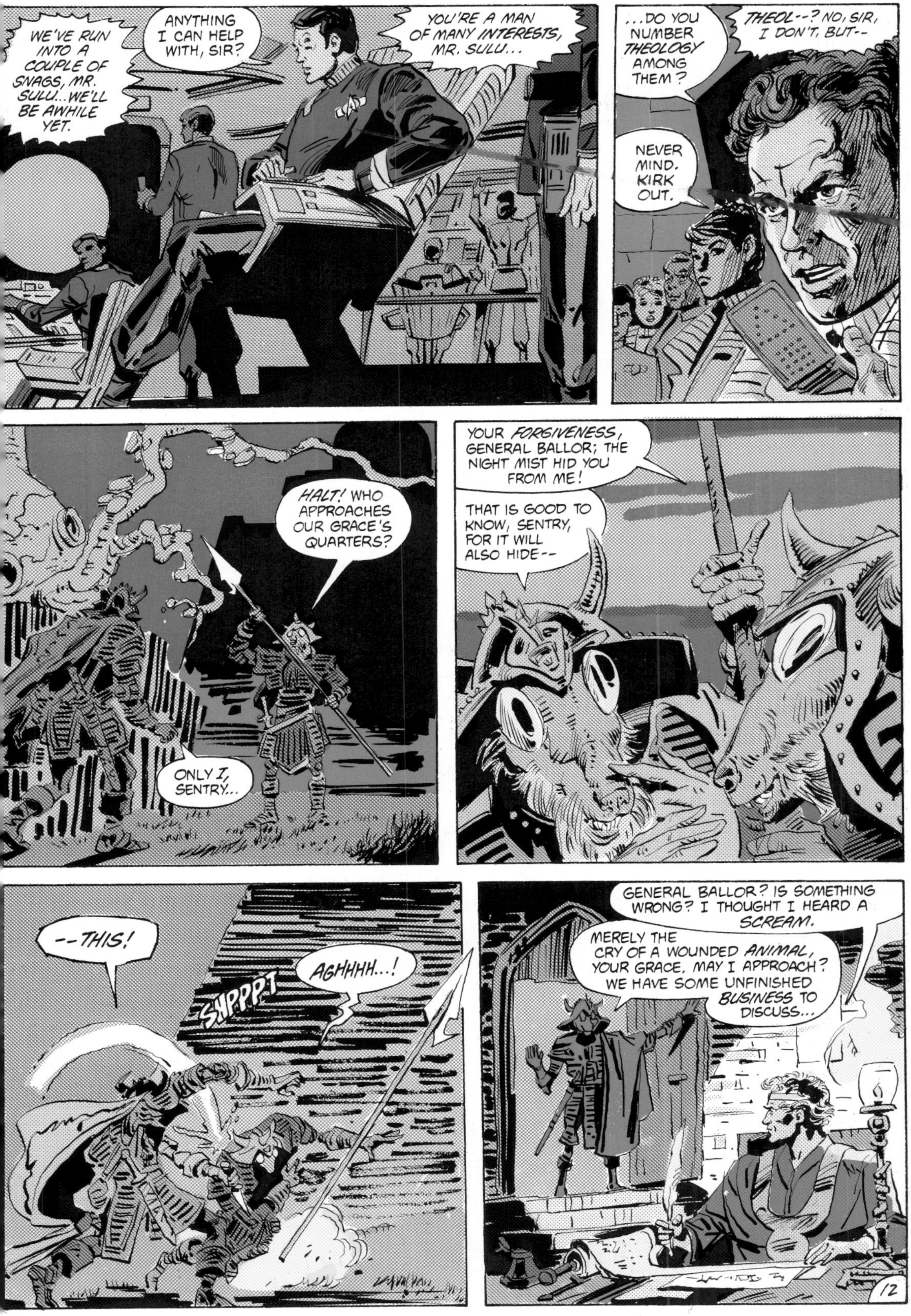
WE'VE RUN INTO A COUPLE OF SNAGS, MR. SULU...WE'LL BE AWHILE YET.
ANYTHING I CAN HELP WITH, SIR?
YOU'RE A MAN OF MANY INTERESTS, MR. SULU...
...DO YOU NUMBER THEOLOGY AMONG THEM?
THEOL--? NO, SIR, I DON'T, BUT--
NEVER MIND. KIRK OUT.
HALT! WHO APPROACHES OUR GRACE'S QUARTERS?
ONLY I, SENTRY...
YOUR FORGIVENESS, GENERAL BALLOR; THE NIGHT MIST HID YOU FROM ME!
THAT IS GOOD TO KNOW, SENTRY, FOR IT WILL ALSO HIDE--
--THIS!
SHPPPT
AGHHHH...!
GENERAL BALLOR? IS SOMETHING WRONG? I THOUGHT I HEARD A SCREAM.
MERELY THE CRY OF A WOUNDED ANIMAL, YOUR GRACE. MAY I APPROACH? WE HAVE SOME UNFINISHED BUSINESS TO DISCUSS...
12

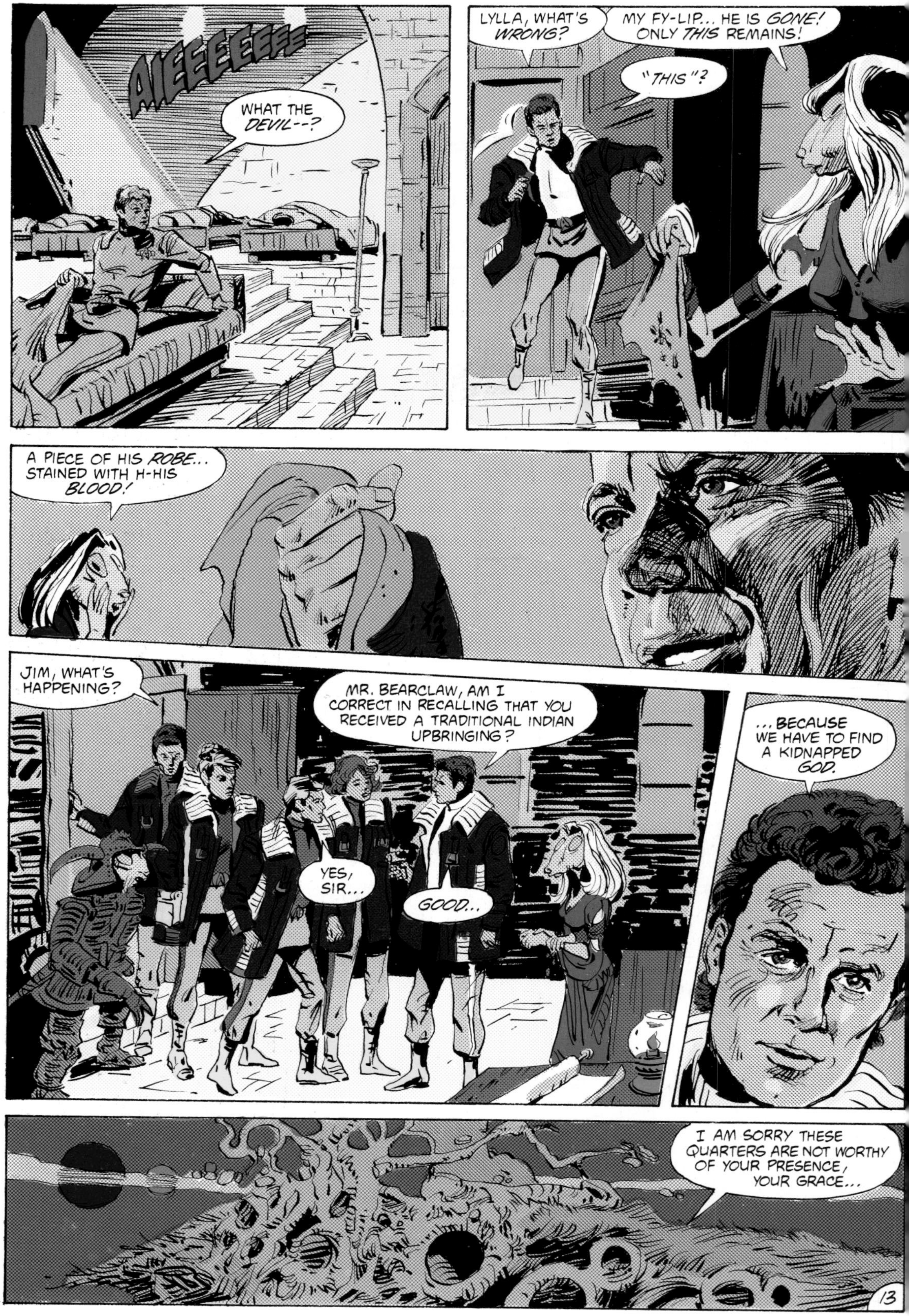
AIEEEEEEEE
WHAT THE DEVIL--?
LYLLA, WHAT'S WRONG?
MY FY-LIP... HE IS GONE! ONLY THIS REMAINS!
"THIS"?
A PIECE OF HIS ROBE... STAINED WITH H-HIS BLOOD!
JIM, WHAT'S HAPPENING?
MR. BEARCLAW, AM I CORRECT IN RECALLING THAT YOU RECEIVED A TRADITIONAL INDIAN UPBRINGING?
YES, SIR...
GOOD...
...BECAUSE WE HAVE TO FIND A KIDNAPPED GOD.
I AM SORRY THESE QUARTERS ARE NOT WORTHY OF YOUR PRESENCE, YOUR GRACE...
13

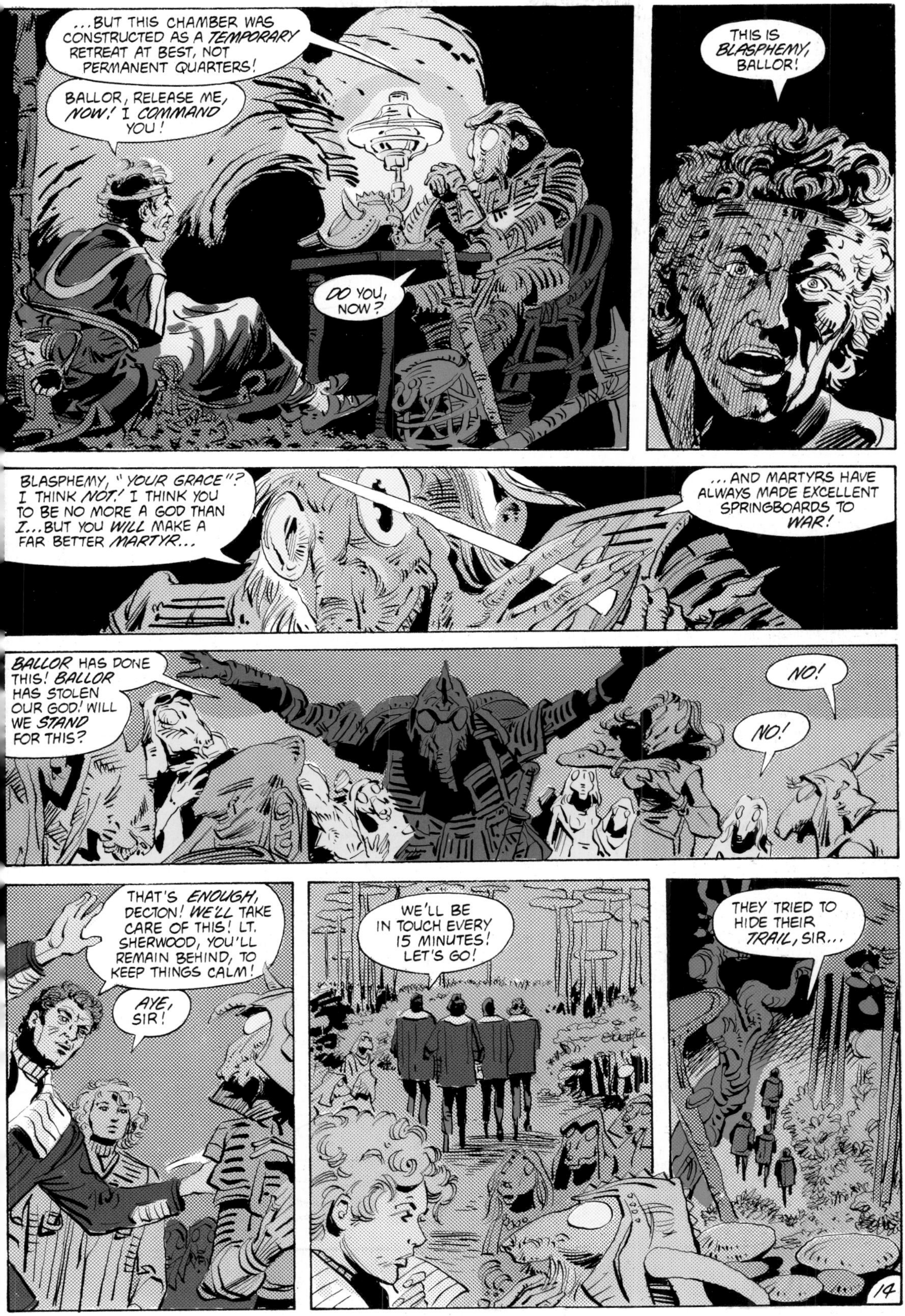
...BUT THIS CHAMBER WAS CONSTRUCTED AS A TEMPORARY RETREAT AT BEST, NOT PERMANENT QUARTERS!
BALLOR, RELEASE ME, NOW! I COMMAND YOU!
DO YOU, NOW?
THIS IS BLASPHEMY, BALLOR!
BLASPHEMY, "YOUR GRACE"? I THINK NOT! I THINK YOU TO BE NO MORE A GOD THAN I...BUT YOU WILL MAKE A FAR BETTER MARTYR...
...AND MARTYRS HAVE ALWAYS MADE EXCELLENT SPRINGBOARDS TO WAR!
BALLOR HAS DONE THIS! BALLOR HAS STOLEN OUR GOD! WILL WE STAND FOR THIS?
NO!
NO!
THAT'S ENOUGH, DECTON! WE'LL TAKE CARE OF THIS! LT. SHERWOOD, YOU'LL REMAIN BEHIND, TO KEEP THINGS CALM!
AYE, SIR!
WE'LL BE IN TOUCH EVERY 15 MINUTES! LET'S GO!
THEY TRIED TO HIDE THEIR TRAIL, SIR...
14

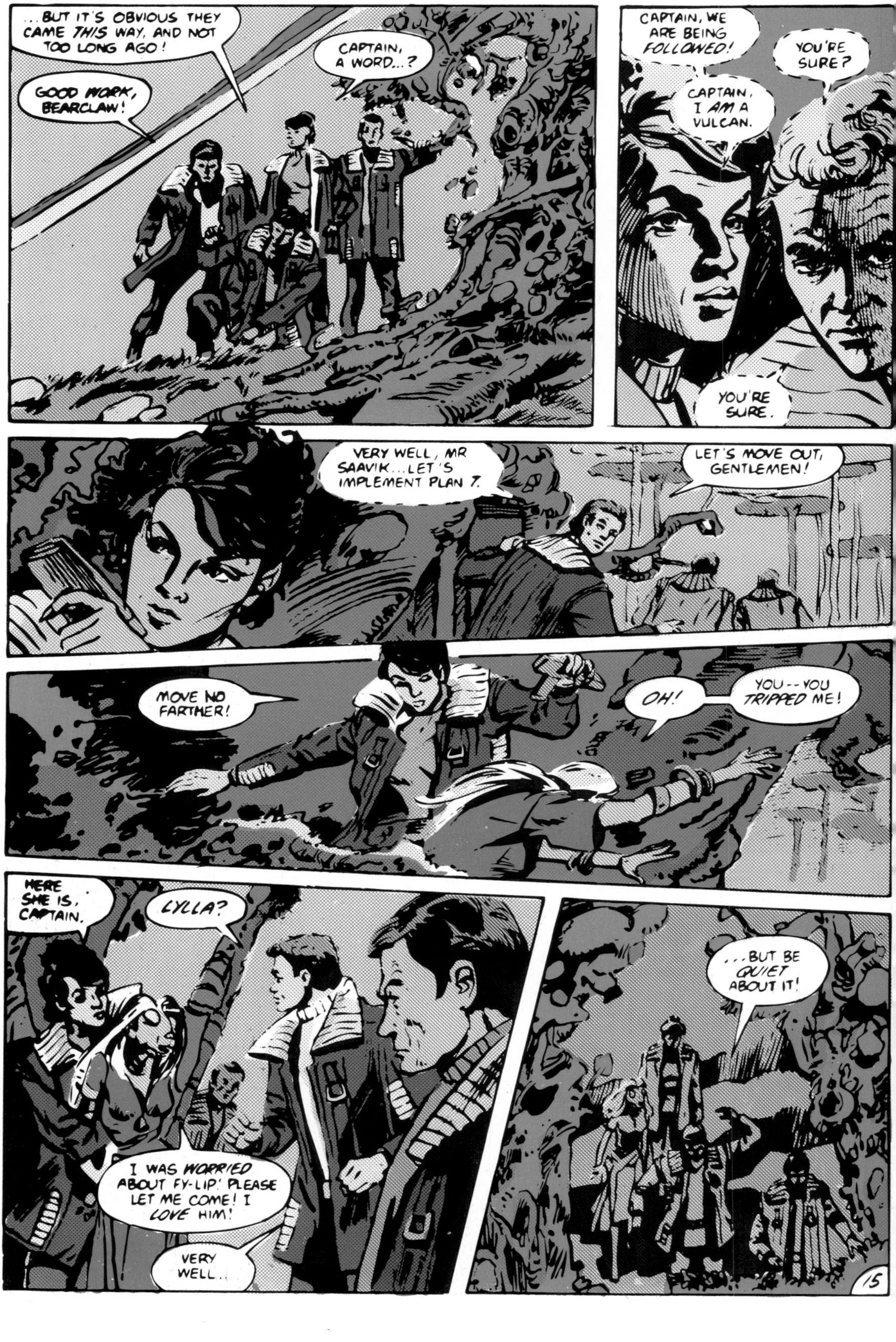

...BUT IT'S OBVIOUS THEY CAME THIS WAY, AND NOT TOO LONG AGO!
GOOD WORK, BEARCLAW!
CAPTAIN, A WORD...?
CAPTAIN, WE ARE BEING FOLLOWED!
YOU'RE SURE?
CAPTAIN, I AM A VULCAN.
YOU'RE SURE.
VERY WELL, MR SAAVIK...LET'S IMPLEMENT PLAN 7.
LET'S MOVE OUT, GENTLEMEN!
MOVE NO FARTHER!
OH!
YOU--YOU TRIPPED ME!
HERE SHE IS, CAPTAIN.
LYLLA?
I WAS WORRIED ABOUT FY-LIP! PLEASE LET ME COME! I LOVE HIM!
VERY WELL...
...BUT BE QUIET ABOUT IT!

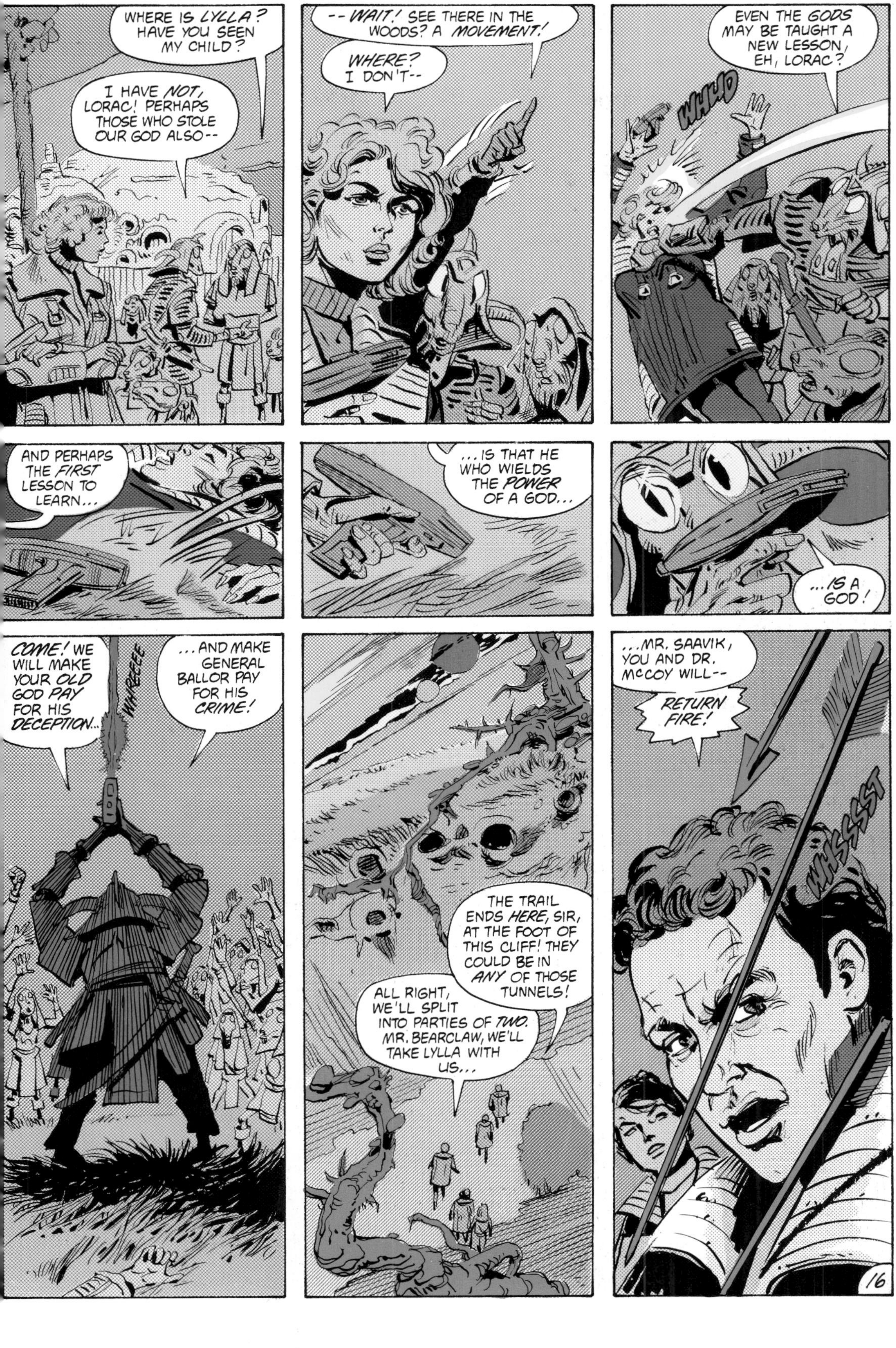
WHERE IS LYLLA? HAVE YOU SEEN MY CHILD?
I HAVE NOT, LORAC! PERHAPS THOSE WHO STOLE OUR GOD ALSO--
--WAIT! SEE THERE IN THE WOODS? A MOVEMENT!
WHERE? I DON'T--
EVEN THE GODS MAY BE TAUGHT A NEW LESSON, EH, LORAC?
WHUD
AND PERHAPS THE FIRST LESSON TO LEARN...
...IS THAT HE WHO WIELDS THE POWER OF A GOD...
...IS A GOD!
COME! WE WILL MAKE YOUR OLD GOD PAY FOR HIS DECEPTION...
WHREEEE
...AND MAKE GENERAL BALLOR PAY FOR HIS CRIME!
THE TRAIL ENDS HERE, SIR, AT THE FOOT OF THIS CLIFF! THEY COULD BE IN ANY OF THOSE TUNNELS!
ALL RIGHT, WE'LL SPLIT INTO PARTIES OF TWO. MR. BEARCLAW, WE'LL TAKE LYLLA WITH US...
...MR. SAAVIK, YOU AND DR. McCOY WILL--
RETURN FIRE!
WHSSSST

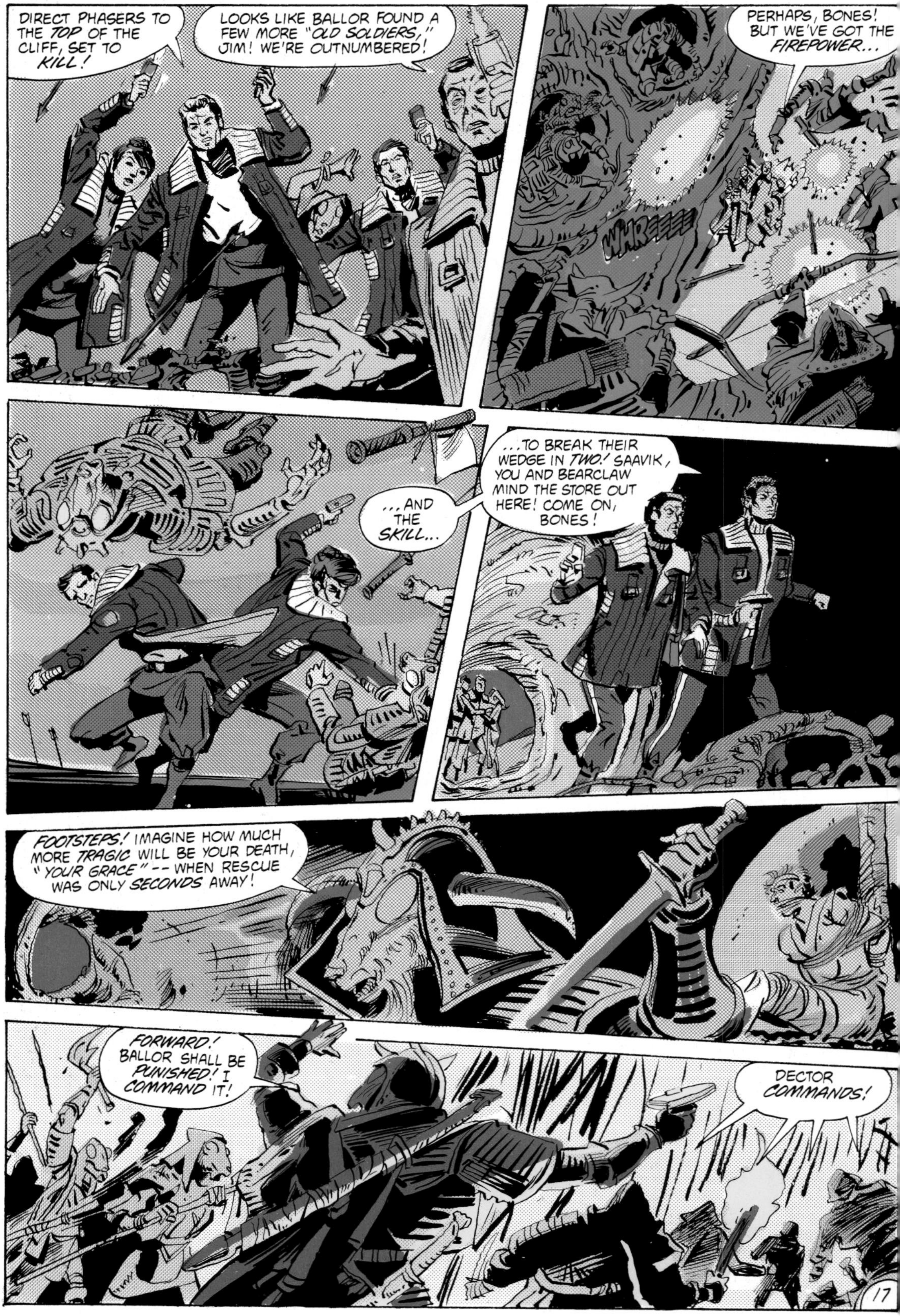
DIRECT PHASERS TO THE TOP OF THE CLIFF, SET TO KILL!
LOOKS LIKE BALLOR FOUND A FEW MORE "OLD SOLDIERS," JIM! WE'RE OUTNUMBERED!
PERHAPS, BONES! BUT WE'VE GOT THE FIREPOWER...
WHREEEE
...AND THE SKILL...
...TO BREAK THEIR WEDGE IN TWO! SAAVIK, YOU AND BEARCLAW MIND THE STORE OUT HERE! COME ON, BONES!
FOOTSTEPS! IMAGINE HOW MUCH MORE TRAGIC WILL BE YOUR DEATH, "YOUR GRACE" -- WHEN RESCUE WAS ONLY SECONDS AWAY!
FORWARD! BALLOR SHALL BE PUNISHED! I COMMAND IT!
DECTOR COMMANDS!

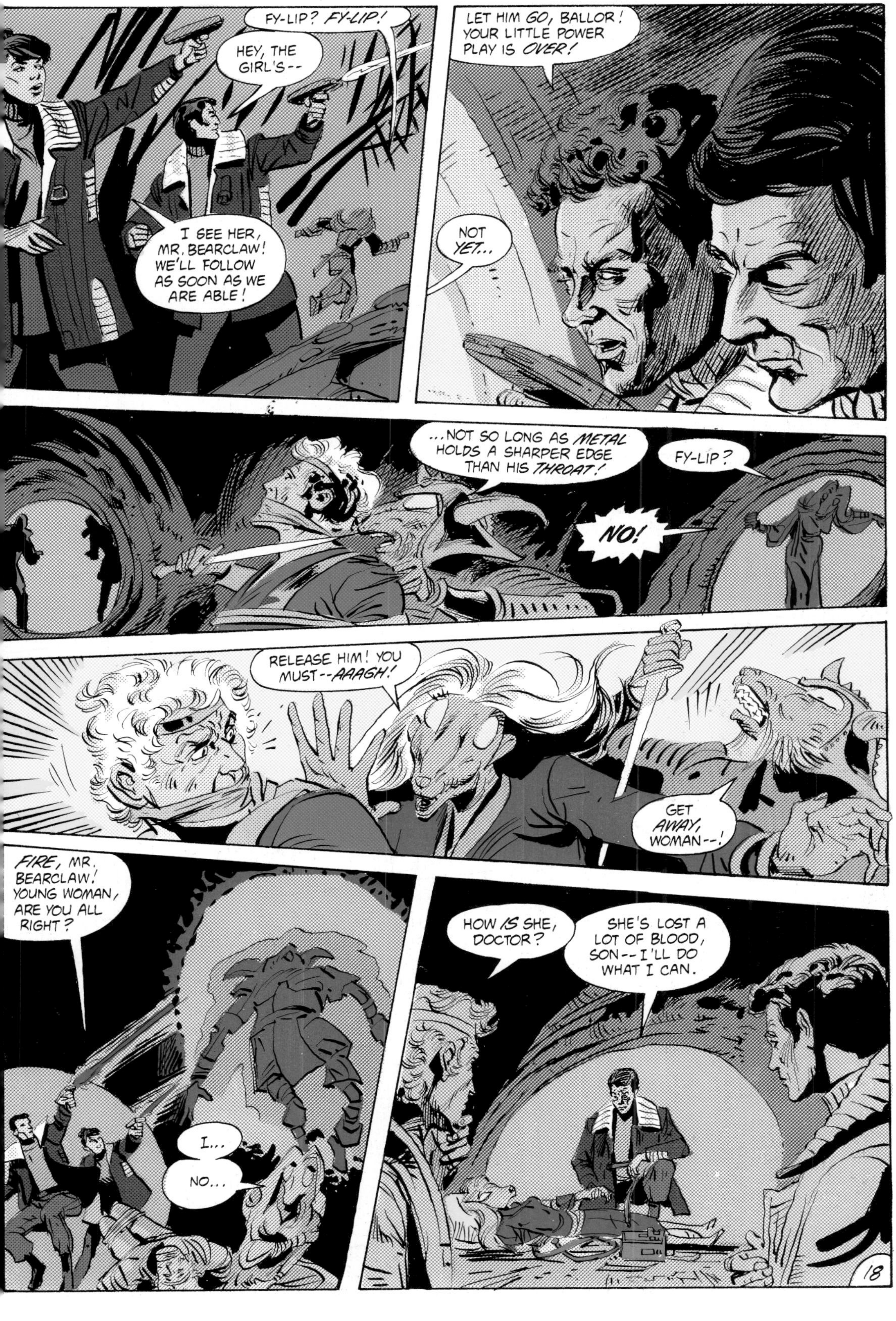
FY-LIP? FY-LIP!
HEY, THE GIRL'S--
I SEE HER, MR. BEARCLAW! WE'LL FOLLOW AS SOON AS WE ARE ABLE!
LET HIM GO, BALLOR! YOUR LITTLE POWER PLAY IS OVER!
NOT YET...
...NOT SO LONG AS METAL HOLDS A SHARPER EDGE THAN HIS THROAT!
FY-LIP?
NO!
RELEASE HIM! YOU MUST--AAAGH!
GET AWAY, WOMAN--!
FIRE, MR. BEARCLAW! YOUNG WOMAN, ARE YOU ALL RIGHT?
I...
NO...
HOW IS SHE, DOCTOR?
SHE'S LOST A LOT OF BLOOD, SON--I'LL DO WHAT I CAN.
18

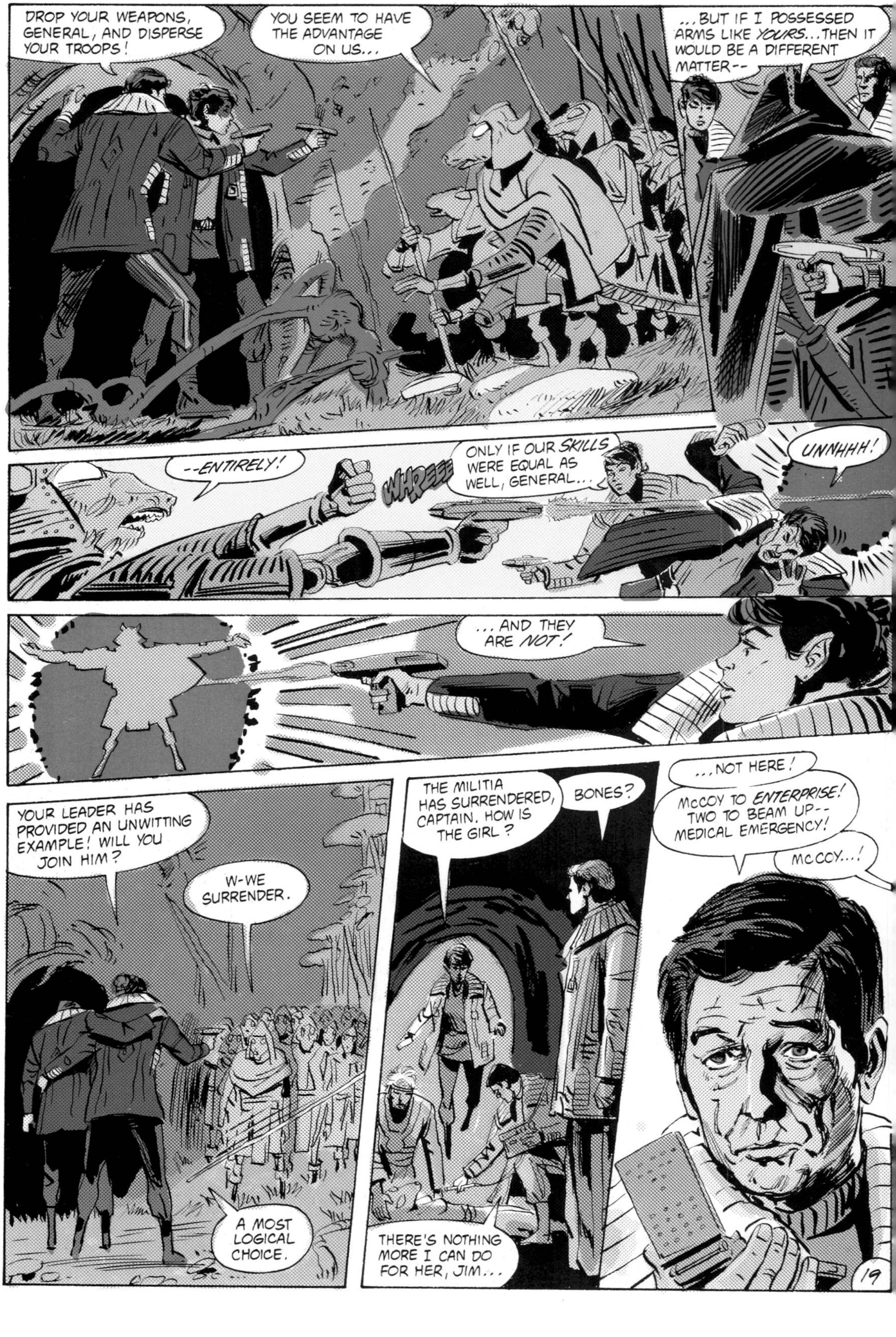
DROP YOUR WEAPONS, GENERAL, AND DISPERSE YOUR TROOPS!
YOU SEEM TO HAVE THE ADVANTAGE ON US...
...BUT IF I POSSESSED ARMS LIKE YOURS...THEN IT WOULD BE A DIFFERENT MATTER--
--ENTIRELY!
WHREEE
ONLY IF OUR SKILLS WERE EQUAL AS WELL, GENERAL...
UNNHHH!
...AND THEY ARE NOT!
YOUR LEADER HAS PROVIDED AN UNWITTING EXAMPLE! WILL YOU JOIN HIM?
W-WE SURRENDER.
A MOST LOGICAL CHOICE.
THE MILITIA HAS SURRENDERED, CAPTAIN. HOW IS THE GIRL?
BONES?
THERE'S NOTHING MORE I CAN DO FOR HER, JIM...
...NOT HERE!
McCOY TO ENTERPRISE! TWO TO BEAM UP-- MEDICAL EMERGENCY!
McCOY...!

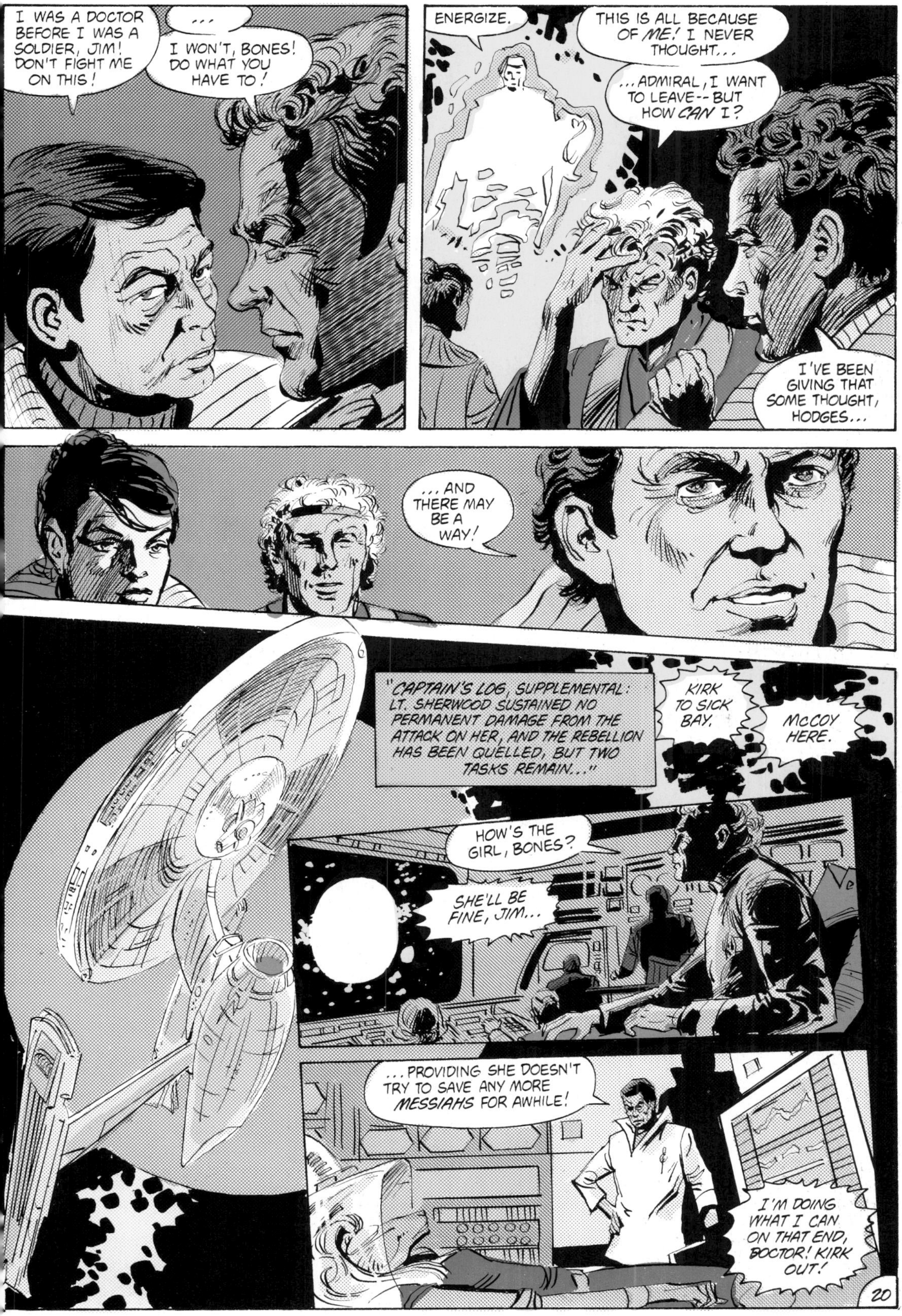
I WAS A DOCTOR BEFORE I WAS A SOLDIER, JIM! DON'T FIGHT ME ON THIS!
...
I WON'T, BONES! DO WHAT YOU HAVE TO!
ENERGIZE.
THIS IS ALL BECAUSE OF *ME*! I NEVER THOUGHT...
...ADMIRAL, I WANT TO LEAVE--BUT HOW *CAN* I?
I'VE BEEN GIVING THAT SOME THOUGHT, HODGES...
...AND THERE MAY BE A WAY!
"CAPTAIN'S LOG, SUPPLEMENTAL: LT. SHERWOOD SUSTAINED NO PERMANENT DAMAGE FROM THE ATTACK ON HER, AND THE REBELLION HAS BEEN QUELLED, BUT TWO TASKS REMAIN..."
KIRK TO SICK BAY.
McCOY HERE.
HOW'S THE GIRL, BONES?
SHE'LL BE FINE, JIM...
...PROVIDING SHE DOESN'T TRY TO SAVE ANY MORE *MESSIAHS* FOR AWHILE!
I'M DOING WHAT I CAN ON THAT END, DOCTOR! KIRK OUT!

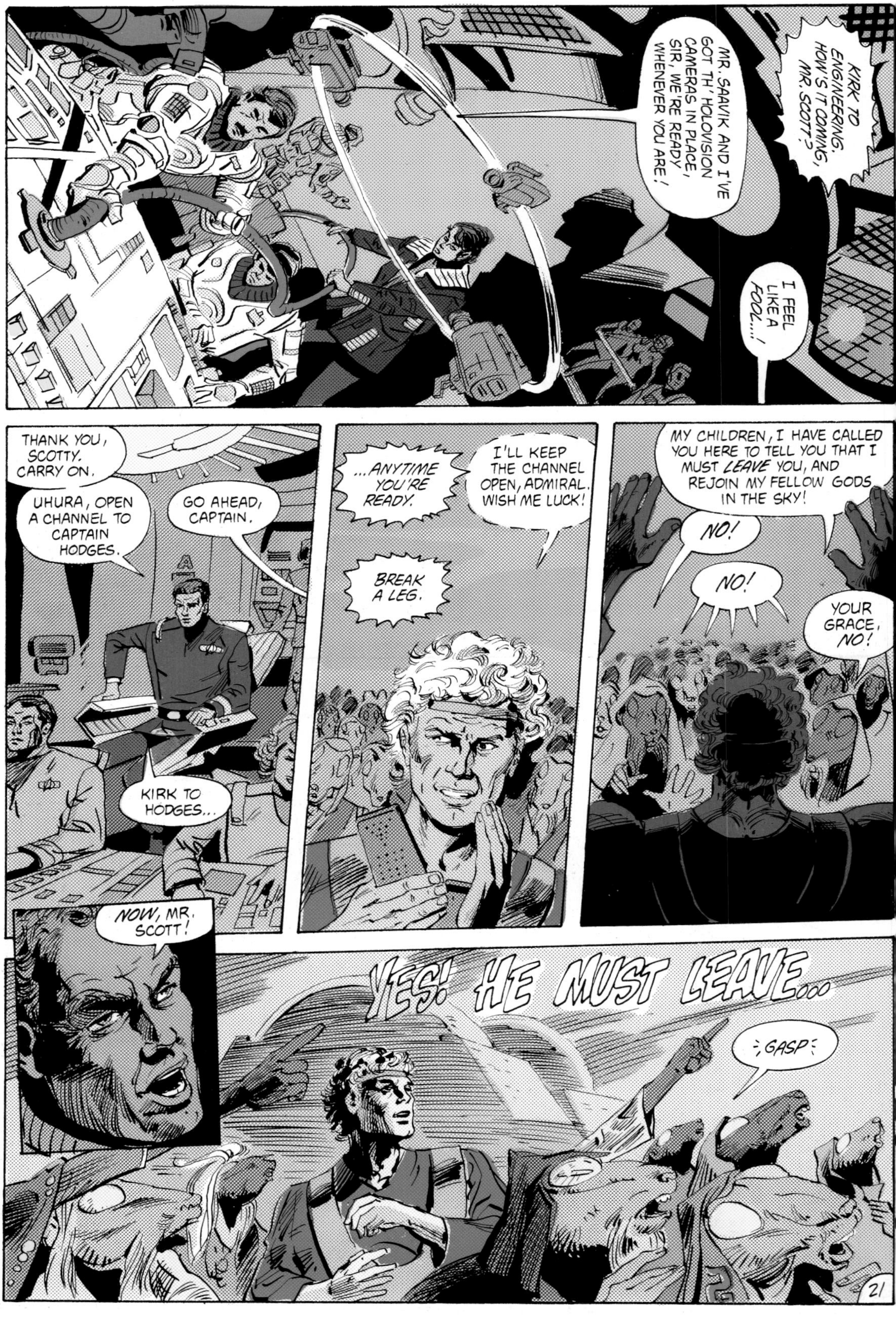
KIRK TO ENGINEERING. HOW'S IT COMING, MR. SCOTT?
MR. SAAVIK AND I'VE GOT TH' HOLOVISION CAMERAS IN PLACE, SIR. WE'RE READY WHENEVER YOU ARE!
I FEEL LIKE A FOOL...!
THANK YOU, SCOTTY. CARRY ON.
UHURA, OPEN A CHANNEL TO CAPTAIN HODGES.
GO AHEAD, CAPTAIN.
KIRK TO HODGES...
...ANYTIME YOU'RE READY.
I'LL KEEP THE CHANNEL OPEN, ADMIRAL. WISH ME LUCK!
BREAK A LEG.
MY CHILDREN, I HAVE CALLED YOU HERE TO TELL YOU THAT I MUST LEAVE YOU, AND REJOIN MY FELLOW GODS IN THE SKY!
NO!
NO!
YOUR GRACE, NO!
NOW, MR. SCOTT!
YES! HE MUST LEAVE...
GASP

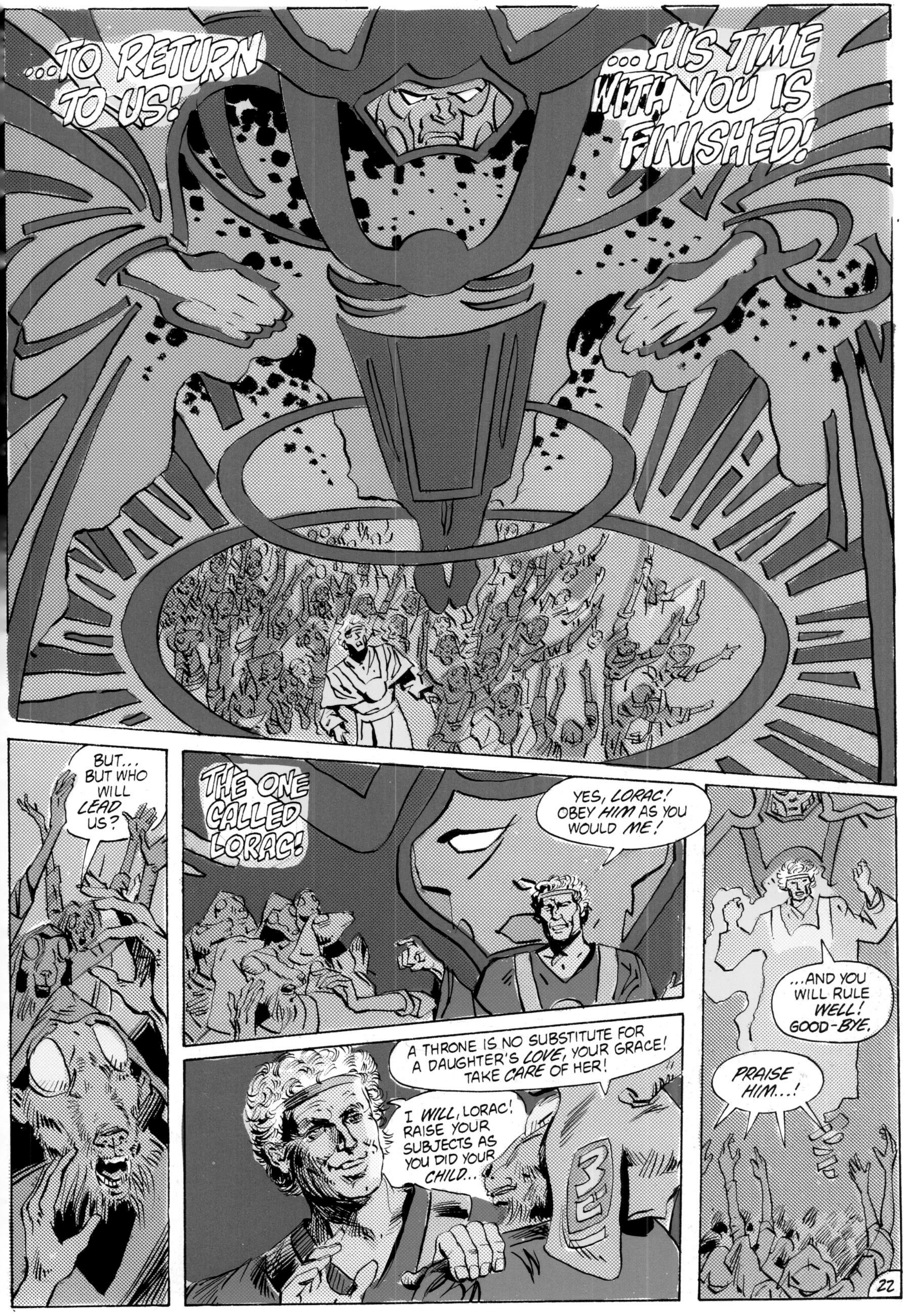
...TO RETURN TO US!
...HIS TIME WITH YOU IS FINISHED!
BUT... BUT WHO WILL LEAD US?
THE ONE CALLED LORAC!
YES, LORAC! OBEY HIM AS YOU WOULD ME!
...AND YOU WILL RULE WELL! GOOD-BYE.
A THRONE IS NO SUBSTITUTE FOR A DAUGHTER'S LOVE, YOUR GRACE! TAKE CARE OF HER!
I WILL, LORAC! RAISE YOUR SUBJECTS AS YOU DID YOUR CHILD...
PRAISE HIM...!

NOW CAN I TAKE THIS STUPID THING OFF?

KONOM, YOU WERE WONDERFUL!

I...I WAS, NANCY?

YOU PROBABLY KNOW THIS BY NOW, LYLLA...BUT I'M NOT A GOD AT ALL!

I DID NOT FALL IN LOVE WITH A GOD, FY-LIP... BUT WITH A MAN!

AH, MR. SAAVIK! AN EXCELLENT JOB!

THANK YOU, SIR...BUT I AM CURIOUS...

YES?

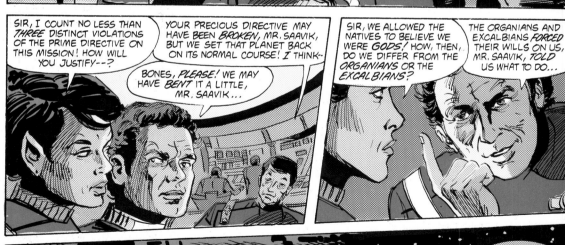

SIR, I COUNT NO LESS THAN THREE DISTINCT VIOLATIONS OF THE PRIME DIRECTIVE ON THIS MISSION! HOW WILL YOU JUSTIFY--?

YOUR PRECIOUS DIRECTIVE MAY HAVE BEEN BROKEN, MR. SAAVIK, BUT WE SET THAT PLANET BACK ON ITS NORMAL COURSE! I THINK--

BONES, PLEASE! WE MAY HAVE BENT IT A LITTLE, MR. SAAVIK...

SIR, WE ALLOWED THE NATIVES TO BELIEVE WE WERE GODS! HOW, THEN, DO WE DIFFER FROM THE ORGANIANS OR THE EXCALBIANS?

THE ORGANIANS AND EXCALBIANS FORCED THEIR WILLS ON US, MR. SAAVIK, TOLD US WHAT TO DO...

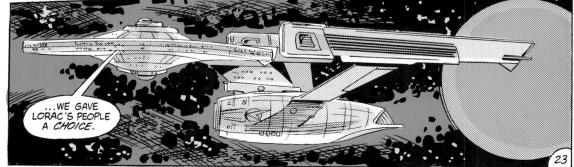

...WE GAVE LORAC'S PEOPLE A CHOICE.

23

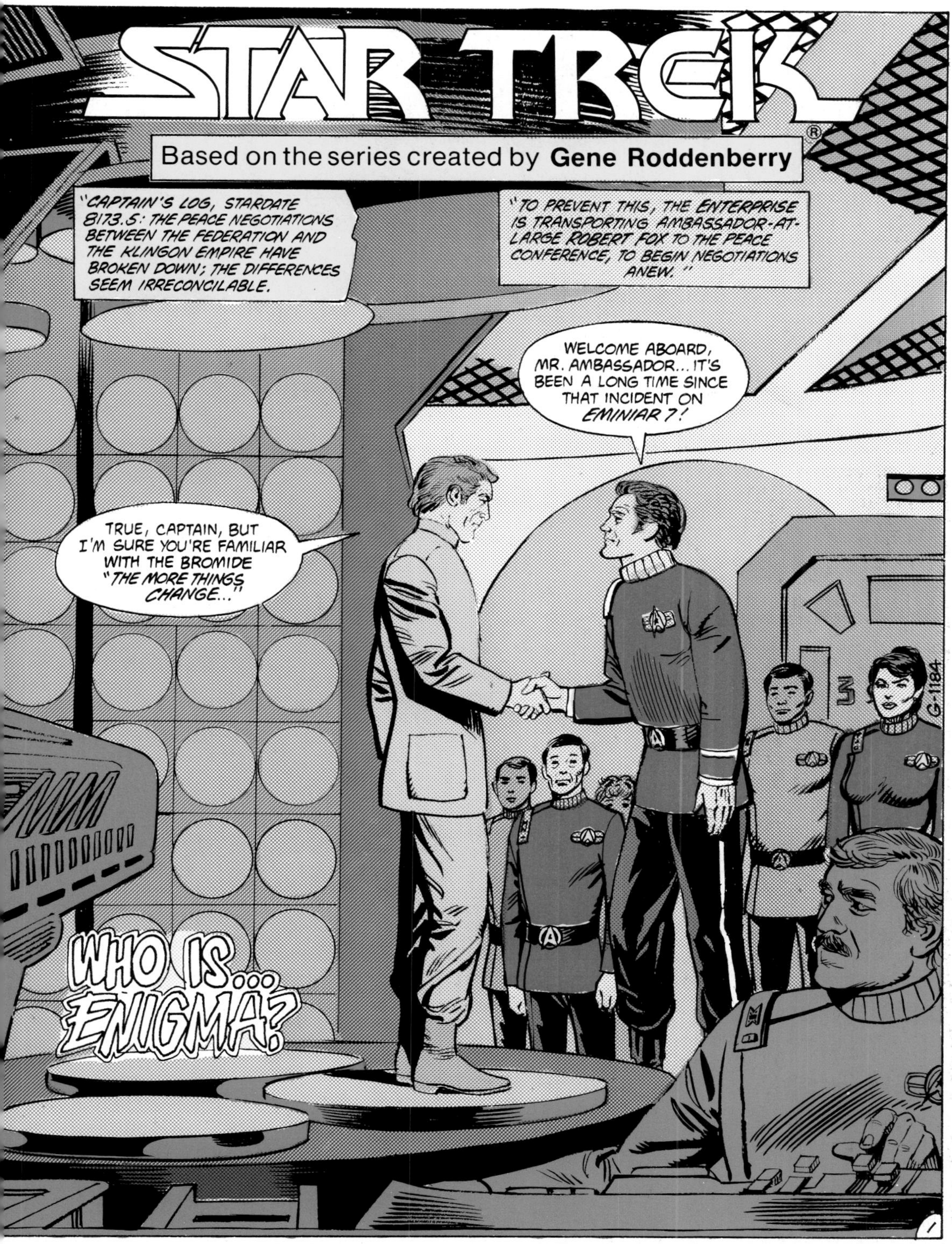
STAR TREK
Based on the series created by Gene Roddenberry
"CAPTAIN'S LOG, STARDATE 8173.5: THE PEACE NEGOTIATIONS BETWEEN THE FEDERATION AND THE KLINGON EMPIRE HAVE BROKEN DOWN; THE DIFFERENCES SEEM IRRECONCILABLE.
"TO PREVENT THIS, THE ENTERPRISE IS TRANSPORTING AMBASSADOR-AT-LARGE ROBERT FOX TO THE PEACE CONFERENCE, TO BEGIN NEGOTIATIONS ANEW."
WELCOME ABOARD, MR. AMBASSADOR... IT'S BEEN A LONG TIME SINCE THAT INCIDENT ON EMINIAR 7!
TRUE, CAPTAIN, BUT I'M SURE YOU'RE FAMILIAR WITH THE BROMIDE "THE MORE THINGS CHANGE..."
WHO IS... ENIGMA?
G.1184
1

Mike W. Barr * **Tom Sutton** & **Ricardo Villagran** **John Costanza** * **Michele Wolfman** * **Marv Wolfman**

Writer — Artists — Letterer — Colorist — Editor

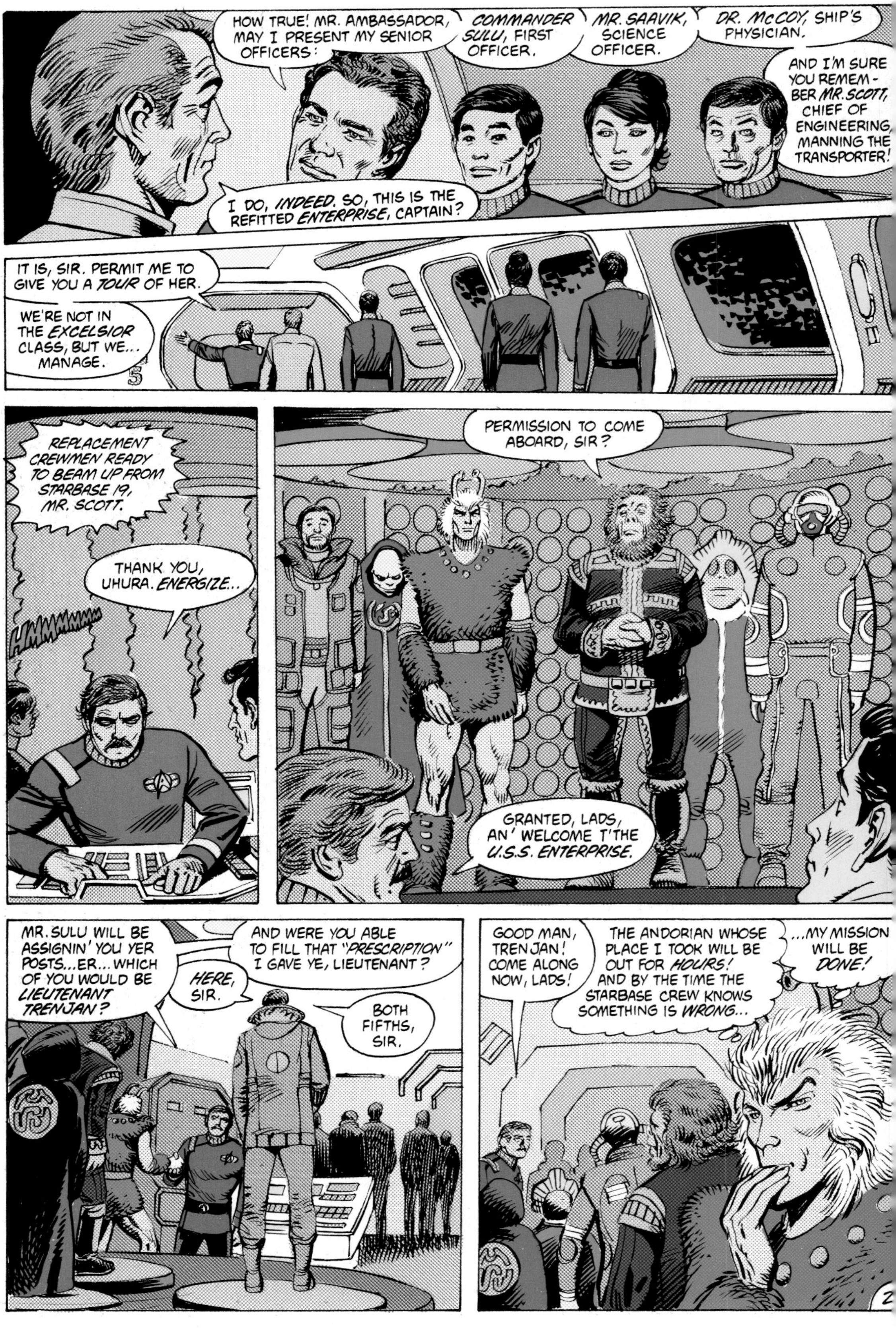

HOW TRUE! MR. AMBASSADOR, MAY I PRESENT MY SENIOR OFFICERS:
COMMANDER SULU, FIRST OFFICER.
MR. SAAVIK, SCIENCE OFFICER.
DR. McCOY, SHIP'S PHYSICIAN.
AND I'M SURE YOU REMEMBER MR. SCOTT, CHIEF OF ENGINEERING, MANNING THE TRANSPORTER!
I DO, INDEED. SO, THIS IS THE REFITTED ENTERPRISE, CAPTAIN?
IT IS, SIR. PERMIT ME TO GIVE YOU A TOUR OF HER.
WE'RE NOT IN THE EXCELSIOR CLASS, BUT WE... MANAGE.
REPLACEMENT CREWMEN READY TO BEAM UP FROM STARBASE 19, MR. SCOTT.
THANK YOU, UHURA. ENERGIZE...
HMMMMMM
PERMISSION TO COME ABOARD, SIR?
GRANTED, LADS, AN' WELCOME T'THE U.S.S. ENTERPRISE.
MR. SULU WILL BE ASSIGNIN' YOU YER POSTS...ER...WHICH OF YOU WOULD BE LIEUTENANT TRENJAN?
AND WERE YOU ABLE TO FILL THAT "PRESCRIPTION" I GAVE YE, LIEUTENANT?
HERE, SIR.
BOTH FIFTHS, SIR.
GOOD MAN, TRENJAN! COME ALONG NOW, LADS!
THE ANDORIAN WHOSE PLACE I TOOK WILL BE OUT FOR HOURS! AND BY THE TIME THE STARBASE CREW KNOWS SOMETHING IS WRONG...
...MY MISSION WILL BE DONE!

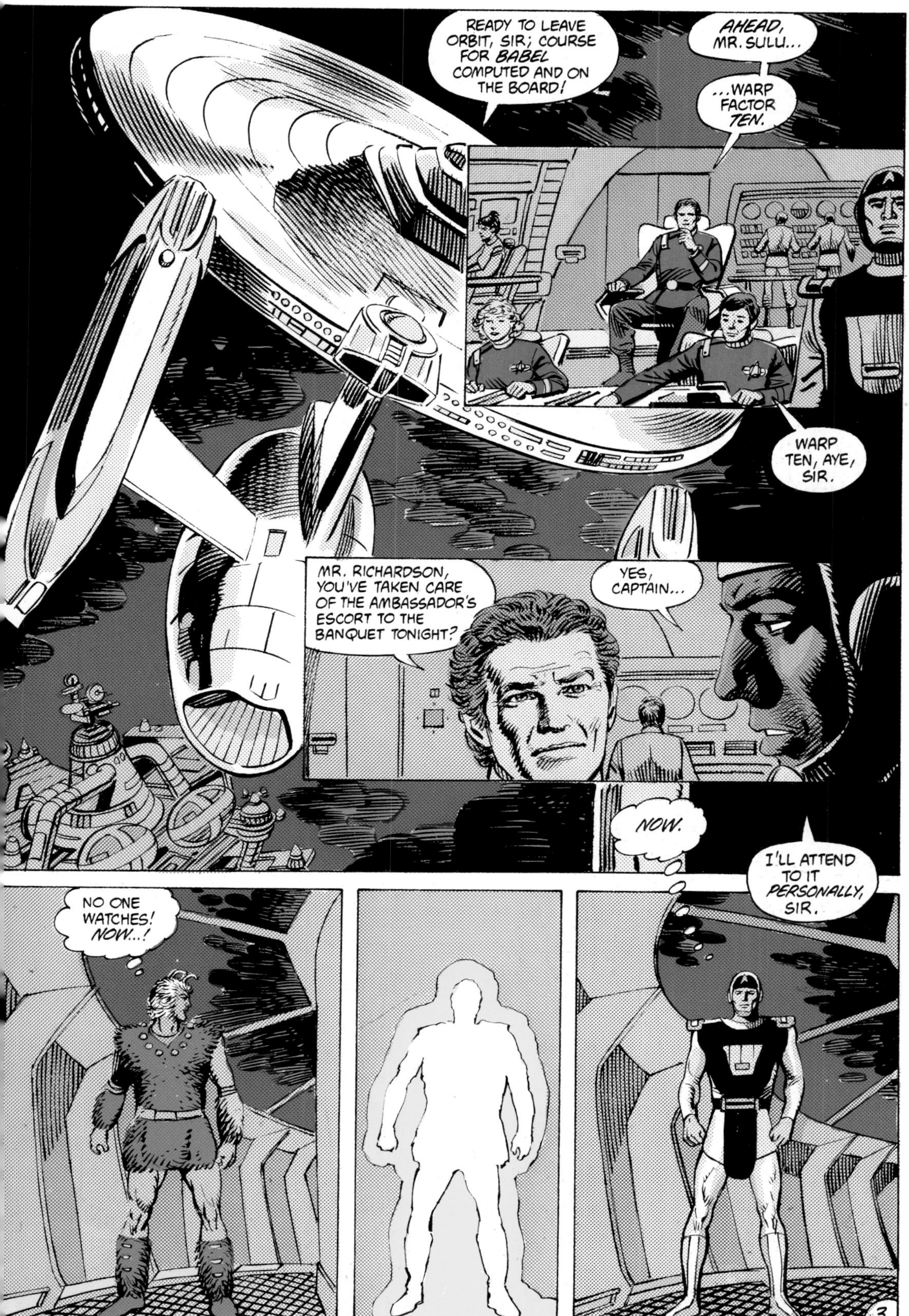
READY TO LEAVE ORBIT, SIR; COURSE FOR BABEL COMPUTED AND ON THE BOARD!
AHEAD, MR. SULU...
...WARP FACTOR TEN.
WARP TEN, AYE, SIR.
MR. RICHARDSON, YOU'VE TAKEN CARE OF THE AMBASSADOR'S ESCORT TO THE BANQUET TONIGHT?
YES, CAPTAIN...
NOW.
I'LL ATTEND TO IT PERSONALLY, SIR.
NO ONE WATCHES! NOW...!

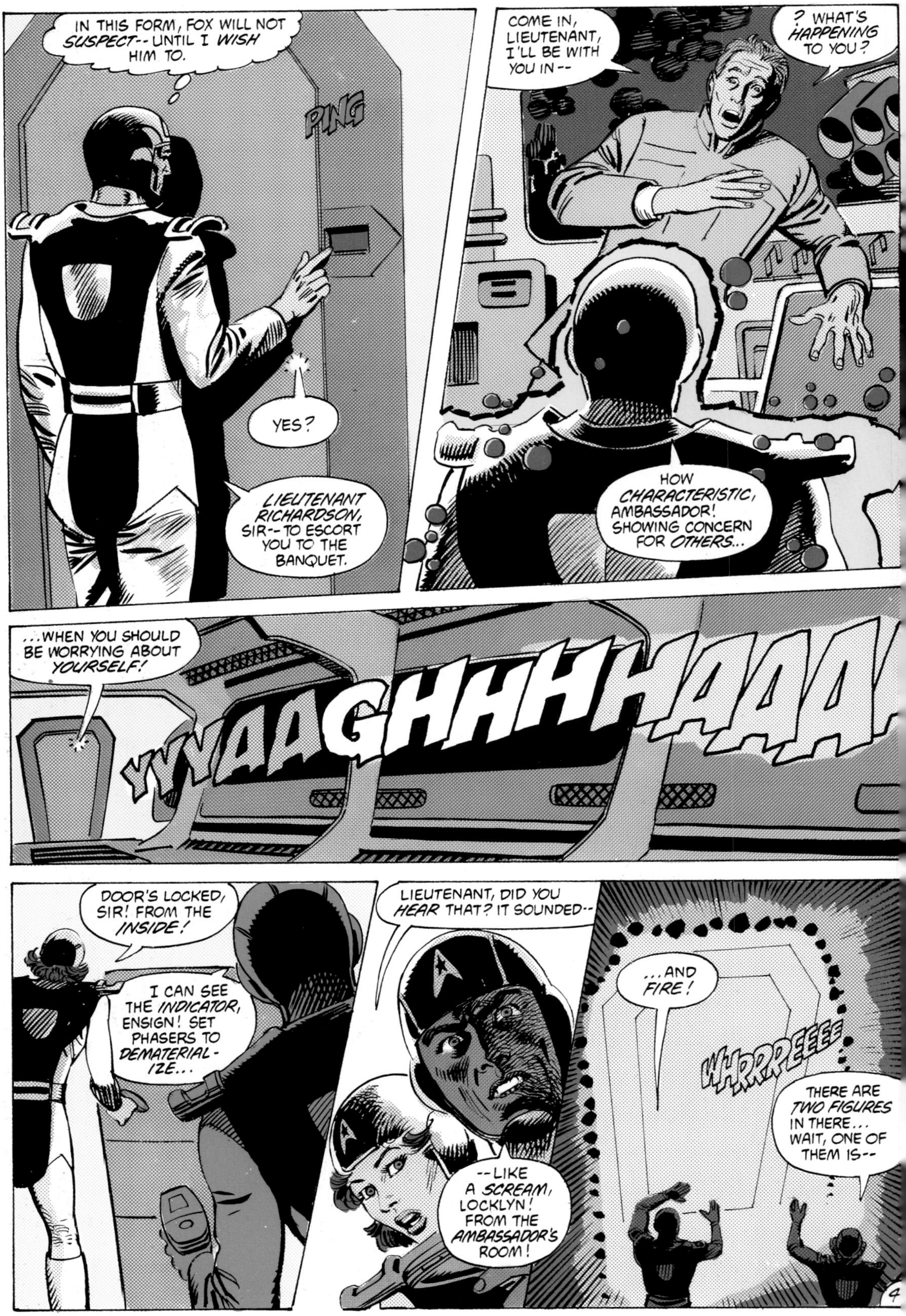
IN THIS FORM, FOX WILL NOT SUSPECT--UNTIL I WISH HIM TO.
PING
YES?
LIEUTENANT RICHARDSON, SIR--TO ESCORT YOU TO THE BANQUET.
COME IN, LIEUTENANT, I'LL BE WITH YOU IN--
? WHAT'S HAPPENING TO YOU?
HOW CHARACTERISTIC, AMBASSADOR! SHOWING CONCERN FOR OTHERS...
...WHEN YOU SHOULD BE WORRYING ABOUT YOURSELF!
YYYAAGHHHHAAA
DOOR'S LOCKED, SIR! FROM THE INSIDE!
I CAN SEE THE INDICATOR, ENSIGN! SET PHASERS TO DEMATERIAL-IZE...
LIEUTENANT, DID YOU HEAR THAT? IT SOUNDED--
--LIKE A SCREAM, LOCKLYN! FROM THE AMBASSADOR'S ROOM!
...AND FIRE!
WHRRPEEEE
THERE ARE TWO FIGURES IN THERE... WAIT, ONE OF THEM IS--

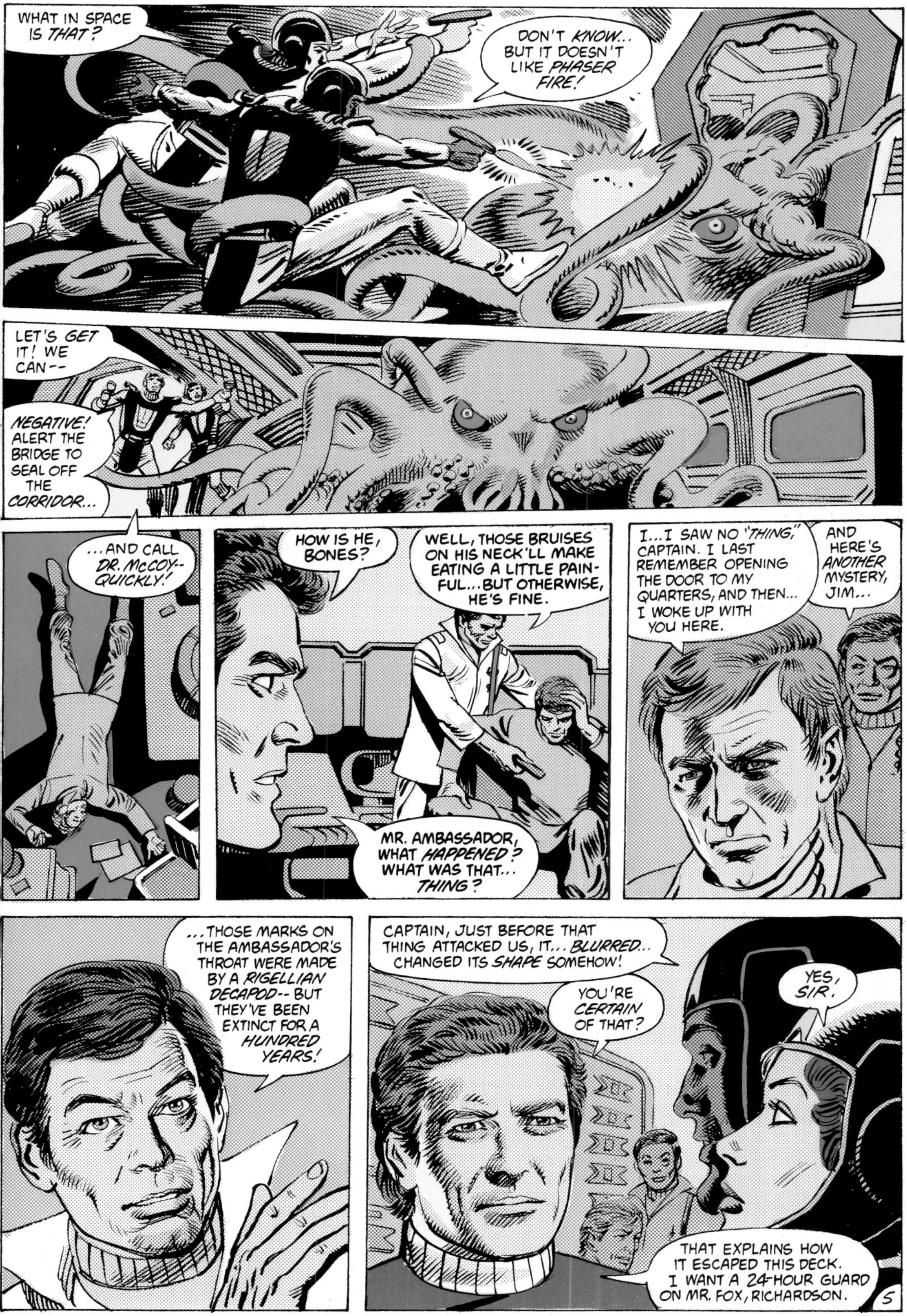
WHAT IN SPACE IS THAT?
DON'T KNOW... BUT IT DOESN'T LIKE PHASER FIRE!
LET'S GET IT! WE CAN--
NEGATIVE! ALERT THE BRIDGE TO SEAL OFF THE CORRIDOR...
...AND CALL DR. McCOY-- QUICKLY!
HOW IS HE, BONES?
WELL, THOSE BRUISES ON HIS NECK'LL MAKE EATING A LITTLE PAIN-FUL...BUT OTHERWISE, HE'S FINE.
MR. AMBASSADOR, WHAT HAPPENED? WHAT WAS THAT... THING?
I...I SAW NO "THING," CAPTAIN. I LAST REMEMBER OPENING THE DOOR TO MY QUARTERS, AND THEN... I WOKE UP WITH YOU HERE.
AND HERE'S ANOTHER MYSTERY, JIM...
...THOSE MARKS ON THE AMBASSADOR'S THROAT WERE MADE BY A RIGELLIAN DECAPOD-- BUT THEY'VE BEEN EXTINCT FOR A HUNDRED YEARS!
CAPTAIN, JUST BEFORE THAT THING ATTACKED US, IT... BLURRED... CHANGED ITS SHAPE SOMEHOW!
YOU'RE CERTAIN OF THAT?
YES, SIR.
THAT EXPLAINS HOW IT ESCAPED THIS DECK. I WANT A 24-HOUR GUARD ON MR. FOX, RICHARDSON.
5

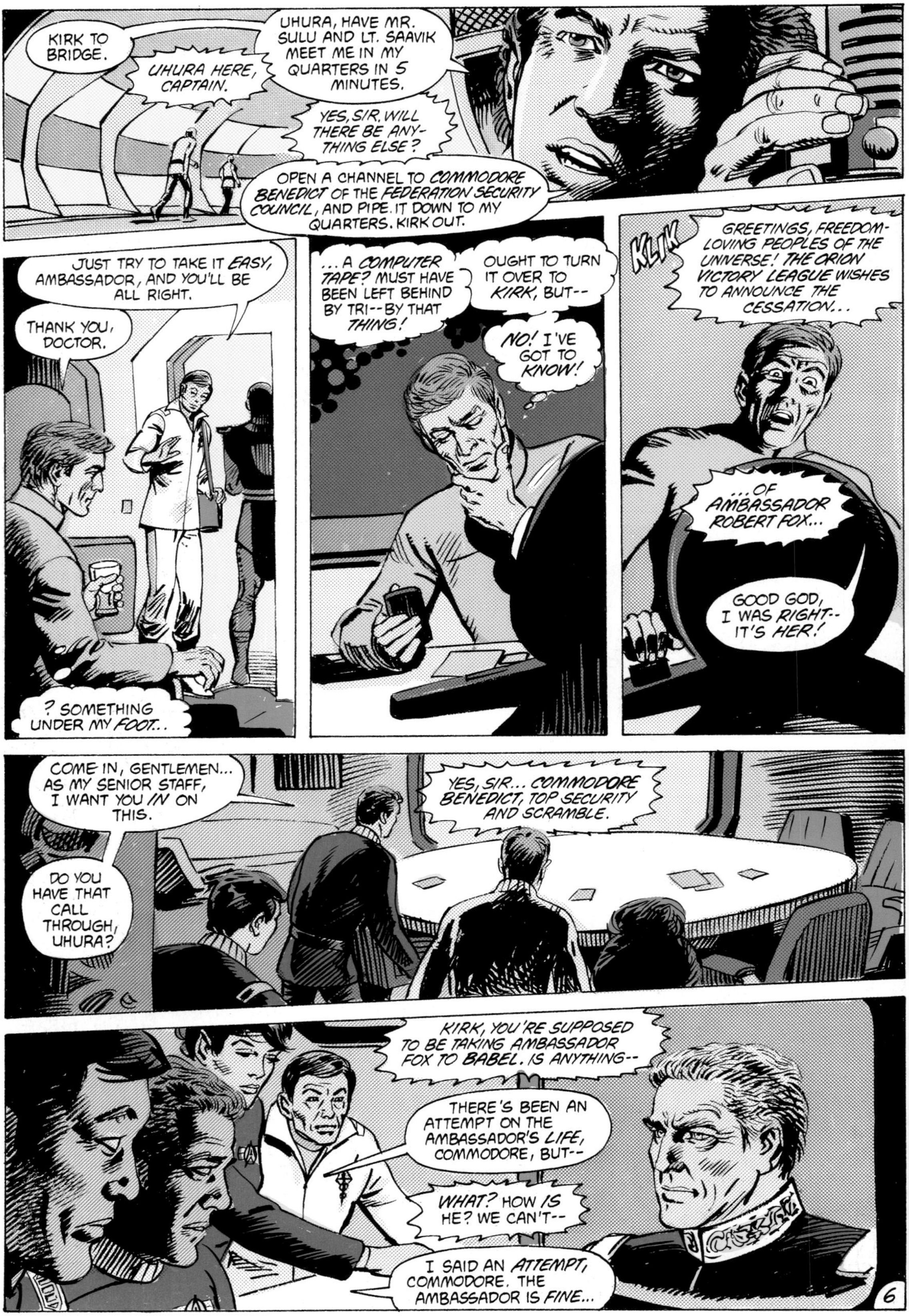
KIRK TO BRIDGE.
UHURA HERE, CAPTAIN.
UHURA, HAVE MR. SULU AND LT. SAAVIK MEET ME IN MY QUARTERS IN 5 MINUTES.
YES, SIR. WILL THERE BE ANYTHING ELSE?
OPEN A CHANNEL TO COMMODORE BENEDICT OF THE FEDERATION SECURITY COUNCIL, AND PIPE IT DOWN TO MY QUARTERS. KIRK OUT.
JUST TRY TO TAKE IT EASY, AMBASSADOR, AND YOU'LL BE ALL RIGHT.
THANK YOU, DOCTOR.
? SOMETHING UNDER MY FOOT...
...A COMPUTER TAPE? MUST HAVE BEEN LEFT BEHIND BY TRI--BY THAT THING!
OUGHT TO TURN IT OVER TO KIRK, BUT--
NO! I'VE GOT TO KNOW!
KLIK
GREETINGS, FREEDOM-LOVING PEOPLES OF THE UNIVERSE! THE ORION VICTORY LEAGUE WISHES TO ANNOUNCE THE CESSATION...
...OF AMBASSADOR ROBERT FOX...
GOOD GOD, I WAS RIGHT--IT'S HER!
COME IN, GENTLEMEN... AS MY SENIOR STAFF, I WANT YOU IN ON THIS.
DO YOU HAVE THAT CALL THROUGH, UHURA?
YES, SIR... COMMODORE BENEDICT, TOP SECURITY AND SCRAMBLE.
KIRK, YOU'RE SUPPOSED TO BE TAKING AMBASSADOR FOX TO BABEL. IS ANYTHING--
THERE'S BEEN AN ATTEMPT ON THE AMBASSADOR'S LIFE, COMMODORE, BUT--
WHAT? HOW IS HE? WE CAN'T--
I SAID AN ATTEMPT, COMMODORE. THE AMBASSADOR IS FINE...
6

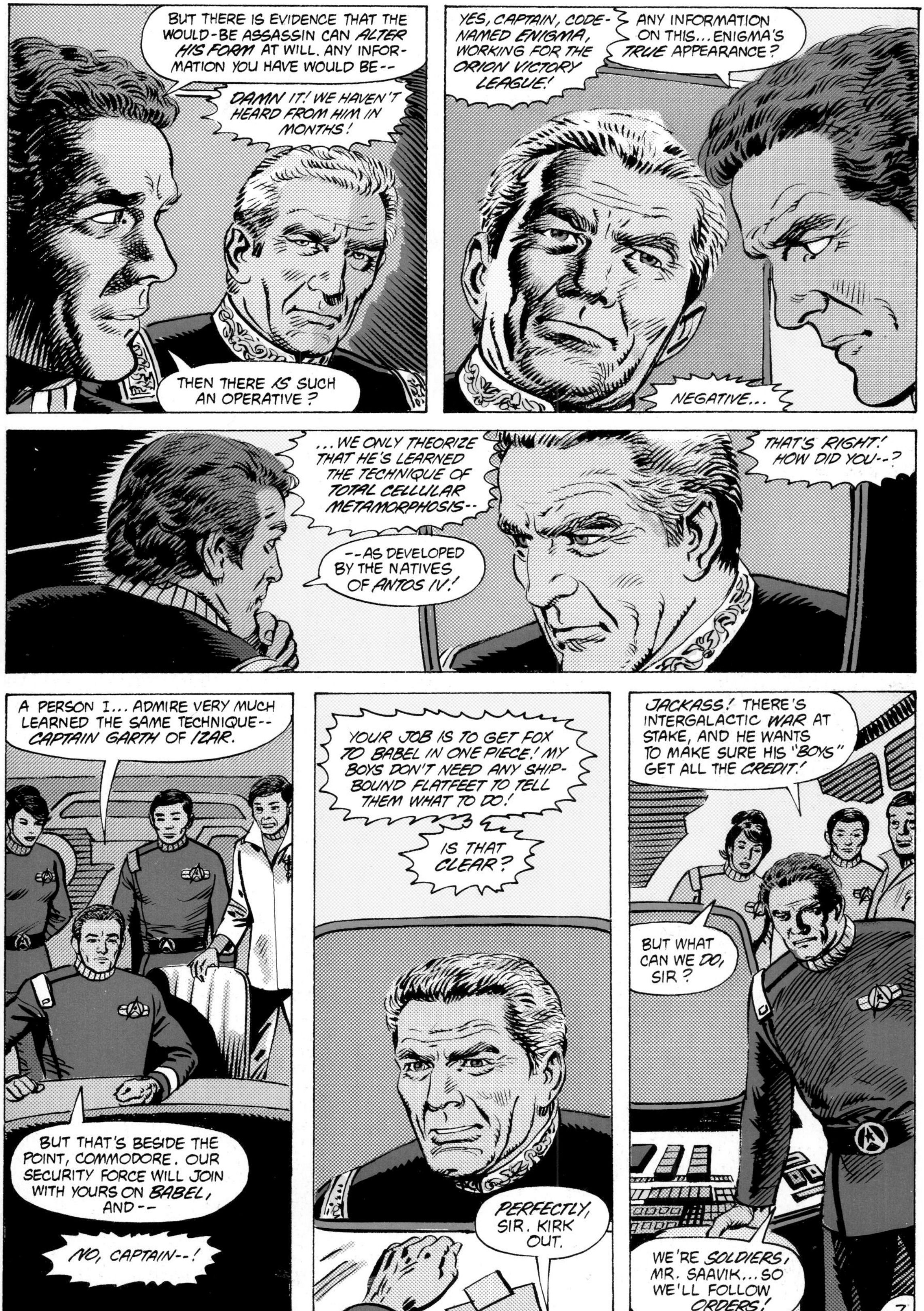
BUT THERE IS EVIDENCE THAT THE WOULD-BE ASSASSIN CAN ALTER HIS FORM AT WILL. ANY INFORMATION YOU HAVE WOULD BE--
DAMN IT! WE HAVEN'T HEARD FROM HIM IN MONTHS!
THEN THERE IS SUCH AN OPERATIVE?
YES, CAPTAIN, CODE-NAMED ENIGMA, WORKING FOR THE ORION VICTORY LEAGUE!
ANY INFORMATION ON THIS... ENIGMA'S TRUE APPEARANCE?
NEGATIVE...
...WE ONLY THEORIZE THAT HE'S LEARNED THE TECHNIQUE OF TOTAL CELLULAR METAMORPHOSIS--
--AS DEVELOPED BY THE NATIVES OF ANTOS IV!
THAT'S RIGHT! HOW DID YOU--?
A PERSON I... ADMIRE VERY MUCH LEARNED THE SAME TECHNIQUE-- CAPTAIN GARTH OF IZAR.
BUT THAT'S BESIDE THE POINT, COMMODORE. OUR SECURITY FORCE WILL JOIN WITH YOURS ON BABEL, AND--
NO, CAPTAIN--!
YOUR JOB IS TO GET FOX TO BABEL IN ONE PIECE! MY BOYS DON'T NEED ANY SHIP-BOUND FLATFEET TO TELL THEM WHAT TO DO!
IS THAT CLEAR?
PERFECTLY, SIR. KIRK OUT.
JACKASS! THERE'S INTERGALACTIC WAR AT STAKE, AND HE WANTS TO MAKE SURE HIS "BOYS" GET ALL THE CREDIT!
BUT WHAT CAN WE DO, SIR?
WE'RE SOLDIERS, MR. SAAVIK... SO WE'LL FOLLOW ORDERS!
7

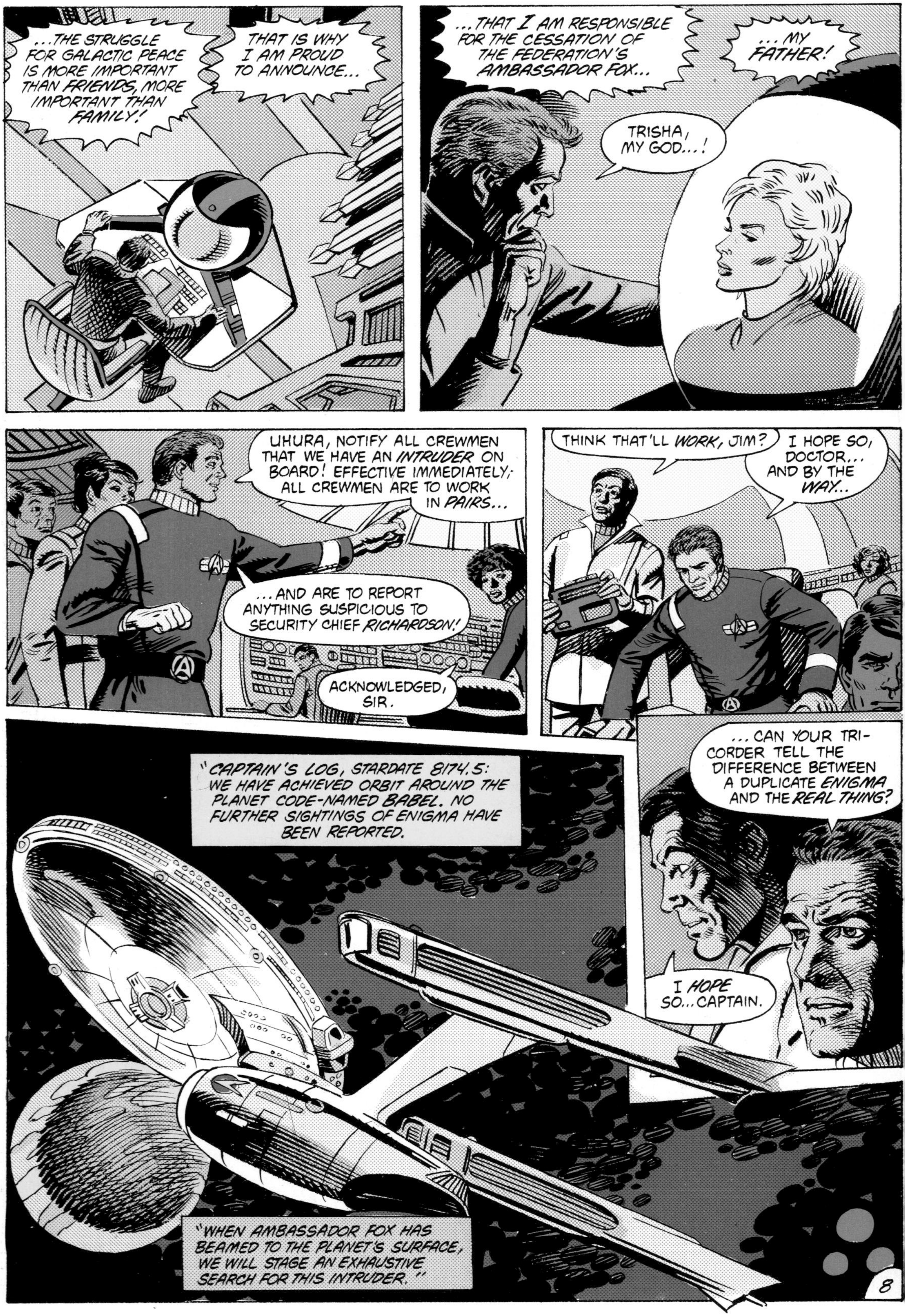

...THE STRUGGLE FOR GALACTIC PEACE IS MORE IMPORTANT THAN FRIENDS, MORE IMPORTANT THAN FAMILY!
THAT IS WHY I AM PROUD TO ANNOUNCE...
...THAT I AM RESPONSIBLE FOR THE CESSATION OF THE FEDERATION'S AMBASSADOR FOX...
...MY FATHER!
TRISHA, MY GOD...!
UHURA, NOTIFY ALL CREWMEN THAT WE HAVE AN INTRUDER ON BOARD! EFFECTIVE IMMEDIATELY, ALL CREWMEN ARE TO WORK IN PAIRS...
...AND ARE TO REPORT ANYTHING SUSPICIOUS TO SECURITY CHIEF RICHARDSON!
ACKNOWLEDGED, SIR.
THINK THAT'LL WORK, JIM?
I HOPE SO, DOCTOR... AND BY THE WAY...
...CAN YOUR TRI-CORDER TELL THE DIFFERENCE BETWEEN A DUPLICATE ENIGMA AND THE REAL THING?
I HOPE SO...CAPTAIN.
"CAPTAIN'S LOG, STARDATE 8174.5: WE HAVE ACHIEVED ORBIT AROUND THE PLANET CODE-NAMED BABEL. NO FURTHER SIGHTINGS OF ENIGMA HAVE BEEN REPORTED.
"WHEN AMBASSADOR FOX HAS BEAMED TO THE PLANET'S SURFACE, WE WILL STAGE AN EXHAUSTIVE SEARCH FOR THIS INTRUDER."

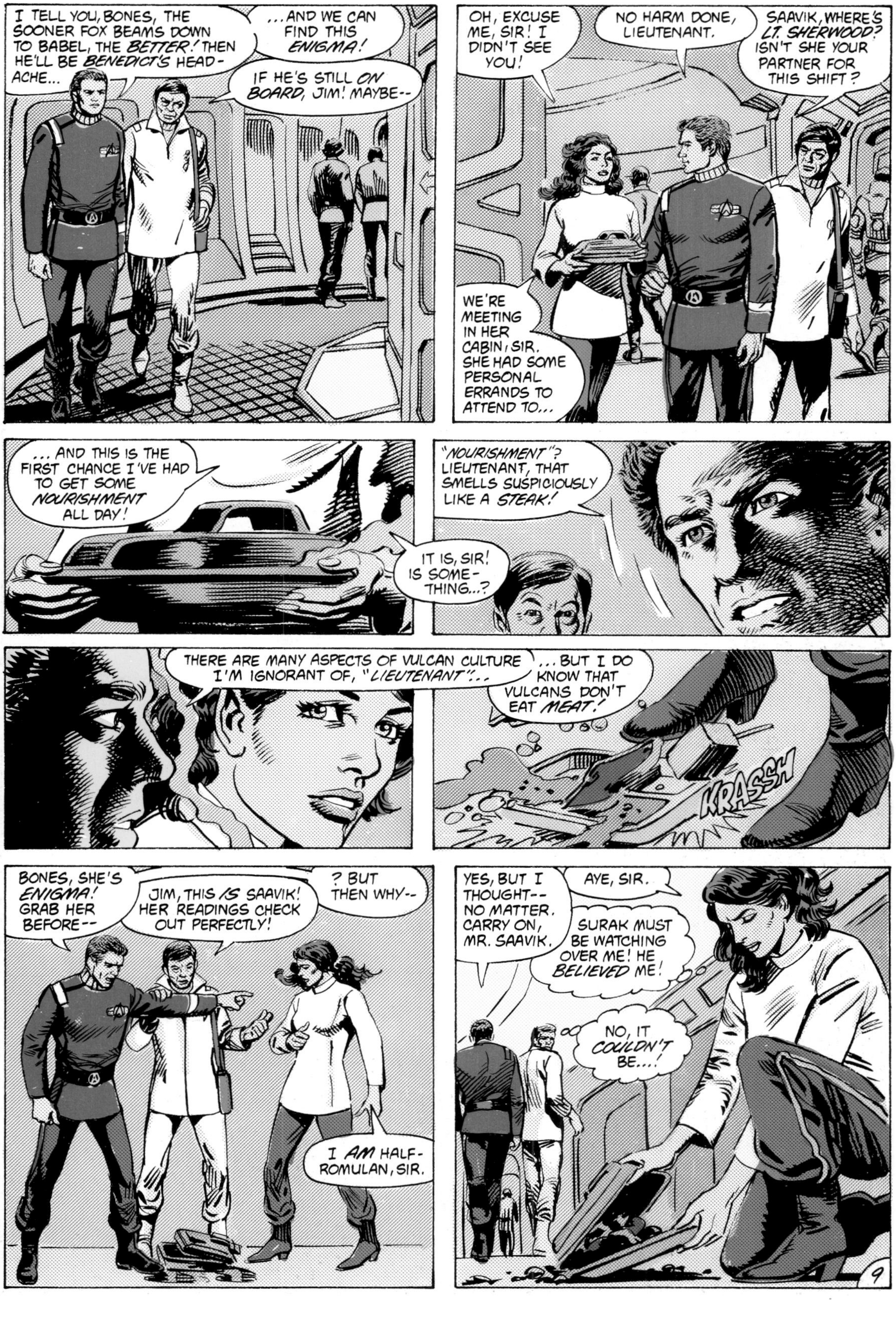
I TELL YOU, BONES, THE SOONER FOX BEAMS DOWN TO BABEL, THE BETTER! THEN HE'LL BE BENEDICT'S HEADACHE...
...AND WE CAN FIND THIS ENIGMA!
IF HE'S STILL ON BOARD, JIM! MAYBE--
OH, EXCUSE ME, SIR! I DIDN'T SEE YOU!
NO HARM DONE, LIEUTENANT.
SAAVIK, WHERE'S LT. SHERWOOD? ISN'T SHE YOUR PARTNER FOR THIS SHIFT?
WE'RE MEETING IN HER CABIN, SIR. SHE HAD SOME PERSONAL ERRANDS TO ATTEND TO...
...AND THIS IS THE FIRST CHANCE I'VE HAD TO GET SOME NOURISHMENT ALL DAY!
IT IS, SIR! IS SOMETHING...?
"NOURISHMENT"? LIEUTENANT, THAT SMELLS SUSPICIOUSLY LIKE A STEAK!
THERE ARE MANY ASPECTS OF VULCAN CULTURE I'M IGNORANT OF, "LIEUTENANT"...
...BUT I DO KNOW THAT VULCANS DON'T EAT MEAT!
KRASSH
BONES, SHE'S ENIGMA! GRAB HER BEFORE--
JIM, THIS IS SAAVIK! HER READINGS CHECK OUT PERFECTLY!
? BUT THEN WHY--
I AM HALF-ROMULAN, SIR.
YES, BUT I THOUGHT-- NO MATTER. CARRY ON, MR. SAAVIK.
AYE, SIR.
SURAK MUST BE WATCHING OVER ME! HE BELIEVED ME!
NO, IT COULDN'T BE...!

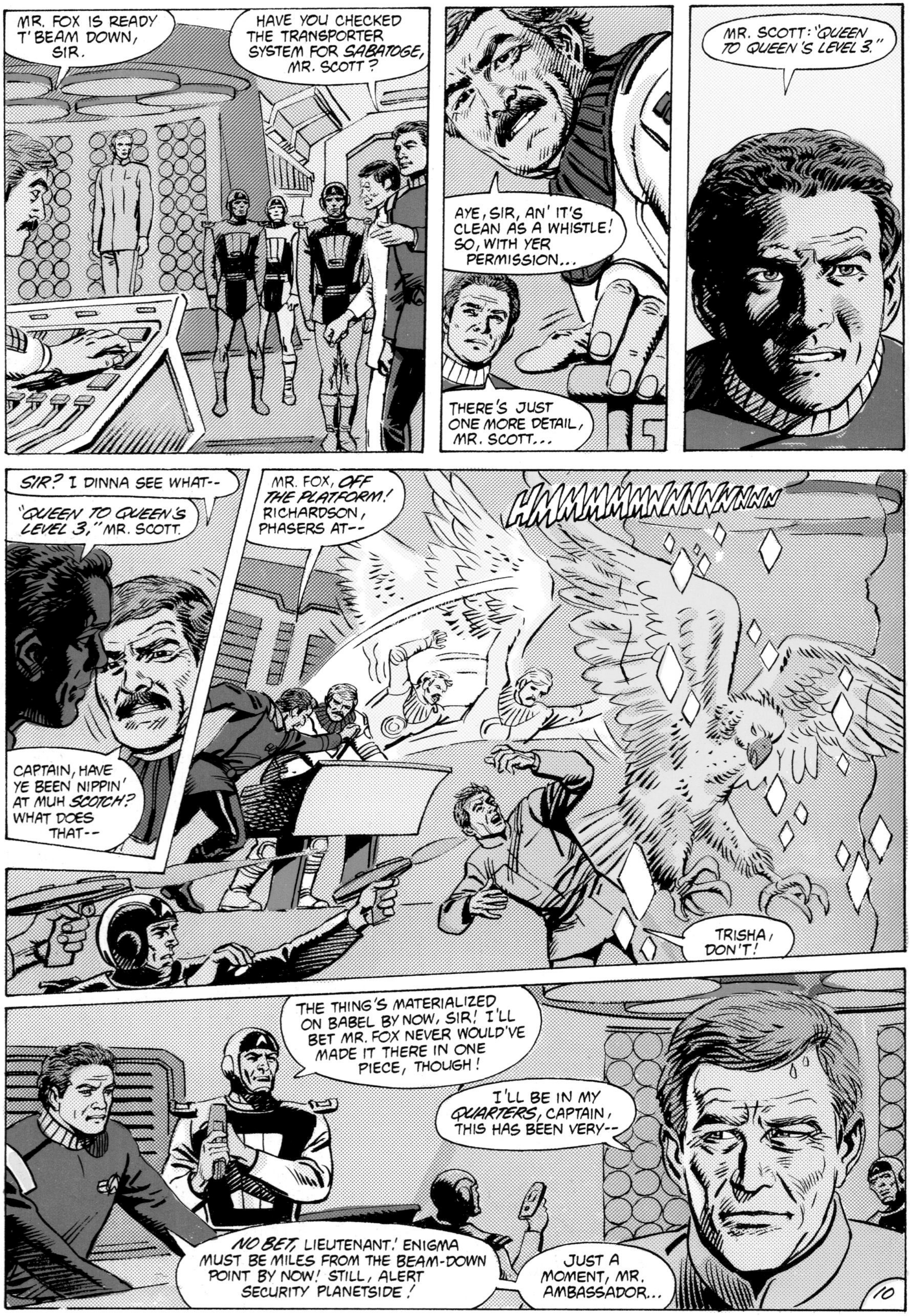

MR. FOX IS READY T' BEAM DOWN, SIR.
HAVE YOU CHECKED THE TRANSPORTER SYSTEM FOR SABATOGE, MR. SCOTT?
AYE, SIR, AN' IT'S CLEAN AS A WHISTLE! SO, WITH YER PERMISSION...
THERE'S JUST ONE MORE DETAIL, MR. SCOTT...
MR. SCOTT: "QUEEN TO QUEEN'S LEVEL 3."
SIR? I DINNA SEE WHAT--
"QUEEN TO QUEEN'S LEVEL 3," MR. SCOTT.
CAPTAIN, HAVE YE BEEN NIPPIN' AT MUH SCOTCH? WHAT DOES THAT--
MR. FOX, OFF THE PLATFORM! RICHARDSON, PHASERS AT--
HMMMMMNNNNNNNN
TRISHA, DON'T!
THE THING'S MATERIALIZED ON BABEL BY NOW, SIR! I'LL BET MR. FOX NEVER WOULD'VE MADE IT THERE IN ONE PIECE, THOUGH!
I'LL BE IN MY QUARTERS, CAPTAIN, THIS HAS BEEN VERY--
NO BET, LIEUTENANT! ENIGMA MUST BE MILES FROM THE BEAM-DOWN POINT BY NOW! STILL, ALERT SECURITY PLANETSIDE!
JUST A MOMENT, MR. AMBASSADOR...

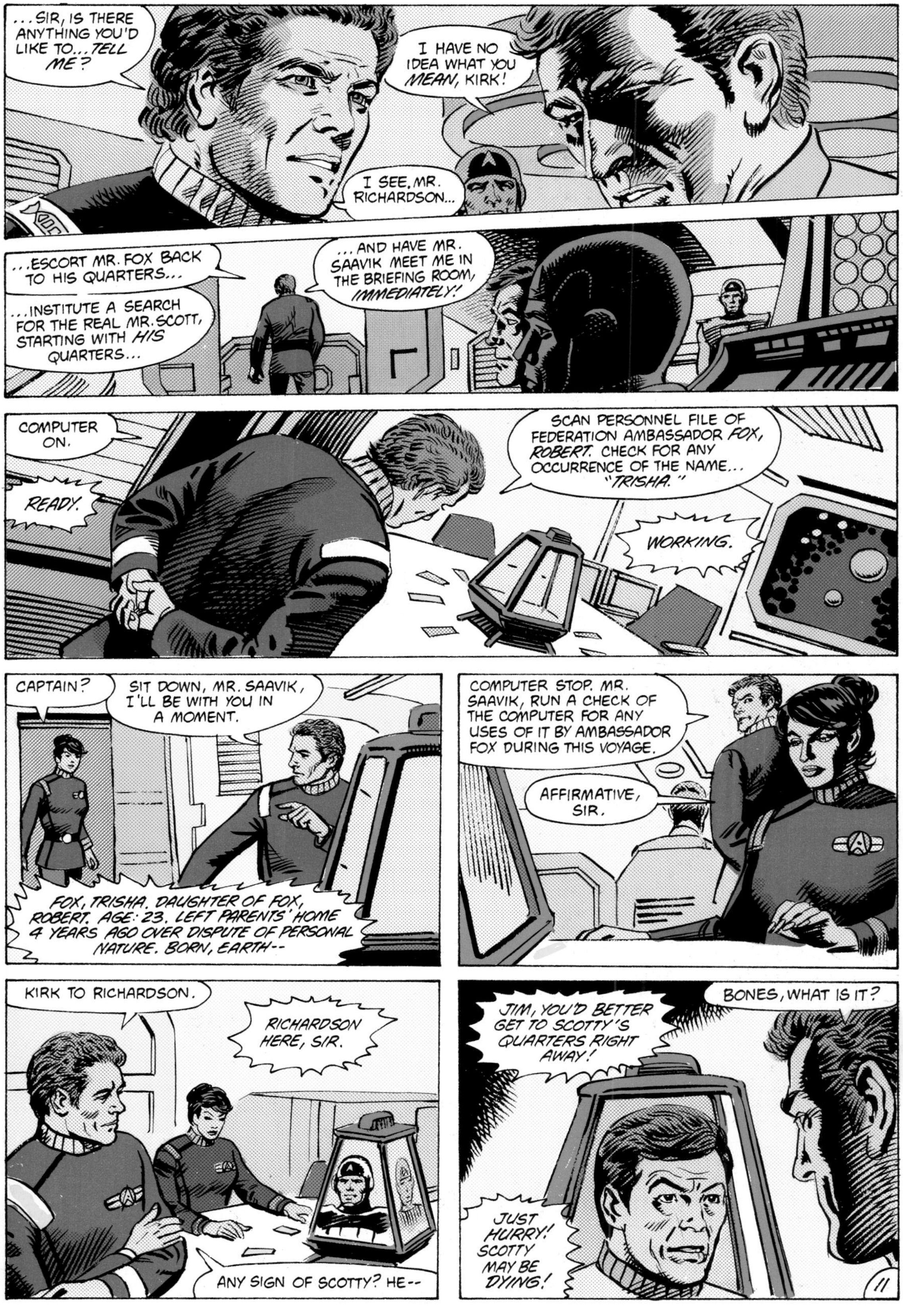

...SIR, IS THERE ANYTHING YOU'D LIKE TO... TELL ME?
I HAVE NO IDEA WHAT YOU MEAN, KIRK!
I SEE, MR. RICHARDSON...
...ESCORT MR. FOX BACK TO HIS QUARTERS...
...INSTITUTE A SEARCH FOR THE REAL MR. SCOTT, STARTING WITH HIS QUARTERS...
...AND HAVE MR. SAAVIK MEET ME IN THE BRIEFING ROOM, IMMEDIATELY!
COMPUTER ON.
READY.
SCAN PERSONNEL FILE OF FEDERATION AMBASSADOR FOX, ROBERT. CHECK FOR ANY OCCURRENCE OF THE NAME... "TRISHA."
WORKING.
CAPTAIN?
SIT DOWN, MR. SAAVIK, I'LL BE WITH YOU IN A MOMENT.
FOX, TRISHA. DAUGHTER OF FOX, ROBERT. AGE: 23. LEFT PARENTS' HOME 4 YEARS AGO OVER DISPUTE OF PERSONAL NATURE. BORN, EARTH--
COMPUTER STOP. MR. SAAVIK, RUN A CHECK OF THE COMPUTER FOR ANY USES OF IT BY AMBASSADOR FOX DURING THIS VOYAGE.
AFFIRMATIVE, SIR.
KIRK TO RICHARDSON.
RICHARDSON HERE, SIR.
ANY SIGN OF SCOTTY? HE--
BONES, WHAT IS IT?
JIM, YOU'D BETTER GET TO SCOTTY'S QUARTERS RIGHT AWAY!
JUST HURRY! SCOTTY MAY BE DYING!

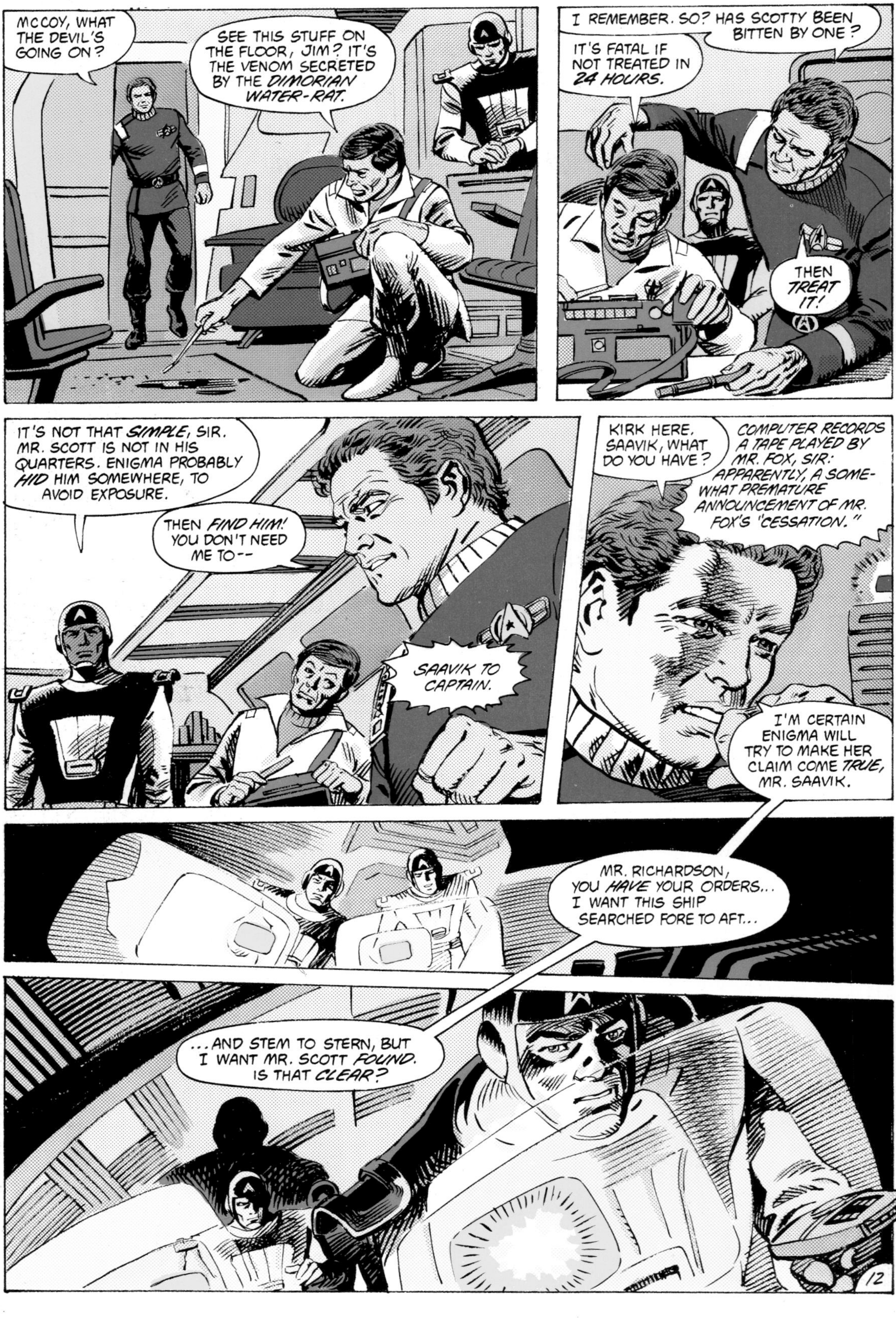
MCCOY, WHAT THE DEVIL'S GOING ON?
SEE THIS STUFF ON THE FLOOR, JIM? IT'S THE VENOM SECRETED BY THE DIMORIAN WATER-RAT.
I REMEMBER. SO? HAS SCOTTY BEEN BITTEN BY ONE?
IT'S FATAL IF NOT TREATED IN 24 HOURS.
THEN TREAT IT!
IT'S NOT THAT SIMPLE, SIR. MR. SCOTT IS NOT IN HIS QUARTERS. ENIGMA PROBABLY HID HIM SOMEWHERE, TO AVOID EXPOSURE.
THEN FIND HIM! YOU DON'T NEED ME TO--
SAAVIK TO CAPTAIN.
KIRK HERE. SAAVIK, WHAT DO YOU HAVE?
COMPUTER RECORDS A TAPE PLAYED BY MR. FOX, SIR: APPARENTLY, A SOMEWHAT PREMATURE ANNOUNCEMENT OF MR. FOX'S "CESSATION."
I'M CERTAIN ENIGMA WILL TRY TO MAKE HER CLAIM COME TRUE, MR. SAAVIK.
MR. RICHARDSON, YOU HAVE YOUR ORDERS... I WANT THIS SHIP SEARCHED FORE TO AFT...
...AND STEM TO STERN, BUT I WANT MR. SCOTT FOUND. IS THAT CLEAR?
12

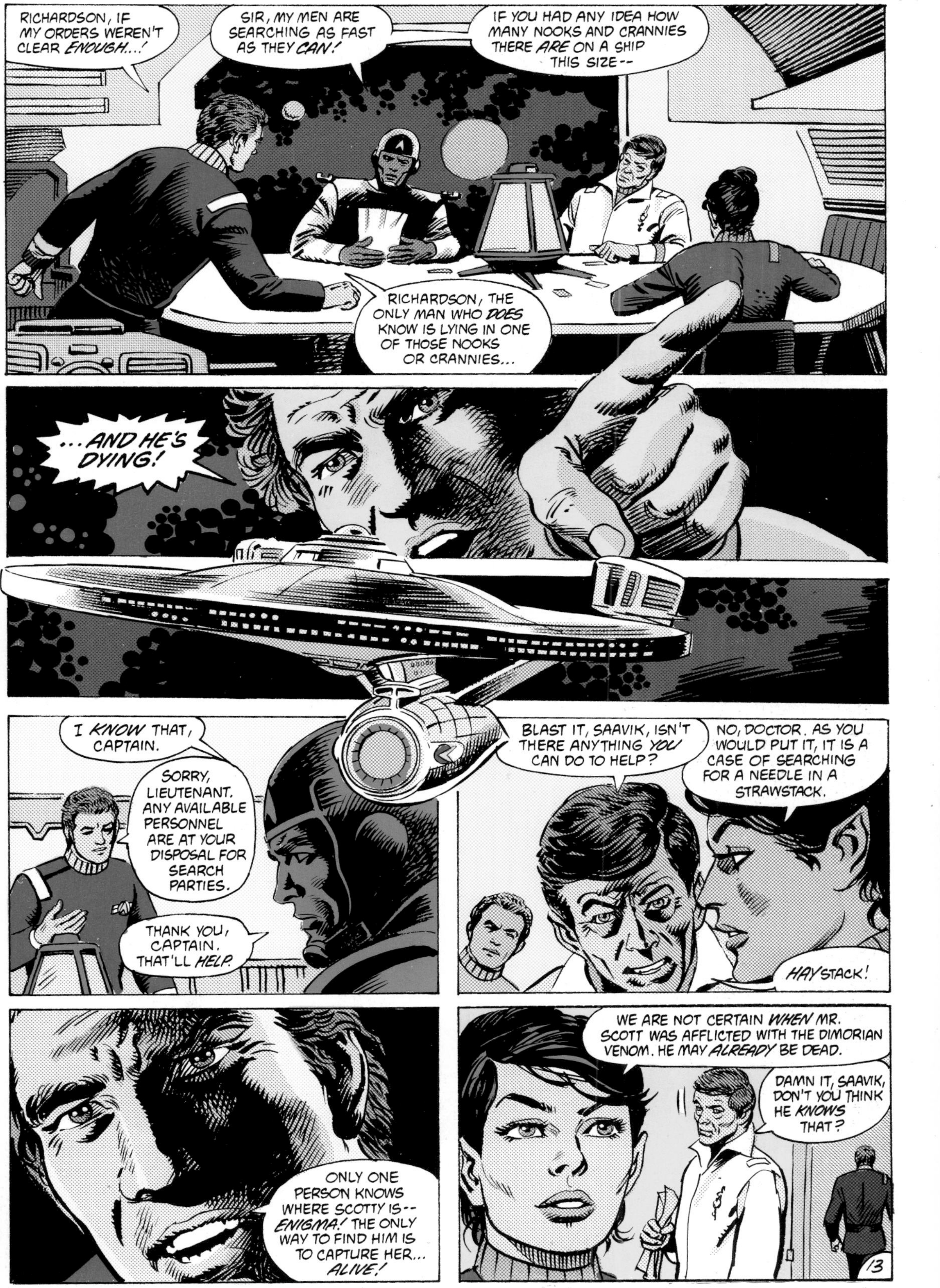
RICHARDSON, IF MY ORDERS WEREN'T CLEAR *ENOUGH...!*
SIR, MY MEN ARE SEARCHING AS FAST AS THEY *CAN!*
IF YOU HAD ANY IDEA HOW MANY NOOKS AND CRANNIES THERE *ARE* ON A SHIP THIS SIZE--
RICHARDSON, THE ONLY MAN WHO *DOES* KNOW IS LYING IN ONE OF THOSE NOOKS OR CRANNIES...
...AND HE'S DYING!
I *KNOW* THAT, CAPTAIN.
SORRY, LIEUTENANT. ANY AVAILABLE PERSONNEL ARE AT YOUR DISPOSAL FOR SEARCH PARTIES.
THANK YOU, CAPTAIN. THAT'LL *HELP.*
BLAST IT, SAAVIK, ISN'T THERE ANYTHING *YOU* CAN DO TO HELP?
NO, DOCTOR. AS YOU WOULD PUT IT, IT IS A CASE OF SEARCHING FOR A NEEDLE IN A STRAWSTACK.
*HAY*STACK!
ONLY ONE PERSON KNOWS WHERE SCOTTY IS-- *ENIGMA!* THE ONLY WAY TO FIND HIM IS TO CAPTURE HER... *ALIVE!*
WE ARE NOT CERTAIN *WHEN* MR. SCOTT WAS AFFLICTED WITH THE DIMORIAN VENOM. HE MAY *ALREADY* BE DEAD.
DAMN IT, SAAVIK, DON'T YOU THINK HE *KNOWS* THAT?
13

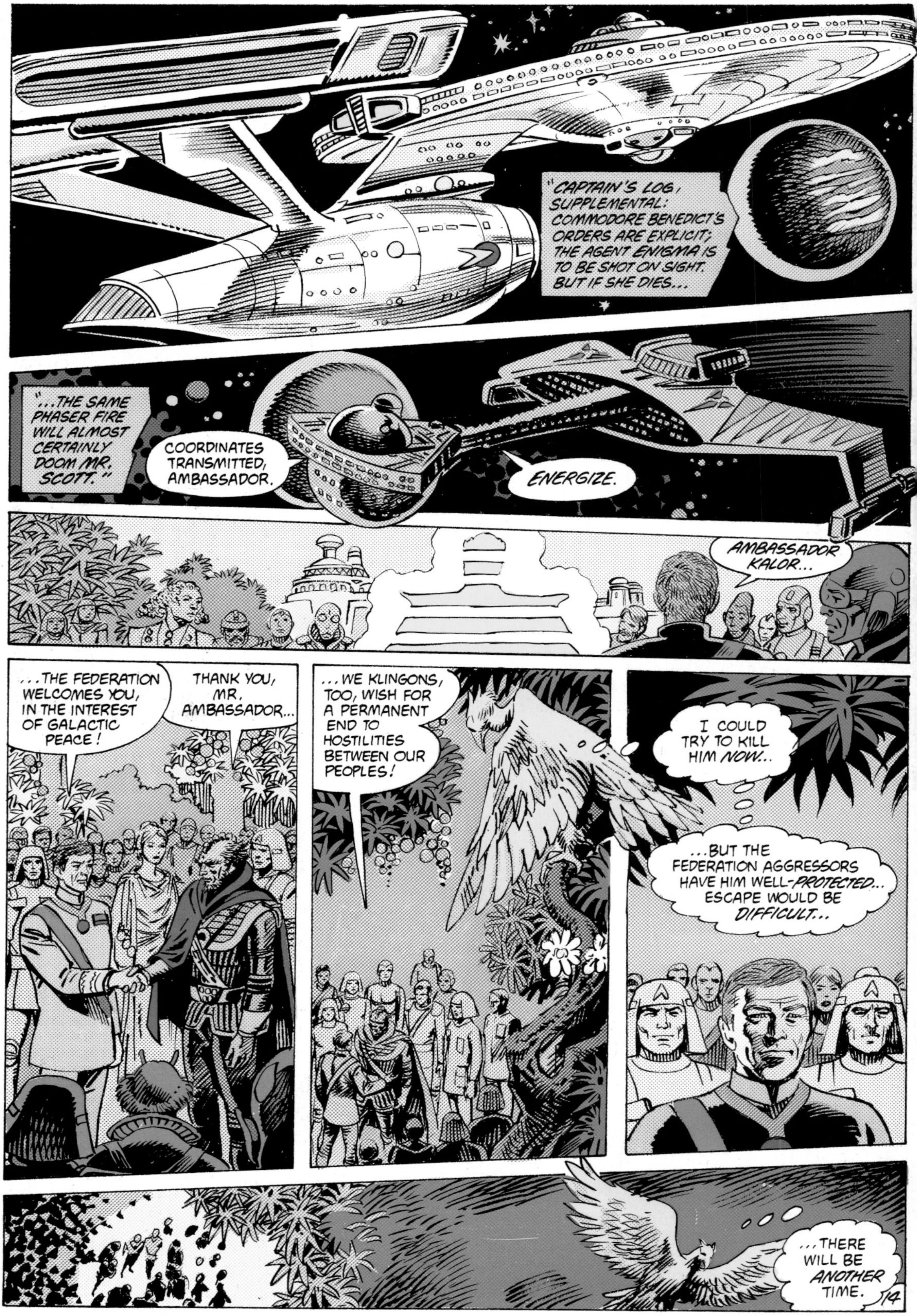
"CAPTAIN'S LOG, SUPPLEMENTAL: COMMODORE BENEDICT'S ORDERS ARE EXPLICIT; THE AGENT ENIGMA IS TO BE SHOT ON SIGHT. BUT IF SHE DIES...
"...THE SAME PHASER FIRE WILL ALMOST CERTAINLY DOOM MR. SCOTT."
COORDINATES TRANSMITTED, AMBASSADOR.
ENERGIZE.
AMBASSADOR KALOR...
...THE FEDERATION WELCOMES YOU, IN THE INTEREST OF GALACTIC PEACE!
THANK YOU, MR. AMBASSADOR...
...WE KLINGONS, TOO, WISH FOR A PERMANENT END TO HOSTILITIES BETWEEN OUR PEOPLES!
I COULD TRY TO KILL HIM NOW...
...BUT THE FEDERATION AGGRESSORS HAVE HIM WELL-PROTECTED... ESCAPE WOULD BE DIFFICULT...
...THERE WILL BE ANOTHER TIME.
14

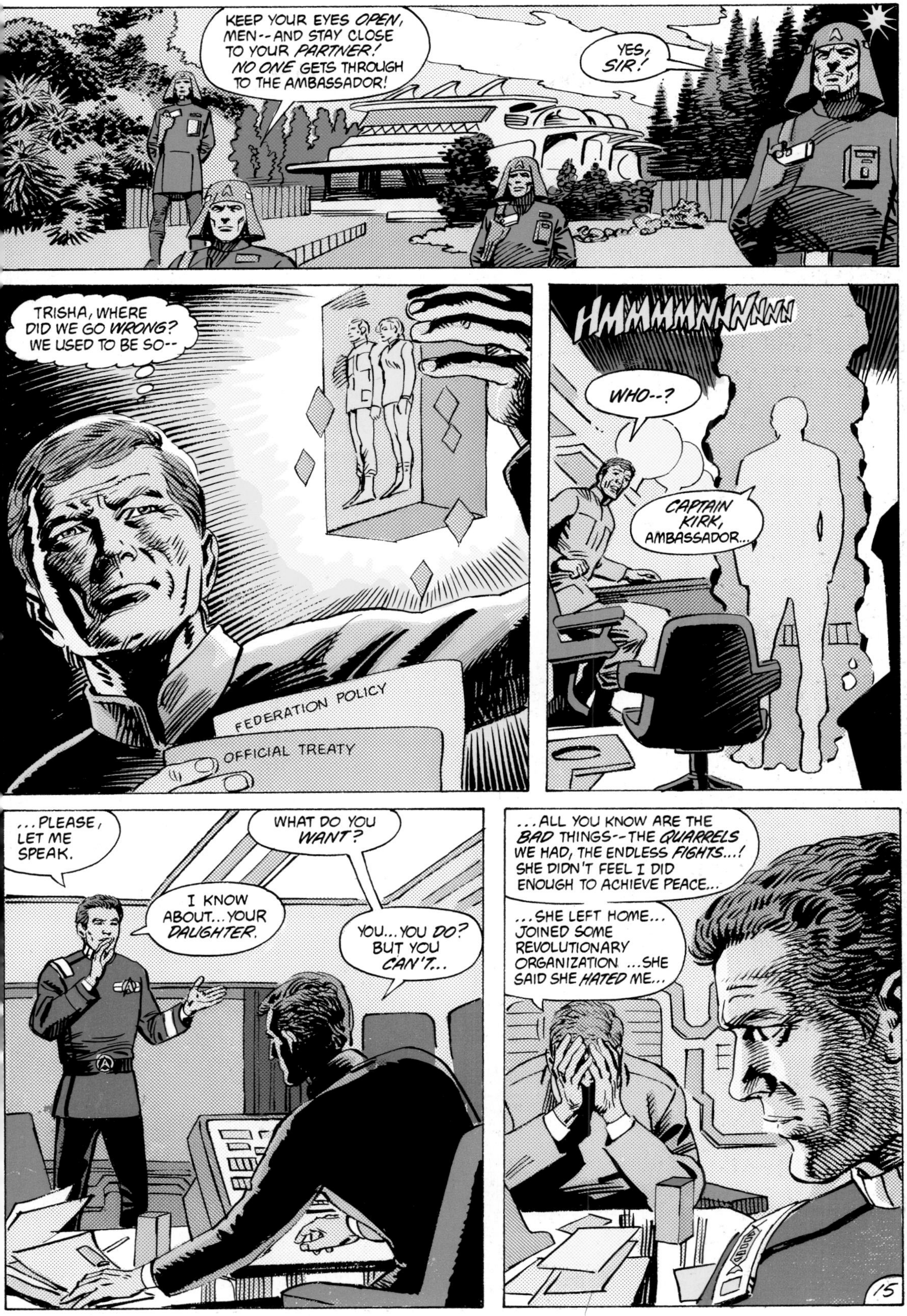
KEEP YOUR EYES OPEN, MEN--AND STAY CLOSE TO YOUR PARTNER! NO ONE GETS THROUGH TO THE AMBASSADOR!
YES, SIR!
TRISHA, WHERE DID WE GO WRONG? WE USED TO BE SO--
FEDERATION POLICY
OFFICIAL TREATY
HMMMMNNNNNN
WHO--?
CAPTAIN KIRK, AMBASSADOR...
...PLEASE, LET ME SPEAK.
WHAT DO YOU WANT?
I KNOW ABOUT... YOUR DAUGHTER.
YOU... YOU DO? BUT YOU CAN'T...
...ALL YOU KNOW ARE THE BAD THINGS--THE QUARRELS WE HAD, THE ENDLESS FIGHTS...! SHE DIDN'T FEEL I DID ENOUGH TO ACHIEVE PEACE...
...SHE LEFT HOME... JOINED SOME REVOLUTIONARY ORGANIZATION ...SHE SAID SHE HATED ME...

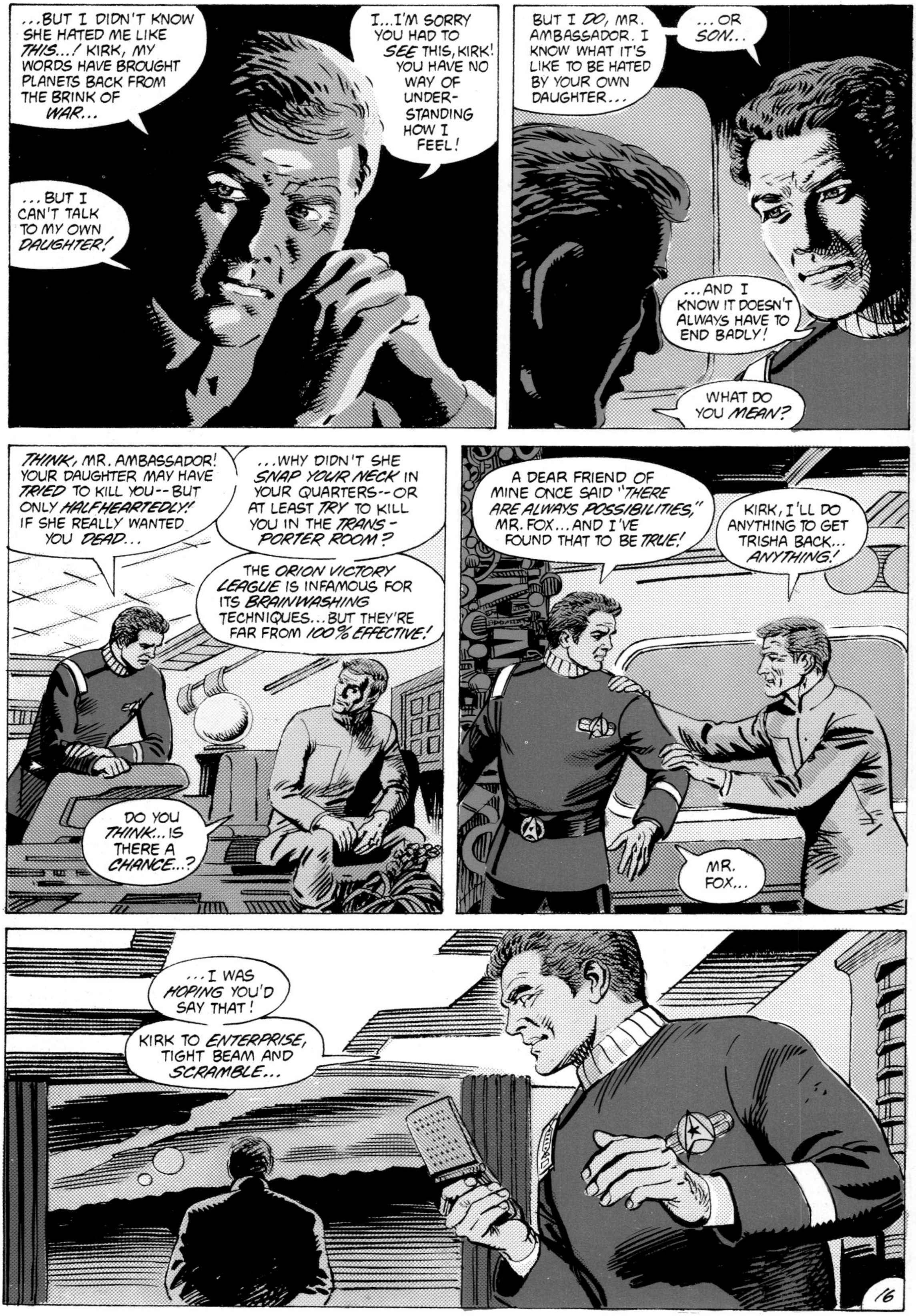
...BUT I DIDN'T KNOW SHE HATED ME LIKE THIS...! KIRK, MY WORDS HAVE BROUGHT PLANETS BACK FROM THE BRINK OF WAR...
...BUT I CAN'T TALK TO MY OWN DAUGHTER!
I...I'M SORRY YOU HAD TO SEE THIS, KIRK! YOU HAVE NO WAY OF UNDERSTANDING HOW I FEEL!
BUT I DO, MR. AMBASSADOR. I KNOW WHAT IT'S LIKE TO BE HATED BY YOUR OWN DAUGHTER...
...OR SON...
...AND I KNOW IT DOESN'T ALWAYS HAVE TO END BADLY!
WHAT DO YOU MEAN?
THINK, MR. AMBASSADOR! YOUR DAUGHTER MAY HAVE TRIED TO KILL YOU--BUT ONLY HALFHEARTEDLY! IF SHE REALLY WANTED YOU DEAD...
...WHY DIDN'T SHE SNAP YOUR NECK IN YOUR QUARTERS--OR AT LEAST TRY TO KILL YOU IN THE TRANSPORTER ROOM?
THE ORION VICTORY LEAGUE IS INFAMOUS FOR ITS BRAINWASHING TECHNIQUES...BUT THEY'RE FAR FROM 100% EFFECTIVE!
DO YOU THINK...IS THERE A CHANCE...?
A DEAR FRIEND OF MINE ONCE SAID "THERE ARE ALWAYS POSSIBILITIES," MR. FOX...AND I'VE FOUND THAT TO BE TRUE!
KIRK, I'LL DO ANYTHING TO GET TRISHA BACK... ANYTHING!
MR. FOX...
...I WAS HOPING YOU'D SAY THAT!
KIRK TO ENTERPRISE, TIGHT BEAM AND SCRAMBLE...
16

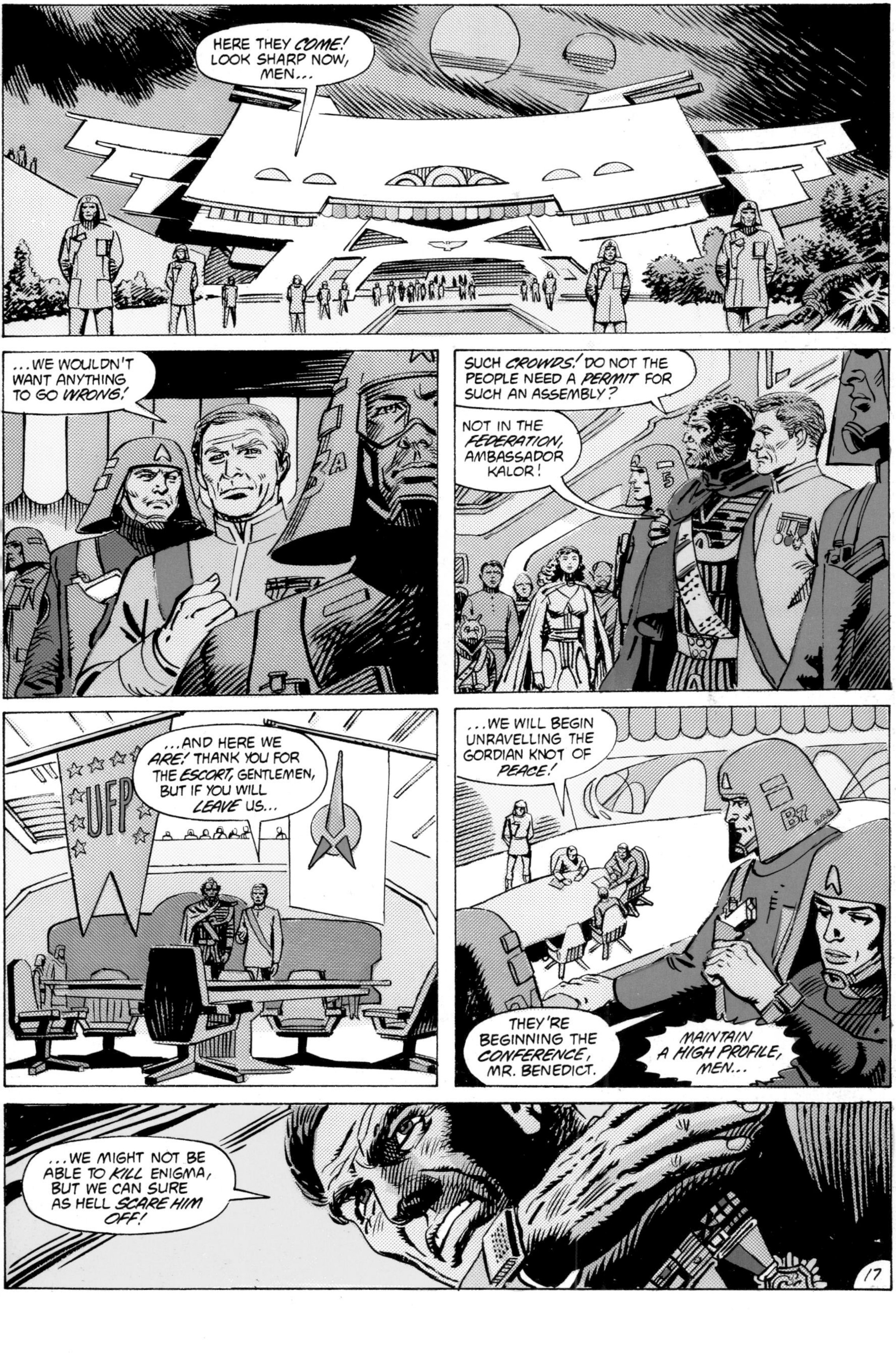
HERE THEY COME! LOOK SHARP NOW, MEN...
...WE WOULDN'T WANT ANYTHING TO GO WRONG!
SUCH CROWDS! DO NOT THE PEOPLE NEED A PERMIT FOR SUCH AN ASSEMBLY?
NOT IN THE FEDERATION, AMBASSADOR KALOR!
UFP
...AND HERE WE ARE! THANK YOU FOR THE ESCORT, GENTLEMEN, BUT IF YOU WILL LEAVE US...
...WE WILL BEGIN UNRAVELLING THE GORDIAN KNOT OF PEACE!
THEY'RE BEGINNING THE CONFERENCE, MR. BENEDICT.
MAINTAIN A HIGH PROFILE, MEN...
...WE MIGHT NOT BE ABLE TO KILL ENIGMA, BUT WE CAN SURE AS HELL SCARE HIM OFF!

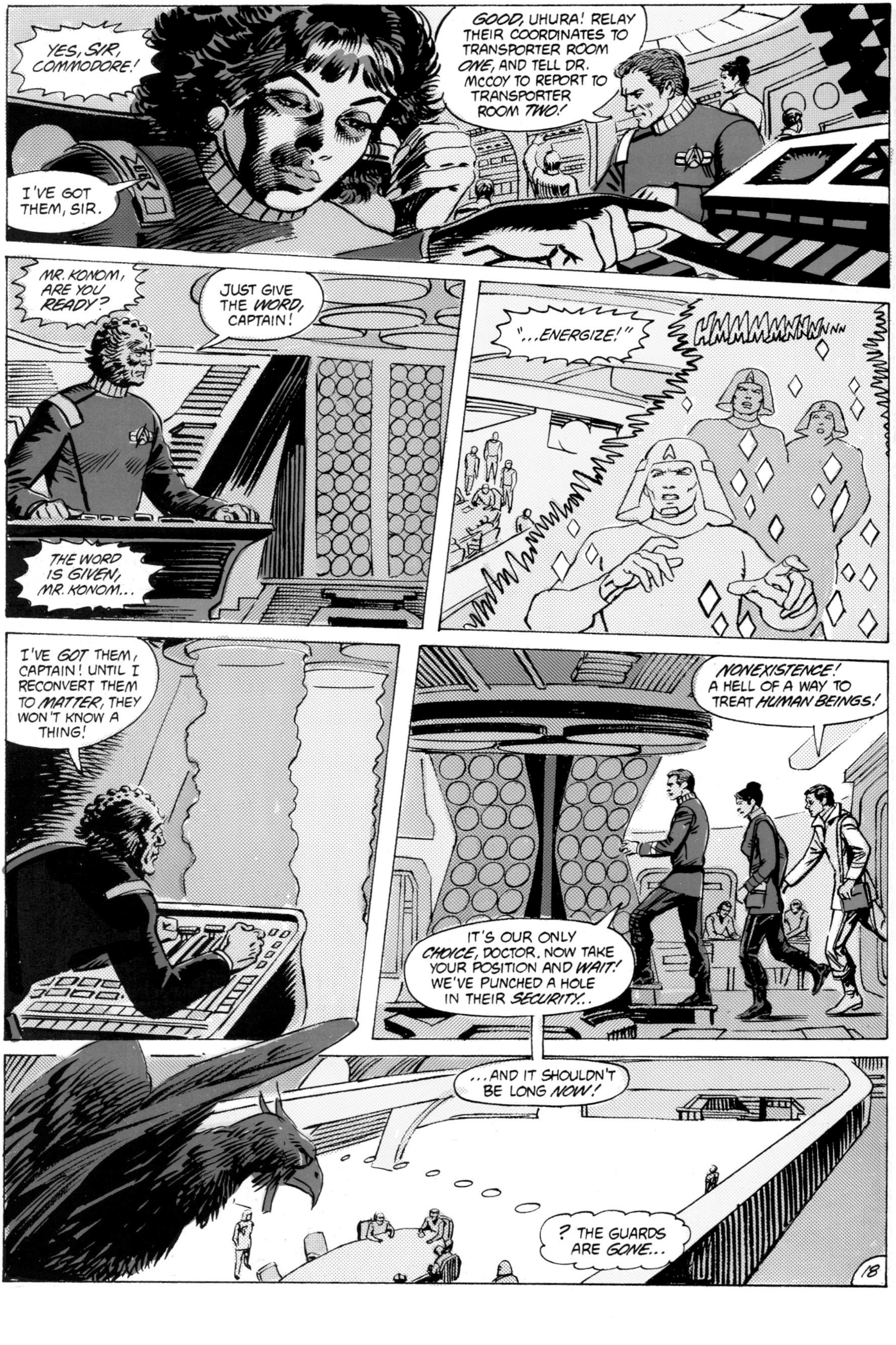
YES, SIR, COMMODORE!
I'VE GOT THEM, SIR.
GOOD, UHURA! RELAY THEIR COORDINATES TO TRANSPORTER ROOM ONE, AND TELL DR. McCOY TO REPORT TO TRANSPORTER ROOM TWO!
MR. KONOM, ARE YOU READY?
JUST GIVE THE WORD, CAPTAIN!
THE WORD IS GIVEN, MR. KONOM...
"...ENERGIZE!"
HMMMMMNNNNNNN
I'VE GOT THEM, CAPTAIN! UNTIL I RECONVERT THEM TO MATTER, THEY WON'T KNOW A THING!
NONEXISTENCE! A HELL OF A WAY TO TREAT HUMAN BEINGS!
IT'S OUR ONLY CHOICE, DOCTOR. NOW TAKE YOUR POSITION AND WAIT! WE'VE PUNCHED A HOLE IN THEIR SECURITY...
...AND IT SHOULDN'T BE LONG NOW!
? THE GUARDS ARE GONE...

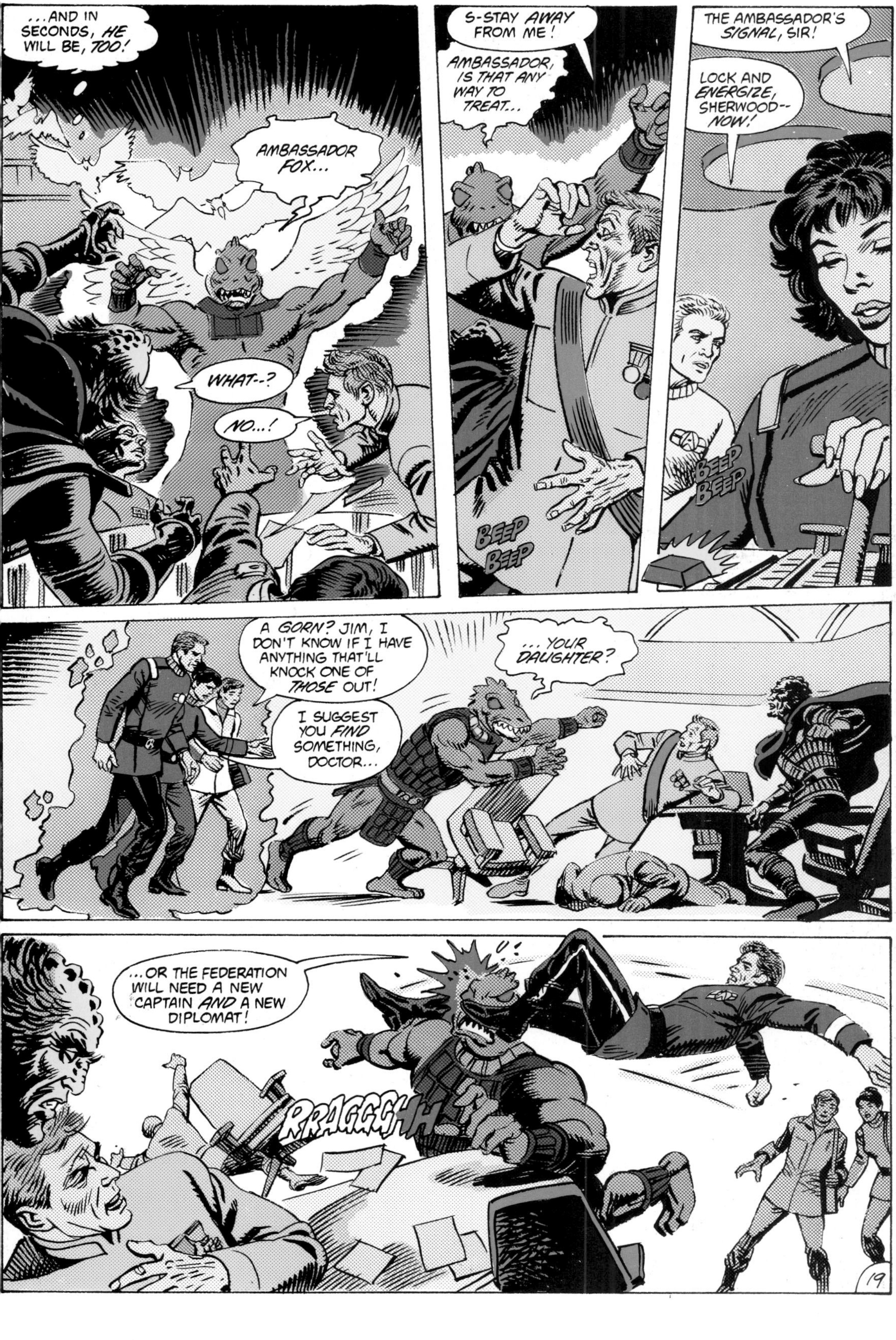
...AND IN SECONDS, HE WILL BE, TOO!
AMBASSADOR FOX...
WHAT--?
NO...!
S-STAY AWAY FROM ME!
AMBASSADOR, IS THAT ANY WAY TO TREAT...
BEEP BEEP
THE AMBASSADOR'S SIGNAL, SIR!
LOCK AND ENERGIZE, SHERWOOD-- NOW!
BEEP BEEP
A GORN? JIM, I DON'T KNOW IF I HAVE ANYTHING THAT'LL KNOCK ONE OF THOSE OUT!
I SUGGEST YOU FIND SOMETHING, DOCTOR...
...YOUR DAUGHTER?
...OR THE FEDERATION WILL NEED A NEW CAPTAIN AND A NEW DIPLOMAT!
RRAGGGHH

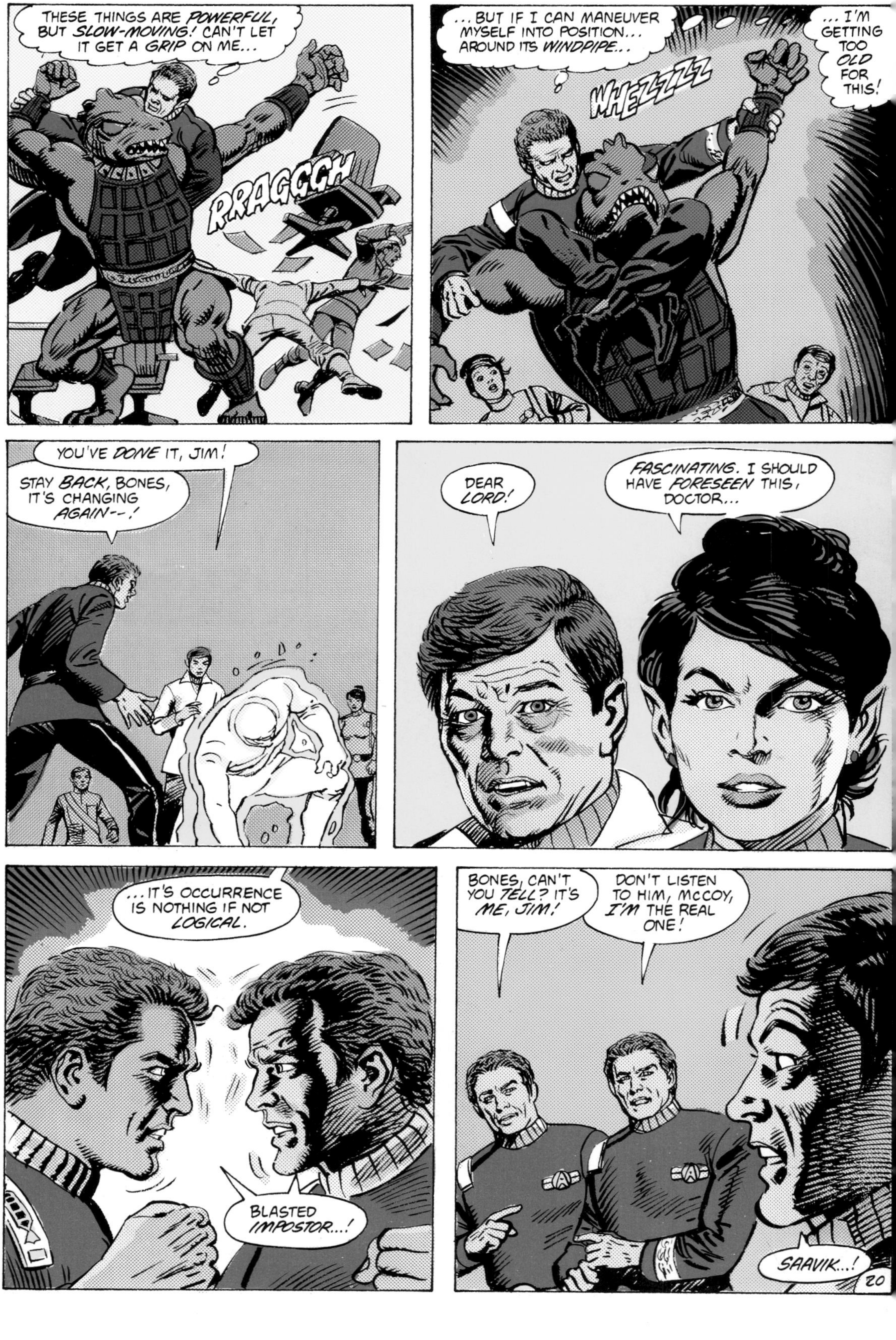
THESE THINGS ARE POWERFUL, BUT SLOW-MOVING! CAN'T LET IT GET A GRIP ON ME...
RRAGGGH
...BUT IF I CAN MANEUVER MYSELF INTO POSITION... AROUND ITS WINDPIPE...
WHEZZZZZ
...I'M GETTING TOO OLD FOR THIS!
YOU'VE DONE IT, JIM!
STAY BACK, BONES, IT'S CHANGING AGAIN--!
DEAR LORD!
FASCINATING. I SHOULD HAVE FORESEEN THIS, DOCTOR...
...IT'S OCCURRENCE IS NOTHING IF NOT LOGICAL.
BLASTED IMPOSTOR...!
BONES, CAN'T YOU TELL? IT'S ME, JIM!
DON'T LISTEN TO HIM, McCOY, I'M THE REAL ONE!
SAAVIK...!

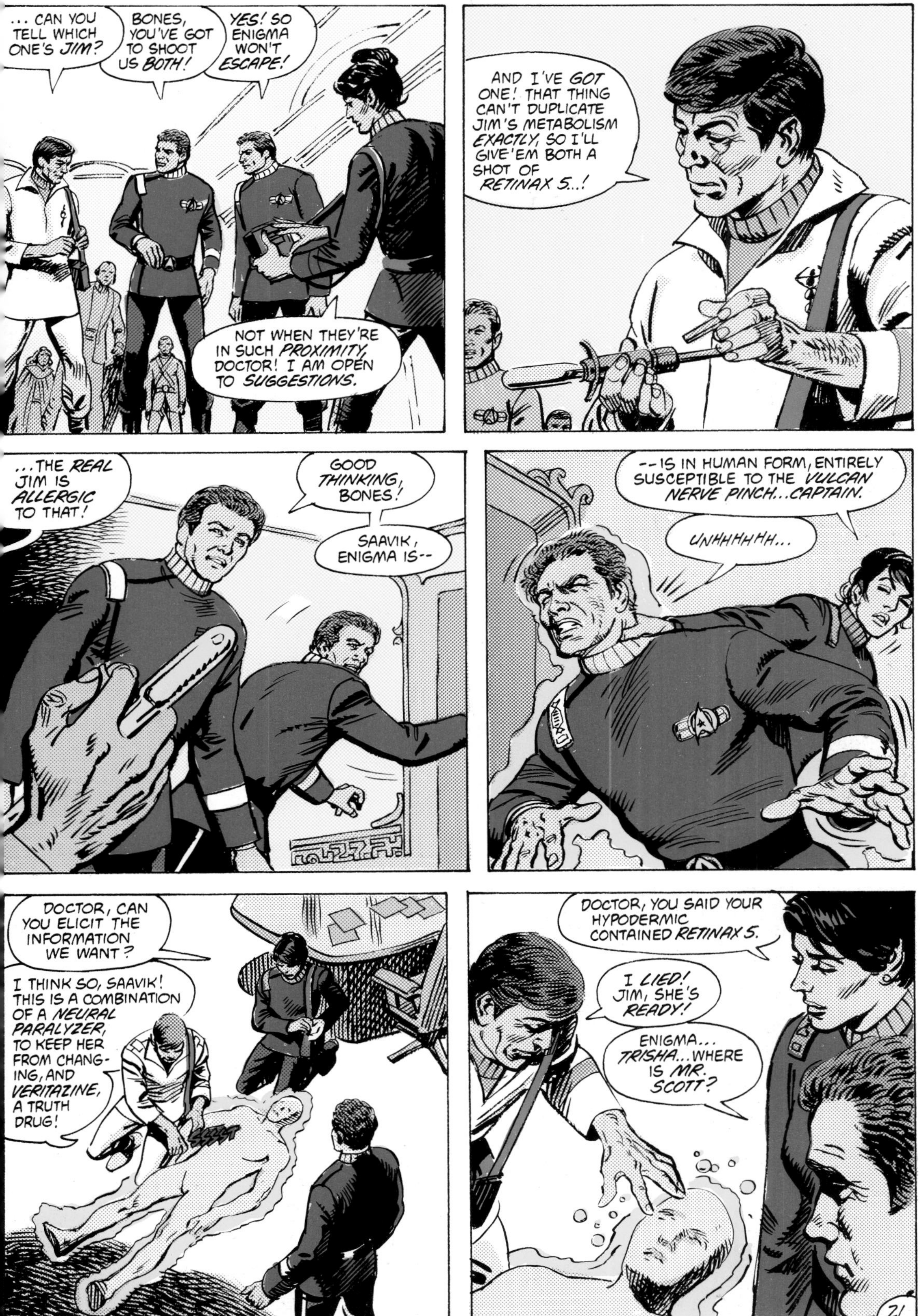

... CAN YOU TELL WHICH ONE'S JIM?
BONES, YOU'VE GOT TO SHOOT US BOTH!
YES! SO ENIGMA WON'T ESCAPE!
NOT WHEN THEY'RE IN SUCH PROXIMITY, DOCTOR! I AM OPEN TO SUGGESTIONS.
AND I'VE GOT ONE! THAT THING CAN'T DUPLICATE JIM'S METABOLISM EXACTLY, SO I'LL GIVE'EM BOTH A SHOT OF RETINAX 5...!
...THE REAL JIM IS ALLERGIC TO THAT!
GOOD THINKING, BONES!
SAAVIK, ENIGMA IS--
--IS IN HUMAN FORM, ENTIRELY SUSCEPTIBLE TO THE VULCAN NERVE PINCH...CAPTAIN.
UNHHHHHH...
DOCTOR, CAN YOU ELICIT THE INFORMATION WE WANT?
I THINK SO, SAAVIK! THIS IS A COMBINATION OF A NEURAL PARALYZER, TO KEEP HER FROM CHANGING, AND VERITAZINE, A TRUTH DRUG!
DOCTOR, YOU SAID YOUR HYPODERMIC CONTAINED RETINAX 5.
I LIED! JIM, SHE'S READY!
ENIGMA... TRISHA... WHERE IS MR. SCOTT?

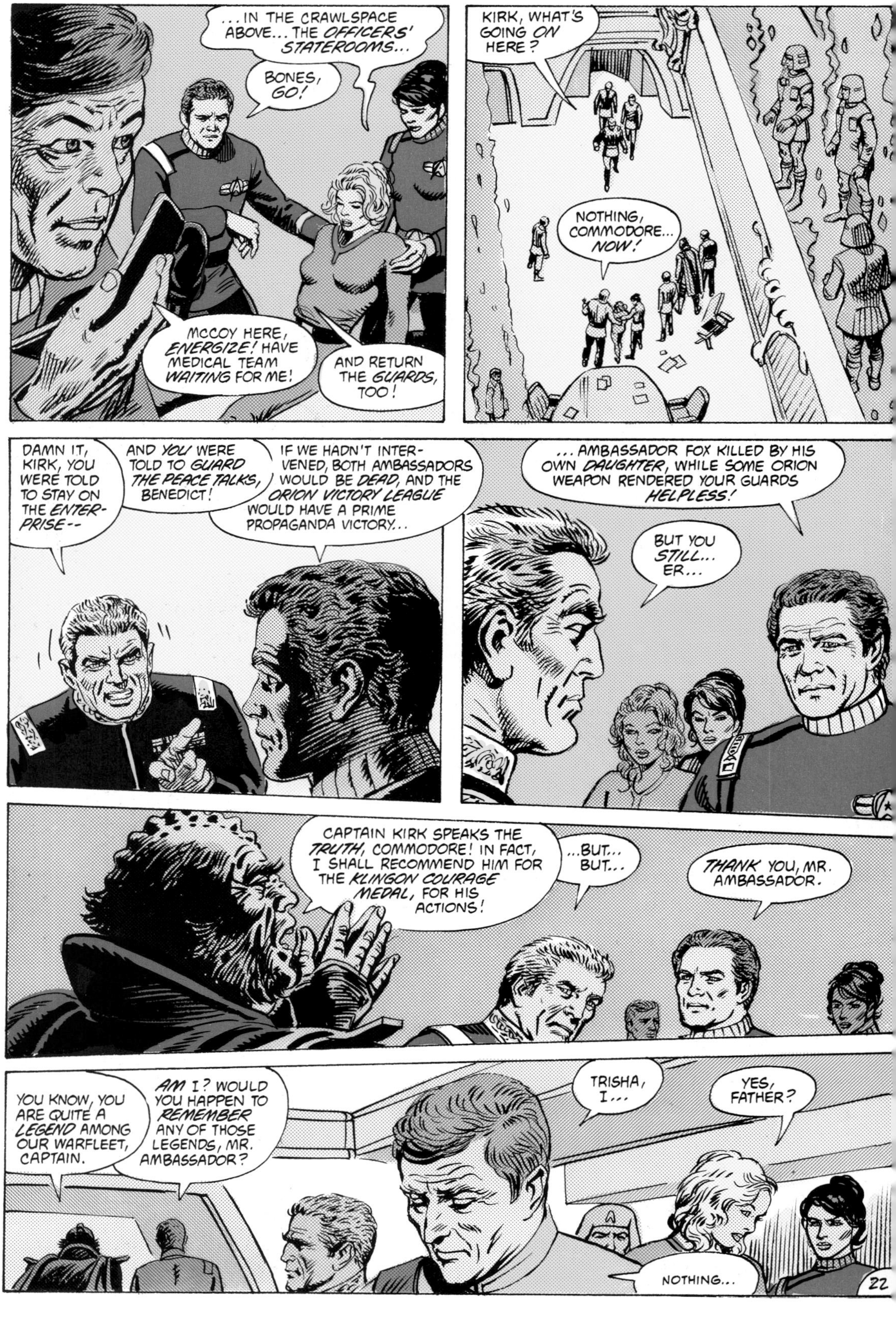
...IN THE CRAWLSPACE ABOVE... THE OFFICERS' STATEROOMS...
BONES, GO!
McCOY HERE, ENERGIZE! HAVE MEDICAL TEAM WAITING FOR ME!
AND RETURN THE GUARDS, TOO!
KIRK, WHAT'S GOING ON HERE?
NOTHING, COMMODORE... NOW!
DAMN IT, KIRK, YOU WERE TOLD TO STAY ON THE ENTER-PRISE--
AND YOU WERE TOLD TO GUARD THE PEACE TALKS, BENEDICT!
IF WE HADN'T INTER-VENED, BOTH AMBASSADORS WOULD BE DEAD, AND THE ORION VICTORY LEAGUE WOULD HAVE A PRIME PROPAGANDA VICTORY...
...AMBASSADOR FOX KILLED BY HIS OWN DAUGHTER, WHILE SOME ORION WEAPON RENDERED YOUR GUARDS HELPLESS!
BUT YOU STILL... ER...
CAPTAIN KIRK SPEAKS THE TRUTH, COMMODORE! IN FACT, I SHALL RECOMMEND HIM FOR THE KLINGON COURAGE MEDAL, FOR HIS ACTIONS!
...BUT... BUT...
THANK YOU, MR. AMBASSADOR.
YOU KNOW, YOU ARE QUITE A LEGEND AMONG OUR WARFLEET, CAPTAIN.
AM I? WOULD YOU HAPPEN TO REMEMBER ANY OF THOSE LEGENDS, MR. AMBASSADOR?
TRISHA, I...
YES, FATHER?
NOTHING...

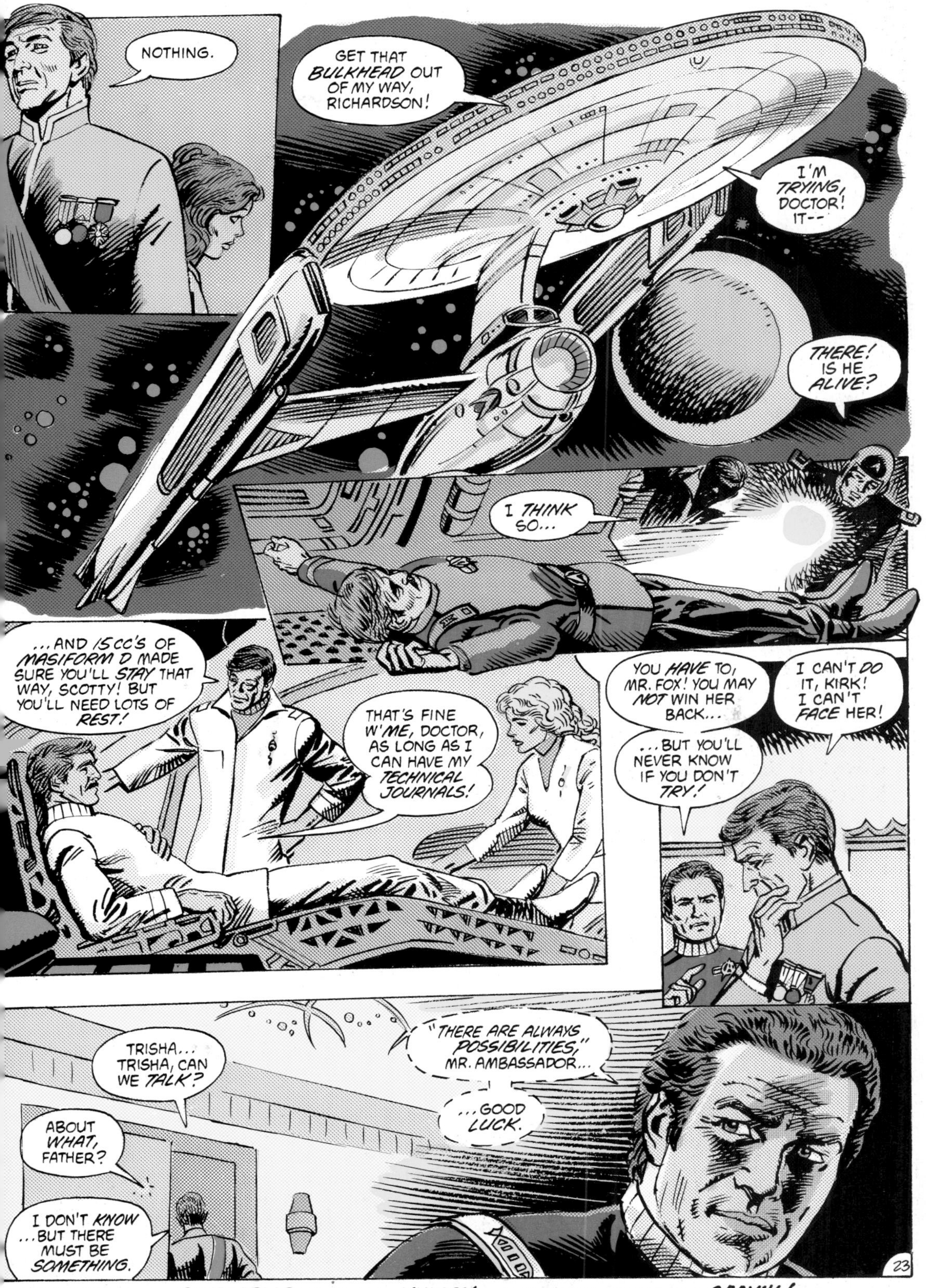
NOTHING.
GET THAT BULKHEAD OUT OF MY WAY, RICHARDSON!
I'M TRYING, DOCTOR! IT--
THERE! IS HE ALIVE?
I THINK SO...
...AND 15CC'S OF MASIFORM D MADE SURE YOU'LL STAY THAT WAY, SCOTTY! BUT YOU'LL NEED LOTS OF REST!
THAT'S FINE W'ME, DOCTOR, AS LONG AS I CAN HAVE MY TECHNICAL JOURNALS!
YOU HAVE TO, MR. FOX! YOU MAY NOT WIN HER BACK...
I CAN'T DO IT, KIRK! I CAN'T FACE HER!
...BUT YOU'LL NEVER KNOW IF YOU DON'T TRY!
TRISHA... TRISHA, CAN WE TALK?
"THERE ARE ALWAYS POSSIBILITIES," MR. AMBASSADOR...
...GOOD LUCK.
ABOUT WHAT, FATHER?
I DON'T KNOW ...BUT THERE MUST BE SOMETHING.

NEXT ISSUE: THE ENTERPRISE RETURNS TO VULCAN... TO LEARN THE TRUTH ABOUT SAAVIK!
(PLUS: A CERTAIN POINTY-EARED GUEST STAR!)

MEMOIRS OF A FIRST FIRST-GENERATION TREKKIE

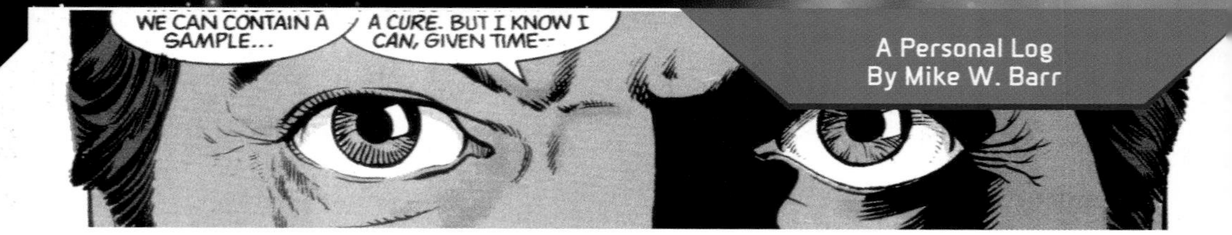
WE CAN CONTAIN A SAMPLE...
A CURE. BUT I KNOW I CAN, GIVEN TIME--

A Personal Log
By Mike W. Barr

Everyone of age 30 or above remembers where they were on November 22, 1963 (and if you're younger than 30, *ask* someone), but, to many, the date September 8, 1966, is equally memorable – and for a much happier reason.

On that latter date, the television series *Star Trek* premiered on NBC TV. Being a tube-carrying member in good standing of the 'TV generation' (though I also carried a library card as well, and used it often), I had heard of the show through network promotion and decided to give it a look. Decided? *Compelled* would be a better word, for though I was not – and am not – a voracious science fiction reader, I was already, at the tender age of 14, a lifetime addict of action-adventure stories in any medium, and this new thing looked like it might be of interest.

So there I was, on that September night, sitting before the old RCA Victor black and white console (affectionately referred to as "Old Ironsides," because to move it was a major undertaking), watching this new show, this… er… *Star Trek*. One hour later, I had seen the first episode and found it good. I would, I thought, as I skittered into my jammies and downed my cookies and milk, be back for the second episode, next week.

Little did I know that I had just made a lifetime commitment. Over the ensuing months I made the acquaintance of the *Enterprise* crew and found that I liked them, lots. This Captain Kirk was a little stuffy, but he had what it took in a crisis, and he was really a good guy, underneath it all. Mr Spock and Dr McCoy were both good second-bananas, but they were also strong characters in their own rights, and more. The structure of *Star Trek* was such that each of the major characters (Kirk, Spock, McCoy) complemented the others, giving each a dimension we never would have seen, had we been introduced to them individually. This, of course, is called *characterisation*, and *Star Trek* was my introduction to it in a TV series.

So, yeah, I was hooked. And beyond the major characters, there were good secondary characters, and beyond *them*, there was a visually interesting, more-or-less consistent *universe* (that is, a background concept

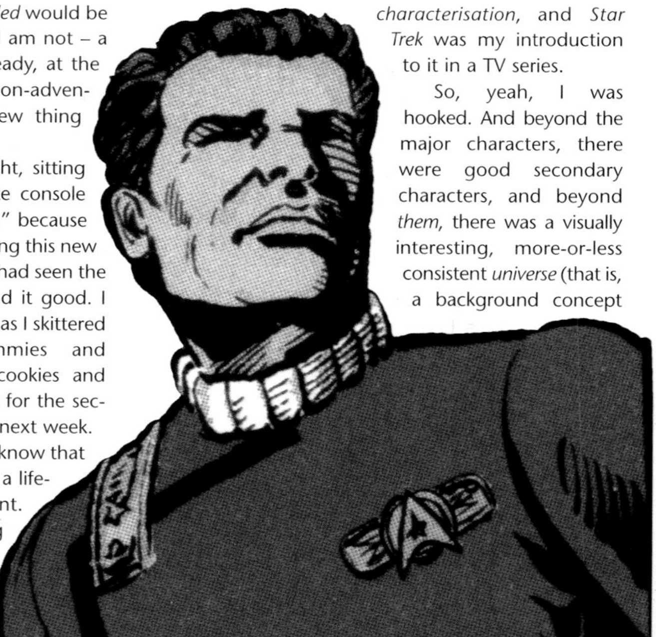

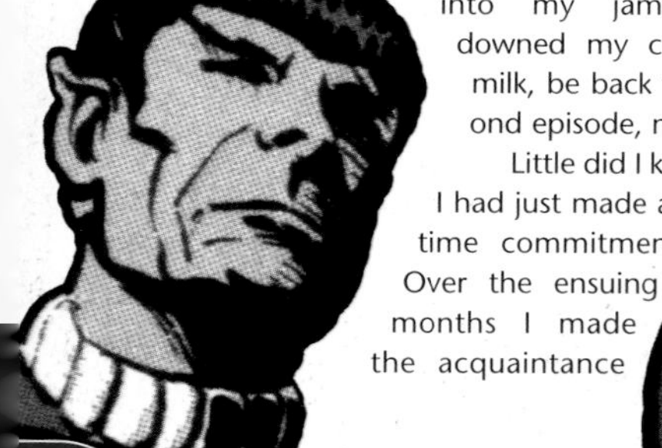

for the show) that I found – and find – consistently compelling. Most of the TV shows I grew up on hold little, if any, interest for me nowadays, but I can watch a rerun – or a re-rerun – of one of my favourite *Star Trek*s and enjoy it just as much as I ever did, perhaps more. The merits of the show are such that they overcome the flaws that erupted occasionally in stories and in production.

And apparently, millions of other people were watching, too, because *Star Trek* lasted three seasons before it was cancelled. Or, to quote the late John Belushi from *Saturday Night Live*'s affectionate *Trek* take-off, "Except for one television network, we have found intelligence everywhere in the galaxy."

(But even in what seemed to be its death throes, *Star Trek* went out in style. The last new episode filmed, 'Turnabout Intruder', was pre-empted by the death of President Eisenhower – I haven't voted Republican since – and was telecast only when the third season was in summer reruns. So the last *Star Trek* telecast was a *new* one, which certainly seemed fitting.)

But *Trek* did look, nonetheless, dead, Jim. Viewers older than myself had for years been mourning the death of what they called "The Golden Age of Television." Now, I joined them...

...Until the series went into syndication, when a strange thing happened. *Star Trek* became more popular than ever, spawning several new generations of Trekkies, and continued commercial interest in the show. Merchandising was stronger than ever, and finally *Star Trek* returned, as a Saturday morning animated (that means *cartoon*) show. Its heart was certainly in the right place, and if you closed your eyes while watching it, the nostalgia was eerily overwhelming. But it wasn't quite the same, and for years *Trek* remained dormant. (For a more detailed history, see Gene Roddenberry's *The Making of Star Trek: The Motion Picture.*)

Then came *Star Trek: The Motion Picture* (hey, *I* liked it!), a second comic book version (the less said about the first, the better), and finally, *Star Trek II – The Wrath of Khan*. A man named Marv Wolfman, whose career wasn't going much of anywhere at the time, saw *Khan*, and suggested, strongly, that DC Comics do another version of *Trek*. "What, *another?*" most people said, and they had a point. But that's where I came in. I convinced Marv to let me write the book (photographic negatives will last a long time, if stored in a cool, dark place), and Marv agreed. With conditions.

"Don't be bound by the television format," said Marv (who by now wanted to be called "Admiral Wolfman"), "take the characters, the concepts, but do *comic book stories*, with comic book pacing, sub-plots, even continued stories. That," he intoned, dramatically, "is your Prime Directive. Beam me up, Scotty."

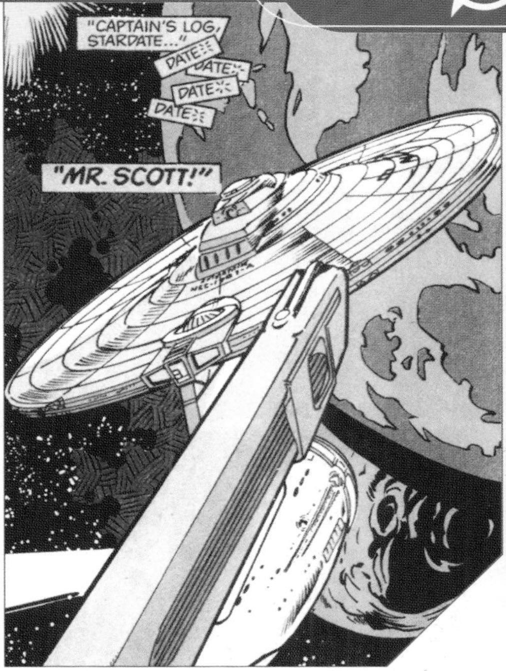
"CAPTAIN'S LOG, STARDATE..."
DATE
DATE
DATE
DATE
"MR. SCOTT!"

But we needed an artist. I suggested Tom Sutton, who had collaborated with me on a science fiction story for one of DC's mystery books years back, but I was told he was too busy. We continued to search, until a High Official of DC tripped me in the hall one day. "We got you a great artist," he said, his voice excited.

"Great," I said, applying a spray bandage to my knee. "Who?"

"Tom Sutton! Aren't you glad we thought of him?" Recalling Mr Spock's patience with the diplomats in 'The Mark of Gideon', I agreed...

Which brings up what is, to me, the most interesting thing about DC's *Star Trek* – Mr Spock, I mean. Since we're beginning our series directly after the ending of the second movie, Mr Spock will not be found on these pages. He is, as far as we're concerned, still on the Genesis planet, awaiting the third movie, and whatever they choose to do with him – if anything.

This makes DC's *Star Trek* unique in that it is the first time the series has ever been done without "that pointy-eared Vulcan." This creates several new ripples in the pool of our continuing characters that we hope you'll find as interesting as we do. And remember, even the many new *Trek* novels now being released still feature Spock, so this book is the only place you'll be able to go to follow the *current* voyages of the Starship *Enterprise*.

We await your comments, of course. Live long and prosper, huh? And a wormhole full of thanks to our own Allan Asherman and Paramount's Edward Egan.

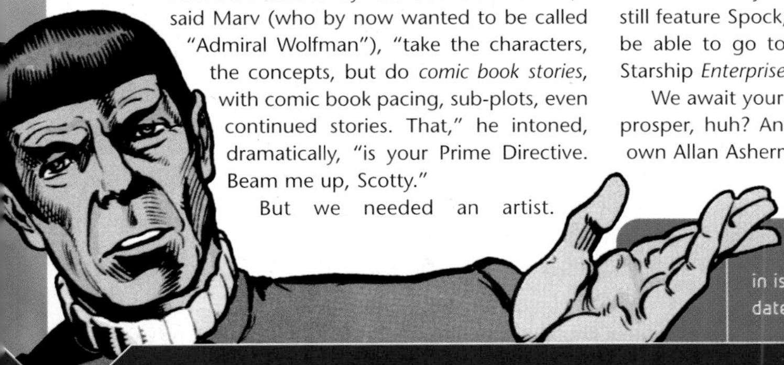

This afterword was originally printed in issue #1 of DC's *Star Trek* series, cover dated February 1984.

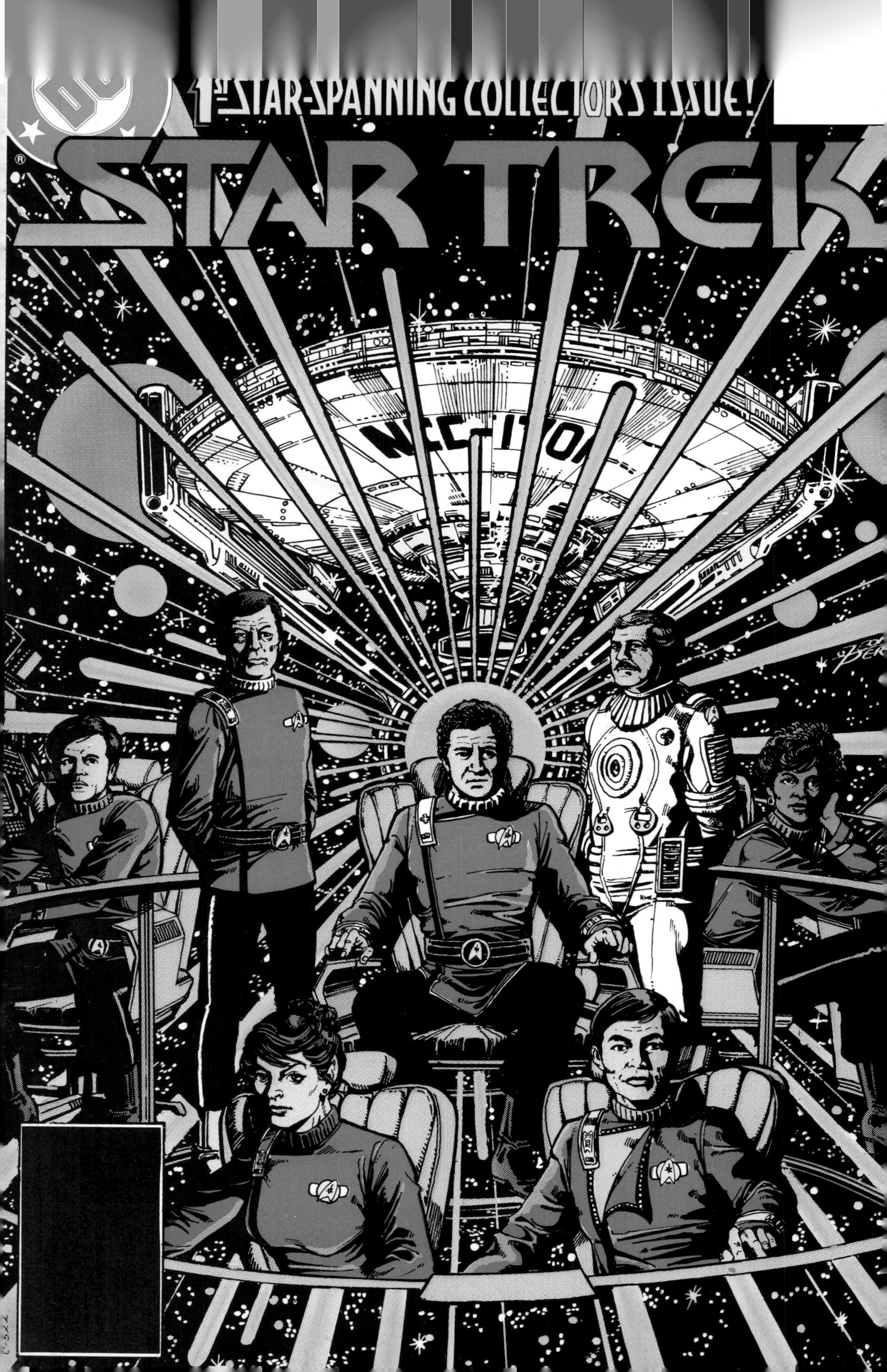
1st STAR-SPANNING COLLECTOR'S ISSUE!
STAR TREK

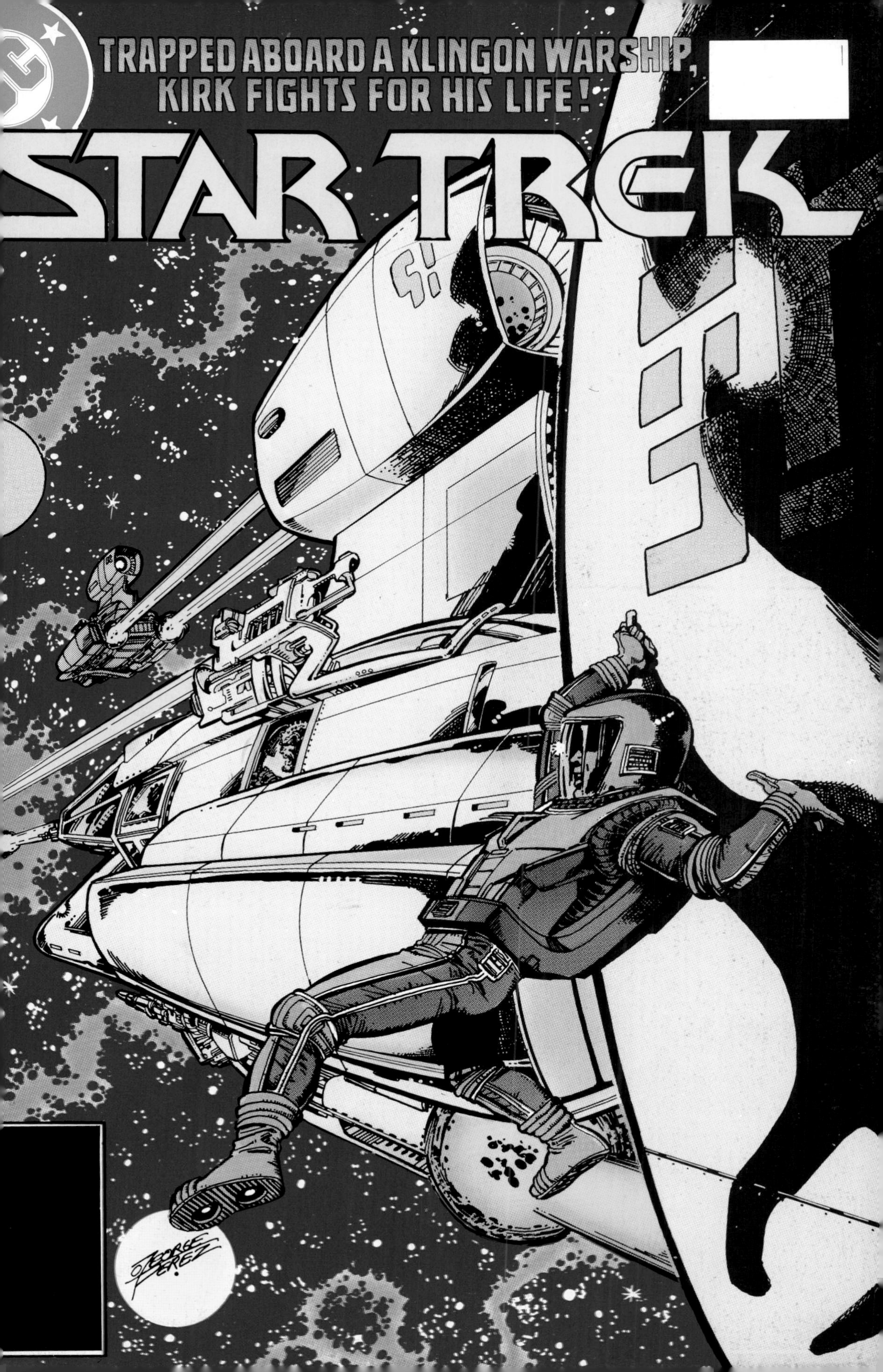
TRAPPED ABOARD A KLINGON WARSHIP, KIRK FIGHTS FOR HIS LIFE!
STAR TREK
GEORGE PEREZ

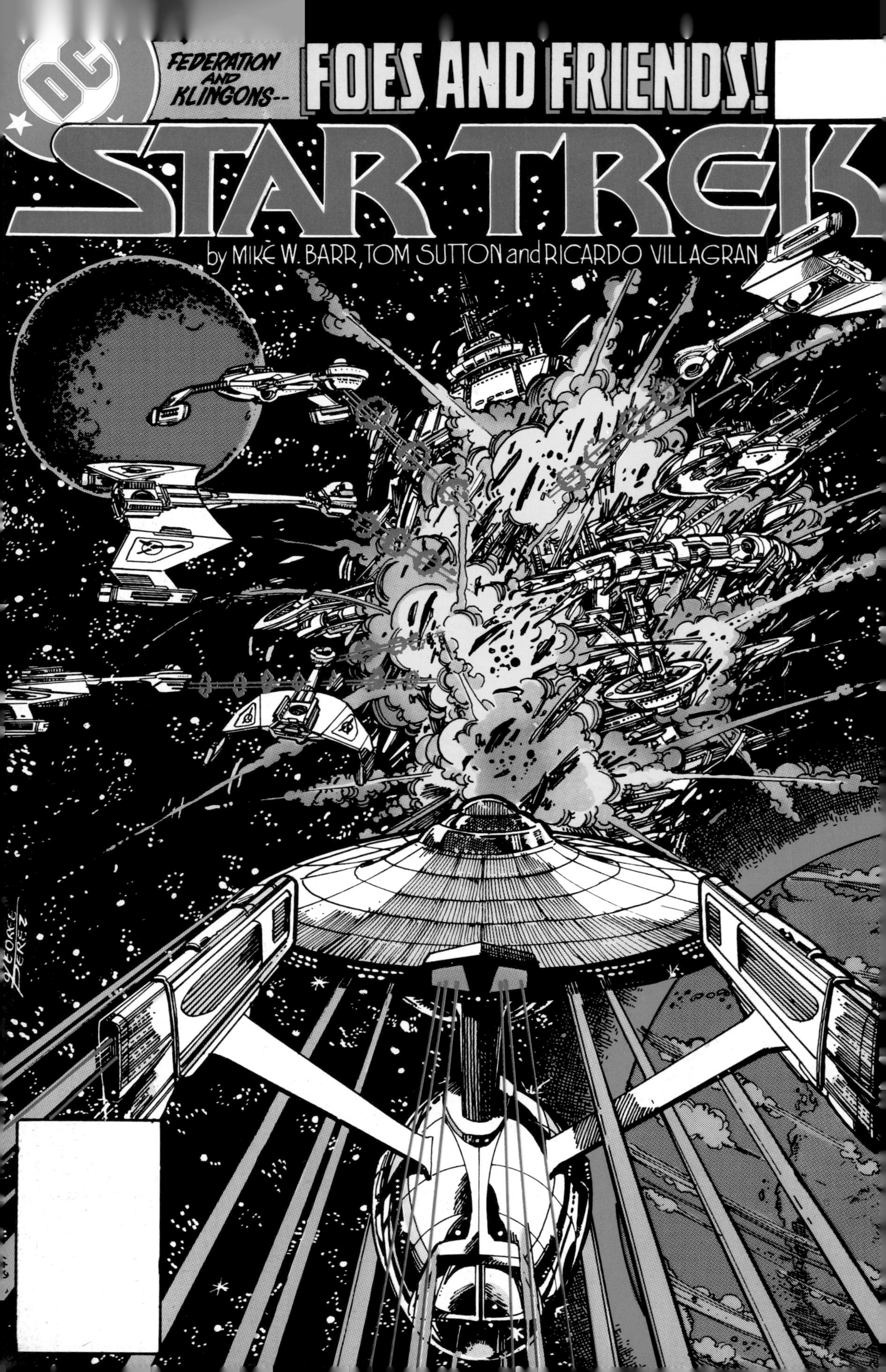
DC
FEDERATION AND KLINGONS--
FOES AND FRIENDS!
STAR TREK
by MIKE W. BARR, TOM SUTTON and RICARDO VILLAGRAN
GEORGE PEREZ